A TALE OF TWO CITIES

D0963694

The future of cities cannot be understood in terms only of the emergence of the post-modern metropole. A large proportion of citizens of Western society will continue for many years to inhabit the old industrial conurbations – from the rust belt in the United States to the originating centres of the English industrial revolution – and will experience contemporary economic and social change in those locations.

A Tale of Two Cities is a study of two such cities in the North of England, Manchester and Sheffield, and of the texture of every-day life within them. It explores the hopes and fears, the memories and folk-beliefs, and the present pre-occupations of young professionals, the unemployed, children and young people, the elderly and ethnic minorities and gay people in these two cities. It offers a detailed sociological analysis of two defining activities of life – shopping and daily travel and transport. The book draws on an international range of theory from Raymond Williams to John Logan and Harvey Molotch to identify and interpret the trajectory of change and development in different old industrial cities. And it provides a series of connected essays on the meaning of different levels of crime and levels of fear in different cities, on begging and homelessness in the city, on the demonisation of racialised enclaves, and on women's adaptive strategies; as well as an investigation of urban redevelopment and extended enquiry into the different futures available to post-Fordist cities in the North of England and in similar regions elsewhere in the world.

A Tale of Two Cities, the product of two years of extensive focus group enquiry, is a demonstration of the importance of locality, even in these 'globalising' times; and, in its theoretical and empirical exploration of local specificity, this study constitutes a vital contribution to the developing sociological and geographical literature on post-Fordist transformations.

Ian Taylor is Professor of Sociology at the University of Salford. **Karen Evans** is Research Fellow in the Institute for Social Research, based at the University of Salford. **Penny Fraser** is Research and Policy Development Officer with the National Association for the Care and Resettlement of Offenders, based in Manchester.

INTERNATIONAL LIBRARY OF SOCIOLOGY
Founded by Karl Mannheim

Editor: John Urry
University of Lancaster

A TALE OF TWO CITIES

Global change, local feeling and everyday life
in the North of England. A Study in
Manchester and Sheffield

Ian Taylor, Karen Evans and Penny Fraser

London and New York

First published 1996
by Routledge
11 New Fetter Lane, London, EC4P 4EE

Simultaneously published in the USA and Canada
by Routledge
29 West 35th Street, New York, NY 10001

Typeset in Baskerville by
J&L Composition Ltd, Filey, North Yorkshire
Printed and bound in Great Britain by
Biddles Ltd, Guildford and King's Lynn

British Library Cataloguing in Publication Data
A catalogue record for this book is available from the British Library

Library of Congress Cataloguing in Publication Data
Taylor, Ian R.
A tale of two cities: global change, local feeling and ever[y]day
life in the North of England: a study in Manchester and Sheffield/
Ian Taylor, Karen Evans and Penny Fraser.
p.   cm.
Includes bibliographical references and index.
ISBN 0–415–13828–0 (hardback: alk. paper). — ISBN 0–415–13829–9
(pbk.: alk. paper)
1. Manchester (England)—Social conditions.   2. Sheffield
(England)—Social conditions.   3. Manchester (England)—Social life
and customs.   4. Sheffield (England)—Social life and customs.
I. Evans, Karen, 1961– .   II. Fraser, Penny, 1966– .
III. Title.
HN398.M27T39   1996
306'.09427'33—dc20   95–37938
CIP

ISBN 0-415-13828-0 (hbk)
ISBN 0-415-13829-9 (pbk)

CONTENTS

Part IV Conclusion

FIGURES

TABLES

PREFACE

We are very pleased that this book is appearing in the International Library of Sociology. We are aware that it is a risky venture for Routledge, as it has been in some ways for us as authors. It is, first, an extended piece of writing – especially on a topic which appears at first sight to have a merely local focus on the North of England (albeit in two rather large localities) – and we are aware that the preference of some publishers (and of many readers) in the accelerated times in which we live is for short, summary texts, preferably in bullet points and with executive summaries, and with international or global significance. But this book is the product of a lot of detailed 'focus group' work with people living in Manchester and Sheffield, and we have found it impossible to do justice to their concerns for their cities in fewer words. We have also wanted to advance an extended and detailed analysis of these cities and their different peoples (the dominant and subordinate groups who constitute their 'general public') which takes account of their own specific industrial history and post-industrial present (that is, actually to attempt to connect 'the local' to 'the global') – an objective which is everywhere recommended, but very rarely achieved. In this last respect, we should say, we were particularly inspired by Mike Davis's wonderful analysis of Los Angeles, *City of Quartz* (Davis 1990), though also convinced that analysis of the 'future of cities' globally must attend not just to post-modern metropoles like 'LA' but also to the hundreds of de-industrialised old industrial cities in the Rust Belt of North America and in Europe as a whole – the declining industrial areas of western societies.

But this book is a risk in another sense. It does not set out specifically to be a theoretical statement as such – though we obviously think it has real theoretical content. There is no attempt in this book to erect and impose a theoretical template, from Marxist political economy, from the new geographies of space or from post-modern impressionism onto some kind of rigid 'analysis' of the city, or alternatively to advance a new Grand Theory of the City, even of the De-industrialised City. We have rather different concerns, probably best described as operating at the middle level between pure theory and outright empiricism. These are spelt out at greater length in the introductory pages of Chapter 1, in terms of an account of the circumstances that initially gave rise to a bid to the Economic and Social Research Council for funding, which made possible this research into what was called 'the public sense of well-being: a taxonomy of public and space'. Fundamentally, the theoretical curiosities informing the proposed research, and running through the two years of fieldwork, arose out of the conviction that it is still sensible, even in these globalising times, to recognise local cultural differences between cities (especially in an 'old country' like England) and to treat them as having a sociological significance and continuing cultural provenance and impact. People may relate increasingly to a global marketplace and mediascape, but they still hold down jobs (or not), or own and rent housing (or not), *in particular cities*, which they still have to negotiate and interpret as places of sociability and pleasure, or, perhaps, of solitude and fear – a recursive practical achievement which, along with many other sociological writers on these matters, we believe involves the development of a practical local knowledge. Along with the cultural geographer Peter Jackson (1989), we were particularly persuaded of the utility of Raymond Williams's frustratingly under-developed notion of the 'structure of feeling'. What began life as an autobiographical preoccupation on the part of one of these authors – to understand the difference between Sheffield (the city of his birth, where he spent his childhood and some of his adult life) and Manchester (the city in which he was now living) – took on a more systematic form as an analysis of the traces and the presence of the industrial past in those two cities, and their continuing production of difference between two cities which might otherwise appear more similar than different. Indeed, these two cities are very often categorised together – for example, in secondary analysis of census material, in political and social policy discussion, and in journalism – straightforwardly as 'Northern industrial cities'. So they are also, unlike Los Angeles (and other major metropoles like Barcelona and Paris, which have been the subject of considerable discussion in recent urban literature), cities which have been the subject of a certain amount of critical comment by the privileged, living no doubt in more prestigious and comfortable metropolitan locations. Only in 1994 was it reported that the queen of England, on a visit to Moscow, mentioned to a party of Russians that 'Manchester is not a very nice place.' Sheffield itself had its own experience of royal acclamation rather earlier, when George III, apparently discouraged by the ebullient politics of that city, uttered his locally famous condemnation 'Damned bad place, Sheffield.' During the course of their industrial and commercial development, it is true, these cities have sometimes been the subject of a muted but appreciative commentary (in Manchester's case by Elisabeth Gaskell; in Sheffield's by Edward Carpenter and John Ruskin), but we are aware that these are not cities which have generally been to the fore in international appreciation. Ironically enough, of course, these old industrial cities are typical of the cities left over throughout the western world from the past period of mass manufacturing and heavy industrial commerce – veritable warehouses of memory and custom which, some argue, may soon be encountered only in heritage museums and nostalgic films and literature, like the industrial working class itself.

We offer this analysis of two old industrial cities as an exercise in comparative sociology, not just to identify their shared and common structural features, but also to understand the cultural differences between them. In this last sense, the work here is located in the tradition of comparative analysis of place (heralded in this country particularly in the work of Doreen Massey). That is, we want to take seriously the idea of unevenness and difference between cities in industrial capitalist societies, which we see to be linked, in particular, to local forms of industrial organisation. Like Massey, and like Geraldine Pratt and Susan Hanson (1994), we will also want to attend to the gendered character of the production process in the two cities of Manchester and Sheffield. In addition to our interest in local industrial forms, however, we will be interested too in the abstract idea of a 'woman's city' and, specifically, in the practical ways in which women seem to make sense of and use these two North of England cities. We will also pay attention to patterns of immigration into, and settlement of, these two cities, as well as local political and social history (for example, that of local labour movements or of the local professional middle class). That is to say, we want to offer a detailed comparative study of two cities, which ostensibly share a great many general characteristics but which on closer inspection reveal significant differences, especially at the cultural level. The strategy pursued, it should also be said, arises very much out of a belief in the importance of introducing 'real' urban voices into the field of urban studies and urban sociology, rather than assuming that such voices can be suppressed in favour of a set of theoretical a prioris of some kind, or alternatively 'deconstructed' according to some set schema in some part of the academy. Not the least of our concerns is that much of the recent literature on the city (Mike Davis notwithstanding) is notable for its lack of attention to local sentiments and lost or present utopias, for example about 'a good city' or local ways of life which have a particularly local provenance.

Thus there are many North of England voices in this book, giving expression to local (as well as national and global) fears and hopes. These voices (gathered in a total of 27 focus group discussions in the two cities, involving altogether 174 people attending these groups, and the 89 school-children with whom we held discussions in three schools in Manchester and two in Sheffield) are not presented here, however, as a seamless and populist narrative. We have tried to hear these voices in what we might call a 'realist' framework – that is to say, in terms of what we want to recognise are the mundane and routinised (rather than the spectacular or newsworthy) patterns in which people (at least, most people in the North of England) make use of their cities, whether they themselves live in the inner city, the old terraced streets, the inner suburbs or even what Northerners sometimes call, simply, 'the nice areas' (i.e., to use another language, whatever their place in the never-ending 'class struggle for housing'). At different places in the book, we will allow these local voices to lead us in different directions – for example, into issues of gender and race in divided and unequal de-industrialised cities, the inescapable contemporary issue of public home-lessness and poverty, the familiar and much-traversed cultural studies field of shopping (but in a rather different, decidedly un-post-modern fashion), 'difference' in sexuality (especially gay lifestyle in Manchester and Sheffield), and the unexplored territory between cultural sociology and transport studies. We also trespass a little into the professional field of gerontology and the study of folklore in our exploration of the memories and mental maps of elderly people living in these two cities. Not the least of our interests in this aspect of our work was to explore the role of nostalgia, memory and the past not just amongst elderly North-erners themselves, but also amongst all locals and residents in what (as we say repeatedly) are both rather old industrial cities well past their nineteenth-century prime, albeit now engaged in different responses to their recent economic 'restructuring'. But we also try to offer a particular analysis of the experience of being a young person in these two cities (the process of becoming a Mancunian – a Manc – or a Sheffielder) in the de-industrialised 1990s.

In pursuing these different enquiries in our tale of two cities, some readers may feel we have fallen between several stools. Perhaps we should more confidently assert that we have tried to grasp (rather than merely reference) 'complexity'. In so doing, we have produced in Part III a series of chapters that could be read, separately and independently, as discrete enquiries into the sociology of gender, race, sexuality and age in the city, as well as the cultural critique of recursive daily travel, and other taken-for-granted aspects of life in the partially modernised and partially de-industrialised North of England. In our final chapter, we open up the study of the city as the site of different life projects. This will include attention to the field of urban development as 'a project' – undertaken by commercial growth coalitions as well as by other entrepreneurs in the visible and hidden economies of the city – but we will also recognise other widespread life projects of urban survival or withdrawal in de-industrialised old industrial cities.

We anticipate a certain scepticism amongst professional sociologists and geographers as to whether we succeed in this book in 'theorising' our different materials satisfactorily, whether in whole or in part. In the United States, Mike Davis himself has been accused of a certain inatten-tiveness to such concerns and, in particular, has been quite firmly taken to task (for example, by Edward Soja) for appearing to ignore the inescapable advance of post-modern textuality and the 'exhaustion' of modernist meta-narratives (like the very idea of the 'good city'). What we would claim for ourselves is a certain kind of critically aware, socio-logical, empirical curiosity – trying to identify the source of the different 'structures of feeling' in Manchester and Sheffield (as well as their shared character as Northern industrial cities); trying to locate the different kinds of dominant and subordinate social group that make up the populations of these two cities; and trying to listen to the anxieties and fears, hopes and desires, expressed by several different publics in these cities. We are aware that we have not solved the conceptual problems inherent in Marxist and post-Marxist approaches to urban process, in geographical debates about the intrinsic meaning of terms like 'the local' or 'the spatial', or indeed in theorising the relation between the play of desire and excess of the post-modern global mind of the young profes-sional or young person in the casualised labour markets, and the material infrastructure of place in post-industrial Sheffield and Manches-ter (the Leadmill, Hillsborough or Coles, for example, in Sheffield; or the Academy, Old Trafford, Kendals, the new Opera House and G-Mex in Manchester). We do strongly feel, after the example of Raymond Wil-liams, that whilst the people's 'ordinary common sense' may need to be theorised in order to be explained, there is always a sense in which that common sense holds true for those people. People continue to think of themselves, we believe, as living 'in a city' and, indeed, in a *specific* city (not in a class structure, urban process or spatial configuration, or even a post-modern pleasure zone). What we hope emerges in this text is a specifically sociological account of organic differences between two cities (which recognises the inequality of citizenship in these cities), which is linked, through the work of Harvey Molotch and John Logan, to a political economy of contemporary urban change, and then 'theorised', in terms of the current trajectory of development and redevelopment in these two cities (urban boosterism in global circum-stances), enquiring critically into their particular local purchase. We take this to be some contribution not only to local thinking about the practical politics and practice of urban rescue, redevelopment and (perhaps) growth, but also to a critical sociology itself. In this last respect, then, we also want to acknowledge another important Amer-ican sociologist (albeit of a different historical moment), C. Wright Mills (1959), in seeing the work we have done on 'the city' as having to do with the interplay between what Mills saw as a public issue (whose kinds of city are now being developed, and to what effect?) and the city as a site of what he called 'private troubles' – the anxieties and aspirations of its citizens. We have done this, however, not in (post-)modern Los Angeles, more or less confidently approaching the Millennium, but in two 'dirty old towns' in the North of England, which, at the end of the twentieth century, are very differently positioned – not least in terms of their 'local structure of feeling' – with a view to transcending their long industrial past.

Ian Taylor, Karen Evans and Penny Fraser
May 1995

ACKNOWLEDGEMENTS

In the course of an extended research project in two cities, engaging with 'members of the public' and also with a large number of individual professional people, it is not surprising that we have accumulated a rather extensive list of debts. In many cases – including the 174 people who participated in our focus groups and the 89 children who took part in our discussions in schools – we cannot name the people who helped us, for fear of breaching the promise of confidentiality which we extended. In the book as a whole, some of these citizens of our two cities appear under fictitious names, but they may recognise themselves.

In Manchester, we would like to thank Jane Hunt and Chris Paris of the Central Manchester Development Corporation; Adolphus Ojinnaka and Sheila Ritchie of Manchester City Council Planning Department; Deputy Chief Constable Malcolm Cairns, Chief Inspectors Paul Cook and John Cantrell, Inspectors Bob Brooks, Margaret Parker and Alan Statham of Greater Manchester Police; Bill Lowe of the Arndale Centre Anti-Theft Group; David Brown of P and O Shopping Centres; Graham Horn and Sue Green of Greater Manchester Research; Ruth Turner of *The Big Issue (North West)*; Barbara Drummond of Manchester Health Authority; James Kenney of *The Chinese Times*, Manchester; Chris Law and Keith Grime of the Department of Geography, University of Salford; Roger Lightup, Public Relations Coordinator, Manchester Social Services; Dr Roger Hall; Dr Jenny Carey-Wood; Kwan Harvey of the Tang Sing Housing Association; Beresford Edwards of the West Indian Centre; Anne Seex, Chief Executive's Department, Manchester City Council; Bernard Andrews, Manchester Taxi Drivers Association (retired); Bill Holroyd, retired bricklayer, of Cheadle Hulme; Tony Young, Jill Lewis, Steve Wright and Steve Cosby, Greater Manchester Passenger Transport Executive; Duncan Broady, Curator, Greater Manchester Police Force Museum; Sandy Ochojna, Harriss Research Centre; and Ms Farah Akhtar, Cheetham Hill, Manchester. Christine Peacock, now of the Oldham Metropolitan Borough Council, was an invaluable Research Fellow on a research project at Salford in which many of our concerns were first 'piloted'. Anna and Jean Taylor were invaluable sources of insider information on the Manchester youth scene.

In Sheffield, we would like to express our particular appreciation to

Janet Perceval, Nigel Buxton, Emma and Sarah King for the hospitality they provided for our Sheffield focus group discussions, held in their home in Hunter's Bar; to Narendra Bajaria, Senior Planning Officer, Sheffield Planning Department; Gurth Wilson and John Weston of Mall Research Services in Meadowhall; Alison Cooke, PR Executive, Meadowhall; Rose Birks of the Don Valley Forum, Reverend Dr John Vincent of the Sheffield Urban Theology Unit; Reverend Barry Parker (now of Prescot United Reformed Church, Huyton); Chief Constable Richard Wells, Chief Inspector John Heritage, Inspector Martin Hemingway, Superintendent John Donnelly, Detective Superintendent Mick Burdess of South Yorkshire Police, as well as Alex Hughes, Architectural Liaison Officer of the South Yorkshire Police; Tony Rodgers of the Kelvin Tenants Association; Mark Arcari of the Sheffield Chamber of Commerce; Martin Lideman, Sheffield Development Corporation; Dr Maurice Roche of the University of Sheffield; Roy Darke, ex-Chairman of Finance Committee, Sheffield City Council, and Jane Darke, both now of Oxford Brookes University; Mr Martin Olive; Sue McGrail of the Directorate of Planning and Economic Development, Sheffield City Council; Kingsley Fosse and Mo Tremble of the Department of Employment, Sheffield City Council; Denise Cabolt, Community Safety Unit, Sheffield City Council; Helen Askham of Sheffield City Libraries' Local Studies Library; John Hicks, Chief Probation Officer for South Yorkshire and his colleagues Milton Samuels and Christine Shann; Steve Arnold of Sheffield Mainline buses; Sarah Drake, South Yorkshire Passenger Transport Executive; Mrs Buckley-Greaves, Sadacca Lunch-club; Farhana, our interpreter with Asian women in Sheffield; and George Fulwood of the Sheffield Disability Forum.

We would also like to thank the five headteachers who gave permission for us to hold discussion sessions in their schools, and the five Personal and Social Education teachers, and 'Heads of Year' teachers, who gave us practical assistance. They will understand that they cannot be named, as this would breach our promise to keep the schools anonymous.

We also want to thank 32 police officers of different ranks who took part in five focus groups in Manchester and Sheffield, discussing their own mental maps of these two cities, and the locations which provoked fear and unease for them. Given constraints of space, we have not been able to make full use of these discussions here, though we will do so in a separate publication. We do think that the sense of well-being and anxiety of those given responsibility for community safety and the maintenance of the peace in individual cities, often in England in cramped and inadequate police stations, is an important topic in urban social research in its own right, rather than simply a managerial issue for the justice system.

Elsewhere, we need to thank Stuart Dickson of British Coal (Public Relations) in Nottingham; Dr Philip Waller of Merton College, Oxford; Dr Andrew Davies of the University of Liverpool; Professor Bob Ratner of the University of British Columbia; and Elliott Currie in Berkeley,

California. We would also like to thank Graham Allsop of the Department of Geography at the University of Sheffield and Gustav Dobrzynski of the Department of Geography at the University of Salford for the production of the maps.

We would like to extend thanks, as well, to the excellent set of street interviewers working in Manchester and Sheffield: Kate Brooks, Chris Brereton, Neil Gaukwin, Charles Makha, Elliott Costello, Marianne Martini, Charlotte Smith, Carol Stanfield, Maria Smith, Garry Ramsahai and Cath Exley. We also need to acknowledge the untiring work done in transcribing the focus groups by Carole Maloney and by Lydia Callaway in indexing them.

We would like to acknowledge the assistance received in funding this research, in its pilot stage and in its more extended, comparative form, from the University of Salford Research Committee, the Greater Manchester Passenger Transport Executive and the Economic and Social Research Council (Grant No. 23–3048).

Ian Loader and Colin Morrison were also a source of support and ideas, especially during the write-up period of this work, and we thank them both.

Greater Manchester

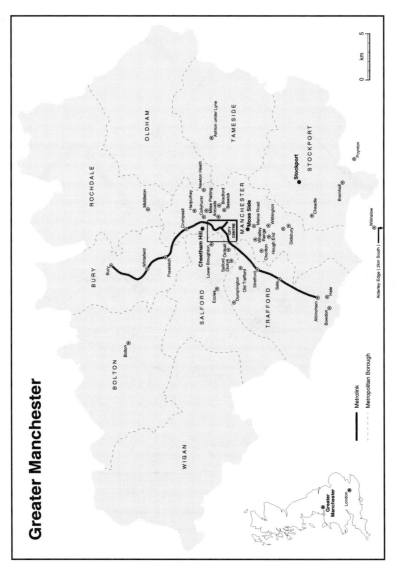

Map 1 The ten boroughs of Greater Manchester
Source: Gustav Dobrynzksi, Dept of Geography, University of Salford

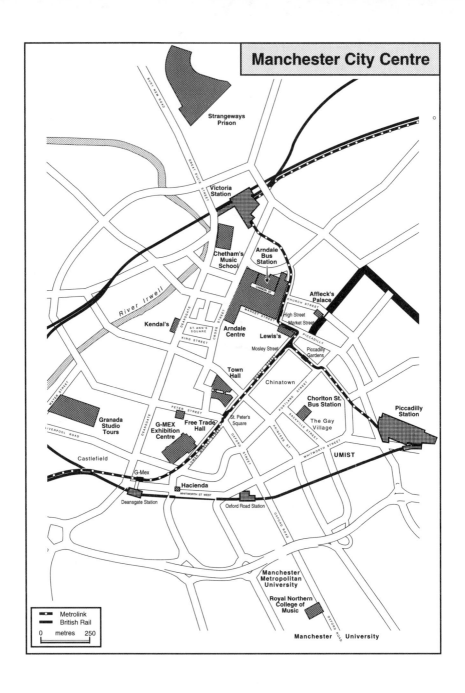

Map 2 Manchester City Centre
Source: Gustav Dobrynzksi, Dept of Geography, University of Salford

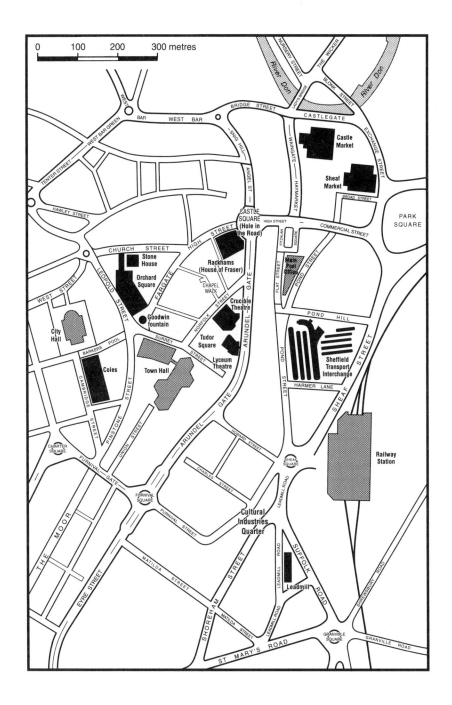

Map 3
Source: Department of Geography, University of Sheffield (G. Allsop)

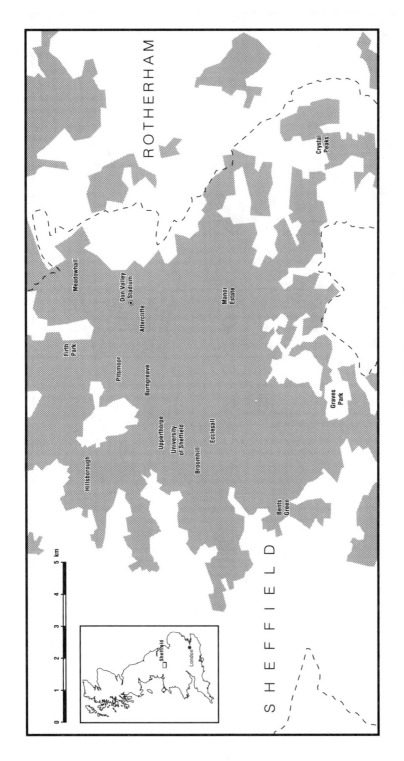

Map 4 The City of Sheffield, 1993
Source: Dept of Geography, University of Sheffield (G. Allsop)

Part I

PAST AND CONTEMPORARY CONTEXTS

1

RECOGNISING LOCAL DIFFERENCE IN NORTH OF ENGLAND CITIES

The 'structure of feeling' in Manchester and Sheffield

INTRODUCTION

This book arises out of three years' sociological fieldwork conducted in the two North of England cities of Manchester and Sheffield in the early 1990s. The research enquiry was motivated primarily by an interest in investigating how different groups of people in these two cities (different 'publics') appeared to be making sense, in the broadest possible, commonsense, philosophical and practical terms, of the rapid changes taking place in those cities – most notably, in the sudden deep changes in the local labour market (the 'demise of mass manufacturing') but also in respect of redevelopment, especially in the core of those cities ('regeneration' and '(post)modernisation'). It was also very much concerned with what we can refer to as 'the public sense of well-being' in these two cities. We shall return to all these issues later in this introductory chapter.

For the moment, we want to offer an account of the origins of this project. However infrequently this is declared, nearly all social scientific research arises, in part, out of some contingency in the personal biography of the researcher(s), and this particular project is no exception. One of the authors of this study, Ian Taylor, grew up and also worked in Sheffield and, after eight years in Canada, 'returned home' to Salford in the North of England.[1] Especially when viewing from a distance, Taylor felt that, although Salford was located in a larger conurbation than Sheffield – Greater Manchester – the character of everyday life and the sense of place none the less would be similar to that of Sheffield: the cities, after all, were only 38 miles apart, and they were both, unmistakably, in and of 'the North of England'.

These presuppositions, of course, were the product of a significant sociological naïveté. There was some awareness on Taylor's part that the sheer size of the Greater Manchester conurbation (2.6 million people, compared to Sheffield's half a million) might make for some difference in the experience of the places (for example, in the relative intensity and intimacy of family and kinship networks), though this insight was never purposively investigated by reference to any of the classic sociological writing on city size (Wirth 1938; Simmel 1950). This lack of sociological reflection – essentially suppressed by a sentimental affinity, in the imagination, with the idea of a generally friendly, down-to-earth North of England as a whole – also meant that this one academic sociologist was unprepared for the fact of urban difference within the North of England – in particular, in respect of what for the moment we should call local culture and the sense of place.

Very little of the scholarly work on localities and local difference that had appeared in Britain in the 1980s (cf. Newby *et al.* 1985; Murgatroyd *et al.* 1985; Cooke 1986, 1989; Harloe *et al.* 1990) had been read when Taylor presented some impressions about the overall condition of the city of Manchester and other Northern cities in an inaugural lecture (Taylor 1990) and, later in the same year, applied for funds to carry out research into 'the public sense of well-being' in two North of England cities: the cities of his birth and current residence.

Running through the original application for research funds was a concern to register – and make sense of – some of the more obvious differences between these two cities (initially, given the pre-existing criminological interest, the apparently much greater level of reported crime in Manchester than in Sheffield and other Northern cities), but also extending to significant differences in respect of the health and morbidity of the local population, as well as the levels of visible or invisible poverty and homelessness.[2]

There was some initial interest in the utility of official measures of local difference of this kind for a comparative sociology of regions within Britain and, indeed, within a larger Europe (increasingly being spoken of, at this time, as a 'Europe of the regions'). Also informing the decision to undertake some comparative research was a persistent awareness of the unmistakable 'difference of feeling' of the two cities. Where Sheffield obviously felt familiar to someone who had lived there for a total of some 28 years, Manchester was new and relatively unfamiliar (and certainly this affected the perception of the two cities). The size of the city and the local accents of the Mancunian and the Lancastrian were also certainly 'unfamiliar'. But – setting these self-evident considerations aside – there was too a sense that Sheffield's familiarity might also be a function of its apparently unchanging character (as a culture which had always, perhaps complacently, prided 'honest graft' as well as the quality of its local crafts and thought these qualities could 'see it through'):[3] many Mancunians, on the other hand, seemed in the early 1990s to be rather enthusiastically involved in the rapid changes and transformation demanded by global change. There was some sense that the idea of change and adaptation was not new – in other words, that the people of Manchester, 'the first industrial city' in England, were in some sense used to being at the cutting edge of change – and that this expressed itself, quite powerfully, in the character of the local culture.

LOCALITY: RAYMOND WILLIAMS AND THE
'STRUCTURE OF FEELING'

Williams's rather anthropological concern, in *The Long Revolution*, where he first advanced his notion of 'the structure of feeling', was to argue that the definitive cultural character of any one social formation (he meant, here, a single society) could best be grasped in the examination of the routine and taken-for-granted 'social practices' that characterised that social formation (Williams 1965). But they must be thought of not as a set of unconnected, distinct practices, but as elements of a complex, organised whole: they were part of a given 'ensemble' of social relations, exercising enormous power over individual behaviour and belief, but, in Williams's perception, according to class patterns within that social formation. However, he argued – very much in opposition to reductionist and deterministic forms of Marxism that were active at the time – that in any individual social formation there would be unexpected, as well as expected, correspondences and also *'discontinuities of an unexpected kind'* (Williams 1965: 63, our emphasis). Moreover, Williams argued in opposition to various idealist and text-based approaches to culture (in English literature and history in particular), in insisting that the analysis of culture should be concerned to grasp 'the nature of the organization which is the complex of these relationships' (Williams 1965: 61) and also the socially patterned relationships within and between these practices. As Stuart Hall observed in a well-known commentary essay:

> The purpose of the analysis [must be] to study how the interactions between all these practices and patterns are lived and experienced as a whole, in any particular period. This is its 'structure of feeling'.
>
> (Hall 1981: 22)

In a later work, *Marxism and Literature*, Williams added a further dimension to his conception of the 'structure of feeling' in arguing that a culture must be understood in terms of past and future aspirations, as well as the contemporary 'lived experience': 'structure of feeling' was about the intangible 'elements of impulse, restraint and tone' as well as the 'specifically affective elements of consciousness and relationships' (Williams 1977: 132).[4]

Williams's concern was with the culture of specific social formations or national societies: he was particularly preoccupied with 'the structure of feeling' of English society, by contrast with that of Wales and the other social formations that make up the 'Celtic fringe' in Britain, and he was also very clear that a sociology of culture that generalised across national societies (for example, from the United States to Britain) begged nearly all the key questions as to how culture is 'lived' and is 'ordinary' in individual societies.

It would be foolish to argue that Williams's arguments in respect of the 'structure of feeling' – for all their significant appeal in terms of the analytical importance of difference and complexity in individual social formations – can be transferred, without any modification, from the level of a 'national society' to that of a city or region. But popular common sense in England would certainly insist on there being important defining differences between the character (and local culture) of the Cockney, the Scouser, the Brummie and the Geordie. Historically, these differences have often registered by reference to differences in local accent, and although the 'meaning' of local accent may now be in the process of modification through television representation, the sense of accent and region remains a powerful source of myths and stereotypes about the character of most major English cities, especially across the Midlands and the North. In the received folklore and televisual representation of 'the North of England', Liverpool and Newcastle historically have had a rather fixed and well-defined regional identity, but Manchester and Sheffield (and other cities in the North of England) have not.[5] Elsewhere in the world – for example, in North America – generic discussions of 'England' would be substantially inattentive to differences between places, other than between 'medieval' and industrial sites, and would in this way pass over the local feelings about individual cities. Understanding the impact of local place on individual personality formation, personal biography and 'orientation to the world' or 'affect' (all of which contribute to what we mean by 'local identity') – influences which parallel but do not reduce simply to what American behavioural scientists call 'residential attachment' (Fried 1982) or to what the human geographer Yi-Fu Tuan calls 'love' or 'fear of place' (Tuan 1974) – is a significantly under-researched field in both sociology and psychology. We do not know what it means to be a Mancunian or a Sheffielder, and whether or how the process of local identity formation works for different sections of the local publics in cities.

THE GLOBAL UNIMPORTANCE OF LOCALITY: LASH AND URRY AND INTERNATIONAL POLITICAL ECONOMY

We will elaborate further on these questions below. Here, we want to ask whether the study of these local differences matters, and in what respect. Social commentators are currently preoccupied with the massive shift that has taken place in the direction of a global economy, with its associated, internationally prevalent effects in terms of patterns of consumption and communication. So, for example, the cogent recent analysis provided by the sociologists Scott Lash and John Urry, *Economies of Signs and Space*, ranges widely across the world, examining what they see to be a general move towards a post-industrial capitalism – essentially and necessarily 'disorganised', they argue, in the sense that capitalist organisations are increasingly required to be speedy and mobile, migrating across different labour and consumer markets in order to survive and prosper (Lash and Urry 1994). In this global economic market, the idea of a city (or any other fixed location) as a given centre of particular kinds of production very much recedes in importance, especially by comparison with what Lash and Urry call the 'new circuits of capital'. The three elements of 'capital' – money, productive capital and commodities – circulate with ever-increasing speed and energy through an increasingly international set of spaces. In the meantime, the rapid development of electronic communications networks threatens to transcend 'traditional' or modernist ways of thinking about the relationship of cities to production and consumption. The guarantees which, it was once thought, a strong, specialised local labour market provided for a single city or conurbation (graft and craft, for example) no longer have the same influence or effect. It is in this sense, Lash and Urry argue (following Karl Marx's observations in *The Communist Manifesto*) that 'all that is solid melts into air' (Marx and Engels 1986).

Lash and Urry's account of these developments – rather like Tony Giddens's analysis of what he calls 'reflexivity' in conditions of high modernity (Giddens 1991) – is very heavily focused on the impact of global economic transformations on individuals, in respect of both individual forms of consciousness and individual behaviour. There is a particular interest, in this body of sociological theory, in the ways in which individuals have recently been dislodged from their familiar or 'traditional' patterns of behaviour (their 'routines'), and also their beliefs and certainties about the world, by the need to adapt to the rapid changes taking place in their economic life or their social and cultural environment. The overall source of this 'de-traditionalisation' is the move towards global markets: the local imperative in Britain and in other older industrial societies is the collapse of the local mass manufacturing industry and the communities associated with it. At every level in such social formations, individuals are left to adapt to the void in what was their working world, their identity, their community and their social life, but in particular local contexts.

There is no doubt that the world Lash and Urry describe (and which Giddens assumes as the background for his thinking about high modernity) represents the 'cutting edge' in the current phase of capitalist development and transformation (Castells 1989). There *are* towns in this country (Cambridge, Swindon, Lancaster) where the essential or core economic activities have very rapidly been transformed in this direction, particularly in the last decade and a half, and where quite significant proportions of the population are now employed in high-technology service industries (cf. Saxenian 1989 on Cambridge; Urry 1987, 1990, on Lancaster). Many of the people employed in these towns, importantly, will no longer themselves be 'locals': staff will be recruited nationally, and significant numbers of the employees may be part of the ever-increasing population of weekend commuters (working in one town, paying a mortgage on a property elsewhere, returning 'home' on a weekend). Even the city-edge shopping malls are recruiting their service staff from national markets: Sheffield's Meadowhall Retail Academy functions as a training school for these nationally recruited staff. These are places, and towns, in which it clearly does make some sense, analytically, to focus on the mobile character of the employed local labour force and, indeed, on the restless, mobile sentiments of many of the local residents as a whole.

It is not clear, however, how many towns and cities, and how many people, can be spoken of in such terms – in particular, how much sense it makes to see cities as comprising 'mobile individuals' rather than the fragments of long-established social classes and the powerful, continuing trace of local cultures – especially in an 'old country' like Britain.[6] Lash and Urry do remark, themselves, that:

> not all local economies are experiencing the same pattern. In Britain, Rochdale is far from being post-industrial and service-dominated.
>
> (Lash and Urry 1994: 212)

A considerable amount of research was undertaken in Britain during the 1980s on the essentially uneven fate and experience of different localities with respect to 'de-industrialisation' and the shift to 'post-Fordist arrangements of production'. It is probably fair to say that the logic of enquiry in these studies, deriving from a realist political economy tradition, rather than from the perspective of a cultural sociology of place, has not so far generated an account of this unevenness in terms of what we are calling a 'local structure of feeling'. It is probably fair to say too that these studies have generated an accurate picture of the contradictory and uneven responses of different localities to the challenges of a 'disorganised', global economic culture, yet have done so without also generating an account either of the 'lived culture' of those local entrepreneurs or new workers who have emerged rather successfully from these challenges, or of the 'lived experience' of those who, in the meantime, have been 'left behind' or residualised. Whilst there is no doubt – as Lash and Urry show repeatedly – that the main source of employment growth in nearly all western societies is in what they call 'producer-services', this clearly does not mean that every person who is so employed (for example, on a supermarket check-out) is likely to adopt a set of values and behaviours thought to be characteristic of the new, mobile, service-industry middle class. Nor does it mean the complete extinction of all employment in manufacturing industry: in Sheffield in 1989, for example, some 26.7 per cent of all employment was still in manufacturing (Seyd 1993: 154) and, in Manchester, in 1989–90, about one quarter was (Peck and Emmerich 1992b: 24). The proportion of the population employed in professional occupations in those cities in 1991 was estimated at about 30 per cent, only marginally higher than the numbers employed in manufacturing.

LOCALITY: TELEVISION AND A GLOBAL SENSE OF PLACE

Any attempt to take the idea of locality or local 'structure of feeling' seriously must contend with the cultural reach of global communication systems - particularly, with the continuing reach of television. The broad-brush generalisations of Marshall McLuhan with regard to the 'global village' in the 1960s have more recently been developed further in a thoughtful analysis by Joshua Meyrowitz (1988), focusing on the electronic media's undermining of individual sense of place. His organising argument (1988: ix) targets 'the once strong relationship between physical and social space' and insists, instead, that individuals now draw up their social world (with its values, meanings, memories, ways of speaking, and behaviours) primarily in a process of socialisation with the global media, rather than through any meaningful engagement in the institutions or practices of a locality. In this view (given American domination of the international media), Americans, above all, are seen as having a shared national (rather than a local or international) identity constructed in and through television: there is no longer any serious possibility of a local history or shared 'local experience', outside the discussions in neighbourhood schools or other neighbourhood 'locales' about national television. There is, in this sense, no locality.[7]

There can be no denying the force of Meyrowitz's argument, especially when applied, we would argue, to new residential developments on the edge of North American cities; and there is no denying their power for the understanding of lived experience of private households in England, whether in the North or the South. Even so, we would argue, the thesis is probably overdone, even for America (where there *is* local news on television – on some television channels, indeed, only local news – and also a mass of local advertising). There are also locally generated cable channels, of uneven quality and impact, but with some consequence in terms of local knowledge of local schools, sports and shopping. There is some – highly mediated – sense of provision and action in local shopping malls, cinemas and sports. Indeed, in another sense, 'locality' intrudes even into prime-time television 'entertainment' programming and comedies on national networks – the troubled condition of the 'rust-belt' Northern states being one of several powerful themes, played for humour but in deadly earnest, on *Roseanne.*

The relationship between national and local television (terrestrial and satellite), local newspapers and radio would be a separate research project from that which we conducted in Manchester and Sheffield. But we do need to make reference, in passing, to a kind of commonsense familiarity with local media which we discovered in our work. For many people living in and around Manchester, the local evening paper, the *Manchester Evening News* (selling 214,077 copies on the average day in the first half of 1994, the biggest circulation for an evening paper outside London), is an institution ('A Friend Dropping In' says its masthead).

There are also local evening television news bulletins directed at the North-west region as a whole (*Granada Reports*, *North West Tonight*): these programmes are primarily produced from Manchester, but regularly revert to the studios maintained by the BBC and Granada in Liverpool. The importance of regional television in scripting a local regional sense of identity is confirmed by the widely used description of the whole region as 'Granadaland'. For many others in the region, particularly the young, Manchester's metropolitan status in the North-west is underlined by the presence in the city of some five commercial radio stations broadcasting 24 hours a day.

Sheffielders, in the meantime, having lost their daily morning paper – the *Sheffield Telegraph* (closed by the United Newspapers Group in February 1986) (Vickers 1992: 207) – have an evening newspaper, the *Star*, a weekly *Sheffield Telegraph* (which began life in 1989) and two local radio stations. But it has been a matter of angry local comment over the years that the regional television news emanates from Leeds, Sheffield's great rival Yorkshire city, 40 miles north up the M1 motorway.

In both cities, the coverage of local matters by these recognisedly public, shared media is also supplemented by a range of local 'community newspapers' – essentially vehicles for an enormous amount of local advertising, and delivered free to thousands of households on a weekly basis. These newspapers rely on the local police and courts for a guaranteed flow of crime stories, but also carry a large number of photographs of local events. In Manchester, many suburbs have a large number of competing editions of such newspapers, as well as the conurbation-wide *Manchester Metropolitan News*.[8] Manchester also has its own listing magazine, *City Life* (akin to *Time Out* in London), with a circulation of 18,000–20,000. The role of these media in constructing a particular sense of local identity, especially in a sprawling conurbation like Greater Manchester, is clearly important in the 'globalising' 1990s. What is being constructed is a very specific, local journalistic sense of 'the locality' that also cuts into a kind of commercial mental map of each locality, through which local advertisers reinforce a sense of their particular location in the neighbourhood and the local 'market'. This is a form of 'local knowledge' that we cannot ignore, either in understanding popular attachment to place, or in understanding how people build up a mental map of the 'symbolic locations' of crime in their own locality (cf. Taylor 1995a).

Nor does this recognition of transformed global circumstances mean that the long-established forms of routine, local common sense that have characterised the life of major industrial cities (the folk beliefs, the routine and 'unreflexive' practices, the mental maps of the city, and local sayings and folklore) – in what is, after all, a very 'old country' (Wright 1985) – are likely to be replaced overnight, 'melting into air'. The historian Patrick Joyce, in his classic study of popular culture and class relations in the North of England in the period between 1848 and 1914, has underlined the persistence at local level of the pre-industrial rituals and customs in rural areas and also in cities (like the annual Preston Wakes) and the way in which these traditions have been actively transformed into more contemporary festivals 'for the whole community'. He has also pointed to the continuing importance of dialect, accent, local superstitions and folk tales, and notorious local personalities in conferring a sense of local identity (Joyce 1991). There is no doubt that the advance of 'mass media' and global economic competition has undermined the processes through which a strong and immediate sense of local identification is adopted by individuals, but it would be a very sweeping generalisation that denied the continuing desire for such a local identity (for example, in local history groups, amongst fans of football clubs or amongst various different kinds of craft group and other hobbyists. The new sociological writing on 'reflexive modernization' (notably Tony Giddens in his commentary on Hägerstrand's geography of everyday work and leisure time) (Giddens 1984) emphasises the importance of what is seen as a routinised set of practices, as a solid basis from which actors proceed to engage in reflexivity and innovation in their lives. But they have tended to ignore the ways in which such familiar practices can serve as a 'hedge' against the changes and risks of the modern world. Some years ago, Gaston Bachelard analysed in some depth the ways in which familiar places, including, here, 'the home' itself (cf. Bachelard 1964), can be the source not only of profound reassurance in the individual life-span but also of activity and pleasure – an alternative to the pleasures of the changes taking place in the 'outside world'.

We are aware of the interest of social anthropologists and social historians in the question of 'social memory' – the way in which social groups may make use of shared understandings from the past to make sense of contemporary changes. Local history has been a continuing theme in English city life over many years, but most recently the level of nostalgic interest has been marked, notably in Manchester and Sheffield, by an explosion of pamphlets on a vast range of topics (including local folklore and dialect as well as memorabilia about particular places), as well as photographs, coffee-table books, and autobiographies written by local people. At a time of fundamental transformation of local labour markets and urban form, one especially powerful strategy may be to establish the past, imaginatively, as a preferred temporal location to the present.[9] A particularly powerful dimension here is the nostalgia which is felt by many people in these cities for the lost world of industrial work – a nostalgia which is underwritten by the opening up of heritage museums, selling sepia-tinted memorabilia and other important monuments to this lost world. In Sheffield and Manchester, there is also an increasingly popular new local industry involved in the production and sale of a vast range of nostalgic memorabilia specifically about the local industrial past.[10]

LOCAL ALLEGIANCE AND POPULATION LOSS IN THE NORTH OF ENGLAND

One of the most sociologically interesting topics to have been suggested in the course of this investigation is that of the differential levels of affection and attachment produced by different cities and locales. We realise that this is no simple field and we also are clear that, whilst notions like the 'quality of life' in a region are relatively new, the phenomenon of emigration from economically troubled regions is itself by no means new. Emigration from some (though not all) North of England industrial areas (as well as from many other areas in the British Isles) has been continuous throughout the twentieth century, though we are not aware of any systematic study of the regional patterns of such emigration. What is emphasised, once again, is the fact that we are dealing with one of the oldest industrial societies, well past the height of its prosperity, and increasingly unable to create the levels of gainful employment to which the area was once accustomed.

Attachment to a particular location cannot be understood via an analysis, simply and only, of the patterns of residential stability and emigration. All kinds of factors are involved in the decision to leave a city, especially the condition of the local labour market. The experience of the Irish over the last two centuries, however, indicates that whilst the condition of the local labour market may provoke emigration, the fact of emigration does not necessarily diminish the sense of pride in one's own place of origin or, indeed, undermine the commitment of emigrants from different localities and places to 'returning home'. There is some evidence of significant unevenness across the cities of the North of England in terms of the rate of emigration and population loss in the last two to three decades:[11] the massive emigrations from Merseyside in the 1970s and from Tyneside and the North-east during the 1980s are well-known, not least because of their televisual representation (*The Boys from the Blackstuff*; *Auf Wiedersehen, Pet*). There was a continuing loss of population from the Greater Manchester area throughout the 1980s (an overall loss between 1981 and 1991 of 131,400 people, or 5.02 per cent of the 1981 population): the city of Manchester lost 24,200 people, or 5.23 per cent. Merseyside's loss over the same period was 4.7 per cent, while the Tyne and Wear lost only 0.12 per cent and South Yorkshire 0.11 per cent, a net loss of only 14,800 people (data from 1991 Census provided by Greater Manchester Research, Information and Planning Unit). Without knowing the destinations of the emigrants, we cannot know what proportion of the 'flight from Manchester' in the 1980s was to neighbouring towns of Cheshire or the Yorkshire hills (the evidence is certainly of an increase of population in the outer suburban areas of Bury and Bolton). The information currently collected on these questions in the national Census is unhelpful on this question, but, on the basis of the Census data presented, there is a suggestion that a significant proportion of the local population of Sheffield and South Yorkshire may actually have responded to the deepening crisis of its local economy in the 1980s simply by 'staying put' – where, by stark contrast, Mancunians (already used to the exigencies of a local business economy and the idea of job choice in a large industrial region) have more enthusiastically searched out better prospects elsewhere in the country or abroad. We will return to this issue in Chapter 3, since it clearly touches on the issue of whether the local 'structure of feeling' contributes to what Philip Cooke (1989) calls 'local effectivity' in terms of 'social mobilisation and initiative', whether it is conducive to 'resignation' or whether, indeed, a 'local structure of feeling' may be a kind of sustaining alternative to the benefits of employment in a global free market economy.

THEORISING SPACE, SENSING PLACE

Even a superficial reading of the literature on locality, well-being and space involves engagement with the epistemological debate which emerged in the mid-1980s on the interface of urban geography and social theory, particularly in respect of the theoretical status of the taken-for-granted concepts regarding space (referring to notion of place, region, city, territory, and even physical buildings) as they had tended to be employed in these disciplines. Doreen Massey (1991) and Savage and Warde (1993) have summarized many of these issues very helpfully: it is certainly not our concern here to suggest that an interest in local differences between Manchester and Sheffield involves us in a purely empirical investigation, searching out a mass of facts to illustrate or prove some difference assumed at the outset. Our interest in what we are calling the 'local structure of feeling' in these two cities does not limit our focus only to the area within the city boundaries, or even to particular definitive sites or symbolic locations in the centres of these two cities, though our fieldwork to some extent focused more on 'the centre' and three carefully chosen local areas rather than the city's larger range of suburbs and inner-city areas. Our interest in local difference also involved curiosity, on our parts, as to the historical processes of production and cultural practice that may make up 'the local'. We quickly became aware of the problems that had been encountered by students of locality in the 1980s, in trying to specify or define the local either as the 'locale' (the 'setting' or the 'resource' for social action) or as the 'local labour market' (in the realist political economies, mentioned earlier) (Duncan and Savage 1989: 185–91). For the moment, we simply remark that the position to which the researchers were drawn was one in which the necessary substantive properties of urban spaces (the focus of realist analysis) (Sayer 1989) were recognised (cities *are* expressions of social and economic processes that can be theorised in the language of class analysis and political economy), but in which the understanding of these urban spaces was being subject, continuously and unpredictably, to human interpretation 'at local level'. We were particularly taken – for example, in our understanding of Sheffield – by Cox and Mair's suggestion, as relayed by Alan Warde, that 'the substance of a locality may be considered as routinised relations, reproduced over time, because of the dependency of actors condemned to geographical immobility' (Warde 1989: 278, commenting on Cox and Mair 1989). Equally – in respect of both Manchester and Sheffield – we were interested in Philip Cooke's continuing emphasis on 'sense of place', referring back to the earlier work of humanist geographers like Relph (1976) and also the well-known work, in the tradition of environmental psychology, of Yi-Fu Tuan on love and fear of places (topophilia and topophobia) (Tuan 1974, 1979). As mentioned earlier, a particular focus here was on the way in which a local structure of feeling, understood as a mediation of the local labour market, in the historical past and in contemporary experience, might help generate a sense of resistance or adaptation to global economic transformation. We hope that the distinctiveness of this work – which will be very detailed and empirical in many ways – lies in this larger theoretical curiosity with respect to the dynamics of local feelings in present circumstances and also in the fact of its comparative dimension.

It was not and is not our concern to pursue an interest in local variation within the North of England out of some concern to 'fetishise' these localities (and to speak as if these localities have some essential character or quality that can transcend historical time and experience). This might, indeed, have led us into what Alan Warde calls 'idiographic geography' – the very detailed, essentially empirical description of every conceivable aspect of a local place (Warde 1989). Nor was it our concern to search out an island of progressivism in the 1990s in a society over-run by free market theologies. Moves of this kind have been subject to a stringent critique by David Harvey in *The Condition of Postmodernity* (Harvey 1989), on the grounds that all such 'turns to the local' inevitably reduce to a merely aesthetic celebration of place and, he argues, to political reaction. The intended analogy is obviously with the sentimental politics of nationalism itself, which have received a powerful boost as a reaction to the moves taking place, throughout the 1980s and early 1990s, towards global economic 'harmonisation'.

Our much more cold-blooded concern was to try to capture and define the 'local structure of feeling' in the two cities, provide an account of its origins and development, and, latterly, to begin to investigate the ways in which local urban populations, whose lives were framed, culturally, by such 'local structures of feeling', were responding to the fundamental changes that had been so rapidly occurring in these two cities. This involved us, in particular, in an attempt to listen closely to the voices of people living in these two cities – hearing their troubles, fears and anxieties as to 'what's happening to our city' (the majority sentiment was one of local decline),[12] as well as the more hopeful aspirations of members of the local professional middle class. In this more classical sociological project, we did not want to assume that matters of local cultural understanding could be settled purely within theory, as both Harvey and Sayer seem to argue. No matter how united they might be around certain cultural self-conceptions and practices, these two cities must also be understood as social structures riven by inequalities of class, gender, age and race, in which the capacity of local (and other) actors to resolve unevenness of economic fortunes or social experience – or to make sense of the unprecedented contemporary character of change in these cities – was in some important sense an open 'empirical' issue, which sociological observers ignore at their peril.

THE QUESTION OF 'THE QUALITY OF LIFE'

We noted early in our research that these matters (of variation in local urban culture) had become increasingly important in other social and political agendas – particularly those of the new, mobile middle class identified by, amongst others, Lash and Urry. In both North America and Europe over the last ten to fifteen years, there has been a marked increase of interest in personal and social 'lifestyle' and 'the quality of life', very broadly conceived.[13] There is a new, very detailed and strategic, consumerist interest in all aspects of a locality, from its crime rates to its schools. For some 'new consumers', especially those who have some private wealth or occupations enabling professional work from home, this search for a better quality of life has led a 'relocation' in some form of rural retreat – a contemporary resort to the pastoral. Others have been committed by necessity of career or by preference (for urban living) to take up residence in the suburbs or, in increasing numbers, in city-centre redevelopments. These processes are reflected in a series of 'consumer reports' in the press as to the relative merits of various towns and cities as places in which to live, usually identified in terms of some set of measures of the 'quality of life'. In August 1993, the *Sunday Telegraph* reported on a survey it had commissioned from Dr Robert Rogerson of the Quality of Life Group at the Universities of Glasgow and Strathclyde. Some 19 different factors were identified, in order of importance, as the key determinants of quality of life in British cities,[14] and on the basis of this evaluative schema, Dr Rogerson identified the top ten British cities, with population greater than 250,000, as being, in this order:

1. Edinburgh
2. Aberdeen
3. Plymouth
4. Cardiff
5. Hamilton
6. Bradford
7. Reading
8. Stoke-on-Trent
9. Middlesbrough
10. Sheffield

It is a matter of remark that so few of these cities in this particular league table are in the South of England which, on many other measures, would emerge as a 'desirable' place in which to live, and it is clear that Dr Rogerson's results are a function of the criteria he adopts for purposes of evaluation and the weighting given to different dimensions of the 'quality of life', which do not seem to be supported by any clear social or cultural argument. (None the less, it is interesting, for our purposes, that Sheffield enters Dr Rogerson's table in tenth position, whereas the City of Manchester and the other municipalities of Greater Manchester do not appear at all.) The meaning of any such formal scheme will be challenged by more detailed, and specific, examination of particular localities, which is in part the concern of the work reported here.

DECONSTRUCTING 'MANCHESTER' AND 'SHEFFIELD'

To many observers outside the North of England, Manchester and Sheffield must have a great deal in common: most obviously, they are Northern industrial cities, born of the Industrial Revolution, and sharing much of the landscape and culture of the industrial North. They are only 38 miles apart across the Pennine Hills. Yet, for all their similarities, the cities certainly 'felt' different to one of the authors of this study, and it soon became clear, on closer examination of various different dimensions of life (for example, in respect of measures of employment, wealth, health, and, as we shall see later, crime), that the two cities appeared to have a quite different profile in many definitive respects. Our research soon suggested that discussions of 'North of England cities' so often found in social commentary writing and in political discourse – formulated as if these cities constituted a unitary economic, social or cultural category – may be quite misleading sociologically, in respect not only of understanding the character or the present condition of the local economy but also of what, for the moment, we will simply call local culture.

At one level the point is quite trite and obvious. It is not at all clear, for example, what the maritime cities of Hull and Liverpool have in common with the landlocked cities of Leeds or Bradford, other than their generally Northern location. Nor is it obvious what smaller Northern cities, founded before the Industrial Revolution – Durham, Lancaster and York – have in common over and above their medieval heritage.

The existing economic and social histories of English cities do recognise the fact of local difference. A favourite comparison amongst English social historians is between Birmingham (the heartland of a confident imperial England and efficient local government) and Manchester (a 'nervous' and 'governmentally disorganised' centre of commerce and trade) (Briggs 1963; Smith 1982). But this writing does not usually enquire with any sociological curiosity as to how widespread these perceptions of difference might be within the local population, according to the key dimensions of class, status, age, gender and race, or how the existence of these perceptions of a local historical continuity feeds into what we are calling a 'local structure of feeling'.

We set out to research specific and local aspects of popular experience in order to try and understand the ways global processes presented themselves to local people in our two cities ('What's happening *here*?') and to explore differences in the way that local publics interpreted and negotiated these changes. In no sense was there any presumption that the Manchester–Sheffield comparison had any necessary, global significance – for example, as a measure of the relative positions of cities in the new world economic order. On many dimensions, the crucial comparison for Manchester is with Liverpool, the only other major industrial city within the North-west of England; and for Sheffielders, the key reference and comparison is nearly always with Leeds, its 'rival' city in Yorkshire. Conversations within the research team – particularly around the apparently very marked differences in crime rate of these two ostensibly similar but differently sized old industrial cities in the North of England – confirmed the original choice of the cities as research sites.

ALL IN THIS TOGETHER: THE COMMON FATE OF THE NORTH OF ENGLAND

Many of the defining features of Manchester and Sheffield life in the mid-1990s, however, are present in all Northern industrial cities, to one degree or another. So one of the most fundamental features of social and economic change in the 1980s and 1990s for the great mass of the public with whom we have had contact was the massive loss of work, especially the loss of 'good jobs', in the old manufacturing industries which had hitherto dominated the local labour markets.[15] The point is graphically put by Mark Dickinson:

> In the decade from 1979, when Mrs Thatcher applied the mone-tarist analysis and freed the market of perceived countervailing forces, 94 per cent of all job losses occurred North of a line drawn from the Wash to the Severn. Of the manufacturing jobs lost, 70 per cent were in the North . . . More depressing still were the figures on investment – since 1979, the real value of manufacturing investment has fallen by 41 per cent in the North.
>
> (Dickinson 1990: 76)

This Northern employment catastrophe was played out, throughout the 1980s, against the background of a massive withdrawal of the institutions of the local and national state from earlier patterns of social provision and welfare (for example, in respect of public housing or income maintenance): one of the inescapable features of the everyday life in these Northern cities was the massive growth of street begging by the homeless (especially in Manchester). This was the most public expression of the difficulties being encountered by many different groups within these cities in 'making ends meet', as a result both of local de-industrialisation and the withdrawal of welfare state social provision. There was a powerful sense that this economic catastrophe represented a real moment of truth in the given popular definition and understanding of the North – namely, that the North has always been a region that is defined by its residual and subordinate relation to London and the South-east. Being 'of the North', in this sense, has always involved a recognition that one is 'peripheral'. Richard Burns titled his essay on Sheffield, for example, 'The City as Not London' (1991): in a country where so many of the powerful political, economic and social institutions (and the governing and 'chattering' classes) are centred on London, being provincial and in the North fundamentally structures and defines one's life experience. The people of the North, in this respect, constitute an example of what Oskar Negt and Alexander Kluge have recently called a 'counter-public' (1993), marginalised from the centres of power, and tending, by virtue of this marginalisation, to develop 'a sense of solidarity and reciprocity rooted in the experience of marginalization or expropriation' (Hansen 1993: xxxvi). The solidarity that exists across the North does not easily translate into a solidarity with 'counter-publics' in other areas or regions: what Negt and Kluge call the 'horizon' of a counter-public is governed by the life experience, including the travel experience, of that public.[16]

This sense of the North as a residual and subordinated region within Britain – some distance from the levers of power – was an inescapable domain assumption in nearly all the discussions we held (from February 1992) with the different sections of the public in Manchester and Sheffield. Even in Manchester, where, as we will see later, there is a keen sense of the city and region as a metropolitan place (which no other Northern city can seriously claim), this sense of the North, economically and politically, as a peripheral place, now in danger of further marginalisation by the demise of its mass manufacturing basis, was fundamental: so obvious it did not always need to be said.

MAKING A RIGHT MESS OF THE TOWN

Independently of the demise of the local manufacturing labour market, a number of other major transformations had been occurring throughout the late 1980s and into the 1990s in the physical infrastructure and layout of both these cities, most notably in respect of the city centre and of out-of-town shopping and leisure developments, and also in respect of public transport. The general direction of these changes in urban form and organisation is common to many late industrial societies: most commentators speak of a global process of reorganisation of consumption (sometimes discussed in terms of the idea of 'post-Fordism') (cf. Hall and Jacques 1989). But it is becoming quite clear that there are enormous variations in the local expression of these global processes: Sheffield has the Meadowhall Centre, proclaimed at the time of opening in 1989 as being the largest indoor shopping mall in Europe, and also an enviable collection of new sports stadia, built for the World Student Games held in the city in 1991. Manchester has significant 'up-market' shopping in St Ann's Square and King Street, the first new light rail urban transit system built in Britain in the post-war period, a range of new cultural facilities, including a new Concert Hall scheduled for opening in 1996, and a number of new sports facilities initially connected with the city's bid for the Olympics in the year 2000; but, as at 1995, it had no major new shopping mall development on the scale of Meadowhall.[17]

In Chapter 3, we trace the development of the major issue of public concern in the city of Sheffield – the 'crisis of the city centre' – which parallels developments in many North American cities in the 1990s. In Manchester, by contrast, the major local issue was the fear of crime, especially crimes of violence, seen, in the public imagination, to be located outside the city centre core. Anxieties in Manchester focused on certain areas in the inner ring around the central core of the city (Cheetham Hill, Whalley Range and especially Moss Side); areas of multiple deprivation, which are widely discussed in the local and national press and in local gossip as ghetto areas housing an exclusively black underclass. The recycling of this view of the inner city in Manchester has a powerful mythic quality – in the sense that there is little pause to evaluate the accuracy either of the gossip or of the press reports. According to the 1991 Census, however, the population of Moss Side itself was actually only 31 per cent black, with an additional 6 per cent of local residents being of Indian or Pakistani background; whilst Whalley Range was 11 per cent black and 20 per cent Indian or Pakistani: the majority population of both areas was poor white.

Given the absence in Sheffield of a comparable, concentric circle of inner-city deprivation, Sheffield's 'ghetto', as we will see in Chapter 8, has grown up and institutionalised in the local imagination in Pitsmoor and Burngreave, a Victorian inner suburb which in the 1930s had a quite genteel reputation. The particularity of these local transformations in urban environments (the presence or absence of a recognisable inner-city area) is one of many features lost in accounts which speak, in highly generalised a fashion, of the shared or common features of 'the North of England industrial city' as a whole.

MATERIAL LANDSCAPES OF THE INDUSTRIAL NORTH

It is important to remember that the different cities of the 'North of England' occupy quite different, and diverse, geographical locations (very close to the Pennine hills, as in Sheffield and in Bradford, and, to a lesser extent, in Leeds; or to the sea, as in Liverpool and Hull), and that the 'natural' features surrounding these cities have had an ongoing influence on the character of local urban industrial development and on local culture: Manchester's sprawling location has always been much more difficult than that of many other cities in the North to identify in terms of specific or determining natural features:

> Manchester lies at the middle of the Lancashire plain, an area which resembles a vast amphitheatre. To the west the plain extends in a continuous, flat expanse as far as the Irish sea. To the south it merges into a low, hilly countryside of Cheshire and Derbyshire. To the north and east the landscape rises in a series of valleys and even higher mountain slopes near the borders of Cumberland, Westmoreland and Yorkshire.
>
> (Messinger 1985: 5–6)

The subsequent development of industry and of the cities themselves in these particular geographical locations has both modified, and added to, these natural endowments of place. In Manchester, one of the key nineteenth-century developments was the opening of the first successful passenger railway in the world, the Manchester–Liverpool railway, in 1830, establishing Manchester's significance as a transport interchange in the North. The determining moment, however, much later in the nineteenth century, was the opening of the Bridgewater Canal in 1893 and, especially, of the Ship Canal a year later, linking the three rivers which meander across the Cheshire and Lancashire plains (the Irwell, the Irk and the Medlock) to the Mersey basin and the sea, so constructing Manchester as an inland port, 36 miles from the sea – of enormous significance for purposes of trade and commerce in and out of the whole North of England.

We shall present a more extended and detailed analysis of the development of Manchester's industry and local labour market in Chapter 2. For the moment, our concern is simply to register the way in which the development of that industry has left an inescapable legacy, a material landscape of canals, railways, warehouses, mills, other industrial buildings (which would be referred to, locally, simply as 'works') and related office buildings, which criss-cross, and demarcate the public availability and use of space across, the urban sprawl of Greater Manchester. So also, of course, did the development of Manchester in the nineteenth century involve the construction of a series of celebrated Victorian buildings in the city centre, ranging from the Free Trade Hall, built in 1846, to the elegant Barton Arcade, opened in 1871 (cf. Dyos and Wolff 1973). At the other extreme, the development of Manchester as the 'first Victorian city' also left behind a material legacy of cramped, unhygienic and dangerous areas of housing reserved for the use of the poor, famously discussed by Engels in his *The Condition of the English Working Class*, first published in 1845 but still pertinent, as we will argue in Chapter 6, as an account of Manchester's inner-city estates and high-rise blocks (Engels 1987).

The development of the steel trades in Sheffield during the nineteenth century bequeathed to the city a harsh and oppressive landscape of steel mills and coal mines, particularly in what came to be known as the East

Figure 1.1 Very old towns: cotton mills of Manchester and the North West
Source: North West Museums Service

End (Attercliffe, Darnall and Tinsley); and it was a visit to the East End which led George Orwell to describe Sheffield in *The Road to Wigan Pier* (published in 1937), as 'the ugliest town in the Old World' – much to the chagrin of Sheffielders at the time. Orwell was upset by the soot and grime deposits emitted from the chimneys of the East End: he does not seem to have visited any of the older manorial homes of Broomhill or Ranmoor, or the new civic buildings of the central city (the Mappin Art Gallery, the Graves Art Gallery and Central Library and the City Hall, all opened in the 1930s) in which the city itself took much pride. He seems also to have been unaware of the great range of public parks, including the vast expanse donated to the city by its major benefactor, J.G. Graves, and other open spaces close to the Derbyshire Peak, which are also a part of its nineteenth-century legacy.

We think it would be idle to suggest that the material configuration of public 'civic' buildings, private and public housing, and the works and warehouses themselves that characterise each old industrial city (or any urban environment) is without social effect – not least, for example, in the way in which the grandeur of particular buildings (the Refuge Assurance Building in Manchester) or streets (Grey Street in Newcastle upon Tyne) might underline the hierarchical and unequal character of the local social structure, whether built around commerce or around landed wealth. Alternatively, the relative absence in a city of such buildings of grandeur might speak, in the imagination, to the existence of a local level of social equality (or, in another view, a lack of ambition on the part of the local dominant commercial or political elites). These speculations aside, it is important not to dismiss the power of Bill Hillier and Juliette Hanson's strictures that:

> architecture structures the system of space in which we live and move. In that it does so, it has a direct relation – rather than merely a symbolic one – to social life, since it provides the material conditions for the patterns of movement, encounter and avoidance which are the material realisation – as well as sometimes the generator – of social relations.
>
> (Hillier and Hanson 1984: ix)

Hillier and Hanson's argument is that the physical layout of buildings and space in a city – independently even of their aesthetic interpretation – provides a basic material structure for everyday life in that city, in ways that many architects and cultural commentators, preoccupied with the symbolic features of buildings and space, have tended to ignore. To recognise the powers of buildings and physical infrastructure (for example, to elevate the mind and imagination or depress the will) is not to deny that the interaction between buildings and local culture is a matter of 'active' and changing social relationships (as Doreen Massey has so powerfully insisted) (Massey 1994: 144), in which buildings can be transformed both in form and function, but it is to recognise that there may be some unevenness of potential: a chemical works in Teesside is less useful and more restricting a legacy in our post-industrial, post-modern times than Central Station in Manchester (now reconstructed and renamed G-Mex: the Greater Manchester Exhibition and Concert Centre) or a riverside Warehouse in London's East End.

The cities of the North of England can, however, nearly all claim, not just a distinct geographical and natural location, but also a quite distinct material legacy in terms of architecture, physical layout of the city, and the infrastructure of industrial buildings and spaces generally left over from the era of mass manufacturing. It is partly in recognition of these differences that we wish to suggest there is no such thing as *the* de-industrialised North of England city (a unitary category of places defined by their distance from London, by accent and by the collapse of their manufacturing base) – although, by the same token, we also want to insist that these are important common features of something called 'Northern-ness' and that these attributes of the Northern region, rooted in its overall industrial history, do enable one to speak of sets of values (e.g. collectivism and a sense of community, but also, perhaps, of hard physical labour – 'graft' – masculinism and insularity) which distinguish it from the South of England, from the Midlands and from other parts of the country.[18] It follows also that the 'North' may have more in common, in terms of the dominant culture (of masculinist collectivism) through which it lives its 'Northern-ness', with other de-industrialising old industrial regions, like the Ruhr in Germany, or some American 'Rust-Belt' cities like Pittsburgh, than it does with other urban areas in Britain.

DIFFERENT FOLKS

In Part III of this book, we will develop another important sociological argument – namely, that there are several publics in the cities of the North of England, other than the modern-day professional consumer of cities, on the one hand, and the male industrial workers who have been so dominant historically in these cities, on the other. This truth became absolutely apparent early in a series of street surveys which we undertook in Manchester and Sheffield in the first months of 1992, in our first attempt to identify the different patterns of use of different urban territories in these two conurbations by different sections of the public. It became possible, very quickly, to identify quite distinct patterns of use by groups whom we could only describe, initially, as shoppers, workers, commuters and leisure seekers. A series of focus group discussions with individuals who had been contacted in these initial surveys enabled a significant refinement of this crude and rather commonsensical grid of city-centre use into a more complex taxonomy of publics making use of these two cities. We will be discussing this notion of 'different local publics' more fully in the Introduction to Part II.

THE MEASUREMENT OF LOCAL DIFFERENCE

We will want to develop these introductory theoretical observations as we go along, and also in the concluding chapter. For the moment, we want to take note of the way in which a great many issues of national and international concern pertaining to the 'quality of life', or well-being, have become the topic, in the late 1980s and early 1990s, of local identification and investigation on the part of those governmental and neo-governmental agencies which in the free market societies of the 1990s are charged with the responsibility of administering civil society. Across nearly all fields of social and educational policy in Britain, we are now regularly being presented with large numbers of different league tables which purport to measure the local effectiveness of different public institutions and 'trusts': in local schools (in terms, in this instance, of exam results), local and regional hospitals and other health-care provisions (in terms, especially, of various measures of cost-effectiveness or 'value for money'), and the performance of local police forces (in terms of the clear-up rate of offences across different force areas, and, if the Sheehy Report into Police Performance had been legislated in 1993, in terms of a system of performance pay-by-results). These particular indices of local variation in service delivery are part and parcel of the government's project of ensuring accountability and cost-efficiency, especially within the public sector. But we are also constantly presented, particularly in the quality press, with many other league tables, giving expression to a wide variety of other instances of local and regional variation – most notably, in terms of levels of poverty, unemployment, ill-health and mortality. Some of these reports (and the league tables that accompany them) are the fruits of the ongoing concern of academics and scholars with the effective auditing and evaluation of government policy, sometimes in respect of certain egalitarian goals that are still held dear in many parts of the academy, and sometimes simply in the name of a stubborn and realistic curiosity with respect to the quality of life of other citizens.[19] Others, however, are the result of attempts by service providers (like the regional fire brigades, ambulance services, or similar locally based organisations) to make a case at national level for improved budgetary appropriations, via demonstrations of the different levels of workload that present themselves in particular regions or localities by reason of their demographic make-up or other officially recognised contingencies.[20]

This new centrally orchestrated 'public consciousness of local variation' of performance has emerged against a backdrop of national and even global processes underlining the idea of 'competition' and efficiency. It is being applied across nearly all significant areas of social and economic activity, and in nearly all related debates within what Laffin (1986) calls 'the policy community'. In that foremost of areas of national concern in free market Britain – the mushrooming problems of property and personal crime and the escalating levels of fear and anxiety

Table 1.1 Worst areas for recorded crime (1991)[22]

Ranking	Police force area	Offences per 100,000 population
1	Northumbria	4,360
2	Cleveland	4,271
3	Greater Manchester	4,001
4	Nottinghamshire	3,934
5	Bedfordshire	3,706

Source: Labour Party (1992: 7)

associated with 'crime' – there is an increasing awareness of the differential expressions and levels of 'the crime problem' at local level. This
first surfaced, one could argue, in 1992 with the release by the Home
Office of figures revealing the differential 'clear-up rates' of all crimes
reported to the police across the 43 police-force areas in England and
Wales. Then, at the very end of 1992, the Labour Party released a report
on rates of car crime across those same 43 police forces demonstrating
enormous variation in the rates of car theft and thefts from vehicles
reported to the police across the country.[21] According to the Labour
Party report, the five police forces under greatest pressure in 1991 on
this dimension of their fight against crime were as shown in Table 1.1.

Our own scrutiny of the annual reports of the chief constables across
the North of England in 1991, early in this research project, confirmed
that the prevalence of crime reported to the police, as recorded in these
reports, and then compared to population figures reported in the
Census, showed significant variation (Table 1.2).[23]

It is not our intention here to endow these figures, covering only one
year of police operations, with special significance. But it does bear
saying that our own examination of the crime statistics for the two cities
for the period 1975 to 1991 – remembering all the caveats that must be
made about the comparative analysis of locally collected crime data[24] –
did none the less suggest that the city of Sheffield throughout the 1970s
and 1980s consistently exhibited a lower level of reported crime per head
of population than did the city of Manchester (Table 1.3). It is also a
matter of some remark, for other commentators on Sheffield, that it was

Table 1.2 Rate of recorded crime in five selected police forces in the North of
England (1991)

Police force	Ratio of reported offences to number in local population
Greater Manchester	1:6.8
West Yorkshire	1:7.0
Merseyside	1:9.4
South Yorkshire	1:10.6
Derbyshire	1:12.9

Source: Annual reports of the chief constables for each of the five forces (1991)

Table 1.3 Crime rates of the Cities of Manchester and Sheffield (selected years 1975–90)

Year	City of Manchester	City of Sheffield
1975	10,368	3,565
1980	13,180	4,893
1985	18,732	6,207
1990	19,724	8,632

Note: Figures for crimes reported per 100,000 population
Sources: Population figures from Central Policy Unit, City of Sheffield, County Planning Department of City of Manchester, and Registrar-General's Final Mid-Year Estimates, and annual reports of the Chief Constable, South Yorkshire and Greater Manchester Police

one of a very small number of cities to have 'escaped' the 'civil disturbances' that occurred in many urban centres in England, notably in Manchester, in the 1980s (Watts *et al.* 1989: 26).[25]

Our initial examination in 1991–2 of the rates of increase in crime in the two cities during this decade and a half of de-industrialisation and social transformation did suggest, however, that the levels and trajectories of reported crime might now be undergoing interesting changes (Table 1.4).

The increase in the amount of crime known to the police for the city of Manchester over the period 1975–91 was in the order of 210 per cent, but the biggest increases were in the period to 1986. Since then, the annual rate of increase in crime within the city of Manchester proper (i.e. within the Census boundaries of Manchester City Council) has only been 2.2 per cent (expressed in terms of the rate of crime per 100,000), with three consecutive decreases reported in 1986–7, 1987–8 and 1988–9. In Sheffield, the increase in the overall rate of reported crime per 100,000 population between 1975 and 1991, on the same dimension, was 291 per cent, with an increase since 1986 of 36 per cent. The relationship between these very different rates of increase in these two cities, and the broader changes taking place in the local economies and infrastructure of these two localities, is surely a matter of significant sociological interest.[26]

Table 1.4 Annual rate of increase in reported crime, Manchester and Sheffield (selected years 1975–91)

Period	City of Manchester	City of Sheffield
1975–6	0.6	−6.5
1980–1	13.1	5.8
1985–6	11.0	17.2
1990–1	10.1	13.3

Note: Figures are for percentage increase over 12 months.
Sources: As for Table 1.3

POPULAR COMMON SENSE ON LOCAL DIFFERENCE: MANCHESTER AND SHEFFIELD

There are a variety of more or less commonsensical ways in which differences between the two cities of Manchester and Sheffield are discussed by Mancunians and Sheffielders themselves, and we think these forms of popular common sense should be heard. We have already indicated that Manchester and Sheffield are not necessarily the natural foils for comparative discussion for the residents of either city, despite their proximity on either side of the Pennines. Nevertheless, when the two cities are compared in popular conversation, the following comparisons are very often made.

One fairly frequent topic, especially for Sheffielders, is the different size of the two conurbations (the population of the Greater Manchester conurbation, according to the 1991 Census, was 2,455,093, whilst the population of the City of Sheffield was only 525,800).[27] Local commonsense talk, however, often goes beyond the fact of size, in its references to the 'feel' of the two cities, or Northern cities in general, to discussion of cities as being more or less crowded or spacious. There is not always any unchallengeable empirical warrant for popular common sense, but popular identification of Liverpool and Manchester as crowded cities does find some support in Census data produced on population and city size (Table 1.5).

Even more common a topic in popular talk is the weather experienced by different cities across the North, but in Manchester in particular. According to an analysis published by the Sheffield City Museums in 1984, the city of Sheffield enjoyed 1,235 hours of sunshine per annum on average over the period from 1931 to 1960, consistently well above Manchester, which experienced only 1,071 hours. Over the same period, Sheffield (at an altitude of 131 metres above sea level) had an average of 809.2 millimetres of rainfall per annum, by comparison with Manchester's consistently higher total, at 38.1 metres above sea level, of 858.3 millimetres of rain per year. It is only in terms of average temperature that Manchester fares better than Sheffield climatically:

Table 1.5 Population and area of major English cities (1961)

City	Population	Acres within city boundaries	Density (population per acre)
Liverpool	747,490	27,810	26.87
Manchester	661,041	27,555	23.99
Birmingham	1,105,651	51,147	21.62
Leeds	510,597	40,610	12.57
Sheffield	493,954	39,586	12.48

Source: Robbins (1994: 311)

from 1931 to 1960, Manchester had an 'average daily mean temperature' of 10.0°C, compared to Sheffield's 9.6° (Garland 1984).

Not the least important commonsense observation often heard in popular discussion of these two cities is the view of Manchester as a grand city of fine Victorian architecture, where Sheffield is seen, by contrast, as a city of little architectural interest. Sheffield's 'virtue' is seen to lie in its situation, on the very edge of the Derbyshire Peak District, built, as local folklore insists, 'like Rome' on seven hills, and somehow, albeit with a population in 1991 of 525,800, 'the largest village in England'. Manchester, by contrast, is largely flat, though, as we indicated earlier, it reaches outwards to the Pennines at different points to the north and east: and the extended conurbation of Greater Manchester contains at least ten distinct towns, each of which exhibits some kind of autonomy from Manchester, not least for purposes of local government (in the form of ten local borough councils).

Social commentators, urban policy makers and academic social scientists ignore these well-established, commonsense appraisals of city location by long-time residents, newcomers and visitors alike, in terms of positive or negative aspects of their geographical location and climate, at their peril. It is also vitally important, we would argue, to understand how popular common sense deals with the given physical and material features of the actual cities themselves (from factory sites, through particular housing estates or high-rise buildings and city-centre shops, to pubs and local municipal parks), and, most notoriously of all, how concrete underpasses, city-centre car parks, and other areas of public resort with low visibility and uncertain custodianship become important topics in popular conversation. The material landscape evokes both celebration and fear and anxiety. Through gossip and story-telling, it may also come to inform local folk belief and myth (albeit sometimes involving 'tricks' of the memory and/or collective belief). Many of these myths are of extremely local provenance, circulating amongst the inhabitants of individual estates, for example, defining the moral character of particular streets or clusters of houses.[28] There are also important myths that are general to the whole Northern region rather than specific cities, which we might think of as 'Northern myths'. The notion that 'what Manchester does today, the world does tomorrow' may have originated in the role which Manchester's theatres once played as a testing ground for new plays before they were launched on the West End of London; but it is also a phrase which speaks to the sense of Manchester's dynamic 'structure of feeling', as well as alluding to what Buck has called 'the regional sense of grievance' that pervades the North as a whole with respect to the hegemony of London and the South-east over the rest of England and the definition of what England is all about (Buck 1979). There is a definite feeling in Sheffield, Leeds and other Northern cities about Manchester as an 'alternative capital', i.e. for 'the North'.[29] There has always been a powerful recognition in Sheffield that Manchester is a big place, which in the past always had much better shops than Sheffield, an airport, and the Hallé Orchestra – which pays a number of visits to Sheffield during the year but is based in metropolitan Manchester. For many years, one of the other attractions of Manchester for Northerners was the Belle Vue Zoo, first opened in 1836 – a 36-acre compound built around a fairground which itself was a popular Northern destination (Kidd 1993: 53). It was also the home to the *Manchester Guardian* – before this voice of dissent, the preferred newspaper of the thinking Northerner, finally departed for London in 1976 – and the Northern editions of many other national newspapers. Manchester was recognised as a centre for national television and radio in the North, and, especially amongst football supporters, there is an envious awareness that Manchester is home to one consistently successful football team, which now regularly represents (the North of) England in national and international competition. In the 1980s, particularly amongst young people, as we shall see in Chapter 11, Manchester emerged as the centre for popular music and the 'club scene' – a fact that was celebrated in the massively popular T-shirts reading 'On the Seventh Day, God Created Manchester' and 'Born in the North, Return to the North, Exist in the North, Die in the North'.

SIGNIFYING LOCAL IDENTITY

The vast range of badges, scarves, shirts and other items of kit worn by football fans across England are one well-known example of the way in which particular places or regions ('spaces') are taken up as signifiers of a local identity or affiliation. Another less widely remarked site for the active recycling of local culture and identity are the signs outside public houses, and the names given to these pubs. Sometimes, this may simply involve the naming of a pub after a significant local folk hero. One of the more prominent pubs in Milnrow, near Rochdale, on the edge of Greater Manchester, is the Tim Bobbin: Tim Bobbin being the *nom de plume* adopted by John Collier, the author of a major piece of comic writing in local dialect, *Tummus an' Meary*, published in 1750 (cf. Joyce 1991: 257–8). At other times, a pub's given name may become the object of some active local renegotiation: on Snig Hill, in Sheffield, there was for many years a public house of dubious local reputation, the Black Swan, known universally to all Sheffielders as 'the Mucky Duck'. In the 1980s, when the pub was reconfigured as a city-centre wine bar, the owners faithfully recognised the power of local myth and decided, indeed, that this new Sheffield leisure spot should be called 'The Mucky Duck'.

It would be idle to suggest that the full range of such redefinitions of 'the spatial characteristics' of particular cities, or localities, can be grasped simply by describing the recycling of local urban folklore. What matters in terms of the retrieval and reimagining of a sense of 'the local', at a time of globalising tendencies on other fronts, is how the inherited themes of urban folklore are renegotiated and reconstructed in particular localities – sometimes, it must be recognised, in the name of 'heritage' or 'regeneration', and at other times less obtrusively, in the spontaneous talk and taken-for-granted ways of thinking of local residents.

LOCAL CLASS STRUCTURES AND URBAN COMPETITION

Our interest in these aspects of local folklore and myth about locality sat alongside the recognition that the character of locality must be understood in terms of the analysis of local labour markets, in ways that had been recommended by locality studies in England and Wales in the early 1980s. We referred earlier to John Urry's interest in moving from the analysis of local industrial history to local class structures, and, in particular, to his argument that such local structural variation in the size, economic focus and relations of classes may have assumed an even greater importance in recent years – paradoxically as a result of the increasing globalisation of capitalist activity. This globalisation has the effect of enlarging the capacity of 'capital', which is increasingly well integrated internationally (both horizontally and vertically) into multiple product markets, to relocate its activity (including its employment of labour) to its best advantage, more or less anywhere in the world. This in turn has the effect of weakening the relationship of dependency which had grown up, particularly during the 1930s and the early post-war period of social reconstruction, between capital and individual nation-states. This also weakens the ability of locally organised interests to represent themselves effectively with capital, through the medium of nationally organised agencies of the state, since capital is no longer so dependent on its earlier relationships with individual national states.

The impact of these changes on the relationship between capital and the state, at local level, is profound, with a key determinant of the economic prospects of any one locality being the character of the particular class structure left over, at local level, from the earlier periods of social struggle. Urry identified four such local class structures in early 1980s Britain, defined primarily in terms of the extent to which employment is organised by private capital or the state, the relative size of the intermediate service and professional class, the size of the traditional working class, and the levels of employment of women in particular localities, though he recognises these are not exhaustive of all possible configurations.

In the meantime, however, the American writers Harvey Molotch and John Logan, examining, in particular, the dynamics of change across American cities in the 1980s, have advanced their own conceptual taxonomy of cities, in part constructed in terms of the different capacities to perform particular roles in respect of the new global economic order (Molotch and Logan 1985). They speak of cities which are 'headquarters' for massive multinational corporations; of cities which perform as centres of innovation, 'border entrepôt' cities located on national boundaries dealing with the international trade of products and of labour; and of cities which function, specifically and strategically, as retirement centres. Each of these first three types of city can potentially survive well in the new global economic order as it presents itself in the United States; but there remain a large number of other cities, which Molotch and Logan call 'module production cities', which lack the attributes that are required for investors and whose futures are tied to routine production tasks, in narrow or outdated areas of industrial activity. This conceptual schema is clearly not transferable directly to Britain: there are very few examples of whole cities which are directly and exclusively involved in innovation (as in California), although there are examples of cities (e.g. Cambridge) where the introduction of significantly sized business or enterprise zones in recent years has changed the balance of the local economy (Saxenian 1989). There are a few examples of cities and towns which are specifically orientated, on a commercial basis, to the servicing of people's retirement years (Bournemouth, Hove, Southport), but the retirement years of many of the more wealthy of Britain's commercial middle classes are spent abroad, in rather warmer climates. But what does make sense is to think of Molotch and Logan's distinction between the 'headquarter city', dedicated to the provision of the full array of services required by international capital and communications, and thereby attaining a lead position in the global competition for investment in places, and the 'module production city', left behind in this competition by virtue of the restricted range and articulation of local capital and local labour force alike.

As we progressed further in our research into Manchester and Sheffield in 1991–3, Molotch and Logan's schema – particularly its distinction between a headquarters city and a module production centre – began to commend itself as a useful starting point, alongside John Urry's approach to local class structure, for our thinking and analysis. Urry's idea of the 'local class structure' is not intended to correspond, in any straightforward sense, to the legal or geographical boundaries of a town, city or even region; it has to do, instead, with the character of the relations of production spread across the area, including, in particular, the types of work available and their given features in terms of wage levels and of prospects for occupational or class mobility; and it also has to do with the level of organisation of the local labour market, including its gender, sectoral and occupational aspects, and the level of development of local trade union and labour politics. All of these aspects of 'local class structures' can be understood in terms of their lengthy local histories, producing a very specific inheritance in the form of a labour force with particular skills and knowledge at the level of a local area as well as, it must be added, a network of local cultural institutions (working men's clubs, pubs, sports clubs, etc.), folklore and taken-for-granted social routines (including, here, certain routines determining when one 'goes to town' for shopping or other purposes). It begins to make sense to speak not just of a local class structure, in Urry's words, but also of a *local cultural structure*, inextricably connected up with a widely understood though implicit sense of the social structure (of power, status and life-chances) in the particular locality.

Our central argument is that this local culture structure can be understood, following Raymond Williams, as a 'local structure of feeling' that distils a set of local wisdoms and folklore about local place. This is not merely the exercise of an idiosyncratic creativity of particular publics, or the social mix of particular neighbourhoods, with the actual physical reality of cities merely a secondary variable. We do not believe that the creative activity of local residents can 'make of their city what they will'. Each urban area, region and locality involves a given inheritance of geographical form (morphology), climate, industrial base, labour market and labour history, patterns of in-migration and emigration, ethnic and cultural mix, conflicts and contest with other neighbouring towns or cities, and many other given features that define it and endow it with an identity which, as we suggested earlier, can perhaps be thought of as a 'local structure of feeling'. We are also interested, here, in exploring how the gendered dimensions of this 'local structure of feeling' (shaped, in the Sheffield case, by the masculinism of the so-called 'Little Mester' – the term which is used, almost universally, to refer to local men employed in Sheffield's 'dual economy' of cutlery and steel) were and are challenged, ignored or reproduced by women – for example, at the high point of the cutlery industry, by the so-called Buffer Girls, employed to polish the finished products of the cutlery trade, locally famous for their profanities and independent mindedness. We will also want to note, in Chapter 2, the gendered aspects of Manchester's 'business' culture: the continuing local references to the founders of the cotton trade and the industrialists of the later nineteenth century as 'the men who made Manchester'. There will be other contested areas in this local structure of feeling, notably over issues of ethnicity as a kind of membership category in local identity (Manchester has a long history of immigration and this has had long-term effects in defining the character of local Mancunian culture). Our argument is that the dominant forms of the local structure of feeling must in part be understood as a product of 'the local class structure' (Urry 1981: 467), which itself must be understood in terms of the particular 'industrial history' of a locality; but that the contested and changing character of that local identity must also be understood. We are particularly aware of the specific and local forms of hegemonic masculinities that have been dominant in these old industrial cities, as in other North of England cities and industrial regions,[30] which carry enormous weight for many local men, with their powerful continuing mythology and imagery about the value and the community of industrial men. But we are also aware that these are contested definitions, which are not now so firmly located and legitimised in local labour markets or industries.

One concern of this book is to understand how industrial histories are lived or actively reinterpreted by the different publics who now live in those de-industrialised locales. This will involve us, in part, in an analysis of the practical strategies adopted by different publics (women, children, gay people, the elderly, and people from different ethnic backgrounds) in making use and sense of each city. It will also confirm the important sociological truth that there are, within each of these two industrial cities, different 'configurations of space and facilities' for each of these different publics. Different buildings and different spaces and areas of these cities help to create discrete 'mental maps' of each city for diverse publics, which then get to be institutionalised for members of each public as 'their' Manchester or 'their' Sheffield, cutting across, in the practical popular imagination, the dominant maps of the city that are mobilised by the local 'heritage industry' or members of the local growth coalition.

In Chapter 12 of this book, our specific theoretical sociological concern will be to try to examine the way in which interconnected structures of class, local gender order and routinised social practices (and also, perhaps, 'the local structure of feeling') are currently being modified by the rapid changes taking place, globally and locally, in the availability and forms of work in the last years of the twentieth century. It is in this particular sense, in fact, that John Urry argues that 'local class structures' have assumed an increasing importance in the context of the fundamental reorganisation of work and capital accumulation that has characterised the last decade and a half. To this we would add the importance of the 'local structure of feeling' of class, culture and routine social practices. It is in this light that we examine the specificity of the local social structures of Manchester and Sheffield, in terms of both their rootedness in the past and their present expression.

2

DIRTY OLD TOWNS

The pre-industrial and industrial histories of Manchester and Sheffield

We have three connected purposes in this chapter. We want, first, to provide a brief account of the topography and geographical situation of Manchester and Sheffield and also some sense of the 'material reality' of the cities (the configurations of buildings and streets that have historically made up their urban form). The provision of this account, of course, involves us in writing something of a local industrial history of the two cities and their larger regions, since the colonisation of space and terrain in these two areas was overwhelmingly driven by the massive expansion of manufacturing, especially throughout the nineteenth century.

Secondly, however, we want to use this geographical overview and historical narrative we provide here as a way into an understanding of the specific 'local structure of feeling' in these two cities and their larger region. In particular, we will see our narrative quickly turn to a discussion of the form of organisation and the culture of local industry and local workplaces – that is, of the organisation of shifts in local factories or mills, the division of domestic labour, the gender divisions in the industry itself, and the associated rhythms of the working day and week. This is not simply a 'class reductionist' argument. We will try to show how cultures originally associated with local workplaces (the cotton mill, the docks, the steel works or the cutlery workshop) 'escape' into the larger local culture generally and leave their indelible imprint or traces over time at several different levels within that local social formation. This process of local 'identity construction' (as, for example, around the idea of 'a Manc', or Mancunian) may originate from the cotton mill, but it will find expression in the everyday cultural assumptions and practices of the masters of local trade and industry themselves: amongst all 'the men who made Manchester'. This local 'Manc' culture (which is about male businessmen and workers alike, relatively attuned, compared to men from elsewhere in the North of England, to the fast-changing boom and slump of the capitalist business cycle) has a provenance across a city region, and bears some comparison with the kind of enterprise culture identified for the East End of London by Dick Hobbs in his excellent study (Hobbs 1989). In this respect, it becomes easier to understand how a city like Manchester – both in the 1990s and in earlier periods – could and can simultaneously present itself as 'the first industrial city', Cottonopolis, and a city of commerce and trade, and also as a shrine to organised labour and its venerable traditions (the site of the Peterloo massacre, home for a period to Friedrich Engels, and, most recently, an appropriate venue for the National Museum of Labour History). Sheffield's 'local identity' (and 'local structure of feeling'), in the meantime, has an altogether different provenance: an unambiguously Labour city, built around a dual economy of cutlery and steel, with close and familiar relations between local labour and local employing class – an enclave of 'community' and mutual dependence. This particular culture of the local workplace in Sheffield also escapes outwards from the workplace, with a very general effect on the character of the 'local structure of feeling' (even, we will argue, on those who never found employment in either of the two local trades). It finds expression in religion – the prevalence of the Methodist church – and also in the character of local Labour politics and local argot and folk culture.

We take it that our project here – that of tracing the origins and current re-representation of 'the local structure of feeling' – is precisely what Raymond Williams envisaged in the arguments he advanced for close study of the complex interconnectedness of the ordinary, lived culture of the people. In *The Long Revolution*, for example, he demanded, in a rather Weberian fashion, that cultural analysis must focus on 'the discovery of patterns of a characteristic kind' (Williams 1965: 61) since it was precisely in this interaction of apparently disparate patterns of activity in particular places at particular times that one could glimpse what he wanted to term 'the structure of feeling'.

Our third intention in this chapter, then, has already been signalled in these opening remarks. As against the thrust of some 'post-modernist' writing on the city, we are interested in seeing the different ways in which the current regeneration of old industrial cities (at least in the North of England) actually reworks and re-represents the facts of local identity and difference, and therefore, importantly, preserves and symbolises these identities, albeit in a modified fashion by comparison with the custom and practice of the modernist period. This is a matter in part of knowing and understanding the 'play' of local culture (the Mancunian 'scally', the Sheffield 'Little Mester') and, in part, of recognising the continuing exercise of memory and local myth (in ways which are not obvious to visiting *flâneurs* from the academy or national press and politicians). We have in mind here the exemplary work on the industrial area of Terni in Italy by Alessandro Portelli (1991) and on London by Raphael Samuel (1994), but we are also particularly interested in the way in which memories and myths may work differently in different places – either as part of a process of acquiescence and surrender to fate and destiny, or as part of an active appropriation of a local culture (like the local culture of enterprise itself) with a view to the future of some contemporary local business or other initiative. The current, quite dramatic regeneration of Manchester involves not a re-representation of 'any city, any time' but a specific reappropriation of local best tradition ('bringing back the trams', as the locals observe) and local sensibilities with respect to work, commerce and the market. Sheffield's preoccupations in the 1980s (with the opening of a series of quite excellent museums of local labour and working history) speak to a lost culture and rhythm of work, and a nostalgic set of cultural feelings, that may signal a wider set of problems in that city at the end of the twentieth century.

SHEFFIELD

Prehistory

Historical information on the history of the city of Sheffield prior to the Industrial Revolution reveals, primarily, that the area was home to a small number of Iron Age hill forts and a single Roman fort at Temple-borough, a little to the north-east of the present city (Bartlett and Preston 1956: 115–16). No local historian tries to claim that there was any really significant Roman settlement in the area. Even after the invasion of the Anglo-Saxons, the area remained quite sparsely settled. The Domesday Book identifies 'Hallam' as having considerable ploughland and meadow and a hall, belonging to Earl Wallef, but gives little detail about neigh-bouring 'Sheffield' (Maxwell 1956: 136). Even in the later Middle Ages, the Sheffield region:

> lying, in the main, on the uplands of the southern Pennines, [the Sheffield region] was comparatively barren, sparsely populated, and inaccessible apart from these eastern parts which were within reach of the main route of north and south communication through the plain of York.
>
> (Lewis 1956: 138)

This summary statement actually catches two themes about the geography of the Sheffield region, prior to its industrial development, which have had a continuing significance ever since: its hilly topography and isolation from major transport routes. The region which was to become the location for Sheffield's industrial development in the late eighteenth and early nineteenth centuries was, above all else, a region of hills and valleys (it was, indeed, these hills and the rivers that ran down from them which were later to provide the water power for the mills and forges of the emerging forges and workshops that were opened up by small craftsmen in the eighteenth and early nineteenth centuries). The proximity of the Derbyshire Peak, and the constantly invoked local belief that the city grew up 'like Rome' on seven hills, are profoundly important features of local Sheffield folklore. Sheffield was always, also, 'off the beaten track', located some distance away from the main lines of north–south (and indeed east–west) communication in England, as opened up by the Romans and then by Scandinavian settlers. Even in the early nineteenth century, the sense of Sheffield's 'apartness' from the main lines of communication within Britain was confirmed by the routing of the main London–Scotland rail links through Doncaster, well to the east of Sheffield. It was not until 1870 that the opening of the Midland Station made available a direct line to London.

The origins of the cutlers

The origins of Sheffield's cutlery trade lie in the presence of iron ore in the area, mined as early as the thirteenth century. The 'subsidy rolls' of 1378–9 listed over 50 smiths and ironmongers in the area of Sheffield, which was already known for its 'whittles' – knife blades in wooden handles of the kind identified by Chaucer in 'The Reeve's Tale' as Sheffield 'thwitels' (Jones 1956: 149). By the sixteenth century, growing numbers of smiths and cutlers were making full use the water pouring down from local hills to power their forges, importing iron from Russia, Spain and Sweden, and established local craftsmen saw the need to regulate entry into the trades and the quality of the product. The oldest set of regulations of the cutlery trade, the View of Frankpledge of the Manor of Sheffield, drawn up in 1565, set up the conditions of a local monopoly, a formal system of apprenticeship and two periods (a fortnight in August and a month from Christmas day) of total cessation of output (still known locally, as late as the 1970s, as 'the stop weeks'). Later regulations of 1590 forbade cutlers to use marks on their products other than those assigned to them, and provided for a special jury to identify and punish such offences. In 1624, these craftsmen of the cutlery trades were established by Act of Parliament as a self-governing corporation, the Cutlers' Company of Sheffield and Hallamshire, with regulatory powers over the industry extending over all of Hallamshire and six miles around it, symbolised in the annual Cutlers' Feast (still held to this day). The Cutlers' Company exercised a continuing influence over the city of Sheffield throughout the nineteenth century on behalf of the small craftsmen (or 'Little Mesters') working in the cutlery trade, with the Master Cutler, elected on an annual basis, having almost as much local importance as the Lord Mayor. The only significant local industries outside the jurisdiction of the company were nail-making[1] and workshops involved in the manufacture of old Sheffield plate (the technique for forging of which had been discovered in 1742 by Thomas Boulsover). So the Sheffield area was a well-established centre not just of the cutlery trade, but also of a specific system for the governance and regulation of that local trade and other trades associated with it, well before the coming of the Industrial Revolution proper.

Sheffield as an 'industrial district'

The organisation of Sheffield's cutlery trade and labour market has been the subject of considerable interest – not least on the part of the liberal economist, Alfred Marshall, writing in the early years of this century.

Marshall extolled the benefits of the system of occupational regulation imposed by the Cutlers' Company, in particular because of the way it was thought to institutionalise cooperative relationships at local level between capital and labour. He also argued that this close relationship encouraged flexibility within the industry, notably in terms of product specialisation and development. In Marshall's view, the cutlery industry of Sheffield shared with the textile industry of south-east Lancashire the attributes of what he called an 'industrial district' – a geographically well-defined district with a level of cooperation and flexibility uncommon in other industrially active areas (Marshall 1919, 1920). Whether or not this characterisation of Sheffield as an 'industrial district', in Marshall's sense, can be sustained is a matter of quite active debate amongst economic and social historians.[2] What is not in dispute is the distinctive character of Sheffield's local labour market, or its 'local class structure' in Urry's terms, in the late eighteenth and early nineteenth centuries, resulting from the parallel development of the established cutlery trade and the newly emergent industry based on steel.

The emergence of Sheffield steel

The key moment for Sheffield's steel industry was the arrival in the district, in or around 1740, of the Lincolnshire-born clockmaker and Quaker, Benjamin Huntsman, who was interested in finding a more reliable method for the production of a refined steel for use in clock springs and pendulums. Huntsman began to experiment with the use of large clay pots, or crucibles, in which he could melt steel, adding a flux which would harden the steel, or 'cast' it. The resulting steel, unlike all previous versions, had little tendency to break and could be used in making razors and knives as well as clockpieces. His methods were quickly taken up by Matthew Boulton, John Wilkinson and others, and by 1787 there were seven large converters in the area working on a version of Huntsman's crucible. Seventy years later, there were 135 steel-making firms in the city. This massive expansion of the local steel industry was to receive a further boost, in 1856, with the discovery by another local 'ironmaster', Thomas Bessemer, of a method for purifying pig iron in its molten state through air pressure. Bessemer's furnace was put into commercial use by Bessemer himself, but much more effectively by John Brown at his Atlas Works in Brightside. By 1862, Brown had a labour force of 3,000 men and boys, and by 1900, their numbers had increased to 15,000. John Brown's then led the way in the acquisition of manufacturing interests elsewhere within the country (for example, the Clydebank Engineering and Shipbuilding Co. in 1899), and also of smaller steel manufacturing companies in Sheffield itself (like Thomas Firth and Sons in 1902). Throughout the last years of the nineteenth century and into the period leading up to the First World War, the ironmasters of Sheffield experienced an almost uninterrupted period of growth and prosperity, much of it bound up with the use of steel in

Table 2.1 Population of the City of Sheffield (1801–1901)

Year	Population
1801	46,000
1821	66,000
1841	111,000
1861	186,000
1881	285,000
1901	400,000

Source: Sheffield Town Planning Committee (1945: 13)

the production of armaments. The population of the city expanded by over 20 per cent in each decade of the century, and, during the period in which most of the major steel manufacturing plants were first opened (1851 to 1861), it grew by 37 per cent (Mitchell and Deane 1962, cited in Thrift 1987: Table 2.2). See Table 2.1.

A 'very resistant culture'

Throughout this period of growth and development in the steel industry, however, the local social structure built around the cutlery trades remained intact, particularly in those districts of the city lying close to the craftsmen's workshops and forges. In each of these districts, according to archival research by Nigel Thrift, there seemed to be:

> a set of class-specific institutions form[ing] the node around which this way of life could be built: the workshop, obviously; the sick clubs (the proportion of artisans contributing to sick clubs was higher in Sheffield than in any other manufacturing town in England); the Sunday schools (often firmly in artisanal hands); the many small inns and beer houses; the numerous Methodist chapels (Methodism was the major denomination in Sheffield and 'democratic' Methodism was very popular); and the distinctively domestic character of the home (it was a male culture; fewer women worked than in Leeds).
>
> (Thrift 1987: 32)

Summarising detailed work undertaken by Smith on working-class life in Sheffield in the early nineteenth century, Thrift concludes:

> Workshop–pub–chapel-house: these were the foci of what was almost an enclave mentality and what was certainly a very resistant culture, *a culture that controlled itself.*
>
> (*ibid.*)

According to both Smith and Thrift, it is these features of the local social structure, and the associated 'culture' of the Little Mesters, which explain the distinctive character of Sheffield as a locale. As Smith observes:

The population of Sheffield is, for so large a town, unique in its character, in fact it more closely resembles a village than a town, for over wide areas everyone appears to be acquainted with each other, and to be interested in each other's concerns.

(Smith 1982: 31)

The rapid development of the steel industry, under the influence of Huntsman's and Bessemer's discoveries, gave rise to what Thrift has called a 'dual economy', comprising the heavy steel trades (in the factories of Attercliffe, Tinsley, Darnall and Brightside), on the one hand, and the cutlery trades, on the other, in clusters of small workshops scattered around the city. In 1891, for example, there were 25,743 people employed in the cutlery trade, as well as in the manufacture of saws, files and tools, in the city (Vickers 1972: 77). The workers in these trades were increasingly dependent on the larger steel industry, but, by virtue of the monopolistic regulation of the trade exercised by the Cutlers' Company, they were able to maintain some autonomy from the steelmasters. The 'Little Mester' was able, stubbornly, to maintain his independence of large capital and also of the mass of semi-skilled organised 'works labour'. In Thrift's memorable phrase:

The typical Sheffield artisan owned his own tools, controlled his hours of work, observed Saint Monday and paid a weekly rent for space at his 'trough' and the use of power.

(Thrift 1987: 35)[3]

A Labour town

Throughout the post-Second World War period, the city of Sheffield has become widely known nationally as a Labour town: five of the six parliamentary constituencies have consistently returned a Labour member, usually by a handsome margin. In Sheffield (Brightside), covering the industrial East End, the Labour vote, in local parlance, was not so much counted as 'weighed'. In many accounts, the strength of this Labour vote (which, during the 1980s, continued to increase, against the national trend) is explained in terms of the benefits which had been brought to the city in the 1940s and 1950s as a result of the careful rebuilding and planning of a city which had been significantly damaged by the blitz of December 1940,[4] and also by the imaginative and generous post-war housing developments (in areas like Arbourthorne, Norton and Wisewood) initiated by 'the Corporation'. But in the 1970s and early 1980s, the city of Sheffield gained a widespread reputation as a stronghold, specifically, of left-socialist politics, the 'Socialist Republic of South Yorkshire' (cf. Clarke 1987). In some commentaries at the time, the development of the Council's politics and policies was seen as a new departure – as a radical break from the solid tradition of 'municipal' Labour politics which, it is argued, were dominant in the city in earlier periods – a local example (albeit a rather prominent one) of a national move on the part of many local authorities, inspired by the Greater London Council, to the left of the political spectrum. But there are reasons for identifying a continuous sense of an autonomous Labour tradition in the city, closely implicated with the local sense of a city set apart by the fact of geography and industrial identity, not least in the middle years of the nineteenth century, and the role played by the city in the Chartist movement.

Chartist activity in Sheffield was early to develop: meetings in support of the franchise as early as 1792 resulted in a violent confrontation (and two deaths) on Norfolk Street – the present site of the Crucible Theatre (Fine 1992: 72). Half a century later, in 1840, Sheffield Crown Court imposed a sentence of three years on Samuel Holberry, the newly emerged local leader of the Chartists, on the grounds that he was planning an armed insurrection in pursuit of the aims of the Charter. Meetings had been held on Skye Edge (the site of the famous Park Hill flats during the period from 1960 to 1993) throughout 1839 calling for extension of the franchise, and there had been riots after Chartist meetings, with the militia called out from Hillsborough Barracks to suppress the trouble. Holberry died after two years in jail, and was subsequently commemorated in the city with a fountain and some residential streets named after him, as a symbol of the city's tradition of protest and defiance in the interests of Labour (cf. Vickers 1972: 97–8).

Even more famous in local history were the local industrial struggles, especially of the saw grinders, in the period between 1820 and the mid-1860s, struggling to improve their wages and also to punish unscrupulous employers, and take vengeance on workers who refused to join their embryonic union. The saw grinders, confronting hours of work in excess of 12 hours a day in a trade where there was a life expectancy of 32, began to resort to the practice of 'rattening' (or destroying) the working grind-wheels used by 'blacklegs'. Eventually, in 1866, the grinders turned to the use of gunpowder, deposited down the chimneys of blacklegs' homes. In 1867, the leader of the Saw Grinders' Union, William Broadhead, was brought to trial, found guilty and sentenced. Broadhead subsequently emigrated, but in the meantime the troubles in Sheffield gave rise to a Royal Commission on Combinations. So the Rattening Outrages have been seen, not only locally, as the event that gave rise to the legalisation of organised trade unionism (in the Trade Union Act of 1871), and, not least because of the repeated successes in several runs in the Crucible Theatre of the play by local playwright Alan Cullen, *The Stirrings in Sheffield on Saturday Night*, the city remains well aware of its key role in this history.

Steel City

The local culture of Sheffield is, in part, a matter of its geography and topography (defining it, in particular, as 'a city apart'), and it must also be understood for its political legacy as a Labour town, and, crucially, in terms of its long period of dependency on the relatively narrow dual economy of cutlery and steel. The key point is how *all* these themes, working together, help to construct the marked sense of personal and civic autonomy in the local structure of feeling (which have also been recognised, *inter alia*, by Thrift and Smith and many other commentators on the city over the last two hundred years).[5] Prior to the early 1980s, the physical reality of the city involved not only the huddle of old cutlery workshops on the hills around the city centre but also the vast expanse of steelworks (the present site of operation of the Don Valley Development Corporation). This was the set of physical locations that gave meaning to the name of 'Sheffield' both nationally and internationally – the places where quality steel ('Sheffield plate') was forged and Sheffield cutlery produced. In all their grimy reality, these industrial places were the 'authentic' sites of quality Sheffield cutlery and steel – which was later to be copied in Hong Kong and the Far East and marketed, inauthentically, as 'Sheffield' cutlery or steel.

The 'heavy trades' that comprised the steel industry have always been the primary sources of employment in the city. In 1921, before the onset of the Great Depression, some 65,724 people were employed in Sheffield in iron and steel smelting, refining and rolling, and in engineering and construction work directly dependent on steel manufacture. A further 40,536 people were employed in cutlery and hand-tool manufacture, in various kinds of jewellery work, precious metal manufacture and screw making, or in the production of bone, horn or ivory making for the cutlery trade (Pollard 1959: Tables 12A, 12B, pp. 335–6). In 1954, some 41,617 workers were engaged in steel production, and a further 51,349 in the conversion of steel to 'a machined product' (Hargreaves 1956: 280). Throughout the period from the mid-nineteenth century to the early 1980s, virtually the entire landscape of Sheffield's so-called East End (Attercliffe, Tinsley, Darnall and the incongruously named Brightside) consisted of mile after mile of massive steel plants, built close up against each other, their front walls and forges towering high into the sky. For much of this period, the rail journey out of Sheffield to the east (through Rotherham to Doncaster and York) took the rail passenger past a jungle of small workshops and engineering works, but then, slightly further out, through a quite unforgettable landscape of blazing forges, red-hot furnaces and thundering steel-hammers. Trains belonging to the Tinsley Wire Industries or to Parkgate Steel would be shunting their loads out of the yards, and black-faced, sweating steelworkers would sometimes be observed taking their 'snap' (their lunchtime or evening sandwiches) outside the sheds. Occasionally, the passer-by could see directly inside the forges and glimpse the workers 'manhandling' white-hot steel girders off the production lines – a process involving the manipulation of enormous pincers. As the train struggled further east, the landscape would thin out into open country of a barren, industrial kind, dotted with the pitheads of the South Yorkshire coalfield and the small colliery villages of the Dearne Valley (itself, to an important extent, an outpost of the steel industry of Sheffield but also, in other respects, the source of some high-grade coal produced for export from Hull and the Humberside ports).

The heavy steel trade in Sheffield, like the mining industry to the east of the city, involved hard, physical work (or 'graft', as it was known locally) and a 24-hour shift-work system to enable continuous production runs on large orders. Though its long-term effects on health were less marked than those suffered by the grinders in the cutlery industry, the foundry was a place in which serious accidents were an ever-present possibility, and in which premature deafness ('hammerman's paralysis') was especially common amongst forgemen and boilermakers (Pollard 1959: 228). It was a physically demanding regime, which was reserved, in terms of the dominant assumptions of both the steelmasters and the local working class itself, for fit men. Of the 65,724 people employed in the heavy trades in Sheffield in 1921, only 6 per cent (4,022) were women, of whom 2,200 were in skilled metal work rather than steel itself. By contrast, some 33 per cent (13,226) of the 40,536 employed in the light cutlery and associated trades were women: 3449 worked as polishers – the 'Buffer Girls' who were famous locally, as we indicated in Chapter 1, for their jaunty and direct sense of humour and resilience. In some ten to twenty thousand households in the East End of Sheffield, husband and wife would both be employed in the light cutlery trade, working different shifts (morning, afternoon or 'afters', or nights).[6] Overall, however, the steel trades and the cutlery industry remained the preserve of the 'Little Mesters'.

In her discussion of transformations occurring in an American steel town (Weirton, West Virginia) during the worldwide demise of the industry, Sharon Zukin draws attention to the enormous symbolic and cultural image of 'steel':

> No industry has a more powerful image than steel. Its symbolic weight in the national economy reflects a host of material factors: the brute force required to make steel, the volume of capital investment in a mill, the size of the work force engaged in smelting, pouring, casting, and shipping, and the omnipresence of steel in all modern structures, from rail trestles and bridge girders, to auto bodies, skyscrapers, airplanes, and ships. Steel has power because it has been the lifeline of industrial society.
>
> (Zukin 1991: 59–60)

What Zukin calls the 'mystical power' of steel, in symbolising 'man's' conquest of nature (and the establishment of mass-industrial society), also has a pre-industrial origin, in her view, in the development of iron ploughshares and tools for use in agrarian cultivation. It is arguable, in our view, that the development of the cutlery trades and the smaller water-powered forges on the river banks of Sheffield and the surrounding peaks of Derbyshire constituted a critical transitional moment in the mastery of nature for purposes of industrial exploitation.

The development of steel in the United States, according to Zukin, involved a particularly 'male production culture', informing the practices and cultural assumptions of steelowners and workers alike:

> Since the days of Andrew Carnegie and Henry Clay Frick, owners and managers have been brusque, forceful, often violent. If the worker was a 'man of steel', he faced no less an adversary than the 'steel baron', surrounded by hired security guards and hand-picked elected officials . . . The legacy of iron manufacture was a craft-dominated production process in which highly-skilled workers accumulated power on the basis of know-how and technique. When a monopoly of ownership confronted a monopoly of skill, the resulting power struggles centred on the privileges of craftsmanship.
>
> (Zukin 1991: 61–2)

Sheffield's steel industry never involved the construction of the kinds of single monopoly that dominated the 'steel towns' of the United States: in the late 1950s, the industry comprised a complex mix of over a hundred firms of various sizes, including some specialised steel firms that have been nationalised (initially as the English Steel Corporation, and, latterly, simply as British Steel). The absence of such monopolisation may be one reason for the relative absence of volatile confrontation between local steelowners and workers, at least until the national strike of 1980 (cf. Kahn *et al.* 1983: 108–12), in that neither owners nor steelworkers were collected together as massed armies of capital and labour. Industrial relations in the Sheffield steel industry took the form, instead, of direct and localised negotiation between relatively small workforces in individual plants and personnel departments, often with the mediation of the local Trades and Labour Council. However much it had to pay attention to national legislation, the settlement of wages and conditions in the Sheffield steel industry was dominated overwhelmingly by local Sheffield men, the masters of the steel and cutlery trades.

The symbolic legacy of cutlery and steel

In the mid-1990s, the legacy of these steel and cutlery trades to the city of Sheffield still expresses itself directly in the physical landscape (the 'set of places') that continues to define the city and the environs of Sheffield. But it does so in the form of a massive expanse of vacant, quite literally de-industrialised territory and space in the East End of the city, where less than fifteen years ago there were steel plants in great numbers. A visual or imaginary history of the city's lost industry is now played back onto its citizens in the form of *contemporary* urban images and myths – for example, in the picture of a helmeted forge worker (complete with his white sweat muffler) constructed from coloured bricks, and finished in 1986, on a gable-end on Castle Street, or the monument to the steelworkers adorning the entrance foyer of the Meadowhall shopping mall (in effect, commemorating the disappearance of the local industry). This mythology of the Sheffield steelworker is also carried forward in the Yorkshire area in television advertising and street hoardings (where, again, the concern seems to be to celebrate local male working-class culture at precisely the moment of its historical abolition).[7] What is being celebrated in the advertisements, and played back onto popular consciousness, is the reassurance of a familiar local culture that was dominant in the earlier years of this century – the muscular masculinity ('grafting') of the steelworker and also, perhaps, the familiar rhythm of the working day (the pint at the end of the shift), an industrial rhythm and camaraderie which the fact of unemployment, and labour market restructuring, abolishes.

At the end of the twentieth century, in a society that is heavily dominated by mass media tuned into national and international (or global) events, trends or personalities, we would not want to argue that the experience of the citizens of any one urban environment can be understood simply in terms of the received local physical environment (the material landscape left over from nineteenth-century industrialisation); the continual recycling, in changed economic circumstances, of local male working-class folk culture; or, indeed, the constant retrieval of a history of the city as it is assumed to have been 'before they closed the works down'. All of that is there in Sheffield (and in any de-industrialised locality). But even in the most well-defined and proud locality or place, a great deal of everyday talk, popular knowledge and behaviour is scripted in terms of messages and themes derived from national and international media, and the idea that we can speak of an autonomous 'popular culture' constructed primarily at the local level, uninfluenced by the global reach of international media, is quite clearly untenable.[8] What may be a key characteristic of the industrial North of England, however, is the inescapable presence of what Raymond Williams once identified as a 'residual' culture of Northern-ness in general, with particular Mancunian and Sheffield expressions, constructed over the last two hundred years of industrial production. This residual culture remains a rich store of essentially local myths and folk wisdoms through which the local identities of citizens continue to be affirmed.

MANCHESTER

Prehistory

Unlike Sheffield, the modern city of Manchester can and does lay claim to a pre-industrial history. At the heart of the modern-day Castlefield development area, near the junction of the Irwell and Medlock rivers, there is now a facsimile of a Roman fort, introduced into the area in the first phase of the area's redevelopment. The original fort built on this site, Mancunium, was actually a minor way-station on the network of roads built by the Romans across their newly conquered territory. References to Manchester's Roman origins, however, are a continuing presence in discussion in Manchester, not least in the later nineteenth century and, more recently, in the imaginations of some developers.

The town that sprang up around the fort and the confluence of the Irk, Medlock and Irwell, however, steadily acquired some importance:

> By Norman times . . . Manchester possessed a large, well-built castle from which the lord of the manor administered the area [and] the Church had designated the town as the headquarters of one of the largest parishes in the realm, and efforts were under way to give Manchester an imposing cathedral.
>
> (Messinger 1985: 6)

In the early to mid-Middle Ages, some of the groundwork was also being laid for the extraordinary later development of the cotton and textile industry. Gary Messinger's account of this earlier period of pre-industrial commerce and trade relates how:

> As early as 1282, the date of the first written reference on the subject, Manchester already possessed an appreciable trade in textiles, probably linen and wool. By the time of the reign of Henry VIII, cloth manufacture had become so vital in the area that the privilege of sanctuary was removed from the town in order to protect the trade from rogues and vagabonds who disrupted the drying of wool and the spreading of linen yarn in open, sunlit fields. By the end of the sixteenth century the town had begun to expand into the production of other fabrics. Usually called 'Manchester cottons', 'cotton wool' and 'fustians', these cloths were made from various combinations of wool, linen, flax and cotton imported from the Near East.
>
> (*ibid.*)

In the evolution of the early Manchester trade, however, the definitive influence – well understood in local common sense – was that of the local climate and local topography and soil. What Messinger calls the 'moist climate' of the area, and the lime-free water of the local rivers, made Manchester far more suitable for the weaving of cotton fibre than was any other area. Other nearby towns (Macclesfield, with its founding charter in 1220 and a flourishing silk trade; Stockport, also given its charter in 1220 and home to a major regional market; and Bolton, a Saxon settlement and a very successful market town) were growing in size and influence. But the development of cotton weaving in Manchester itself over the following five centuries was significant enough, in terms of population growth and the development of urban buildings and roads, for Daniel Defoe, in 1724 – to describe Manchester as 'the greatest mere village in England'. Though relatively small (with a population no higher than 8,000 at the turn of the eighteenth century) it was a major stronghold of the Puritans during the Civil War, and was also a headquarters of the Stuart cause during the Jacobite uprisings of 1715 and 1745.

Halfway through the eighteenth century, however, Manchester was in no sense a major centre of population or even a really major centre for industry and commerce. Contemporary oil paintings and pictorial maps show cattle grazing on the meadows close to the centre of the town, and orchards on the bank of the river Irk. St Ann's Square, now the centre of fashionable shops and the site of the Royal Exchange Theatre, was still the site of a sheep market in the late seventeenth century. In 1774, at the time of the first Census, the town was still only a small centre of 22,481 people, primarily involved in hand weaving and the processing of cotton fabrics. When finished, the fabrics had still to transported – by 'Manchester packmen' in convoys of horses – along the roads to Liverpool or over the hazardous bridle paths across the Pennines to the eastern towns and counties, both of which routes were infested with highwaymen and other dangers. The development of Manchester as a major centre of industry and population had to await breakthroughs in respect of more reliable methods of transportation in the later eighteenth century.

We shall turn to these developments in a moment. But it is important to recognise the three themes in Manchester's pre-industrial past that have continued to exercise an unmistakable influence on the 'structure of feeling' of the city, even in the de-industrialising late twentieth century.

First, as we have already indicated, Manchester does have a pre-industrial Roman point of origin: it is, in that sense, an old city, sharing a claim in terms of age, if not in terms of continuing character of its later development, with cities like Chester and York. Most local historians of the city like to quote from John Leland, an essayist of the early Tudor period, describing Manchester as 'the fairest, best buildid, quikkest and most populous tounne of all Lancashire' (quoted in Briggs 1963: 88 and in Green 1959: 58). We shall see later how some Mancunians, including many of those involved in regeneration work but also some residents of the southern surburbs and Cheshire commuter villages, do see themselves as living in an old city, whose age – although the city is actually and overwhelmingly a Victorian creation – is referenced in terms of the presence of Roman settlement.

Secondly, Manchester's pre-industrial history is, indeed, bound up with the fact of its natural and geographical attributes – most obviously its flatness and its climate. In the visit he made to Manchester during the course of his *English Journey* in 1933, Bradford-born J.B. Priestley could not restrain himself from observing how:

> Manchester weather is a popular joke. I do not care what the local meteorological statistics are, that joke has a solid basis. It is true that I have never visited Manchester in summer, but at every other season I have visited it the weather has been foul, combining in varying proportions rain and sleet and fog
>
> (Priestley 1934: 255)

It is curious that Priestley, himself from a textile district, does not discuss the way in which local residents of the city region, particularly its working population, tended to make sense of the local climate – as a key support for the staple industry of the region. The rain of Manchester, like the sea off Hull, Liverpool and other maritime cities, may have been seen by others as cruel and unforgiving, but it was understood locally as performing a productive service for local trade and industry – a welcome endowment of nature for both labour and capital.

A third and final feature of the pre-industrial past of Manchester was the existence of a set of local and specialised trades, initially concentrated within one relatively confined area, the town of Manchester: those of the handloom weaver. Around Manchester, the handloom weavers and early cotton traders laid the basis for a local regional economy that was to become far more extensive geographically than steel ever became in South Yorkshire. But in both Manchester and Sheffield, the early years before mass industrialisation did leave behind two icons (the handloom weaver and the Little Mester) as powerful signifiers of local craft and local pride, which have continued to have important influence, we would argue, on the local 'structure of feeling' – on what it means to be a Mancunian or a Sheffielder throughout the last two centuries, and even in the late 1990s.[9]

King Cotton

Economic and social historians speak of the 1770s and 1780s as a period of boom in cotton manufacture and trade, a period which 'made Manchester', 'when Cotton was King'. L.P. Green identifies the opening of the first full-scale cotton mill as being in 1776 by a Mr N. Hall, on the banks of the River Tame in Stalybridge, east of Manchester (Green 1959: 55). Mr Hall's intention was to take advantage of the long-established wool industry in the neighbouring sheep farms. Many similar mills began to be opened in Manchester and the areas to the north and east, benefiting equally from local sheep stock and access to natural water power. Three crucial further developments involved the invention in 1733 of the flying shuttle by John Kay of nearby Warrington and Bury, the spinning jenny in 1764 (by James Hargreaves of Blackburn and Thomas Highs of Leigh, commercially developed by Sir Richard Arkwright of Bolton), and, later, the spinning mule, which made possible the spinning of fine thread (by Samuel Compton, also of Bolton, in 1779). The manual craft monopolised by skilled members of a local 'labour aristocracy' in the hinterlands was quickly transformed, and mills opened up in their hundreds across south-east Lancashire, alongside the tributaries flowing out of the Mersey, the Irwell and the Irk:

> In Oldham there were 6 cotton mills in 1785. By 1815 there were 47, and in 1839, 94. In Stalybridge, the Sootpokes were providing employment for 14,000 people 60 years after Mr Hall's first venture, and while Macclesfield continued to specialise in silk, Bury had 26 cotton mills and 12 woollen mills by 1850. The cotton industry reached Rochdale in 1795, stormed Glossop and Middleton, soon

employed nearly half the population of Hyde, and began to transform Wigan, Leigh, Worsley and the other towns of the western
border, already opening up the rich coal measures lying beneath
them. Wigan alone had 26 cotton mills by 1846.

(Green 1959: 60)

The size of the labour force employed in the cotton trade in the region
grew extraordinarily rapidly. By 1851, some 80,000 people were directly
employed in cotton (Briggs 1963: 133) and there was a ten-fold increase in
the population of Manchester itself between 1760 and 1830 (from 17,000
to 180,000). According to a survey of 1835, there were 1113 cotton mills
in Britain and 943 were in the north-west region (Bee 1984: 1):

Manchester was the capital of cotton, and as the industry grew so
did 'Cottonopolis'. The open space which lay between Manchester
and its surrounding towns was shrinking rapidly and, by the middle
of the century, these towns were so close together and had so much in
common that we can consider each of them to be part of a single
entity – a giant Manchester with a population of a million people.
This was Britain's largest urban region by far, excluding London,
and it was the largest manufacturing centre in the world.

(*ibid.* 1–2)

A large proportion of the expanding population consisted of migrants,
attracted into the Manchester area in their thousands, in many cases
with a view to establishing businesses and trades of their own, so looking
to make their fortune. As in Chicago later in the nineteenth century, this
in-migration had significant effects, not least in producing a pattern of
axiate urban growth not unlike that of Chicago itself, but also in over-
laying the Manchester area with a sense of cultural and national diversity
that is less obvious elsewhere within the North of England:

Manchester was an extraordinarily open town which took full
advantage of its position between a geographic frontier to the north
and an economic frontier to the south. It became a kind of Eldorado.
From the farms, villages and towns of neighbouring areas, successive
waves of English labourers migrated towards it. From across the sea
came the poor of Ireland. From the north came Scotsmen fleeing the
harsh life of the Highlands and the slums of Edinburgh and Glasgow.
And from the Continent more settlers arrived; some fleeing religious
persecutions, others fleeing civil strife, such as Greeks during the
revolution of 1821 and Italians during the wars leading up to
national unification in the 1840s; others, under clandestine conditions, either offering to sell or hoping to steal the secrets of new
industrial techniques; still others, particularly the large number of
Germans from Hanseatic cities, attracted by the chance of high
monetary return for their business skills.

(Messinger 1985: 8)[10]

Later in the nineteenth century, as Manchester's commercial trade took off, many more German and mid-European families (like the Behrens, the Frankenbergs and the Simons) moved into the city, and were later to play a vital role in the development of the city. The bulk of the migration into the Manchester area, in the early nineteenth century, however, consisted of the workless poor, struggling to find work and also shelter. Thousands of the poor migrants found accommodation in an already overcrowded city-centre area adjacent to the mills, warehouses and workshops. Some localities quickly became colonised by particular migrant groups: a high proportion of the 30,000 Irish residents in the town in 1836 clustered together in the area known as Little Ireland at the lower end of Oxford Street, alongside the River Irwell (Tupling 1936: 22), and a significant number of rural migrants from Cumbria – the 'sojourning poor' – settled in different areas, surviving precariously between recessions by work in the Elizabethan poorhouses (Taylor 1989–90).

The rapid, and highly profitable, growth of the export trade was certainly aided by the sudden availability of a mass of cheap labour, but the key advantage helping Manchester was the development of technical aspects of manufacture and production. In the early 1800s, industrial development in cotton was:

> several decades ahead of places such as Lyons, the Rhineland or the New England region of the United States where sophisticated cotton manufacture was to appear in the latter half of the nineteenth century. This meant that the whole world was Manchester's potential market, especially after the defeat of Napoleon in 1815, when the major trade routes of the world were controlled by British sea power.
>
> (Messinger 1985: 21)

British cotton exports leapt from £1-million worth of yarns and other fabrics in 1785 to £16-million in 1816 and £31-million in 1851 (*ibid.*). The growth of an export trade in the ever-increasing variety of cotton fabrics and cotton products being produced was also facilitated by Manchester's access to the developing regional system of canals and waterways. Legislation permitting the canalisation of the Mersey and Irwell rivers between Liverpool and Manchester had been passed as early as 1720; and the opening of the Duke of Bridgewater Canal in 1761 was a major boost to cotton commerce and trade, allowing cotton owners to move goods to the coast by water rather than over the treacherous turnpike routes. Canals through Ashton, Bolton, Bury and Rochdale were all open by 1800.

The railways

Manchester's importance was further underlined by the opening of the Manchester–Liverpool railway, the first passenger rail service in the world, in 1830, which was very quickly followed by the opening of rail links to Bolton, Bury, Leeds, Sheffield and Birmingham (Green 1959:

60–1). The train to Birmingham meant that travellers from Manchester could now travel all the way to London by train, and also that residents of the larger north-west region could get to London through Manchester. So by the middle of the nineteenth century, Manchester had become a terminus for rail lines crossing between most of the manufacturing towns and cities of the industrial North of England, and over the next fifty years four other major rail stations were built to handle the expanding passenger and goods traffic. Two of these railway stations (Central and London Road) had an imposing frontage, and this, along with the number of lines coming into the city, confirmed Manchester's status as a major regional and national centre of transportation. The city was in this sense 'industrialised' not simply in terms of the presence of the cotton mills and massive manufacturing activity, but in the broader sense of being connected up, in a relatively short time, to other major centres of industry and population. The location of these four stations in different sites across the city also introduced users of the railways in Manchester, in the late nineteenth century, to a problem that was to continue to define the city throughout the next century – that of moving between these stations and bus termini. No connecting underground system was ever built, though it was frequently discussed.

The problem of the four rail stations of Manchester, at the beginning of this century, was one of the first expressions, we would argue, of the city's unplanned growth, resulting from the explosion of population and trade in the nineteenth century, but with long-term consequences later. In Chapter 4, we will be exploring how this same issue – of personal movement across Manchester's 'travel-to-work' region – continues to define the problem of everyday life in this city of business and trade. The growth of the cotton export trade also had all kinds of profound effect on the organisation of space and the architecture and layout of the whole, wider region. By 1840, according to Asa Briggs:

> Manchester was far more than a 'metropolis of manufacturers'; it was above all a centre of trade of a whole region, linked with the whole world.
>
> (Briggs 1963: 105)

As a consequence of the explosion of commerce and trade, indeed, what has since been called an 'industrial region' – in contrast to Sheffield's characterisation as the heart of an industrial *district* – emerged, with Manchester at its centre. Leon Faucher, in a famous commentary written after his visit to the city in 1844, observed how:

> Nothing is more curious than the industrial topography of Lancashire. Manchester, like a diligent spider, is placed in the centre of the web, and sends forth roads and railways towards its auxiliaries, formerly villages, but now towns, which serve as outposts to the grand centre of industry.
>
> (Faucher 1969: 15 quoted in Pons 1978: 54)

By this time, right across the region, but especially in the centre:

> the warehouses of Manchester were more impressive than the mills; massive, simple, austere, they were later to be praised for their 'real beauty'. They were held to represent 'the essentials of Manchester's trade, the very reason for her existence'.
>
> (Briggs 1963: 106)

By 1842, the Love and Barton handbook to the town for the first time carried a separate chapter on Manchester's commercial buildings, dealing at length with the mercantile establishments in the Mosley Street area and also with the Royal Exchange itself – the 'parliament house of the lords of cotton'. Manchester was the 'shock city of the 1840s', growing at great pace, and throwing up a new landscape of mills and warehouses, as well as commercial offices and trading houses, and also appearing, to very many commentators at the time, to symbolise the promise of 'a new age' of industrial development tied directly into international commerce and trade.

City of free trade

Though it may be declining in importance in the 1990s as a concert hall and meeting place, compared to other sites in central Manchester, the Free Trade Hall on Peter Street is a continuing reminder and symbol of a defining theme in Manchester's nineteenth-century history. A.J.P. Taylor, writing in 1957, caught the point well:

> The Free Trade Hall [has] a special claim to fame, though not from its architecture. It stood on St Peter's Fields, where the battle of Peterloo began the break-up of the old order in England. Its name announced the greatest victory against that order. Other great halls in England are called after a royal patron, or some other figure of traditional religion. Only the Free Trade Hall is dedicated, like the United States of America, to a proposition, one as noble and beneficent as any made. Richard Cobden formulated it in the words, 'As little intercourse as possible between Governments, as much intercourse as possible between peoples of the world.'
>
> (Taylor 1957: 9)[11]

The Anti-Corn Law League, the political force dedicated to the idea of free trade, emerged from a meeting at the York Hotel, Manchester, in September 1838, under the leadership of Richard Cobden. The pressure to create the League resulted from the depression of the late 1830s and early 1840s, which had substantially reduced business profits and increased working-class unemployment. The price of bread, the most staple product of all, had increased significantly as a result of taxes imposed by government in the interests of agricultural classes and landowners. The demand for the repeal of the Corn Laws was seen as a way of liberating businessmen from this tax burden and also of 'relieving' working people, and thereby enhancing commerce and trade. The League itself proceeded to organise thousands of meetings in London and throughout the country, and it was at these meetings that Cobden voiced the refrain that 'Manchester' spoke for all the provinces of England, against or in advance of London. Asa Briggs has also observed how it was in this period that the specific reputation of Manchester's business class was first forged. He quotes a correspondent to the *Morning Chronicle* as observing that Cobden was always surrounded by:

> rich men who made little figure in public but whose wealth and mercantile operations are known for their vastness throughout the whole civilised world. Several of them who are there every day employ each from 500 to 2,000 workpeople . . . All the members being habituated to business they go about their work of agitation with the same precision in the minutest details as they do in their work of cotton spinning.
>
> (Briggs 1963: 120)

These 'Manchester men' were wealthy on a scale that few steel-masters in Sheffield ever achieved. They were dedicated to a version of economic liberalism, as the bearer of some notion of the popular interest, which (for all that Ebenezer Elliott, the pamphleteer known as the 'Bard of Free Trade', lived in Sheffield) never gained any serious footing in that city. In Manchester, the doctrines of economic liberalism had been institutionalised in talk of 'the Manchester School', based at the Free Trade Hall, propagandising against all government interference in business, and in favour of unleashing a new era of commerce and trade, driven by private capital based on manufacturing industry, especially in the North. The refrains were widely supported in many Northern cities and towns, especially in the textile districts, and in some centres in the West Riding of Yorkshire (Bradford, Halifax and Huddersfield) these radical versions of economic liberalism continued to have an influence on local culture and voting patterns well into this century. The Corn Laws were repealed in 1845 and the League disbanded the following year. By 1846, the industrial middle classes of Manchester, in the middle of an explosive period of economic growth, were beginning to confer their favours on Conservatives like Peel rather than on the Free Trade liberals.

But the legacy of Manchester liberalism and the struggle against the Corn Laws continue to find expression, we would argue, not just in the continuing presence of a building called the Free Trade Hall or in the other grand office buildings, arcades, theatres and museums that were erected by wealthy Manchester capitalists during this period (though these are vital physical aspects of Manchester's Victorian city centre), but also in the 'structure of feeling' of Mancunian culture itself – a self-confident and even brash form of classless populism, orientated to the pursuit of wealth and personal success through commercial enterprise and cunning. The dominant image of the Mancunian in the 1990s, of the street-wise 'scally' (scallywag) doing business across the world or profiting from local initiatives in the entertainment business (the pop groups of 1980s 'Madchester' or the Olympic Bid in 1992), we would argue, is no overnight invention.

The two nations of industrial Manchester

In the mid-1990s, Manchester may be well known nationally and even internationally as the city of initiative and enterprise, the carrier of the British Olympic Bid in 1987 and 1993 and now the host of the Common-wealth Games bid for the year 2002, the European City of Drama for 1994, and the home of the first new light rapid-transit system in Britain (the Metrolink, opened in 1992). But it is also widely known for the violence and trauma of its inner-city riots in 1981, with this reputation being confirmed in the popular imagination in the early 1990s by a series of incidents of violence and murder associated with the inner-city areas of Cheetham Hill and, in particular, Moss Side. In other commentaries, especially by health and welfare professionals and housing pressure groups, it is well known for the quite extraordinary levels of ill-health, poverty and housing need of a very significant proportion of the popu-lation of the larger Greater Manchester region. It is a city with many areas of extreme poverty and deprivation, sitting alongside areas in which the much-celebrated pursuit of private success and wealth continues unabated.

The close proximity but *de facto* separation of areas of wealth and poverty in Manchester was first noted by a Canon Parkinson, who observed in the 1830s that:

> There is no town in the world where the distance between the rich and the poor is so great and the barrier between them so difficult to be crossed.
>
> (quoted in Bee 1984: 5)

This refrain was taken up again by Alexander de Tocqueville, after his visit to the town in 1835, and perhaps even more famously by Friedrich Engels, in his famous commentary on the city, written in the first two years after his arrival in 1842, *The Condition of the Working Class in England in 1844*:

> Manchester . . . is peculiarly built, so that a person may live in it for years, and go in and out daily without coming into contact with a working-people's quarter or even with workers, that is, so long as he confines himself to his business or to pleasure walks. This arises chiefly from the fact that by unconscious tacit agreement, as well as with out-spoken conscious determination, the working-people's quarters are sharply separated from the sections of the city reserved for the middle-class . . . Manchester contains at its heart a rather extended commercial district, perhaps half a mile long and about as broad, and consisting wholly of offices and warehouse. Nearly the

whole district is abandoned by dwellers, and is lonely and deserted at night: only watchmen and policemen traverse its narrow lanes with lanterns. This district is cut through by certain main thoroughfares upon which this vast traffic concentrates, and in which the ground level is lined with brilliant shops . . . [These] shops bear some relation to the districts which lie behind them, and are more elegant in the commercial and residential quarters than when they hide grimy working-men's dwellings; but they suffice to conceal from the eyes of the wealthy men and women of strong stomachs and nerves the misery and grime which form the complement of their wealth.

(Engels 1987: 85–6)

Engels also commented on the areas lying further out from the town centre, observing how they almost entirely comprised:

unmixed working-people's quarters, stretching like a girdle, averaging a mile and a half around the commercial district.

(*ibid.*: 86)

Engels's observation retains a powerful truth to this day. With the important qualification that some inner-city zones in Manchester, like Trafford Park, have been zoned for industrial development, and that others (Hulme) have been the site of major post-war public housing development, Manchester still remains a city that is fundamentally defined, in terms of its spatial layout, by an enormous and inescapable 'girdle' of inner-city working-class housing. In the late nineteenth century, the central city areas – Dolefield (Deansgate) and Angel Meadow (Rochdale Road) – were the location of the town's 'rookeries' and, during the twentieth century, many of the inner-city areas of working-class houses, adjacent to the city centre and this same inner 'girdle' (Moss Side, Hulme), have developed equally ferocious reputations. In the 1950s and 1960s, in the meantime, hitherto respectable areas of more middle-class housing adjacent to these inner-city areas (Whalley Range, Cheetham Hill) have accrued their own reputations as centres for prostitution and the drug trade respectively.

Engels's characterisation of spatial organisation and the separation of the classes in Manchester has been the subject of widespread discussion and criticism (cf. Marcus 1973; Pons 1978); and it is certainly arguable that the separation of social classes is more fundamentally and effectively achieved in cities like Sheffield, where the successful middle class in the nineteenth century established its residential enclave in Ranmoor, Endcliffe and Tapton, well to the west both of the city centre and of local steelworks, and their areas of housing intended for workers (cf. Briggs 1963: 36). Similarly wholesale geographical separations of the middle class from concentrations of industry in well-defined, quite autonomous residential areas are apparent in other Northern cities: for example, in Leeds, where many of the successful commercial middle class have migrated north of the city towards towns like Otley, or in Newcastle (where the middle class has an enviable corridor of possibilities north of the city centre through Jesmond into Gosforth). What has not been challenged about Engels's account is the size and scale of Manchester's problems of inequality and poverty, which he described in the earlier years of the Industrial Revolution.

Manchester and its Bridge of Tears

Only two hundred yards from Manchester Cathedral lies the main bridge across the River Irwell, linking the city of Manchester to its neighbouring, politically autonomous city of Salford – which in the mid-1990s remains one the poorest areas in the whole Greater Manchester conurbation. This bridge, which has featured in many an image of Manchester over the years, once led Samuel Bamford (a working-class Radical of the early nineteenth century) to observe that whilst 'Venice hath her Bridge of Sighs, Manchester [has a] Bridge of Tears' (quoted in Briggs 1963: 90). This Bridge across the 'turbid and black' River Irwell from Manchester's fast-developing commercial centre led to a veritable warren of squalid, overcrowded and dangerous working people's dwellings, and a similar type of housing also extended north and east from the Bridge (into infamous 'rookeries' like Newtown, Angel Meadow, Ancoats, Gibraltar, Little Ireland, Chorlton Row and Hulme). In 1832, one of these inner-city warrens, Ancoats – inhabited mainly by Irish immigrant labourers and textile workers – was the epicentre within the Manchester region of an epidemic of cholera which had been sweeping through Europe. The senior physician of the Ardwick and Ancoats dispensary, James Phillips Kay (later Sir James Kay-Shuttleworth), had been appointed to coordinate the responses of the various local boards of health to this epidemic, and he went on to publish his findings in an influential pamphlet, 'The Moral and Physical Condition of the Working Classes Employed in the Cotton Manufacture in Manchester'.[12] Kay-Shuttleworth's descriptions of the poverty, morbidity and squalor in the heart of the 'exploding' industrial City of Manchester were unflinching. In a widely quoted passage, Kay-Shuttleworth insisted that:

> He whose duty it is to follow in the steps of this messenger of death [cholera] must descend to the abodes of poverty, must frequent the close alleys, the crowded courts, the overpeopled habitations of wretchedness, where pauperism and disease congregate round the source of social discontent and political disorder in the centre of our large towns, and behold with alarm, in the hot-bed of pestilence, ills that fester in secret, at the very heart of society.
>
> (Kay-Shuttleworth 1832, quoted in Mort 1987: 21)

Kay-Shuttleworth's 1832 report on 'inner-city Manchester' pre-dated the more famous studies of the poverty and squalor of London by Chadwick and others by some years, and it was also important for its commitment to the essentially social rather than moral account of poverty and ill-health, by contrast with the many contemporary accounts of such poverty and illness as arising out of the 'ignorance or moral errors' of the poor themselves. James Donald observes:

> Kay-Shuttleworth refused to dissociate [the evils of poverty] from appalling living conditions, wretched diets, inadequate or non-existent sanitation, the supposedly 'pernicious' moral examples of Irish immigrants, and 'the prolonged and exhausting labour' which resembled 'the torment of Sisyphus' and deadened their minds.
>
> (Donald 1992: 427)

As Donald and other observers have noted, however, Kay-Shuttleworth's critique is not so much of the commercial or industrial system itself as it is of the particular form that urbanisation had assumed in Greater Manchester. The critique is of an urban system that has developed at speed, in an uncoordinated way and with insufficient attention to the human consequences of such rapid, unplanned and incoherent growth. At one level, as nearly all social historians writing on Manchester observe, this was a matter of the scale of population growth across the whole south-east Lancashire region. By 1851, the census population for this area reached 1,063,000, by comparison with only 132,000 fifty years earlier (an increase of over 705 per cent). Over the following 60 years, the region's population increased a further 70 per cent to 2,328,003 (Green 1959: 66). The sheer speed of this increase in population, and the resulting size of the industrial population across the region, absolutely overwhelmed the capacity of local government agencies to cope. In nearly all contemporary commentary, there was an awestruck admiration for the explosion of the cotton industry of south-east Lancashire as a whole, and for the grandeur of the office buildings, the warehouses and exchanges thrown up (once again, with great speed) as headquarters of the domestic and export cotton trade in the centre of Manchester itself.[13]

But simultaneously there was widespread anxiety as to the implications of such a sudden and explosive growth of the population of one urban region, particularly in terms of matters of sanitation and health, but also in respect of order. Asa Briggs summarises the concerns well:

> With no adequate police force, no effective machinery of modern local government, a disturbed social system which lacked the 'benevolent influence' of 'natural gradations', and an economy subject to fluctuations and developing on the basis of obvious conflicts of interest, Manchester was felt to provide a persistent threat to that 'good order' on which statesmen and moralists loved to dwell.
>
> (Briggs 1963: 92)

In Disraeli's novel *Coningsby*, published in 1844, Sidonia tells Coningsby, as they meet in an inn in the forest, that 'the age of ruins is past'. Coningsby famously replies 'have you seen Manchester?' Thomas Carlyle remarked in the 1840s that he personally thought Manchester 'every whit as wonderful, as fearful, as unimaginable as the oldest Salem or prophetic city'. The 'shock city' of the 1840s provoked both admiration (as 'the first industrial city', the shape of Britain's commercial future) and fear and anxiety.

Recession and 'restructuring' in the nineteenth-century textile trade

Mass unemployment is not a new experience in Manchester. The recessions and slumps of the nineteenth century (in 1819, 1826, 1837 and 1842) threw thousands of textile workers out of work. Technical advances within the textile industry (particularly the development of the power loom and its introduction into factories in the mid-1830s) also had devastating effects on the handloom-weaving trade. The numbers of handloom weavers fell from 250,000 across the region in 1835 to 10,000 over the following 25 years (Bee 1984: 6), and it was during the course of this massive attack on the handloom-weaving trade that one of the key incidents in Manchester's political and industrial history occurred. At the end of the eighteenth century, 'radicals' in the textile areas began to pressurise Parliament to legislate for a minimum wage for the handloom weavers. After a succession of essentially peaceful rallies and demonstrations over a number of years failed to provoke a response from Westminster, local handloom weavers, inspired by the example of hosiery workers in the East Midlands under the leadership of 'General Ned Ludd', began in 1812 to engage in the sabotage of power looms. These Lancashire 'Luddites' gained support from a network of 'Hampden Clubs' (named after John Hampden, a seventeenth-century radical who had campaigned against arbitrary taxation), and for the next eight years the campaign for the defence of the weavers and the extension of the suffrage to 'all male persons of mature age and sound mind' gained momentum. On 16 August 1819, after weeks of anxious anticipation (especially on the part of the local magistracy), a mass meeting called in St Peter's Field attracted 60,000 workers, the biggest radical demonstration yet in early nineteenth-century England. Henry Hunt, one of the most famous of the radical leaders, was scheduled to speak at this meeting, but early in the build-up to it, a magisterial order to arrest Hunt was passed by the Deputy Chief Constable to the two groups of troops stationed nearby. The Manchester Yeomanry, a group of inexperienced part-timers, were the first to arrive, and they responded to the call to effect the arrests by surging into the crowd with sabres. Eleven demonstrators were killed and several hundred injured.

The Peterloo Massacre, as this incident came to be known, has a vital place in popular folklore in Manchester, as well as in local history teaching in schools. 'Peterloo' continues to be the topic of complex mythology, nurtured, in particular, through the local labour and trade union movement, and the location of the confrontation is itself a stopping point on tours of the city organised for visiting socialists.[14] The immediate outcome of the Peterloo massacre in reality was not an heroic victory of labour: Henry Hunt and the other orators in St Peter's Field were arrested and legislation was passed to prohibit the holding of large public meetings. The campaign of industrial radicalism rapidly lost momentum and effectively ended in 1820 as trade improved and there was an upturn in employment. The only remaining major event in Manchester's labour history was a mass Chartist meeting (of some 50,000 people) on Kersal Moor in Salford in 1840: otherwise, the 'hungry forties' witnessed a series of unfocused and relatively disorganised local disturbances, which petered out by 1850.

In the 1990s, with the opening of the Museum of Labour History in central Manchester and a number of other symbolic locations throughout the region, claims have been made for Manchester as a key 'labour city'. There can be no doubting the importance of the events or the individuals who are remembered within this heritage of labour which is being (re)invented for the city. But this nostalgic representation of the history of labour has no obvious reference to any moment of labour triumph or hegemony: the history of Manchester, we would argue, is a continuing history of social divisions and social segregation (first observed by a mass of writers on nineteenth-century Manchester, but still very apparent today). It is this restless flux of the utopias of organised labour and the utopian dreams of urban fortunes, won through free trade and enterprise, that defines the parameters of local Mancunian 'structure of feeling' – a culture that sees itself as connected up to a larger world and a larger set of possibilities, rather than simply an industrial Northern city caught within a narrow labour metaphysic.

3

'THIS RUDDY RECESSION'

Post-Fordism in Manchester and Sheffield

As late as the mid-1960s, the City of Detroit, Michigan, the home to Ford, General Motors and Chrysler – the home of 'Fordist', production-line mass manufacturing – was still seen in America as a blueprint for future prosperity, a massive company town which had successfully neutralised the local unions and also created massive economies of scale in one large 'industrial region'. The famous refrain of Henry Ford – 'What's good for Ford is good for America' – still had some popular purchase.

Thirty years later, in the mid-1990s, Detroit and its surrounding area were caught in one of the steepest declines of all American urban areas. Following the riots of the 'long hot summer' of 1967, when 43 people died in Detroit, a massive exodus began of both the white and black middle class to the suburban areas in neighbouring Oakland and Macomb counties, progressively undermining the property tax base on which the City Council depended. The flight to the suburbs reduced the population of Detroit city from 1.67 million in 1960 to just over 1 million in 1994; whilst the city's share of the Greater Detroit region's tax income declined from just under 50 per cent in 1960 to 16.5 per cent in 1980. Only Washington DC has a higher murder rate than Detroit, with 57.9 people out of every 100,000 being the victims of murder in 1992. According to one commentator, Detroit has moved from being 'Motown to No Town' in the course of just three decades (Greig 1994).

Nearly all the industrial cities of the North of England have experienced a similar overall process of de-industrialisation over the last twenty to thirty years, as the prevailing conditions in the world economy have forced a shift away from the 'Fordist' reliance on mass-manufacturing industry. The shift is succinctly described by Stuart Hall and Martin Jacques:

> In economic terms, the central feature of the transition is the rise of 'flexible accumulation' in place of the old assembly-line world of mass production. It is this, above all, which is orchestrating and driving on the evolution of this new world.
>
> (Hall and Jacques 1989: 12)

The emergence of what many commentators speak of as 'post-Fordist' forms of economic organisation involves massive changes in the labour market, particularly in respect of the structure and composition of the local labour market and also the security attaching to any one type of employment. The changes have brought redundancy to millions of workers, predominantly men, whose skills were specific to mass manufacturing, as well as to the political and cultural infrastructure (trade unions, working men's clubs, traditional labour parties, etc.) which were an expression of those economic realities. In Britain, through the 1970s and 1980s, the new economic realities were experienced, in turn, in the local economic crises of Liverpool,[1] Newcastle and the North-east (including Teeside)[2] and, most recently, Sheffield and South Yorkshire. As we observed earlier, in the ten years 1979–89, '94 per cent of all job losses occurred north of a line drawn from the Wash to the Severn' (Dickinson 1990: 76) and 70 per cent of all manufacturing jobs lost were in the North. The brunt of de-industrialisation was being borne in the cities of the North of England, as in the Rust Belt of the United States, primarily by households that had previously been dependent for their economic well-being on heavy manufacturing.

THE LOCAL CRISIS OF THE GREATER MANCHESTER REGIONAL ECONOMY

The best estimates we have suggest that at least 207,000 manufacturing jobs were lost in Greater Manchester between 1972 and 1984, with about three-quarters of these losses occurring in the period after 1978 (Peck and Emmerich 1992a: 2). In the last thirty years, more than half of Manchester's industrial jobs have disappeared (*ibid.*). In the 1980s, up to 1989, there was a loss of 18.2 per cent of manufacturing jobs in Greater Manchester (somewhat greater than the 16.5 per cent average rate of loss of such jobs nationally). In the meantime, there was an increase of only 10.9 per cent in the total number of jobs available in the service industries. By 1981, Manchester – 'Cottonopolis' – was employing only 31,400 people in the textile trades – a figure that continued to decline until 1989, when it touched 21,200 (Peck and Emmerich 1992a: 49). As Table 3.1 shows, the textile industry was now only the fifteenth largest industrial sector in the Greater Manchester region.

The changes in the pattern of employment in Greater Manchester are clear. By far the largest absolute increase in jobs (34,900) has been in the banking, insurance and building service sectors, with the second most significant area of increase being in hotel and catering (17,400). In no sense, of course, have the increases in the number of jobs created in these and other sectors offset the massive losses in manufacturing. This crisis of mass manufacturing actually began thirty years ago, but accelerated considerably in the late 1970s and on into the 1980s. Unemployment on official measures reached a peak at 16 per cent in 1986 – compared to a national average of 12.9 per cent. The national 'recovery' of the late

Table 3.1 The structure of employment, Greater Manchester (1981–9)

Area	Employment (thousands) 1981	Employment (thousands) 1991	Employment change (per cent)
Public administration and defence	162.4	163.0	+0.37
Retail distribution	102.8	96.8	−5.84
Insurance, banking, business services	76.4	111.3	+45.68
Medical and other health services	58.5	64.4	+10.08
Mechanical engineering	56.6	43.7	−22.79
Other services	55.1	65.8	+19.42
Construction	53.3	53.9	+1.12
Wholesale and distribution	51.6	56.0	+8.53
Transport	45.3	42.7	−5.74
Hotels and catering	37.3	54.7	+46.65
Electrical and electronic engineering	36.0	34.2	−5.00
Food, drink, tobacco	35.5	31.4	−11.55
Paper, print, publishing	33.7	22.0	−34.72
Leather, clothing, footwear	32.4	28.1	−13.27
Textiles	31.4	21.4	−31.85

Source: Adapted from Peck and Emmerich (1992a: Table 4)

1980s did produce a reduction in Greater Manchester's unemployment rate, but only to 8.2 per cent (compared to a national average of 6.6 per cent) (Peck and Emmerich 1992a: Table 2b). Even more ominously, Peck and Emmerich have recalculated the data available on patterns of job loss and growth between the 'peaks' and 'troughs' of recent economic cycles. Their gloomy conclusion is that:

> during the years of economic buoyancy in the late 1980s, Greater Manchester was continuing to carry two-thirds of the unemployment which it had accumulated at its 1985 high-point, in the wake of the previous recession. At the low point in 1990, unemployment in Greater Manchester was 126 per cent higher than it had been at the previous low point in 1979. The conurbation is consequently carrying a 'hard core' of at least 144,000 unemployed people (88,000 on the partial, official count) which a cyclical upturn alone is extremely unlikely to return to work.
>
> (Peck and Emmerich 1992a: 24)

Approximately one-third (some 30,000) of the unemployed people, in the meantime, had been out of work for a year or more, and long-term unemployment was increasing, especially among the young (Peck and Emmerich 1992a: 31). There was a clear concentration of the worst levels of unemployment in the central Manchester and Salford areas, with official levels of unemployment in these areas at around 30 per cent (*ibid.*).

Peck and Emmerich's account of the structural weakness of Manchester's local economy is significantly gloomier than the picture which is painted by the local 'growth coalitions', especially the Urban Development Corporations and the City Council in their new-found role as partners to private development. The Prospectus produced to accompany the so-called 'City Pride' bid from Manchester, Trafford and Salford councils in 1994, underlining the city's claim for significant British government and European funding, sketches out an optimistic vision:

> Despite two recessions in the last fifteen years, the City Pride area continues to be a comparatively strong manufacturing centre, with some 43,000 jobs in the City Pride areas in this sector. It is no longer, however, over-dependent on heavy industry or any other sector of the local economy. It is an important regional banking and financial services centre and has experienced growth in services, in high technology and in tourism over the last decade. Manchester is the most important centre in the North of England for media and cultural industries whilst, in the public sector, our Higher Education institutions and hospitals are very significant players in the local economy. At times of considerable economic change and new challenges, the diversified nature of the economy is an important strength.
>
> (Manchester City Council 1994: 14)

Certain parts of the larger Greater Manchester conurbation and 'travel-to-work region' are doing well: the Borough of Stockport added 18.5 per cent more jobs within its boundaries in the period between 1965 and 1989 – a stark contrast to the 32.5 per cent losses sustained in Salford and Manchester in the same period (Peck and Emmerich 1992a: Table 24). What is crucially at issue in Greater Manchester is whether the particular mix of service industry, mass communications and high technology now in place will create new employment to any significant degree; and, in particular, whether any such growth might directly foster a sense of alternative future employment opportunities for the mass of local people made redundant by the demise of local manufacturing.

THE CATASTROPHIC DECLINE OF SHEFFIELD'S INDUSTRIAL DISTRICT

The economic problems confronting Sheffield take the same general form (the collapse of the major manufacturing industry that has sustained the local labour market), but the challenge looks more intractable – in no small measure because of the absence of any real alternatives to the long-standing 'dual economy' of cutlery and steel. The potential dangers of this dependency had been well known in Sheffield for years, but, for reasons discussed by the classical economist Alfred Marshall and others, few corrective initiatives emerged from the city's entrepreneurial and industrial structure itself. As late as 1981, therefore:

Sheffield had the third highest employment dependence of any urban area in Britain on mining, iron and steel and other metal sectors of the economy.

(Seyd 1993: 152)

In 1981, unemployment in Sheffield – at around 6 per cent – remained just below national average. However, any complacency on the part of local capital and local labour was about to be shattered: an organic collapse of the city's manufacturing base (especially in steel) had already begun. The first responses of organised labour, locally, were contained in the pamphlet 'Sheffield: The Second Slump', published in March 1982 by Sheffield Trades Council: this pamphlet sold out its first printing, and, on reprinting, was widely distributed throughout the local trade union and Labour movement. The pamphlet is important for its clear recognition of the scale of Sheffield's economic crisis ('unparalleled since the 1930s') and also for its sense of the social disaster unfolding in the industrial East End. It is remarkable too for its attack on the idea of continuing company loyalty amongst some steelworkers: some of the heaviest 'lay-offs' were occurring in firms like Firth Brown's, which had traditionally attracted considerable loyalty, especially amongst skilled forgemen. Consequent on a worldwide 'over-production' of steel and the new Conservative government's deflation of the economy (involving the imposition of a cash limit on British Steel), the bulk of the Sheffield steel industry (Brown Bayley's, Hadfield's, Osborn's, Tinsley Wire Industries, Steel Peech and Tozer, and British Steel at Tinsley) was in the process, quite straightforwardly, of closing down. On one analysis of this process, some three-quarters of the 45,000 jobs in existence in Sheffield's steel industry in 1981 had disappeared by 1987. Nearly 70 per cent of the 70,863 redundancies reported in Sheffield in the seven years from 1979 to 1986 (nearly 50,000 jobs) were in 'metal manufacture, metal goods and engineering' (Pollard 1993: 278). During the brief 'recovery' of 1987–9, only 1,000 'new jobs' were created in metals and manufacturing, whilst some 8500 new positions emerged in distribution, financial and other services. The City Council's Department of Employment and Economic Development has plotted the demise of Sheffield's steel industry as shown in Table 3.2.

Table 3.2 Employment in the Sheffield steel industry (selected years 1971–93)

Date	Total steel workforce	Percent of total workforce (Sheffield)
June 1971	45,100	16.0
June 1978	34,600	12.6
September 1981	24,700	9.5
September 1987	6,200	2.8
September 1989	7,200	3.1
September 1991	6,800	2.9
December 1993	4,700	2.2

Source: Sheffield City Council Department of Employment and Economic Development Library

In the period from 1981 to 1987 (in contrast to the earlier post-war period), Sheffield's unemployment rate increasingly moved ahead of the national average, and in 1987 reached 16.2 per cent on official measures, as against the national average of 12 per cent. In the period since 1987, the city's unemployment rate, as measured on the ever-more restrictive official definitions, had declined – to 13 per cent in 1994. But it is important to underline how Sheffield's unemployment now seems stuck, stubbornly, at some 2 per cent above national levels, and that in a city which before 1979 had been used to having a better than average local labour market. Significant numbers of the 36,000 officially registered as 'unemployed' in January 1994 were concentrated in the city's post-war housing estates – the new homes in the 1960s of the city's thousands of steelworkers. The official unemployment on one of the more infamous local estates, the Manor, ran to 29 per cent for the estate as a whole, but local sources indicated that there were clusters on this estate – on particular streets – where the real rate was more like 50 per cent. About a quarter of the unemployed on the Manor, according to one local job-centre worker, had been unemployed for more than 10 years (Halsall 1994) . Over roughly the same period (1979–89), to take another measure of local decline, the city's 'gross domestic product' was shown, in a survey commissioned by the Opposition's spokesperson for Industry, Derek Fatchett MP, to have declined from 95.7 in 1979 (against a national average of 100) to 79.1 by 1989 (reported in the *Guardian* 20 December 1993). Locally, the scale of the economic catastrophe was signified visually – and in terms of an inflection to that collective social psychology which we are calling, after Raymond Williams, the 'local structure of feeling' – by the transformation of Sheffield's industrial area, 'East of the Wicker Arches'. Subsequent to decisions taken collectively and collaboratively by the steel owners and the City Councils, the steelworks were razed to the ground: by 1986 the same thoroughfares which had previously wound past the high frontages of massive steel plants stretching out towards Rotherham and Doncaster now cut across vast, open stretches of wasteland (some 301 hectares in all), broken up only by a few new-build office blocks, including the headquarters of the Urban Development Corporation itself.

The response of the local public and private sector in Sheffield to this economic collapse has taken three forms: the move towards a 'new realism' in the partnerships of the local Council with local business, the hosting of the World Student Games and the City of Sport, and the Campaign for a new City Centre. We will discuss each of these in turn.

'Market' realism at a local level

The 1980s witnessed a transformation in the character and assumptions of local Labour politics in Sheffield, for which there are undoubtedly many parallels in other Northern cities, as well as in the politics of old industrial cities in other national contexts (the Ruhr in Germany and the

Rust Belt of the United States). But the change of direction in Sheffield –
in what had only recently been the heartland of what had been called the
Socialist Republic of South Yorkshire – was fundamental and involved
several moments of 'crisis of conscience' for many local councillors and
their thousands of local supporters. Not least of these moments was the
final and painful vote of the City Council in May 1985 to agree to a
'legal rate' under the national government's Rates Act of 1984 and
thereby knowingly set in motion a train of events which would, inevitably, financially undermine the extended infrastructure of local social
services (from 'special schools for maladjusted children' to old people's
homes) which the local Labour administration had proudly built up over
the years.

The second moment arrived in March 1986, when the South Yorkshire County Council – shortly to be abolished – indicated that it could
no longer sustain the subsidies which had been making possible the
celebrated 'cheap bus fares' policy across the county. In moving towards
what one commentator (Seyd 1994) called 'a new realism', the City
Council began quite publicly to modify its attitude to local business,
entering into a series of joint initiatives with the Chamber of Commerce
and the so-called 'Ranmoor Church Forum', a gathering of powerful
business people and community activists meeting in a church building in
one of Sheffield's western suburbs. By December 1986, the City Council
was a full participant in the business community's Sheffield Economic
Regeneration Committee and, some 14 months later, in March 1988, the
Council was able to accept without demur the establishment of the
Urban Development Corporation, entirely taking over the Council's
responsibilities for the regeneration of the industrial East End. The
Sheffield Urban Development Corporation, one of the second phase
of UDCs launched nationally that year, opened up on Savile Street,
looking over the wastelands which had once been the site of a massive
kaleidoscope of different-sized, specialised and mass-production steelworks. The UDC had a budget of £50 million to underwrite its activity
over a seven-year period, and confidently committed itself to the creation
of 20,000 jobs.

Creating the City of Sport

In the meantime, the City Council was involved in a desperate search for
a viable strategy to sustain some kind of future for the local economy. A
series of working parties and special units of the Council, supported by a
host of progressive local academics, struggled with various kinds of local,
essentially Keynesian, visions, meanwhile pinning their hopes on the
return of a Labour government at national level. The key conversations
in the early 1980s, in the event, were not with these committees, with the
Labour Party or with the local trade unions (which had been heavily
defeated in national political confrontations and were not in a creative
period). Discussions between key local councillors and industrialists quite

clearly indicated that the 'City of Steel' was desperately in need of a new self-definition and vision. The Council's financial advisors, Coopers and Lybrand, released a report in early 1987 strongly recommending that the city must make 'a flagship investment' (as had other cities in the North of England: Liverpool as the Garden Festival city, Newcastle and Gateshead as a Centre for Shopping, and, in the Midlands, Birmingham as a city for conventions). Sheffield had also to identify a specific niche for itself in the new – national and international – competition for 'profile' and 'image'. This report finally confirmed the Council in the commitment it had made, initially somewhat tentatively, in December 1986, to a bid to be the host city for the World Student Games of 1991. This was to be the first move in establishing Sheffield as a major centre for international sports events. The marketing of Sheffield (with the set of sports stadia that would then have been built) as the City of Sport would help redirect, reposition and reorganise the local economy, with potentially significant benefits in respect of economic growth and job creation. The Council's Department of Employment and Economic Development (DEED) in 1990 released a report estimating that the work associated with the construction and the 'after-use' of the facilities built for the Games would generate some 13,500 new jobs over the four years to 1992 (Sheffield City Council, DEED, 1990, quoted in Darke 1994: 16)

The bid for the World Student Games was successful and eight major sports facilities were established, either *ab initio* (the Don Valley Stadium, the Sheffield Arena and the Ponds Forge International Swimming Pool) or via the refurbishment of existing sites. But the build-up to the Games was accompanied locally by strong criticism, especially by the local Liberal Party, particularly of the neglect by the City Council of the existing facilities used by local people, and also by persistent accusations of corruption within the organisation, Universiade GB, to which the Council had delegated the organisation of the event itself. There was also some scepticism with respect to the actual stature of the Games (which, indeed, were not purchased by any television company or by the BBC). In one journalistic report, an unnamed person – no doubt Sheffield-born and bred – was quoted as saying 'If the World Student Games are that bloody important, who held the last bugger, then?' In 1992, the worst fears of this section of the Sheffield public, and of the Council itself,[3] were realised when the first set of accounts for the Games suggested a financial loss of £10.4 million.[4] Reports in the local press and radio – and some in the national press – subsequently began to concentrate on the extra burdens that this loss was going to place on local taxes (the council tax) and to speculate on the scale of the further reductions that would occur in council services, and on public-sector redundancies. Predictably enough, in 1993, a 3.25 per cent pay cut was agreed in a vote of 12,500 council staff, members of the then National Association of Local Government Officers, as the only way of 'staving off' redundancies in the council (Wainwright 1993: 3).

In the last months of 1992, the fundamental crisis of the local economy in Sheffield came to the attention of most of the quality national press.[5] In the annual *Business Review* released through the *Sheffield Telegraph*, spokespeople for the local Chamber of Commerce, the Urban Development Corporation and the Council tried to conjure up some areas of optimism (Hambridge 1992),[6] particularly in connection with beneficial spin-offs from Meadowhall, the plans being developed for the City Centre and the opening of the Supertram, scheduled for 1994. It was predicted that the opening of the transit system would bring 80,000 visitors a day into the city. We discuss some of these issues below. In the meantime, however, the economic prospects of the whole South Yorkshire area took a further body-blow, as rumours circulated about an acceleration of British Coal's pit-closure programme. The rumours were confirmed finally in a speech by Michael Heseltine on 19 October 1992, followed by a cruel few months in which a moratorium was announced on closures, pending further enquiries: the closure process was then completed in two separate moves early in 1993. The consequences of these closures on the economy of South Yorkshire, particularly on employment, were devastating (and continue to be so): in the period from 1985 to 1994, all 24 pits in South Yorkshire were closed, with a loss of 10,311 jobs known to British Coal at the time of the closure announcement.[7] By the early 1990s, indeed, the whole employment structure of Sheffield and South Yorkshire had experienced a profound and very sudden transformation. In Sheffield itself, for example, the 'City of Steel', the vast majority of the 235,000 people in employment in 1993 were actually employed in shops, hospitals, offices, education and recreation. The three largest employers in the city were the Council, the health authority and the university, and only one employer from the old 'dual economy' featured in the top ten employers in the City (Table 3.3).

Table 3.3 The top ten employers in Sheffield (1993)

Ranking	Employer	Employees
1	Sheffield City Council	27,000
2	Sheffield Health Authority	12,800
3	University of Sheffield	3,740
4	British Telecom	3,500
5	British Steel Stainless	3,155
6	Midland Bank	3,150
7	South Yorkshire Passenger Transport Executive	3,000
8	Trent Regional Health Authority	2,519
9	Royal Mail	2,500
10	Department of Employment	2,300

Source: Sheffield Chamber of Commerce, mimeo information sheet (1993)

The crisis of the city centre

The development of the 'city centre' in Northern cities over the last two centuries may have had some shared 'organic' features (for example, in most instances, the retention of the town market, although in a changed relation to its surrounding environment or the building of a central railway station), but the specific development of each city centre also exhibits important idiosyncratic features. In Chapter 1, we described the particular influence of a city's geographical and topographical location. Liverpool's city centre cannot be understood except in relation to its location on the Mersey Estuary and, similarly, Newcastle and Hull are very clearly defined by their waterside location: entry to Newcastle and its centre, in particular, for most people is via the famous Tyne or High Level bridges. Elsewhere in the North, the layout of the central core of cities at the confluence of rivers or valleys is determined by the proximity of the Pennine Hills (Bradford, Huddersfield and, to some extent, Sheffield itself). It is in these sites and locations that particular config- urations of commercial offices, warehouses and other industrial buildings have sprung up, and it is in the context of this 'material infrastructure' that the particular and specific character of the city centre has emerged.

We have indicated earlier how Sheffield's location 'on seven hills' has become a key motif in local folklore.[8] Less frequent attention has been given, until the 1990s, to the curious character of its city centre, though periodically the City Council and planners have glimpsed that it is an issue (cf. Sheffield, Town Planning Committee 1945). The 'centre' of Sheffield actually consists of one long thoroughfare running south-west (Moorfoot) to north-east (Fitzalan Square) across the geographical mid- dle of the city, changing its name at several different points from The Moor, through Pinstone Street, Fargate, High Street and Angel Street, to 'below' Fitzalan Square Commercial Street and Castle Street. (At the central point, by the Town Hall, there is a triangular road system, involving Church Street and Leopold Street, routing some buses and cars through the centre, as well as a short road, Barkers Pool, containing the City Hall and Coles Department Store.) This 'long and thin city' developed in this fashion from the eighteenth century onwards; and there is a well-developed local understanding of how this particular kind of city is to be used, particularly for different kinds of shopping. We discuss these issues further in Chapter 5.

This is the 'material infrastructure' around which all subsequent development has had to occur. There was one fundamental modifica- tion to this pattern in the post-war period, in the decision, taken in the early 1960s, to redesign the northern end of High Street/Angel Street to create easier access to the city for cars. The new design of this junction involved the removal of a whole side street (Change Alley) and the routing of an urban throughway (Arundel Gate) to connect up to High Street. The absolutely definitive feature of this re-engineering of the city centre was the decision to separate pedestrians from cars, routing pedestrians underground by means of underpasses, walkways and esca-lators to a large concourse, open to the sky, to be known, according to the planners, as the Civic Circle. The 'Circle' was quickly renamed 'Castle Square' by local politicians and finally opened in 1967: great hopes were held out for the square as a new kind of shopping arcade, linked into surrounding shops, and, indeed, as a place for casual resort (seats were installed around the central concourse, and a large fish aquarium in one of the concrete walls).

The 27-year history of Castle Square in central Sheffield is a powerful case study for students of urban fears and local myth-making in the second half of the twentieth century. The Square itself was very quickly renamed by Sheffielders 'the Hole in the Road' (a.k.a. 'Hole in the Ground', with all its negative connotations) – a succinct subversion of the intended civic ambitions attending its opening. By the mid–1970s, the concrete walls of the square were fairly heavily graffitied; the escala-tors from High Street were regularly found to be out of order (along with the toilets situated on one wing of the square); the aquarium was becoming covered by algae and other deposits; and the owners of the fruiterers, bakers, newsagents and kiosks in the underpasses were begin-ning to experience considerable loss of trade. The 'Hole in the Road' was progressively reconstructed in the local imagination into what Yi-Fu Tuan (1979) has called 'a landscape of fear', fuelled by reports in the local press of incidents of theft or harassment, and by the physical decline and neglect of the space itself. There is no question, however, that the increasingly agitated debate in Sheffield about the condition of 'the Hole in the Road' (which, throughout this period, remained the only pedes-trian route from High Street to the markets or vice versa) was very quickly becoming a metaphor for a much larger concern about the future of the whole city centre.

The originating moment of this sense of city-centre crisis in Sheffield was the announcement by a local entrepreneur, Eddie Healey, in the mid-1980s, that he was to build a massive new shopping city on derelict industrial land (the site of Hadfield's steel works, closed in 1983) in Sheffield's East End, adjacent to the M1 motorway. This new develop-ment, to be known as Meadowhall, was to house all the major UK retail chains and to provide space for a total of about 270 new shops. When it was eventually opened, in September 1990, Meadowhall proclaimed itself the largest such development in Europe. The publicity distributed by Meadowhall positioned the new mall as a shopping centre for the whole Northern region, suggesting that it was situated within easy driving distance for 10 million people. The anxieties of the local Cham-ber of Commerce and all other traders and business people in Sheffield's existing city centre were intense. The fear was that Meadowhall would very quickly siphon away city-centre shopping custom and add a further fatal blow to a city centre already struggling with the problem of bus deregulation. We discuss these problems in some detail in Chapter 4: it is sufficient here to note that the deregulation of municipal bus services in

the 1985 Transport Act had brought massive problems of traffic congestion and pollution to Sheffield's city centre and, coupled with the ending
of the 'cheap bus fares' policy in South Yorkshire (itself a product of this
Act), there arose a widespread, and new, local disenchantment with the
idea of 'going to town'. Clearly what was feared by local politicians and
the Chamber of Commerce was the development in Sheffield of a local
version of the problem experienced by many American cities during the
early 1980s – that of a wholesale evacuation of the city-centre core (with
that city centre then being beset by problems of crime and dereliction),
and the relocation of most people's shopping and leisure activities to
large urban mall developments in the suburbs or on the outer edge of
cities (Garreau 1991). By the early 1990s, this process seemed well in
train in Sheffield: the loss of trade to city-centre shops resulting from the
opening of Meadowhall by the summer of 1992 was estimated to be in
the region of 20 per cent.[9] Significant numbers of city-centre traders (like
the electricians Bunker and Pratley's) who had been very strong 'local
names' in critical locations (in this case, at one exit from the 'Hole in the
Road') closed down and boarded up their windows. This 'boarding-up'
of the city centre (in particular in evidence around the old Schofields
store, situated by another exit from Castle Square) was a frequent topic
of remark and despair in our focus group discussions in Sheffield, as a
signifier of a more general sense of decline and abandonment.

In 1992, the City Council, Development Corporation and local
Chamber of Commerce commissioned an urgent investigation into the
problem of resurrecting the city centre as what they called a Quality
Central Area (cf. Foley and Lawless 1992). The resulting report, written
at speed by academics in the city's two universities, received widespread
attention in the local press, and seems to have informed subsequent
deliberations of what Molotch and Logan would call the 'local growth
coalition'. After the award of a £2.3-million grant from the Departments
of Employment and Transport, the 'Hole in the Road' was finally closed
to the public on 10 January 1994, and filled in, with a view to the
construction, at road level, of a pedestrian square and Supertram
station *Sheffield Telegraph* 3 December 1993): in the words of the designer
employed on this project, 'the people were put back on top' (*Sheffield
Weekly Gazette* 26 August 1993). By October 1994, key members of
Sheffield's urban partnerships were being quoted, throughout the local
press, as saying that the 'rescue' of the city centre had been successfully
accomplished, and the City Council initiated a marketing campaign
under the slogan 'City Centre Alive and Kicking' (Kay 1994a, 1994b).

Undoubtedly the most fundamental modification to the 'material
infrastructure' of Sheffield city centre has been the opening of the
Supertram, which we discuss in Chapter 4: what is at issue, in terms
of the local decline of the city centre in Sheffield, is whether the Supertram (which also connects Sheffielders very quickly to Meadowhall) will
contribute to a resurrection of the centre, or merely be a quicker, more
congenial means of travelling bypassing it.

Figure 3.1 Attempted rescues of the city centre: the Orchard Square shopping arcade, Sheffield
Source: photo by Penny Fraser

This account of the dereliction in Sheffield city centre provides a complete contrast to recent discussions of the city centre of Manchester, where the focus is currently on further moves towards the construction of city-centre Manchester as a 24-hour city, the home to a network of theatres, night clubs, wine bars, Chinatown, downtown apartments and the Gay Village itself (see Chapter 7). We will discuss some of these developments later: for the moment, our concern is to underline the fact of difference in the 'conjunctural' situation of these two old industrial cities.

COMMONALITY AND DIFFERENCE

These contemporary facts of difference in the situation of the two cities are inescapable. However, our analysis is also informed by a recognition of the ways in which these different trajectories are played out against some shared common understandings and assumptions, which would be recognisable to the local 'growth coalitions' and 'local rescue squads' respectively. We spoke in Chapter 1 about the 'Northernness' of these cities as a constituent element in their 'sense of place'. There is also a shared general sensibility in these cities, we would argue, in respect of the sense of time and history, which specifies the industrial North (and equivalent urban industrial regions in some European cities) as a particular 'object of analysis' – quite different from cities in the New World, the Pacific Rim or elsewhere. The real heyday of the industrial city in the North of England – and certainly, of Manchester and Sheffield – was not, as in Detroit, the 1960s (or even the 1930s) but, almost without question, the last years of the nineteenth century. Manchester, in particular, the 'shock city' of the 1840s, matured as a major city throughout the following half-century and, in the estimation of Dame Kathleen Ollerenshaw, 'was probably at her peak just before the outbreak of the first war, or somewhat earlier, say at the turn of the century' (Ollerenshaw 1982: 21). Sheffield, in turn, was 'the unrivalled centre of world cutlery production' in the period between 1870 and the end of the nineteenth century, with 97 per cent of Britain's 13,756 cutlers working in the city (Taylor, S. 1993: 194). As late as the 1870s, Sheffield steel industry's monopoly of crucible manufacturing seemed to guarantee the future of local firms: thereafter, Sheffield's distance from major natural deposits of iron ores, and its relative geographical isolation, fed into a slow process of decline, interrupted by the boosts of armament production during the two world wars (Tweedale 1993).

Close understanding of the 'structure of feeling' of industrial cities in the North of England does depend, we would argue, on recognising that these cities, unlike Detroit and the American Rust-Belt cities, were already in the 1970s quite old industrial cities with their origins in the Victorian period and well past their prime. There was (and is) no strong immediate memory of a prosperous and successful period of economic growth and well-being – the 'golden age' spoken of by Eric Hobsbawm in his recent magisterial history of the twentieth century (Hobsbawm 1994). These were also cities in which many of the older population defined themselves in terms of their experiences during the war, either as serving soldiers or as civilians who had borne the brunt of the blitz which the Luftwaffe targeted on many Northern cities. They were cities in which large proportions of a certain age-cohort in the population, by reason of their specific experience of economic depression in the 1920s and 1930s and the war of 1939–45, felt themselves, not without justification, to be 'hard done by', but also had developed a talent for 'making do', 'getting by' or – in Sheffield – 'mucking through'. The capacity of the Northern industrial working class, in particular, to be long-suffering in its deprivation has frequently been the subject of comment in television soap operas (*Coronation Street*) as well as in the famous Northern 'kitchen-sink' films of the early 1960s (*A Taste of Honey, This Sporting Life, Billy Liar* and many others). This emphasis is not new: Patrick Joyce follows Gareth Stedman-Jones in seeing popular culture in nineteenth-century England as a highly controlled cultural form, concerned to discipline and restrict self-indulgence and pleasure. Even in music-hall humour, there was:

> a marked sense of stoicism and fortitude bringing order and dignity out of the implacable material of life.
>
> (Joyce 1991: 158)

But this 'mucking through' did not take place in a vacuum. Throughout the post-war period, and, we would argue, as late as 1970, the Northern industrial cities were sustained not by a sense of a 'golden age' of economic possibility but rather by the fact of 'full employment' (that is, of the male working class). The local expression of this in Sheffield was the stubborn assumption that the well-established 'dual economy' of quality Sheffield steel and cutlery was essentially impervious to international competition (this involved a certain suppression of the fact of rapid development of the Japanese cutlery industry in the 1950s). The critical point here was that unemployment in Sheffield remained at about 2 per cent of the registered labour force throughout the post-war period to the end of the 1960s (Pollard 1993: 276–7). It was not until the mid-1970s that the scale of job losses that would follow the collapse of the dual trades was fully appreciated. In Manchester, during this same period, a range of different job opportunities was being thrown up in a diversified economy spread across the whole of south-east Lancashire, generating some local sense of the Greater Manchester region as relatively immune from changes in international patterns of demand and trade and in some ways reproducing the sense of possibility that had characterised Manchester in the 1840s. Manchester – the city of business, trade and commerce – was seen by many key local politicians and commentators throughout the post-war period to be abreast of the changing times:

> Joseph Whitworth [had] standardized the pitch of manufactured screws; Craven Bros. supplied the world with cranes from Miles Platting and later led the manufacture of heavy-cutting tools, Platt Bros. produced looms and spinning machines . . . Rolls-Royce built their first cars in Hulme; Crossley's motor works were in Gorton; Mather and Platt were famous world-wide for their pumping machinery; Metropolitan Vickers at Trafford Park made electricity available the world over with their generators. Charles Beyer and Peacock of Gorton exported locomotives world-wide. Henry Simon exported milling machinery. Hans Renold and his son Charles (who gave much to the later development of 'the Tech') were famous for chains of all kinds, particularly fine driving chains. Alliott Vernon Roe (AVRO – later Hawker Siddeley) built Lancaster bombers in a factory still standing in Great Ancoats Street. William Mather brought Edward Hopkinson to Manchester, hence the Manchester (Edison-Hopkinson) dynamo. Sebastian de Ferranti, who developed the alternator (his family originally from Bologna) settled in Man-

chester after building the first British power station in Deptford, seizing the opportunities of diversification in manufacturing by pioneering the developing of alternating electrical equipment. Followed by his son Vincent, Ferranti's moved on to be leaders in electronic control mechanisms and computers.

(Ollerenshaw 1982: 8–9)

MANCHESTER: REVIVAL IN THE 1990S

We discussed the depth of the crisis that confronted Manchester's local economy in the 1970s and 1980s – the 'crisis of Fordism' – in some detail in Chapter 2. Our concern here is to present an account of Manchester's attempt, beginning in the 1980s and continuing into the 1990s, to respond to this crisis by positioning itself as what Molotch and Logan call a 'headquarter city' – particularly with respect to Europe (for example, in the City Pride bid of 1994).[10] This campaign to establish Manchester's stature as a major European and international city is most clearly evident in the investment of £570 million in a new terminal for Ringway Airport, identified by many in the early 1990s as the 'fastest-growing airport' in Europe, in the City's two bids to host the Olympic Games, and in many other developments with profound impacts on city space and 'feel' (which we will discuss more directly in Chapter 12). In part, these developments are an expression of the availability in the wider region of a relatively large number of highly skilled workers and professionals. These developments may also be seen as an expression of what A.J.P. Taylor identified as Manchester's 'restless and dynamic' character, signified locally in the oft-repeated refrain that Manchester is 'a city of firsts' (the 'first industrial city', the site of the 'first commercial passenger railway', of the first computer, etc.). Victor Keegan has argued that the 'economic correction' which he believes is taking place in Manchester in the 1990s may actually be confirmation of the advantages that larger regional economies may have in respect of capital investment and human skills in adjusting to the new global economic competitive environment (Keegan 1993).

Certainly the scale of development in Greater Manchester since the early 1980s is remarkable. The ambitious schemes of the Greater Manchester Council – for example, to transform Central Station into G-Mex, the Greater Manchester Exhibition Centre (now a massive open exhibition space, doubling as a concert hall) – were accompanied by major developments taking place, across the River Irwell, in Salford – in particular, the transformation of 160 acres of land around the old Manchester Docks by Edward Hyams, a local entrepreneur, into 'Salford Quays'. Hyams's initiative – in part taking advantage of national government's designation of the area as an Enterprise Zone, attracting large reductions in local taxes – has helped create a major development of office blocks, restaurants, a multi-screen cinema and new-build waterside apartments, and brought some £330-million worth of investment into the area between 1984 and 1991.

In the meantime, in the southern suburbs of Manchester, major developments were launched to 'upgrade' and extend Manchester International Airport: under the chairmanship of Sir Gil Thomson, the airport committed itself not only to the building of a £570-million new terminal but also to the construction, in partnership with British Rail, of a new rail station in the airport itself. These new facilities opened in 1993, with the airport declaring that it was now the thirteenth largest airport in the world in terms of patronage. The third arm of the development strategy – the building of a second runway – remained stalled in the courts, because of local objections, at the time of writing.

Probably the most important development in the resurrection of Manchester in the 1990s – certainly in terms of the lived experience of the city for thousands of local people – was the opening of the Metrolink light transit system in July 1992. The origins of this scheme lay in discussions taking place between the old Greater Manchester Council, British Rail and the Greater Manchester Passenger Transport Executive in 1982, convened to tackle the continuing problems of access to the city-centre core – including the problem, inherited from the nineteenth century, of the dispersal of the main rail stations and the lack of any connecting link between them. A high priority in these discussions was the idea of building an underground link between Manchester Piccadilly and Victoria rail stations. In Chapter 4, we provide a fuller account of the progress of these developments in the 1980s, always against the background of ever-increasing estimates of the volume of car traffic coming into the city. The concept of the Metrolink emerged as an alternative to an underground system, and involved the purchase by the Passenger Transport Executive of the British Rail lines to Bury and Altrincham, then linked together through lines through the city streets (Ogden and Senior 1991). The Metrolink opened in 1991, with 25 stations and a 6-minute service frequency throughout most of the day.

Many of these initiatives for regeneration in Greater Manchester have been initiated by local entrepreneurs, though it is vital to record the key role of public authorities, like the Greater Manchester Council. The GMC (like its counterpart in South Yorkshire and in five other large metropolitan areas, as well as the Greater London Council) was a creation of the Local Government Act of 1972. It was heavily involved, during the early 1980s, in a variety of initiatives to reclaim tracts of derelict ground in the city-centre cores, but was also at the forefront of movements to reclaim waste land alongside the old valleys and riversides of the urban regions. In the Greater Manchester area, for example, the GMC planted several thousand trees and also established five new country parks in the period to 1983 (Dickinson 1990: 11). The Council was also instrumental, as we indicated earlier, in attempts to create a conurbation-wide transport strategy. The achievements were not insignificant and the traces of the County's original initiatives are still clearly visible across metropolitan areas like Manchester, though increasingly overshadowed by the Development Corporation's retrieval of buildings and spaces. It seems clear, however, that the activities of these county authorities, abolished by the Conservative government in the Local Government (Interim Provisions) Act of 1986, did not have the same cultural impact in all county council areas. The creation of a strong sense of 'Greater Manchester' in a region built up, from the eighteenth century, initially around six significant local towns, and, latterly, around ten borough authorities, was a rather different enterprise to that of the South Yorkshire County Council: the idea of being a citizen of somewhere called Greater Manchester was always weaker than the sense of identity that comes from birth or residence in individual towns, including Manchester itself, at different locations across that conurbation.

Constantly informing all these developments in the later 1980s and the early 1990s was the coverage given the City Council and local growth coalition's interest in being chosen as the UK bid to host the Olympic Games. Under the chairmanship of Mr (later Sir) Bob Scott, the City did gain the right from the British Olympics Committee (against competition from London, Birmingham and, on the second occasion, Sheffield) to be the British bid for the Olympics of 1996 and 2000. In 1989, bidding for 1996, the city lost out to Atlanta and in 1993, bidding for the 'Millennium Games' of 2000, it came third to Sydney and Beijing. One measure of the local cultural impact of the regeneration that had been taking place in the city, however, was the widespread belief, on the second occasion, that Manchester could win. The voting of the International Olympics Committee on 23 September 1993 was televised live to thousands of Mancunians assembled in the Castlefield arena, with Metrolink providing free travel for all and local newspapers printing memento editions. The leader of Manchester City Council, Graham Stringer, predicted that the success of the bid would unlock some £2.3 billion of capital investment in Manchester, with some 11,000 new jobs (*Manchester Evening News* 10 September 1993). The disappointment in the city at the final vote was palpable, but leaders of the local growth coalition quickly pointed to the £75 million of capital investment that was to be put into the city in any case (by national government), emphasising how this would enable completion of the Velodrome in east Manchester (already chosen as the site for the 1996 World Cycling Games), the 'Olympic' Indoor Athletics facility being built by Bovis over and around Victoria Station, and other sites. In February 1994, Manchester was selected to bid for the Commonwealth Games in the year 2002 and announced its commitment to build a new 65,000-seat stadium (the 'Wembley of the North').

These initiatives in the area of sport were a direct challenge to the attempts which Sheffield had been making to establish itself as an international city for sport and, indeed, to claim this particular niche for itself in the North of England. There was evidence of some despair in

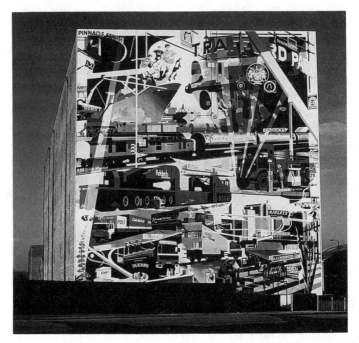

Figure 3.2 Memorial to modern industry: the Trafford Park mural
Source: photo courtesy of the Trafford Park Development Corporation

Figure 3.3 Industrial nostalgia and hegemonic masculinity: Sheffield steelworker
wall mural (1986) Castle Street, Sheffield
Source: photo by Ian Taylor

Sheffield in February 1994, when Manchester beat Sheffield, quite easily, in the process of selection of a UK city to bid for the Commonwealth Games. But there was by now a range of other developments in Manchester which was enabling its growth coalition to make a more general claim for Manchester as a 'headquarter city' – not confined to one area of activity or niche. Already chosen on the basis of its 15 active theatres as the City of Drama for 1994, Manchester was completing the building of a new home for the Hallé Orchestra, the Concert Hall (due for opening in 1996), and was also generating publicity on the range of museums, art galleries, restaurants and night life available within the city. In the autumn of 1994, Regional Railways collaborated with the local council in distributing a glossy brochure 'It's Magic in Manchester', in ticket offices across the Midlands and the whole of the North of England. A very different image of Manchester was obviously being mobilised here to that of a city of poverty, inequality, guns and violent crime that was constructed in the popular press and elsewhere. A real struggle was in progress over both the representation of Manchester and also the experience of living in that city.

THE WORLD THAT WAS LOST: EVERYDAY LIFE IN THE URBAN NORTH

We want to punctuate this contemporary history of these two cities with some comments on the changes that are widely identified in their everyday life by their inhabitants, in particular in the form of widespread reference to changes 'within living memory'. We want to offer this account to provide some background to the material from our focus group enquiries which begins to be introduced in Chapter 4, and which shapes many of our concerns throughout this book. The account we develop is also drawn from a variety of sources, including our reading of a variety of local histories (esp. Vickers 1972, 1992), newspaper cuttings, biographical accounts by long-time residents of Greater Manchester (Roberts 1973) and Sheffielders (Hattersley 1981; Shaw 1993), and the personal experience of two of these researchers in living in these two cities for significant periods of their own lives. There is a conscious attempt on our parts to avoid the reduction of the experience of the city or the city/region in all its complexity to the biography of any one individual – an obvious methodological problem that confronts any such approach to social explanation (for example, life histories). We have decided to try to freeze the two cities at an historical moment at around the end of the 1960s or, at least, in the period between 1968 to 1973. We do so, in the company of many other commentators,[11] in order to try to capture the patterned and material character of life in those cities (as revealed in the organisation of work, family and neighbourhood life and leisure) at this particular 'historical moment' – and, perhaps, also to speak to their 'structure of feeling' at this moment. We will do so, rather crudely, by trying to speak of the 'middle-class and working-class experience' of these two cities and regions in 1968–73. We obviously do not believe that such a dualism covers all the social divisions structuring urban experience at this time (our later chapters underline the diversity of city populations and uses of the city thirty years later, especially the idea of a 'woman's city') and we do not believe that 'the city' itself reduces merely to 'class' or other social group definition: the city is also, as we have argued, a material infrastructure of buildings, routes and spaces. What we do believe is that the experience of industrial cities in the North of England, at the end of the post-war Keynesian period of social settlement between capital and labour, was very heavily influenced and defined by the social divisions of class.

Middle-class Manchester

For the substantial middle class of Manchester in the later 1960s, the city itself was a place that would be visited for purposes of work (in office buildings or inner-city industrial factories and workshops) or perhaps to shop. Kendals department store on Deansgate and the range of other fashionable shops along Market Street would be the first port of call on many shopping trips. For some sections of the middle class, the city – much more than in other Northern towns – was also the venue for music, most publicly in the famous concerts of the Hallé Orchestra (first established in 1848) at the Free Trade Hall, but also in special events held at Chetham's School (first founded in 1656, but re-established on original premises in 1969 as a boarding school for 200 young boys and girls of exceptional talent in music). In 1973, the Royal Northern College of Music was opened to carry forward the long-established tradition of musical education and performance in the city. The City Art Gallery and the Whitworth Art Gallery at the University of Manchester achieved considerable fame amongst painters and sculptors across the North of England, whilst the City Library in St Peter's Square and the John Rylands Library in Deansgate must have been two of the most comfortable libraries in which to work anywhere in the North. Middle-class pride in Manchester in the mid-twentieth century was also excited by the widespread recognition of Manchester as a centre of good theatre, with many a play tried out on the discerning audiences of Manchester before being launched in the West End of London. Manchester's middle class was also well known for the pride it displayed in the quality of the secondary education available in the city, most famously at 'Manchester Grammar' (the boys' Grammar School), the Girls' High School, Withington High School and William Hulme's. This celebration of quality education, especially for worthy and talented offspring of the elite local middle class, also extended to the University of Manchester itself, nearly always referred to in local discussion as 'the Victoria University' or 'Owens', in order to emphasise the heritage of this university, on the one hand, and its origins in the patronage of a local dignitary of the early nineteenth century, on the other.[12]

The bulk of the actual leisure time of the Manchester middle class in the late 1960s was spent in and around private homes in the residential suburbs to the south of the city – or even in the towns and villages beyond the boundaries of the City of Manchester proper. In her lengthy lecture and essay on Manchester, prepared for the Literary and Philosophical Society in 1980–1, Dame Kathleen Ollerenshaw gave voice to what remains a powerful complaint in political circles in Manchester to this day: specifically, that so few members of the political classes or the other influential classes of the region actually lived within the Borough of Manchester itself, having joined the rush to the suburban areas in Trafford and Stockport or to the Cheshire towns and villages further south, or, in some instances, into West Yorkshire or the Derbyshire Peak. The 'flight from Manchester', which is widely discussed in the 1990s amongst estate agents and moneyed 'home-seekers', is no new phenomenon.

Working-class Manchester

By contrast, the world of working-class Manchester in and around the city centre, and extending north into the old cotton-producing towns, remained in the late 1960s a relatively restricted one, very much contained within a 5-mile radius of the city core. For most Mancunian men, everyday life was focused on the place of work, 'the house', the garden or allotment (in some instances), and, perhaps, the local pub. For working-class women, whether or not they were also employed in the waged labour market, the world revolved around the house, the street, perhaps the wash-house, and the corner store. In inner-city areas like Levenshulme and Bradford, and over the Irwell in Salford (the site of the original Coronation Street and also of Manchester Docks, the terminus for the Manchester Ship Canal), the pattern of life seems to have corresponded closely to descriptions made famous (for Leeds) by Richard Hoggart, but perhaps more graphically described for Salford itself in Robert Roberts's *The Classic Slum* (Roberts 1973). The rhythm and pattern of life described in these two accounts changed very little between the 1920s and 1960s. Weekend life in Salford and Manchester in the 1920s and the 1930s had been punctuated by Saturday-night street markets (Davies 1987) and by the occasional 'monkey walks', when young men and women paraded up and down the street in their best clothing (Davies 1992: 102–10). Street life in the rows of terraced houses that dominated Salford and inner-city Manchester remained extraordinarily important throughout the early post-war period – up until the so-called 'slum-clearing programme' and the rehousing of large numbers of the population in high-rise buildings or outlying estates in the 1960s. It was clearly not a life in which women were encouraged to play much more than a subservient, domestic role, restricted to 'the private sphere' of the household (Tebbutt 1992), though it is also clear that the role of the woman (as 'matriarch') in regulating the behaviour of young men and boys in the household and on the street was significant. In the meantime, the skyline of inner-city Salford and Manchester continued to be dominated, as it still is, by the central rotunda of the massive Strangeways prison (built in 1868), appearing to tower over the inner city as an omnipresent signifier of punishment to potential wrongdoers in the immediate locality.

From 'a den of thieves' to Gunchester: a criminological history of Manchester

The prevalence of 'crime' and 'trouble' in central Manchester over the last 150 years ought to be the subject of a separate study. In the early nineteenth century, according to S.J. Davies (1985), Manchester was already perceived as having an exceptional problem in respect of crime, and especially as 'a den of thieves'. In the first decades of the nineteenth century, an almost pathological fear of the lower class and its criminality (focused in particular on new immigrants into Manchester) was the main stimulus in the acceptance of a 'New Police' force in the city, after the example of London. The force was established in 1843, replacing the pre-existing system of a day and night watch (essentially a body of rather elderly men, who were commonly regarded as unfit for the chase). Davies argues that the relationship between the New Police in Manchester and the local working class remained 'highly fraught' at least until the 1880s. In particular, the aggressive tactics of the New Police vis-à-vis the continuing problems of 'prostitution, vagrancy and begging, drunkenness and gambling' in the city created considerable tension and certainly militated against the possibility of the Manchester police acting in the role of 'domestic missionaries'. Towards the turn of the nineteenth century, the city (and some adjacent Lancashire towns) became very widely known for the activities of the so-called 'scuttling gangs', fighting for the control of territory in particular working-class neighbourhoods.

The significance of these moments of urban stress and trouble in the 1840s and 1890s – in terms, say, of the larger issue of Manchester's 'reputation' for crime, the apparently very high incidence of recorded crime, discussed in Chapter 1, or the impact of crime on working-class life in Manchester at different moments in the twentieth century – is in no sense straightforward. Manchester's nineteenth-century reputation seemed to have receded somewhat in the first half of this century – particularly in the 1930s, when other cities (Liverpool, Glasgow and London itself, in the East End) achieved or were ascribed powerful reputations as the centres of organised crime or gang delinquency. Sheffield in the 1920s and 1930s gained some reputation as the home to a number of ruthless 'criminal families' (cf. Bean 1981; Sillitoe 1953). Crime in Manchester in the inter-war period, and indeed into the early post-war period, seemed neither spectacular nor untypical, though there were definite opportunities for organised crime in the 1950s to take advantage of the growth of Manchester's gambling clubs.[13] The changes that have occurred in police organisation and in local government in the ensuing period make it almost impossible to develop any reliable measure of incidence of crime in a particular police-force area.

The key moment in the construction of Manchester's current reputation as a centre of high rates of crime and violence, almost without question, was the 'riot' in Moss Side on the 7–8 July 1981. This confrontation between hundreds of angry young black (and white) Mancunians and about a thousand police officers on Princess Road was actually part of a series of similar 'disturbances' taking place across the country, beginning in Brixton in April, and also taking place in Liverpool (there was, however, no such 'disturbance' in Sheffield). The violence and anger underlying this confrontation are clearly engraved in local memories in Manchester, as are also the findings of the Report on the Unofficial Enquiry into the events by a respected local barrister, Benet Hytner, in which *prima facie* evidence was discovered of the use of violence by Greater Manchester Police on people in custody.

Similar memories exist in those other localities where disturbances occurred in the summer of 1981. What has been so distinctive in Manchester, though, in the construction of 'Moss Side' in the imagination as a place of fear, is the continuing well-publicised occurrence of incidents, especially involving firearms. The culmination of this sequence of events was the murder of the 13-year-old Benji Stanley in January 1992 whilst he was waiting in a queue in a fast-food shop on a main road through the area. Although Moss Side itself is not routinely the scene of murders, this particular incident pushed the area into the national press, television and radio, where it was persistently discussed as a kind of North of England equivalent to south central Los Angeles, which itself had recently been the scene of massive and violent disturbances. The power of the Moss Side metaphor is extraordinary, and we will be examining this issue in more detail in Chapter 8. The relationship of the 'construction' of Moss Side to any kind of lived experience in that area is at best very indirect. What is clear is that the public mobilisation of this fearful discussion of Moss Side occurred at a time – the late 1980s to the early 1990s – when recorded rates of crime throughout the Greater Manchester Police-force area, especially burglaries and car thefts were reaching 'record highs'.[14] It is also important to say that this escalation of public anxiety, in part around the dystopia of Moss Side, occurred alongside the deepest and longest economic recession experienced in Manchester's local economy and against the continuing decline of the traditional economic base of the local labour market, in mass manufacturing industry. However these crime figures were presented in local and national press reports – and sometimes the representation of Manchester (as 'Gunchester', for example) was exaggerated and sensational – the picture presented was of a city in trouble. Residents were being presented by local media with this sense of their own city, an account which they were somehow asked to make sensible alongside its image as being in wholesale economic recovery and regeneration: the Manchester of the Olympic Bids and 24-hour culture and entertainment.

Places of public resort in industrial Manchester

We noted in Chapter 1 how the city of Manchester, from the time of its first commercial development, was thought remarkable by observers for the degree of 'residential segregation' between particular neighbourhoods and spaces, and thereby between social classes. But it was also distinctive for the overwhelming domination of the physical landscape by buildings dedicated to trade and industry. It was not a 'green city', in which the material effects of industrial growth had been carefully contained, with a close attention to the spiritual importance of open space, or the maintenance or retrieval of some sense of nature, or the provision of a shared public space. In particular, as Kay-Shuttleworth first noted in his famous report, there were no parks. The only space left over from industrial development in the inner core of Manchester in the 1840s was a few, dusty turnpike roads on which Mancunians might occasionally engage in sports and play. It was not until 1868, when the Corporation purchased 60 acres from Lord Egerton, that the first municipal park (Alexandra Park in Hulme) was opened. There were further acquisitions of land in the 1890s (including the 145-acre Boggart Hole Clough, in Blackley, north Manchester) and some donations of land in the early years of this century (including Whitworth Park, next to the present-day University of Manchester, and the largest of all Manchester's parks, Heaton Park, in the north of the city). Manchester did not benefit from the donation of land from local industrialists that had occurred in Sheffield (and some other Northern cities) and has never caught up with other Northern cities in its provision of park space for the use of the general public. Shena Simon also observed in 1938 how the parks which had been created were extremely unevenly distributed across the conurbation:

> The inner ring, which contains 33 per cent of the population, has only 2.4 per cent of the open spaces [whilst] the outer ring . . . on the north, east and south . . . with 38 per cent of the population enjoys 84 per cent of the open spaces.
>
> (Simon 1938: 311)

In the absence of major areas of publicly provided green spaces,[15] Mancunians had to adapt to their local environment for purposes of leisure and recreation in whatever ways they could. Casual walks were possible, but rare, in the smaller open spaces in the centre of the city (particularly Piccadilly Gardens, completed in 1934). Fishing in the local canal system was for many years one of the most popular working-class pursuits in Manchester, but there was also widespread resort to commercially provided forms of leisure (the greyhound tracks at the White City and Belle Vue, the horse races at Castle Irwell). For many young men in

Manchester, there was also the experience of playing Sunday football – for example, on Hough End Playing Fields, the largest publicly provided set of football pitches in England, other than the Hackney Marshes in London's East End. Later in the 1970s, there was to be a new place of public resort in city-centre Manchester for purposes of leisure in the form of the Arndale Shopping Centre, opened in 1976, on what had once been one of the prized shopping streets of the city, Market Street. But, in the early 1970s, the city as a whole was no more 'a city for walking' than at any earlier period – not simply because of its size, but also (at least according to one observer) because of a general lack in the earlier post-war period of civic interest in, or awareness of, the benefits of urban preservation in the inner-city areas. Writing about this sense of civic neglect in Manchester, some twenty years earlier, and defending America's city governments and American 'Admass' culture from the critique of J.B. Priestley, the then editor of the *Manchester Guardian*, Alistair Hetherington, observed with great prescience how:

> if Manchester's authorities had a fraction of Chicago's foresight they would not be turning the banks of the Mersey into a rubbish dump, and if its pre-'Admass' citizens were not sunk in stupor they would have organised something like the Allegheny Conference on Community Development in Pittsburgh . . . The 'Admass' society has a creative side which Mr Priestley seems to have missed.
>
> (Hetherington, in Brown 1955–6: 19)

In the absence of downtown parks and walkways (a problem which the contemporary Urban Development Corporation is now trying to address), there was a significant absence in Manchester of 'public space' and 'public assets', which could be prized by the local working-class population at large. One of the most prized examples of shared 'public assets' in the city of Manchester – not always discussed in the authorised histories of this 'Victorian city' – were its professional football clubs, which, though not public institutions in any formal sense, certainly belonged to the public's imagination. Old Trafford, the home of the great Manchester United team of the 1960s but in the 1940s something of a shell (as a result of bombing raids in March 1941 on the nearby Manchester Ship Canal and Trafford Park industrial estate), experienced rapid redevelopment, with the opening of the new United Road cantilever stand in 1964 and the investment of a further £76,000 in the stadium for the 1966 World Cup. In 1973, the club was to become one of the first in Britain to install private boxes for the following it built up amongst the local professional class. It had not yet attained the status of what Bobby Charlton in the 1980s called 'a theatre of dreams', but it was well on the way, and the stadium was used as background in several feature films (*Charlie Bubbles*, with Albert Finney, in 1968; *Hell is a City*, with Stanley Baker, in 1960, *Billy Liar* in 1963 and *The Lovers!* in 1972) (Inglis 1987: 57–61). Very suddenly, 'Old Trafford', a football ground that had originally been established on this site in 1909 by a football club, Newton Heath, originally established in 1878, had become one of the most powerful symbols of modern Manchester to the broader society of the United Kingdom, and by 1970 was one of the most prized local features of the city and region for working-class and middle-class Mancunians alike.

Over the city, somewhat hidden away in a densely populated area of back-to-back terraces later to be identified with Moss Side, the Maine Road stadium of Manchester City, originally established in 1923 as the biggest football stadium in England outside Wembley (holding 82,950 spectators for a league match against Arsenal in 1948), had also been recently refurbished at the scoreboard end, but otherwise seemed more content with the prevailing facilities. In some local folklore, in part because of its location in the inner city of Manchester, City continued to be identified as 'the people's team' in Manchester, whilst United, even as early as 1970, was associated – especially after its introduction of private boxes – with national and international, or alien and 'capitalist', influences.

The six other professional football clubs within the Greater Manchester area (Bolton Wanderers, Bury, Oldham Athletic, Rochdale, Stockport County and Wigan Athletic) seem to have attracted a specific, very local, 'loyal' support – affirming the character of Greater Manchester as in some sense a region of different towns, rather than one single, undifferentiated urban space. In some of these towns, indeed, the fact of 'difference' was symbolised by the presence and influence of a professional Rugby League Club, notably in Wigan and Salford, connecting them up especially in the local, male, working-class imagination to the network of towns across south Lancashire in which Rugby League was the sport of first choice. (Sheffield, by contrast, had historically never been a Rugby League town, until the opening of the Don Valley Stadium and the opportunistic foundation of the Sheffield Tigers club in 1991.)

The football grounds of Manchester (like those of Sheffield and other industrial cities) have always been 'a male space' – the key location for the male-dominated weekends that characterised working-class and middle-class households alike. On Sundays and other times in the week, however, other aspects of Manchester as a location and an urban space took on importance. Many Mancunians would 'take to the hills', to go walking in the Peak District, the hills of south Lancashire or the West Riding.[16] Family groups might make use of available public parks. Significant numbers of men, sometimes with their sons, would take up an early Sunday-morning pitch with fishing rod and other equipment on the side of one of Manchester's many canals, particularly the Bridgewater. Many others, in some cases deterred by difficulties of public transportation, would simply stay in the city, perhaps putting some time into the garden or an allotment, whilst the Sunday lunch was prepared by 'the wife'.

Annual holidays would still be taken, by most working-class households in Greater Manchester, as in the rest of the North of England, during 'stop weeks' – the two weeks in early August when factories and mills would close for general repair and refurbishment. Mancunian working-class households would look to the North-west coast resorts, directly accessible by rail, as the first possibility (in Sheffield, the destinations were Skegness – 'Skeggy' in local parlance, or 'Sheffield-by-the-sea', according to other local observers – Bridlington – 'Brid' – or, for the more aspiring household, Scarborough). Tony Bennett and Patrick Joyce's accounts of Blackpool in the first half of this century insist on its domination by the people of Bolton (Bennett 1986; Joyce 1991), but there is no question that Blackpool was preferred by Mancunians too. Even today, one of the more telling, though unpublicised, rituals of the summer in Manchester is the charity day-trip to Blackpool for deprived local children organised by the Manchester Taxi Drivers, Association: traffic on the A6 has to contend with a vast convoy of about 80 taxi drivers in fancy dress driving some 200 excited local children in the direction of the coast.[17]

Sheffield: 'the most proletarian city in England?'

We have already alluded to the absence of Victorian scale and grandeur (for example, in respect of architecture) in Sheffield in Chapter 1, as well as to its self-definition as 'the largest village in England' – an attribute we argued was produced through local topography (surrounded by the hills, cut off from other places) and industrial organisation (the dual economy of cutlery and steel). On the basis of Census data, Sidney Pollard described Sheffield in 1851 as 'the most proletarian city in England', with 187.6 people per 100,000 employed in local manufacturing industry (by comparison with only 146.1 in Leeds) (Pollard 1993: 260). Only 41 people per 100,000 were employed in professional occupations, as against 65.8 in Birmingham, and 43.1 in Leeds (ibid.). Pollard also singled out, as we did in Chapter 2, the particular form of organisation of the cutlery trade in Sheffield as the key to the lack of massive polarisation in the city. So far from the city being dominated by the large armies of capital and labour in the first half of the nineteenth century there was, instead, a complex 'network of contract and sub-contract' between the cutlery workshops, run by the 'Little Mesters' (the skilled cutlery craftsmen), and the merchant houses who brought the orders into Sheffield. As a consequence:

> The difference between 'worker' and 'employer' was small . . . both socially and economically, and while there were few large fortunes in the city, there were also few who were grossly underpaid.
>
> (Pollard 1993: 260)

The rise of the steel industry in the latter half of the nineteenth century changed the actual composition of the local labour market and, indeed, created a massive workforce of steelworks labour, but there can be no mistaking the continuing strong sense of an organic city that was not so fundamentally fractured by forms of class inequality present in other cities, as well as a powerful sense of the city as the home to an organised craft specific to Sheffield as a locality engendered, initially, in the cutlery trade.[18] Even as late as 1981, there was far less social polarisation in Sheffield, as measured in terms of the Registrar-General and Census definitions, than in many other cities. Fully 62.1 per cent of Sheffield's population was employed in skilled or unskilled manual labour and only 4.6 per cent were classified as 'professionals'.[19] The 'local structure of feeling' of industrial Sheffield was still firmly, or materially, grounded.

Sheffield may not have added a significant number of 'professionals' to its population in the period between 1945 and 1981, but the city and region was transformed in many other respects. The negative reputation of the city as a dirty industrial environment was high on the agenda of the post-war Labour Council. Subsequent to the passage of the Clean Air Act in 1956, the Council imposed a series of local smoke-control orders throughout the industrial areas and, in little over a decade, analysis of the quality of the local air allowed the Council to make the claim that Sheffield was now 'the cleanest industrial city in Europe'.

Perhaps the most important moment in the transformation of the city in the years after the War was the appointment of J. Lewis Womersley as City Architect in 1953. Under Womersley's lead, the Corporation Housing Department became a pioneer in the design and layout of public housing development. The Corporation was responsible for the high-rise deck-access development on Park Hill, overlooking the Midland Station, which, though much disparaged in the 1980s, attracted considerable acclaim in the early 1960s as 'the streets in the sky', from architects in Britain and continental Europe. Womersley also pioneered the development of medium-density neighbourhood estates on greenfield sites in suburban areas (Gleadless Valley, Arbourthorne and Norton), which have now attracted the attention they deserve, and are now desirable properties in their own right. Throughout the 1960s, the Corporation succeeded in completing some 2000 new homes a year, and by 1973 there were some 75,000 council houses in the city – some 20,000 more than the Town Clerk in 1950, in what he thought was a wildly utopian moment, had estimated were necessary to solve Sheffield's problems of slum clearance (Hampton 1993: 128–31).

Sheffield's reputation as a clean industrial city, with an admirable stock of public housing, was to receive a further boost in the 1970s from the decision of the South Yorkshire County Council, led by councillors from Sheffield, to subsidise the operation of local buses on the grounds of social need.[20] With the continuing expansion of other social services and hospitals in the city, many local residents were confirmed in their belief that they had the good fortune to live in a well-managed city, with a real commitment to the population. The City Council continued to return an ever-increasing Labour majority. The only clouds on the horizon were the continuing complaints of local businesses about the levels of tax they were required to pay in Sheffield (which some members of the Chamber of Commerce claimed was, in effect, a business subsidy for socialist policies) and a creeping awareness of a lack of flexibility and competitiveness in the local economy. In the city and region as a whole in the period between 1968 and 1973, however, there was a widespread sense, from the affluent West End to Womersley's garden estates, that Sheffield was a 'good city'.

The degree to which this sense of satisfaction (quite pronounced in local politics and press coverage at the time) worked into everyday life in the city is a pertinent issue for sociological analysis, though no such work seems to have been undertaken in Sheffield at the time.[21] For many working-class and middle-class men in Sheffield, one of the routine weekly considerations would have been the city's two football teams: there was a considerable amount of pride in Sheffield at Hillsborough's selection as one of the sites for the World Cup games in 1966 as well as in Sheffield Wednesday's appearance in the Cup Final the very same year.[22] Regular walks through neighbourhood parks and rambling in the Derbyshire Hills would also have played a large part in the life of many working-class and middle-class men, especially in family groups. There was also a pronounced local interest amongst Sheffield men in golf, cutting across the social classes – two local municipally owned courses being heavily patronised.[23] Amongst Sheffield people, in this period (as in the earlier post-war period), there was widespread affection for Coles – the department store now relocated from its original position on Fargate to Barkers' Pool – and, to a lesser extent, for Walsh's and Debenhams, although undoubtedly the heaviest use of these stores would be made by women from the wealthier suburbs. Women living in other parts of the city would be heavy users of the markets, Woolworths on the Haymarket, and other shops 'below the Hole in the Road'. Women of all classes would do a good deal of shopping on the two main thoroughfares of Fargate and the Moor. (We discuss the routinised use of both our two cities for shopping in the early 1990s in Chapter 5.)

'Family outings' in Sheffield in this period remained quite a common form of recreation. In the late 1960s, however, visits to local museums (Weston Park, first opened in 1887), to an art gallery (the Graves, opened in 1934), to the parks or to a concert (usually in the City Hall, opened in 1932) seem to have played an important part in family life in the city. Young people by themselves might visit the parks in the day for games of football or to meet friends, make use of one of many municipal swimming pools, or go to the small number of city-centre cinemas. In the evening, teenage Sheffielders would gravitate to Josephine's or to another of the night clubs opening up for young people, around the concrete walkways by the bus station, an old-established bus terminus redeveloped in concrete in the early 1960s.[24] What is of interest to us, here, is the relative lack of polarisation of leisure interest amongst Sheffield's middle-class and working-class populations: there seems to have been a continuing overlap in the recreation practices of

Sheffielders, with some sharing of urban space, the green belt areas and civic social provision to an extent not apparent in Greater Manchester.

We have introduced this lengthy discussion of the 'lost world' of recreational and social life in Manchester and Sheffield to a purpose. This close examination of patterns of use of the city in an earlier post-war period is not only a useful background to our later analysis of the memories of the city given us by the elderly. It also is quite clear to us that some of the places we have discussed (the public parks, the canals, the football stadia, particular shops or urban spaces) *continue* to have a powerful symbolic significance amongst a large proportion of the local population, many of whom go on organising their lives and use of the city in an imitation of earlier patterns of use. The Bridgewater Canal in Manchester during the summer months is colonised every Sunday by hundreds of Mancunian men and boys involved in angling competitions, a very traditional and gendered practice. The 'big shops' in Manchester and Sheffield are still, despite new competition, the focal point of suburban trips into town. Families do make for the Peak District or the Pendle Hills on the weekend. There are many other examples. What we were concerned to do in this chapter was to outline the parameters of these traditional practices in Manchester and Sheffield, in order to illuminate, in particular, their relationship to the local industrial structure and the forms of 'family life' associated with it (and thereby the local gender order and also the general pattern of organisation of adult and child relationships). By undertaking this kind of historical retrospect on local forms of social life in industrial Manchester and Sheffield in the 'Fordist period', we will be in a better position to make sense of the radical changes in everyday life and practices (for example, of the young) in these cities in their post-Fordist reincarnation, characterised, in particular, by the loss of a guaranteed job in heavy industry and a series of connected changes in 'family life', orientation to the workplace and, indeed, the city itself ('what it offers'). The detailed excavation of these changed definitions, and of the rearticulation of 'local structures of feeling', will be one of our primary objectives in Part III of this book.

Part II

GETTING TO WORK AND GETTING ABOUT: A REALIST SOCIOLOGY OF EVERYDAY LIFE IN THE NORTH

INTRODUCTION

At this point in the book, we want to change mood and focus. We have spent three chapters providing a history of our two industrial cities in the North of England and offering an account of their common and different experience of 'the end of Fordism' and the demise of mass manufacturing – beginning in the early 1970s and accelerating through the 1990s. Our concern has been to provide what we see to be an essential context for and background to the analysis of 'data' we want to present in Part II and Part III. These data consist largely of observations made by citizens of Manchester and Sheffield in the early 1990s about what was happening to their cities. Some of these voices were heard, and indeed, recorded, in four 'focus group' discussions which formed part of an exploratory study conducted by Ian Taylor and Christine Peacock in Manchester in 1990;[1] and, in 1992–3, when the authors of this study conducted 28 further one-and-a-half-hour discussions with a total of 178 people we had contacted in the two cities, primarily through a survey conducted on the streets of Manchester and Sheffield.[2] A list of these (28) groups can be found in the notes to this section.[3] We also made contact with groups of people who appeared to be under-represented in public spaces, through direct contact with relevant agencies. In addition, we talked to 89 schoolchildren, aged 13 to 15, in a series of 10 discussions held in three Greater Manchester and two Sheffield schools.

The street survey which was the starting point of our detailed research in Manchester and Sheffield was administered in August 1992 to a sample of passers-by (aged 16 or over) at all hours of the day and early evening (until 8.30 p.m.) and on weekdays and weekends, with a total of

1825 completed responses. This gave us some basic information on these respondents (including present destination and purpose of journey, regular use of city facilities, age, sex, occupation, address and phone number), which we were then able to use to identify eight categories of 'users of city space' and six categories of 'non-users or avoiders' of public space in one or other of our two cities. We then invited individuals identified within these categories to discussion group sessions at which we could talk further and in more detail around the general theme of 'the changes happening' in Manchester (or Sheffield). These focus group discussions were held between March and September 1993.

Space does not permit a full discussion of either focus group methods in the social sciences or the particular organisation of our focus group sessions here.[4] However, we should indicate that the majority of the focus group discussions we conducted in 1993 (each lasting approximately an hour and a half), were held in a small room in a comfortable mid-market hotel in Castlefield, Manchester, and in the sitting room of a friendly house in the Hunters Bar area of Sheffield. Taxi transport was provided from home and back for all who agreed to attend. In five cases, particularly in respect of people identified as 'non-users' of our cities (or, more specifically, the central core of these two cities), the focus group sessions were held in rooms provided by neighbourhood centres or local organisations. One of the striking features of this method of research – at least in the cities of Manchester and Sheffield in 1993 – was the willingness, not to say enthusiasm, shown by the people we approached by letter and by phone to attend our sessions, even on the part of those who had initially been identified as 'avoiders' of public space in our cities.[5] Rather against our expectations, we had least difficulty in persuading women of all ages and the elderly of both sexes to attend.[6]

We do not believe that the small gift which was promised (a £10 Marks and Spencer gift voucher) was a major factor in this willingness to help, except, perhaps, in the case of some of the unemployed people who joined us. The names of all participants which appear in the text have been anonymised.

We obviously must make some comments about this choice of research method, and its utility in taking further our interest in the local social structure and local 'structure of feeling' of our two cities. Most important was the confirmation which these focus group discussions (which the group leader had to facilitate as a naturally occurring though very focused conversation) provided of the mundane, routinised and recursive character of everyday life in the city. The exploratory survey, conducted in 1990, revealed that the use of certain city-centre locales in Manchester (bus stations and bus stops, rail stations and shopping centres or streets) was a highly patterned phenomenon – an expression of what might be described as a taken-for-granted micro-sociology of the city. Use of some bus routes in the Greater Manchester area, for example, was dominated by students, and use of others by the elderly and/or the poor. There was a clear suggestion that this kind of routinised use of other 'non-transport locales' (especially the different types of shopping area in the city) was similarly socially patterned – in terms of age, income, social status and even ethnicity. There was a marked sense of city-centre urban space in particular being used very differently indeed by different 'publics' (one could almost speak of 'different cities' within the same, historically given material infrastructure). Some of these patterns of use seemed to have a long history (in Manchester, the patronage of Kendals department store) but others were a consequence of recent changes in the broader economic and social sphere. There was a real sense that these different patterns of use of the city were an important sociological indicator in themselves – a definitive marker of the effects, in terms of the scattering across the city of very different 'lived experiences', of the intense restructuring taking place in personal economic and social power and resources. The most obvious expression of this in Manchester, within a very small urban space, was the colonisation of Market Street by groups of 'visibly homeless' people or beggars (a matter of frequent comment in our focus group discussions), contrasted with the routine domination of St Ann's Square – a matter of 300 yards from Market Street – by young professionals en route between expensive fashion outlets and wine bars. One sociological issue was whether such an active reappropriation of urban space was occurring in other, geographically proximate, conurbations experiencing a similar crisis of de-industrialisation, joblessness and a very generalised loss of economic security and well-being, or whether this colonisation of locales by different publics was a phenomenon of larger metropolitan centres.

In having our attention drawn, initially in this small survey, to the routinised character of patterns of use, and indeed of behaviour, in certain given locales, we were reminded of a range of different socio-logical literatures. Within the literature of contemporary criminology, for example, attention is being given to Marcus Felson's analysis of the impact of crime on what he calls 'the routine activities of everyday life', though it must be said that Felson's essentially empirical approach eschews any analysis of structural inequalities and cultural assumptions associated with such inequality (Felson 1994). Erving Goffman's classic study of 'behaviour in public places' certainly recommended itself as a framework for analysing in some detail a variety of behaviours we routinely encountered during the course of our survey – for example, the rules governing 'avoidance behaviour' by women making use of public space (Goffman 1963). We were also already sensitised, by Tony Giddens's prolific recent writings, to the importance of the daily round of human behaviour as a key theme in the matrix of time and space framing all human action (Giddens 1984). Partly through this interest, we were also drawn to the essentially phenomenological and philosophical enquiry of Michel de Certeau into 'the practice of every-day life' (de Certeau 1984). These conceptual schemas informed the research we conducted – for example, in the construction of the ques-tions used in our focus group discussions or in the interpretation of the discussions that developed. But we did find, in practice, that the answers which were given to us to our survey questions, and the discussions which developed in groups – for all that they could be analysed in terms of an abstract sociology of action or a pure phenomenology (interested in the meaning of places or practices and the recursive, strategic and rhythmic dimension of everyday life) – were also underpinned, to an enormous degree, by a sense of the turbulence of the present historical moment as it presented itself in their city (the crisis of paid employment and mass manufacturing, rapid urban change, 'the threat to our city', etc.) as well as by a powerful sense of local identity (accompanied, even on the part of the young, by a quite startling sense of the city's definitive local history and character: its 'structure of feeling'). It is also very much the case that the range of everyday routine practices discussed by de Certeau – in terms of a benign phenomenology focusing on the problem of repetition of everyday experience, for example, of rail or bus travel – does not really catch the uncertain and risk-governed essence of everyday experi- ence of using British Rail trains or the re-deregulated bus services of Manchester and Sheffield in free market Britain in the 1990s. It does not address the specific character of the daily experience of travel in Man- chester and Sheffield and, we suspect, in most other North of England cities in the late twentieth century – the daily struggle of embodied social actors who are in employment to 'get to work', or the general struggle reported by nearly all local people, and not only the poor, in 'getting about' the city. We discuss this issue in Chapter 4.

So the voices which are heard in the following chapters are the voices of historically situated and embodied individuals who are both the authors and readers of a significant corpus of local knowledge about the locality and the larger city they inhabit. We should stress that much of this local knowledge had a certain moral, mythical and sometimes fanciful quality. In Sheffield, for example, one widespread refrain was that the route of the South Yorkshire Supertram (to outlying Mosbor- ough) was to be explained by the fact of the Leader of the Council living there. In Manchester, some of the discussion of the private bus compa- nies suggested that these companies had, in effect, been bought up by well-known local crooks. We have not set out, here, to 'test' this 'local knowledge' or folk belief against 'the facts', so much as to listen carefully to the local play of stories and speculation, rumour and gossip, and perhaps contribute in this way to the understanding of urban folklore in the North of England, as well as interrogating these modalities of local knowledge as an expression of the 'local structure of feeling'.

4

GOING TO WORK
The daily struggle

Much of the so-called 'post-modern' writing on the city at the end of the twentieth century is preoccupied with images of the casual affluent shopper – a modern-day *flâneur* cruising the fashionable shops of a gentrified downtown street or the latest up-market suburban shopping mall. Images of this kind are also the stock in trade of much contemporary television and billboard advertising: the city is constantly reconstructed as a site of playful activity as well as a place of comfort and aesthetic pleasure, whether by reference to bright city lights or, as in so many recent examples in Britain, to European-style arcades and squares in the evening light.

This 'discursive' construction of the city in the imagination as site of pleasure and play does speak to real changes that are occurring, and have certainly had real influence, in most cities in the industrial world – including the old industrial cities of the North of England – although, we would want to argue, with very uneven effect and, in some ways, in different ways in different cities. We will discuss in Chapter 7 the reclamation of certain downtown, canal-side locales in Manchester as the 'Gay Village' and in Chapter 12 the return of young professionals into city-centre apartment living there. In Sheffield, the closest parallel is the creation of the Cultural Industries Quarter and, more recently, the reclamation of the Canal Basin. Other cities across the North of England can point to similar projects of city-centre regeneration. The transformations that have occurred in shopping in recent years are fundamental, though the local expression of these changes is very uneven. So metropolitan Manchester in the mid-1990s, for example, still had no major shopping mall the size of Sheffield's Meadowhall.

This attempted reconstruction of the city centre as a site of pleasure and a place of casual or even whimsical resort (as against the place for boring, routinised, everyday 'recursivity'), through the rebuilding of physical infrastructure and the imaginative renaming of places and functions, does involve a suppression of certain other key features of cities, which are less accessible in terms of the post-modernist theories of pleasure and actually very rarely examined by cultural sociologists. What is ignored here is the inescapable daily necessity, for the bulk of the employed population, as well as for those children and young people in formal education, to travel across urban space by one means or another – to 'get about' the town. A kind of division of labour, however, has arisen, whereby these matters are left to urban and transport planners, whilst cultural sociologists debate an ideal typical urban figure, browsing the consumer palaces, rather than the city-based worker, caught in a disciplined daily regime of paid employment and therefore, necessarily, the 'journey to work'. Writing in theoretical terms about the organisation of time and space in general, Tony Giddens observes how:

> The origins of the precise temporal regulation of the day may perhaps be found in the chime of the monastery bell, but it is in the sphere of labour that its influence became embedded in such a way as to spread throughout society as a whole.
>
> (Giddens 1984: 144)

and he comments later in the same text, that:

> The journey to work (or school) probably indicates as much about the institutional character of modern societies as do carceral organizations.
>
> (*ibid.*: 154)

Giddens is clear, as are we, that cities remain, for the majority of their users, places of work or schooling, encountered repetitively through the working week: people's encounter with those cities – certainly within the North of England – is essentially either a mundane, routinised activity, most often referred to in terms of metaphors like 'the daily grind', or, alternatively, it is actually 'a struggle', taking on a slightly different form each day – most of all, with the problem of everyday transportation, or 'getting to work'. We would want only to add that this problem of transportation is particularly severe for the many thousands of city dwellers who work at night – for example, hospital nurses, security staff or cleaners, and staff in a variety of other public service occupations (social workers, residential home staff, etc.). We concentrate here on the 'daily' journey to work in the morning and evening.

In some metropolitan urban centres in what we used to call 'advanced industrial' societies, the daily journey to work in the late 1990s has taken on an almost heroic dimension. In the United States, a powerful popular mythology has been constructed around the daily two-hour gridlocks on the highways of Greater Los Angeles or the ever-extending rush-hours on the fearful New York subway. In London, nightmarish stories circulate about breakdowns and delays (as well as bomb scares) on the London Underground system in general, and the Northern Line in particular: the London Underground's own discussion document of 1992, 'Making Visions into Reality', indicates that the creation of a modern underground system in London, on a par with similar systems elsewhere in capital cities, really requires an investment of £900 million a year for the next ten years (Aitchison 1994). A major Department of Transport study, co-authored with the London Research Centre in 1994, revealed that the numbers of cars entering central London increased by 24 per cent between 1981 and 1991. Although the population of London had fallen from 6.6 to 6.3 million over the period, Londoners made 8 per cent more journeys than they had ten years before, with the largest increase (18 per cent) being by car (Cusick 1994). The discussion point in many newspapers, and also in popular conversation, was that traffic in London was now slower than it was in the horse-drawn carriages of the Victorian period, at an average speed of about 10 miles per hour.

Similar general tendencies are observable for our two North of England cities. In the South Yorkshire area as a whole, which in the 1970s had a significantly lower level of car ownership than the national average, the number of families with one car remained stable (at 41 per cent of all households) between 1981 and 1991, but the number of households with two cars increased to some 22 per cent (compared to just 15 per cent in 1981) (University of Oxford Transport Studies Unit 1992). The 'modal trip rate' by car increased in South Yorkshire from 0.4 trips per person per day in 1981 to 0.5 per person per day 10 years later, whilst use of buses declined from 0.55 trips per person per day in 1981 to 0.35 in 1991 (*ibid.*: 5). In Greater Manchester, the decline in the use of buses over the latter part of this same period looks to have been almost equally marked: where some 346 million passenger journeys were recorded on Manchester buses in 1984, there were only 256 million such journeys in 1993 (Farrow 1993: Figure 1). Car use in the Greater Manchester area was, and is, much more extensive and intensive than in Sheffield, or in other Northern cities, not only because of the size of the conurbation, but also, as we discussed in Chapter 2, because of the way in which the area is linked by a set of motorways, the M56, M61 and M62, built in the 1960s and 1970s (White 1980a). Car ownership in Greater Manchester was up 32 per cent in 1993 on 1984 (Farrow 1993: Figure 1).

As early as 1985, however, in the larger conurbation of Greater Manchester, there was already widespread concern over traffic congestion on arterial roads and motorways and particularly in the city-centre core. Anticipating developments in Sheffield some five years later, there was particular anxiety with respect to the effects on the health of the local population from atmospheric pollution from car exhaust fumes and also, especially, from emissions of lead. Research by the Passenger Transport Executive revealed that some 53,000 vehicles were coming into Manchester city centre every day. Some 40,000 individuals, in the meantime, travelled into work every day by bus (a large reduction of usership compared to ten years before) and a further 16,700 by train.[1] A University of Oxford study undertaken for South Yorkshire PTE indicated that whilst use of buses by the elderly had remained very constant over the 1980s, there was now some evidence that younger people were turning, between the ages of 16 and 19, to other modes of travel, and especially to the car. In a promotional video produced by the South Yorkshire Passenger Transport Authority to encourage greater use of public transport in 1990, *Together We Can Go Places*, the prediction was that, for all the absence of any developed road network in the county, car ownership was still likely to increase by 20 per cent over the next five years.

In Greater Manchester, navigation of the larger conurbation by car is far more prevalent than in the smaller, more compact cities in the North of England. According to 'The Greater Manchester Travel Survey' commissioned by the Passenger Transport Executive in 1990, some 61 per cent of all travel journeys to and from work were by car, with a further 10 per cent accounted for by the passengers in the car (Farrow 1990). We are particularly curious about the importance for Greater Manchester as a whole, as for all larger metropolitan conurbations, of the kind of private mental map of the region that is constructed for car users by the presence of particular 'place names' on motorway signs. There are at least two issues here. The first is whether a town is a significant enough 'node' in a larger, metropolitan network of major roads to get a mention on an overhead sign: the relationship between the significance of place, so defined, and the size or significance of place defined in other terms (the quality of the architecture, the level of public provision), is clearly not direct.[2] But perhaps even prior to this is the issue of whether the evolution of a city's motorway and major road network in the last thirty years has generated anything like a cosmopolitan consciousness in respect of the design and content of road signs and other directional markers – i.e. an awareness of how the city's layout, street names and place names, and location *vis-à-vis* other urban areas might appear confusing to newcomers. One of the most striking features of Greater Manchester to newcomers coming into the area by car is the frequency with which they get lost, and the dearth of clear road signs or directional indications for strangers. The assumption in the North of England appears still to be that most of those driving into and around the city will be local (though this assumption does not inform the renovated city centre in Manchester – where the pavements are dotted with Victorian-style directional signs, erected by the Urban Development Corporation – or the immediate vicinity of the airport). In Sheffield, ironically enough, as a result of the World Student Games in 1991, there are new road signs throughout the city, pointing to the various sports stadia, local museums, and other tourist sites.

There is more that can be said on these themes, not least, of course, around the observation that the 'gaze' at the city from a motor car tends to have a particular and gendered character. In Greater Manchester, as in most other North of England cities,[3] the overwhelming majority of car drivers, especially in the morning and evening rush-hours, are men (albeit, quite frequently, with women passengers): some 79 per cent of all car-using commuters amongst those we contacted in our street survey. So also is there a pronounced social class bias in the use of cars through the Greater Manchester conurbation: in 1990, 25 per cent of all motorists driving in Manchester were from Registrar-General Social Class AB, and another 57 per cent from Social Classes C1 and C2 (Farrow 1990:

20). So too we can see that the decision to travel by private car is also, usually, a decision taken to travel privately, i.e. without the company of other citizens (the public). It is in this sense a decision taken against the idea of being with other members of the public – in this instance, on buses, trains or 'the trams' – participating in the messy democracy of everyday public life.[4] We do think that a sociology of these two cities as seen and understood by car drivers from the road (a markedly male, professional middle-class and skilled working-class constituency) would be an important addition to our understanding of how these cities and their various localities are understood, especially in an age in which such large proportions of car users infrequently leave their cars.[5] In the late twentieth century, we need a sociology of the city seen from the private car as well as a sociology of the publicly encountered street.

We discussed the growth of railways in Manchester and Sheffield in Chapter 2 of this book. The problem of the grand Victorian stations of central Manchester originally being built, in the 1860s, at some distance from each other, unconnected up by other local systems, was never resolved during the following century. The strategy of urban planners in the 1960s and 1970s (of building a connecting underground system between Piccadilly and Victoria) was never realised, until the two stations were connected via the Metrolink light transit system,[6] which we discuss below. In the meantime, commuters and other travellers had for many years to endure the neglect and decline of what had once been a celebrated station – Manchester Victoria – much prized for its mural map of the North of England, its cavernous marble entrance hall, the longest passenger platform in England, and the stained glass canopies fronting onto the taxi ranks, indicating destinations to Burnley, Halifax, Leeds and Belgium [sic]. In the years preceding its recent renovation as a Metrolink stop and home to the new Indoor Sports arena, however:

> It [was] a true nightmare to arrive at, if you [were] carrying a case. It [was] a nightmare trundling a case and going through the tunnels . . . It [was] dreary. It need[ed] money spending on [it] or closing down, one or the other. It [was] not a welcoming station at all.
> (Mrs Whitehouse, 67-year-old pensioner, Cheadle)

In the case of Manchester Victoria, these aspirations have recently been fulfilled. Manchester Piccadilly has also been upgraded, in part as a result of its integration into the Metrolink system, but it remains, by local observation, one of the most lopsided stations in Britain, with the bulk of its local services and all through trains departing from platforms 13 and 14, some five minutes' walk from the main concourse and ticket offices.

In 1985, 16,700 people were making use of the local services provided by British Rail Regional Railways into Piccadilly and Victoria every morning, operating on a subsidy from the 10 local borough authorities of Greater Manchester. Many of the local lines were notorious for Regional Railways' deployment of ageing rolling stock and the unreliability of their timetables. In the pilot research undertaken in Manchester in 1991, indeed, one of the most telling discoveries was the sophisticated level of constantly updated local knowledge that was shared, for example, by city-centre office workers about the reliability of train services on particular lines within Greater Manchester and the quality of the rolling stock being deployed on these lines.

The use of trains for the routine journey to work in the Sheffield area in the early 1990s was negligible, involving a small number of commuters from Rotherham, Barnsley and the Dearne Valley coming into Midland Station from the East: for most people working in Sheffield, the three options were to take the bus, drive or, in a significant number of cases, walk. In 1991, more people in Sheffield walked or cycled to work than took the bus (University of Oxford Transport Studies Unit 1992: 5). In Manchester, in 1990, by comparison, only 2 per cent of travel journeys to work in Manchester were by bike (Farrow 1990).

GETTING ABOUT

In this section, we want to frame our account of daily life and transport in our two Northern cities around the voices of the Mancunians and Sheffielders attending our focus group discussions, and responding to our enquiries about the means they use to get about the town and their experience of their use of transport. Our group discussions were conducted in April and May 1993 – in Manchester, therefore, some eleven months after the opening of the Metrolink light urban transit system in April 1992, and in Sheffield, some ten months before the opening of the Supertram, on 21 March 1994: both new systems remained for many of our discussants a matter of hearsay rather than direct experience.

We want to organise this discussion, first, in terms of some features of daily transport in Manchester and Sheffield common to both cities; and, secondly, in terms of some differences. We take it that an understanding of the difference in the types of transport available and patterns of actual transport use is an important index of 'real differences' between cities and city regions in the North of England – a key defining aspect of the experience of those cities for significant sections of the population. Our concerns are similar to those of Michael Cahill's in his interesting book *The New Social Policy*: we want to ground our discussion, as he wants to ground his, in the actual daily practices of citizens as they live now (Cahill 1994). For Cahill, the daily struggle of citizens with transport is a major issue for public policy: we agree, but our specifically sociological concern is to understand how different groups of citizens living and working in different localities interpret and adapt to the changing patterns of transport provision in their cities. First, let us deal with the common aspects of the daily struggle with transport in our two cities: 'the new trams', the buses and the trains.

Bringing back the trams

The cities of Manchester and Sheffield have in common in the early 1990s the introduction of the first light rail transit systems in Britain to operate, in part, 'on-street'. The Metrolink uses British Rail track and extends 31 kilometres from Altrincham in the south to Bury in the north. It is said to have cost £130 million and uses rolling stock built in Italy: the construction was completed by a consortium created for this project, the GMA Group, consisting of GEC Transportation Projects Ltd, John Mowlem and Company PLC and AMEC plc (Ogden and Senior 1991: 11). A major engineering achievement was the linking of the British Rail line to the street via a specially designed viaduct off Lower Mosley Street, next to the G-Mex Centre.

The £240-million Sheffield Supertram, contracted by Balfour Beatty, the local subsidiary of Power Corporation, employing rolling stock built in Dusseldorf, connects outlying suburbs in Mosborough with the city centre and proceeds onto Meadowhall shopping centre in the East End of the city, past the new sports facilities in the Lower Don Valley.[7] Amongst public transport professionals, Manchester and Sheffield are now taken as exemplars of the future shape of urban transport – the envy of many other cities. There are currently large numbers of cities making bids, through the Department of Transport, to build similar systems.

The timing of the fieldwork did not enable us to conduct any systematic investigation of our local publics' experience of the new transit systems.[8] But there was a clear sense, none the less, of the parameters of local responses. For many people – especially the elderly – the Metrolink and Supertram were equated, straightforwardly, with the 'return of the trams', and their appearance was evidence that 'they' (usually meaning 'the Council') had at last seen the error of their ways after 'they' closed down the trams in the first place. This populist sentiment was particularly frequently voiced in Sheffield (at a time when the Council was already a target for resentful popular criticism on other grounds) and where nostalgia for the trams, closed down in 1960, was widespread.[9]

In both cities, there was also a keen awareness that the routes taken by the new 'trams' would restrict their utility to people who were living near the stations:[10] this was connected, in Sheffield, to some vitriolic criticism of the route chosen for the first phase of the Supertram, particularly by people living in the more affluent West End of the city, which is not yet touched by the Supertram. Another key element in this popular assessment of the new trams was the issue of cost: for many local people in Manchester, in particular, the cost of a Metrolink ticket was clearly a significant calculation in terms of daily management of money. We shall return to some of these issues later.

Local bus knowledge

For the majority of people, particularly women and the elderly, in these two Northern cities (and, we suspect, in other cities across the North of England) travel around the city was by bus. In 1991, 26 per cent of all users of Greater Manchester buses were past retirement age, many of them taking advantage of concessionary fares. Of all users, 53 per cent, as measured on this particular Passenger Transport Executive survey, were women.[11] The Greater Manchester Travel Survey of 1990, using a different measure, suggested that fully 65 per cent of all bus journeys in the area were made by women, and also indicated that 28 per cent of all women travelled exclusively by bus, and only 17 per cent of men (Farrow 1990: paras 2.21, 3.12). One of the most important features of this historic reliance on buses by women, the elderly and other users in the North of England has, indeed, been that of encouraging some mobility around the city, enabling members of extended families and friendship groups to keep in touch. There is evidence, for example, that publicly provided buses have been essential for people rehoused onto city-edge estates to maintain contact with friends and also 'to get to town' – now some considerable distance from home. Amongst nearly all users of the buses in our two cities, we encountered a quite remarkably detailed knowledge of the way in which the city's bus routes used to be laid out 'when they only had the Corporation buses'. This 'local bus knowledge' related not only to the routes which were taken by particular buses ('the number 88') but also to the frequency of service on that route.[12] Mr Thompson, a 47-year-old college lecturer living in Poynton, south Manchester, put it this way:

> Well, one of the things of value about bus service – whether you like being on buses or not – has always been a predictability. Routes didn't use to change very much. The generations who used buses from Poynton – used to leave twice an hour at a given time for Stockport.

The knowledge of the city developed by frequent bus use seems to have endowed Mancunians and Sheffielders not only with a useful, practical stock of knowledge about Corporation bus services themselves, but also with a more abstract, aesthetic assessment of the city as a set of places seen from the bus and now connected up in the memory. One of the remarkable features of our discussion sessions was the range of strong views evinced by particular buildings or places (usually negative: the Electricity Board station on Charter Row, Sheffield, or 'No. 1 City Road' on Medlock Street, Manchester) coupled with a near universal inability to identify the names of the streets on which they were situated: bus users, however, would know 'where to get off' to get there.

One of the most fundamental sources of ill-feeling and distress amongst heavy users of buses in these two cities was the fundamental disruption of this form of practical, bus knowledge of the city which deregulation produced. This deregulation, resulting from the Transport Act of 1985, was fuelled by the Thatcher government's attack on 'public monopolies' and by the accompanying belief that such services would necessarily be improved by the release of competitive market forces even into local bus service provision.[13] From the perspective of nearly all users of buses in Manchester and Sheffield, however, the consequences have been disastrous. Most obvious to all observers, including citizens who do not use buses, has been the massive increase in the number of buses, in varying degrees of repair,[14] in use on the city streets, and accompanying increases in congestion. In November 1994, there were some 70 bus operators in Manchester and fully 66 in the much smaller city centre of Sheffield (South Yorkshire Transport 1994). The marketisation of municipal bus provision has produced a massive problem in Sheffield, particularly on High Street – the only thoroughfare in the city centre where buses can stop to discharge and pick up passengers – and the resulting congestion there has been the subject of discussion even in the national press. Much better known to the bus users of these two cities are the problems experienced in terms of a loss of local knowledge and the human costs of the local competition between bus companies.

Mrs Whitehouse, the pensioner from near Cheadle, south Manchester, quoted above, thought it was 'a shambles':

> When I go into Cheadle from where I am, there are one, two, three, four buses in 20 minutes. No – sorry – going into Cheadle there are two buses in ten minutes and then there is another in 20 minutes. Then there is another two buses. But coming home from Cheadle there are four buses in 25 minutes and then nothing for 35 minutes. Then you start again with your four buses.

Part of the problem was that the large number of small bus companies have adopted different liveries and route numbers. Mrs Joan Fowler, a 77-year-old pensioner from Middleton, north Manchester, remembered how:

> When the buses were all the same colour, you knew them as a Corporation bus. But now you cannot tell what they are.

The strategic problem is to try and glimpse exactly what and whose bus is approaching,[15] but, says Mrs Fowler:

> Meanwhile they have gone past you.

And, she observes:

> It's no good asking the opposition. They won't tell you.

Mr Thompson, the college lecturer referenced earlier, commented:

> Because of privatisation, knowing where a bus is going or when it's coming is an art almost involving genius. You've got to look in the

Evening News and read the small column that gives you the bus changes every week. There always seems to be about twenty.

All respondents understood this new unpredictability as an effect of privatisation. Mrs Whitehouse again:

Because they are run by different companies, and they are trying to cut each other's throats, one comes four minutes before the other. Then you get the next company coming along ten minutes later and one a few minutes after that . . . so that's your four buses. Then you have a big gap and they all start this game over again.

There was also some awareness in both cities that the free market in local buses provided no guarantee that a particular private firm would necessarily continue to operate from one week to the next. Common to both cities, indeed, was a widespread sense that 'the pattern has been lost' and that there is no way of knowing when the buses will come or which routes they would follow.

Local responses to the deregulation of buses have involved various adaptations. For some, the response has been one of resignation, involving cessation of the use of buses altogether (with terrible consequences for personal mobility and the possibility of maintaining friendships and use of the city). Even amongst those who can afford the alternative of purchasing a car, there are real costs in terms of local knowledge. Typically, Kirstin Lloyd, a clerical worker in Sheffield, told us:

I wouldn't know where to catch a bus to get home right now, because I use a car. Before, when I lived at home, I always knew the bus times by heart.

There are much more complicated strategies in both cities, involving twin or multiple use of buses (during peak hours), trains, the Metrolink or Supertram, and even taxis. There is absolutely no sense, in these practices, of a casual playful daily encounter: these strategies are difficult, practical accomplishments, engaged in 'heroically' by many on a daily basis. Many bus users in Manchester and Sheffield were clearly constantly engaged in a calculation as to the viability of their personal strategic 'transport-to-work' strategy. Many seemed to have submitted themselves conditionally to the situation of riskiness and dependency involved in travelling in a privatised bus market, but were in a state of readiness to try alternatives (trains, the Metrolink or Supertram, or even a car) if the bus experience became untenable. There was evidence, too, of a range of different combinations of transport (bus and train, tram and walk, etc.), nearly always 'for the time being'. Many individuals adopted different strategies on different days of the week. In many ways, we would argue, the constant deliberations over daily transport strategies are a good example of the kind of reflexivity of modern urban actors discussed by Giddens and Beck (Beck *et al.* 1994). But it must none the less be emphasised that for the majority of people in our focus groups, use of the buses was an absolute necessity, either for financial reasons (no other means of transport were affordable) or, especially for the elderly living away from the Metrolink or the Supertram, by reason of physical capacity ('they're too far to walk').

Whilst the daily bus commuter or other frequent bus user has to find practical adaptations to the 'shambles' of deregulation in these cities[16] or, alternatively, withdraw from this daily struggle, the one area that does attract angry response is the issue of safety. A group of clerical workers from Sheffield focused resentfully on the perils of crossing High Street. Heather Moody explained how:

> you've got to have three pairs of eyes getting across there.

The strategic issue here was not just the sheer number of buses, but also the aggressive competition between the drivers and the speed at which some of them drove. This point had first been raised in the course of our pilot research in 1991, when secretarial staff at the University of Salford commented on the speed of the buses entering the Arndale Centre bus station in central Manchester, and the problems this created, in particular, for mothers with children in prams and/or 'toddlers' in hand. In May 1994, indeed, a mother of two children was crushed to death between two buses precisely at this location: local traders were quoted in the evening newspaper reports as saying that this was 'a tragedy waiting to happen' (*Manchester Evening News* 12 May 1994).

Gender and public buses

One of the topics to provoke the most engaged and committed responses and discussion in our focus group enquiries about use of both these North of England cities was, indeed, the behaviour and demeanour of local bus drivers. In our session with eight clerical workers in Manchester (four women and four men), for example, we had asked people what made them feel anxious on the buses. Sally Glover replied:

> That's if it's just you and the driver if some lunatic decides to get on, sit next to you.

Penny Fraser:	By lunatic, you mean somebody you wouldn't feel happy with?
Sally Glover:	Yes.
Penny Fraser:	You don't feel that the driver would be any help to you in that situation?
Steve Fearnley:	Do you feel secure on the buses with the driver?
Sally Glover:	No.
Steve Fearnley:	I don't think the drivers are very responsible here. I've noticed the negative attitude from them. In Glasgow, the bus drivers are so much nicer. That's one of the things I noticed when I came here.

There were many other such references, and also a number of accounts or explanations offered for the attitudes and demeanours of Northern bus drivers, including, in Manchester, some sympathetic recognition of the job insecurities introduced by privatisation itself.[17] Some drivers working for the smaller companies in Greater Manchester, however, were seen as 'cowboys', uninterested in the idea of 'serving the public' and committed only to being paid to do some driving. Mention of these drivers working for the smaller companies provoked excited discussion:

Steve Fearnley:　　When you walk on, they think they are doing you a favour by giving you a ticket, and letting you pay for it. It's not an effort to press the buttons and issue a ticket.

Oscar Lee:　　Now that they have been sort of privatised . . . you'd think they'd want to stop to pick you up. They just won't, will they? They see you running for it, and that's it. It's a case of if you get there . . . but, if you're a few yards away, that's it.

Constantly threatening to surface in these discussions was some indirect, guarded discussion of the contradiction between the masculinity of these Northern men and the idea of service to other citizens. In discussions during our pilot research, the more elderly respondents harked back to the friendlier and more helpful atmosphere that had obtained when the buses were staffed either with a conductor as well as a driver or, even more so, with a conductress. Our discussions of women's fears in the cities confirmed the extra sense of security provided by twin staffing. Conductors were withdrawn from buses in Greater Manchester over the period 1967–86 (in Sheffield, over one year up to April 1986);[18] and, in terms of the gender composition of the bus services, women have still a lot of headway to make up. Only about 1 per cent of drivers in Greater Manchester in 1986 were women, and there are no records of the proportions of conductors who were women: in the Manchester and Salford depots, there were none, but in other boroughs across the conurbation, we were told (though it seems contradictory) 'there might be fifty per cent'.[19] This 'exclusion of women from the skilled and semi-skilled transport trades' and the consequences of this exclusion for 'sympathetic' understanding of the transport needs of children, the elderly and other women are discussed by writers on public transport such as Gavin Smith (1984: 15), but the resilience of the monopoly control exercised by men over this field of employment in Britain, especially in the North, is neither explained nor really comprehended.

The future of bus travel in Northern cities is primarily being fought over in terms of competing claims of privatisation versus some notion of buses operating as part of an integrated local transport system. In a later section, we will point to some differences in the form which this 'local transport struggle' assumes in our two cities, with some brief discussion of developments elsewhere. But we want to suggest that this struggle is only the official one – the authorised debate between local corporate organisations like the PTEs and the Development Associations – open for discussion in the local press or on local radio and television programmes. Our focus group discussions repeatedly uncovered the persistent, nagging contradiction between the fact that the customers of buses, in contemporary market terms, are overwhelmingly women (followed by children and the elderly) and the 'service providers' are overwhelmingly men. The belief that this produced lack of sympathy towards the users of the buses is compounded, in many accounts, by the sense that the men who are driving the buses, unrestrained by the presence of a friendly conductor or conductress, are having real difficulties with the new roles they are asked to perform in a rapidly changing, service-orientated economy. The problem of masculinity in the North, then, is in no sense confined to 'the underclass', but is intimately linked to the closed job markets operated by organised labour.

We are not suggesting that the domination of local bus service provision by men is an actively contested area in either Manchester or Sheffield, although it is noticeable that the Metrolink and Supertram, after doing some market research, have appointed significant numbers of women to driver jobs, and that the male domination of railway stations is now challenged by Intercity's employment of women 'welcoming agents'. In Manchester and neighbouring Salford, a group of women volunteers, Elles Belles, started an evening and night-time taxi service for women only. The Passenger Transport Executive had discussed a similar arrangement of women-only night-time buses in 1989 as a part of a programme directed at vandalism and assault, but had not acted upon it: throughout 1993, there were calls for this voluntary service to be adopted by the private bus operators and the PTE (*Manchester Evening News* 8 June 1993). What was not widely realised is that the provision of such a service would now have to be viable commercially to have any chance of operation.

In both our two North of England cities, indeed, a key feature of the constant talk about the buses is the widespread and continuing popular belief (completely out of kilter with the wholesale marketisation of actual bus provision and the delegation of public powers of local councils to development corporations, multi-agency partnerships, etc.), that there is somehow still a single, powerful public authority (the Council, 'the Corporation', or just 'they') that is making decisions, in the best local public interest, about a sensible future for public transport as a whole. The continuing hold of this inaccurate and outdated mix of populist sensibility and local state dependency in the North of England is certainly very marked in both Manchester and Sheffield, and may indeed hold for other cities of the North of England where there is a recent memory of an activist local Labour council.

Local rail journeys in the big city

We have already indicated that the use of trains to get to work in Sheffield is very limited. In Manchester it is also a minority form of travel, though any curious observer of the city map would be puzzled, since the conurbation is crisscrossed by a series of rail lines heading into Piccadilly and Victoria stations.

We were interested in enquiring into the reasons for this relative lack of use of rail services in Manchester, in part in order to grasp whether there is anything specific about the city which might explain this under-use or whether there is a general problem about regional railways provision, not specific to Manchester. There is a widespread recognition in Britain in the mid-1990s that rail travel has become one of the most palpably risky ventures in a society perceived as comprising a wide variety of new risks – in the specific sense that the British Rail timetable cannot be seriously relied upon as a guarantee of train arrival times. There is also a sense of distaste at the communal character of the train experience and (especially, for example, among women) fear of encounters with unpleasant Others, particularly groups of football fans on a Saturday. In an increasingly privatised market society, too, there is some sense, on the one hand, of the challenge of a forced conversation with others, but also a dislike of the silent isolation of a train journey, especially during delays.[20]

On local commuter trains, these concerns are compounded by passengers' daily personal reliance on ageing rolling stock and disenchanted rail staff in the daily struggle to get to work. For many professional workers, especially in Manchester, the co-presence in public transport of some of 'the disreputable poor' of the larger conurbation also seems to be a strategic problem – on some routes more than others. All commuters with whom we discussed these issues spoke of the 'trade-offs' involved in the choice of daily transport. The anxieties raised in discussions, in fact, remained fairly general – to do with the quality of rolling stock and the general unreliability of British Rail (which had not at that time been finally broken up into separate agencies). Mrs Trueman, a 60-year-old part-time cleaner from Newton Heath, Manchester, was quite firm:

> where you are going, you know what to expect. If you are going from Poynton to Manchester, on a train from Stoke, your legs are going to be roasted. The rolling stock . . . well, it's not dreadful, I've been in worse, but not much worse. Going, say, short distances like Bolton or Sheffield, if you get a Sprinter, they are fine. Although I would hate to have to travel to Ipswich on a Sprinter, because I don't think the seats are comfortable enough.

Mr Cockburn, a 63-year-old financial controller who had lived in Manchester for 10 years, was equally forceful and knowledgeable in his dislike of Regional Railways' Sprinters:

You *are* packed tightly in. There is not enough leg room. On some you have a little table which you can pull down, rather like aircraft seats. If you put a cup of tea on it, ten to one it will spill. It's not very well planned. You can't see out of the windows. They are correcting that on the new set of Sprinters . . . And they are not very reliable.

In the meantime, Mrs O'Shea, a 65-year-old voluntary worker from Poynton, thought:

on the Poynton–Macclesfield line, you are still on the old-style train, which I think are very solid in comparison to the Sprinters. The Sprinters are very clean but when you put your bottom on them and shuffle, you move the seats.

A topic of considerable sociological interest in the early 1990s was the way in which knowledge about the condition of railway rolling stock and the reliability of particular lines on the Greater Manchester network was locally circulated.[21] One quite widespread folk belief was that the Regional Railways were using the Greater Manchester rail system as a dumping ground for decrepit rolling stock from elsewhere in the country: this was usually accompanied by resentful claims that this was because 'all the money' was in the South of England or, sometimes, the Midlands. In the meantime, however, a set of informal systems had built up for coping with this situation of risk and unreliability.[22] John Dickens, a 21-year-old bank clerk from Altrincham, insisted that:

We have this bloke in our office who knows everything about the trains . . . He just tells you during the day. He knows what they are like. If you are working late, he comes in and says 'Do you know your train isn't going until twenty-five to seven?' . . . where he gets it from? He just amazes me. I plan through him mostly. If he leaves early, I do as well.

It is obviously important not to take these statements at face value. It is also important to see what seems not to be overtly discussed, at least in open focus group discussions. The issue of personal safety on trains did not occur spontaneously in any of our discussions, even in the wake of a series of accidents on trains across the country. Subsequent to our discussion sessions in Manchester, considerable publicity was given in the community newspaper press to persistent throwing of missiles at commuter trains in Manchester by children hiding on railway embankments: some half a dozen 'blackspots' were named as being an object of fear to drivers, and the object of intensive surveillance by British Transport Police (*Manchester Metropolitan News* 20 August 1993).[23] Very little of this information fed into our discussion groups, however, where the persistent concerns – consistent with most other recent studies of public transport – had to do with their frustration over the reliability of services and timetables and the quality of the rolling stock. Sometimes, and perhaps not specific to North of England cities, there was also the frustration felt by passengers in dealing with 'gruff' or unhelpful members of British Rail's staff.

DIFFERENT LOCALES, DIFFERENT PROVISIONS

The specific experience of public transport by long-time residents of a city does depend on the particular provision available in that city – not just the reliability of service and the quality of the interaction with the bus drivers, but also the character of the bus stations, the bus stops and other transport 'stopping places', to use Giddens's term, in a local transport system. The character of such provision in any one city is, inescapably, a matter of its detailed local history, of the relations between local authorities, passenger transport authorities and private interests. This is not to say that the only solution to problems of provision in any one city region (as in South Yorkshire in the 1970s) is for all local provision to be publicly owned: the example of a deregulated West Yorkshire transport system, Yorkshire Terrier, much admired by competitor authorities and by local residents in the late 1980s and early 1990s, provides a counterpoint to any such argument.

What is clear is that a lack of resolution in such local political discussions can have important consequences for actual provision. One of the most powerful areas of public complaint about the condition of Manchester in our discussion sessions was the state of the city's bus stations. Probably one of the most important 'landscapes of fear' in the whole city, indeed, is the Chorlton Street bus station, ostensibly the terminus for the National Express bus company.

Mrs O'Shea, a voluntary worker from Poynton, south Manchester, recalled with Mrs Elland, a full-time housewife also from Poynton, how she had been at that bus station 'three months ago':

	Really . . . it's like the black hole of Calcutta . . . it's terrible.
Ian Taylor:	In what respects?
Mrs O'Shea:	Dirty, dark, facilities are poor. What is there about it? *Nothing.*'
Mrs Elland:	It is dark . . . and it's very difficult to find the bus stops because they are always moving them around . . . I mean, there really aren't any facilities provided. Just a rundown old café. And the toilets are dreadful. I've never seen anything like it in my life . . . it is disgraceful. And for information about buses you just have to wander around until you find someone who knows.

In a discussion group of young people, Sue Vilar, a 20-year-old student from Manchester Metropolitan University and originally from Liverpool, ventured the view, which was universally supported, that all Manchester's bus stations, including the Arndale Bus Station under the Arndale Shopping Centre, and the Piccadilly terminus in Piccadilly

Figure 4.1 Landscape of fear: interior, the Arndale Bus Station, Manchester
(photograph taken during the daytime hours)
Source: photo by Jenny Young

Gardens, were 'dirty and horrible'. Both Chorlton Street and the Arndale were indicted for their gloomy, not to say threatening, interior. Piccadilly bus station was seen both by the elderly and the young as having been colonised by 'down-and-outs' – 'vagrants', 'beggars', 'tramps' and 'those types of people'. In the mental taxonomy of space and people adopted by many Mancunians (young and old alike) there seemed to be a clear distinction made between the 'vagrants' and 'down and outs' taking up residence in the bus stations and Piccadilly Gardens, on the one hand, and the homeless young people and *Big Issue* sellers, congregating on Market Street or in other city centre locations, on the other. The bus stations of Manchester almost without exception were negative 'symbolic locations' – places to be avoided if at all possible, but which, if used at all, would require strategic negotiation with caution and care. There was some evidence as well in Manchester that this widespread dislike and fear of the city-centre bus stations connected to an inescapable popular sense of resignation with respect to the city's bus services in general, as essentially and inherently unfriendly to the local citizen bus user.[24] The row of bus stops at the Piccadilly terminus, alongside a much-maligned row of 'greasy-spoon' take-out cafés – was almost universally disliked. The signs on the bus stops and platforms were thought indecipherable and the quality of information provided to the public from the Information Booth was subject to merciless critique:

Mrs Fowler: I was wanting to go to the Crematorium last week and I couldn't find where the 84 bus went from.

Ian Taylor: Was this Piccadilly?

Mrs Fowler: Yes. I was told at the Information Office that it was just round the corner of Market Street, opposite . . . (I forget the name of the shop). It *wasn't* opposite at all. It was in front of it. And I was walking round and round and nobody knew. Why can't they put the numbers at either end of the bus station and the people can just go and look? At the moment you have to queue in the long queue to find out first of all where it is. *They* don't know and just give you an approximate answer. . . because they change the people in the Information Office.

One of the most common devices used by Mancunian residents to emphasise their discontent was to make an animated reference to a better facility in another city, usually in the North:

Halifax . . . they've got a list of where the buses are going from. They are clearly marked – A,B,C,D, etc. – and you can see from a distance.

(Mrs Fowler)

At the time of our discussion groups, the major construction work at bus stations in South Yorkshire was of very recent completion. The South Yorkshire Passenger Transport Executive had obtained grants in the mid-1980s from the European Regional Development Programme to underwrite the creation of a new Transport Interchange in Sheffield and the renovation of six rail stations. They followed this with a successful bid to the European Integrated Development Operations Programme (IDOPS), a European Community programme established to assist the restructuring of steel areas, and were able to finance new Interchanges in Barnsley, Rotherham and Doncaster town centres and at Meadowhall. Sheffield Interchange itself, opened in December 1990, cost £9.6 million to build, and is described by the PTE as one of the most 'up-to-date transport facilities in the world'. Bus and coach departure details are displayed on a system of monitors, with information changing by the minute; the waiting areas in the Archway Centre are lined with well-lit retail units, and there is a departure lounge for coach users. A direct link into the neighbouring rail station was still due to be completed. Similar transformations have occurred to the other old bus stations in South Yorkshire. It is a matter for remark that there was little overt discussion, in our focus group discussions, of these new facilities, but we think it is important to recognise that the designation of 'the bus station' as a key city-centre landscape of fear was not a part of the repertoire of most of our Sheffield discussants, in a way that it *was* in Manchester and in a way that it would always have been in Sheffield itself, for example, in the thirty years from 1960 to 1990.[25] Two evaluations (in 1991 and 1994) of the new Interchange by the Harriss research organisation for the South Yorkshire Passenger Transport Executive reported very high levels of public approval of the new facilities, with 95 per cent of respondents scoring the Interchange on a 10-point scale at 6 or above (Harriss Research Centre 1991, 1994).[26]

To recognise these real achievements on the part of the South Yorkshire PTE, however, is not to say that the PTE or the Council have succeeded in the local struggle for hearts and minds over the future of transport in Sheffield.[27] We have already referred to the widespread critique by suburban professionals of the route chosen for the South Yorkshire Supertram, which will really only connect to the West End of the city in its later stages of development, some years in the future. The actual building of the Supertram, in the meantime, has been accompanied by considerable resentment from commercial interests near the City Centre, especially on West Street, whose trade was badly hit by the construction programme, which required the closing of some roads to cars for many months. There was also notable confusion and anxiety, especially for suburban and middle-class professionals, over the future of the car in Sheffield: the issue here being whether a city with as compact a centre as Sheffield can simultaneously cater for the bus, the tram and the car (not least in respect of city-centre car parking).[28] On 22 June 1993, the city organised a so-called 'Green Transport Day', asking drivers to leave their cars at home, but reports in the local press suggested that this had made little difference to the level of congestion in the city-centre.

In the folklore of many smaller North of England cities during the earlier post-war period, the development of local road-congestion problems, especially the rush-hour, has acted as a kind of signifier of city growth and development, the arrival of a sort of metropolitan status. Manchester shared with Birmingham (perhaps a more widely discussed example during the 1960s) the kinds of road problem that were taken for granted in London: moving to Manchester for a job would mean that one would have to encounter the kinds of daily travel time to which 'people in Manchester and Birmingham' had become accustomed. In Sheffield, in the late 1970s, these kinds of problem were thought to have been avoided by the popularity of the County Council's subsidised bus fares policy and the significant reduction of car usership which this produced. By the mid-1990s, however, Sheffield had problems of road congestion on a par with Manchester's, made worse by the fact of their sudden development over a short period of time as the product of the bus deregulation of 1986 and the building of the Supertram. We had a strong sense in Sheffield of a set of publics who could not develop, and had not developed, the kind of risk strategies which were necessary for commuters and other transport users travelling across the extended conurbation of Greater Manchester. These two Northern cities had in common, in other words, the problem of the deregulation of the municipal bus service and were both involved, in local parlance, 'in bringing back the trams', but they differed quite significantly in the extent to which the 'local structures of feeling' factored in a long struggle to work (including the danger of gridlock and an extended rush-hour) as a part of daily experience. There is an inescapable sense, we think, in which these issues – conventionally treated in the social sciences as a technical area of study for transport specialists – are also an expression of the definition of our Northern cities as 'metropolitan' or 'headquarter' places, or of the collective local desire for (or toleration of) such a symbolic urban status.

5

SHOP 'TIL YOU DROP
The 'Nice Shops' and the Markets in Manchester and Sheffield

The representation of the English city – for example, in commercial advertising – as a slick, modern 'consumer paradise' is the preferred vision of those with a professional interest in it. It is also characteristic of a certain section of the academy, especially in cultural studies, involved in a kind of idealist and celebratory interpretation of consumer culture. We want to argue that its empirical reference is sometimes more problematic, especially in the North of England. One of the more obvious effects of this kind of representation is the suppression of the widespread evidence of poverty and destitution in the city and the way in which this poverty structures the practice of shopping for a large (and perhaps an increasing) proportion of the urban population. We are also aware that this kind of ideological representation of the city may bear only a partial and indirect relation to overall patterns of use of that city across the social formation as a whole, not just amongst the poor. In that sense, such representations miss the specifics of how people shop in individual cities; and of how the local knowledge which different publics develop, whilst shopping, relates to their local 'sense of place' and, perhaps, also to what we are calling the 'local structure of feeling' of particular cities and city regions.

The approach we want to adopt in the examination of shopping in our two cities in the old industrial North of England is rather different, resting on the more traditional sociological project of gathering accounts of shopping from a wide range of shop users in our cities and trying to situate these accounts against a larger understanding of continuities and change in specific cities. We will be particularly interested in patterns of decline or development in some urban shopping areas and of provision and the rise of the out-of-town shopping mall in others, and in the connected question of access to these shopping spaces on foot, via public transport, or by car. We do not operate with an assumed conception of shopping as a leisured and playful activity, but with an interest in the different types of shopping activity engaged in (with different degrees of difficulty as well as pleasure) by different fractions of 'the public' (the divided social formation which constitutes those cities). We are also very much aware that the 'social character' or social composition of the shopping population in the North of England differs very radically from the commercial and professional middle-class shoppers who have been the focus of studies of consumption in North America and even elsewhere in Britain.

This is quite a long chapter. In part, this is because we agree with many contemporary commentators on the city in emphasising the centrality of shopping in everyday life (though, as will become clear, not simply for the purposes of identity construction or the assertion of personal 'distinction'). Shopping took up a considerable amount of time in the lives of nearly all the people of Manchester and Sheffield with whom we held discussions, though our research method did not involve any attempt to quantify this time investment. We heard enough to convince us of the vital importance of shopping in the process of social reproduction itself – that is, in the recruitment of individuals into the gendered division of household labour, and its intimate relationship with the capacity of individuals to contemplate work in the wider labour market or any other social activity in wider civil society. We want to develop an account of the diversity of shopping practices in our two cities that takes account of the different roles of different shopping locales (the local High Street and the local supermarket as well as the city-centre stores and, in Sheffield, the out-of-town mall). We are hopeful that our attempt to capture the different kinds of shopping practice in our two cities will help inform our comparative analysis of the two cities as being 'different mixes of places' and comprising different combinations of consumer provision (which is then potentially understood in relation to the 'local structure of feeling').

This particular chapter is organised, therefore, as a sequence of different sections on different shopping locations and shopping practices. These sections could, in theory, be read independently as short contributions to the sociological understanding of particular types of shopping, but it is our intention that the range of shopping locations in each conurbation should be seen as quite a complex local structure of shopping provision, more or less well understood by inhabitants and users of each local urban region. Our account will focus quite heavily on the stories provided by users themselves as to the place which consumption (shopping) plays in their lives, the relationship of this activity to personal pleasure and also to the everyday business of feeding and survival, and the relationship between the familiar locales in which shopping is done and the larger image of the city held by different publics in the city.

In order to ground the accounts given us of this activity by Mancunians and Sheffielders and our own interpretative work on these accounts, however, we want first to provide an overview of the recent history of the key shopping sites in the two conurbations, particularly the historical evolution of what architects refer to as the 'built form' of the central city. The locations we want to discuss occupy key places in the 'mental maps' of residents of the two cities (Lynch 1960, 1972); they also play an important role in the folk memories that are retained about the city, especially by its established residents. Moreover, although the point may seem trite, it is primarily these particular locales (with all their given physical characteristics) that the residents of these cities (especially the long-term residents – the locals), who are not themselves the highly mobile vanguard of the new global economy, have to utilise 'in their imaginations' in order to define their own relation to the international consumer market that dominates television, radio and video's symbolic world, as well as most contemporary magazine and billboard advertising.

SHOPPING IN THE NORTH: PAST MEMORIES AND PRESENT CONTEXT

We are not aware of a social history of shopping in the North of England as a whole, though we believe that any such history would have some distinctive features. In particular, given the larger cities and towns of the North of England's long involvement with heavy industry, the associated development of working-class neighbourhoods and the 'weekly-wage' economy, any history of shopping would be an account of the recursive round of daily shopping for essential items, which (given the assumed division of labour in the working-class household) would have primarily been conducted by women, most often in the local corner store or on the local High Street.

Roger Scola's comprehensive analysis of 'food supply' in Manchester in the period 1770 to 1870 shows how the only competition to the corner store in this period came from the traders on the street ('barrow boys'), from the development and relocation of the medieval market centre, and from 'hawkers' – people selling particular goods from door to door (Scola 1994). Scola's account of the social organisation of food shopping across the exploding and sprawling Victorian city of Manchester probably holds true in its generality for other North of England cities, although the specific lines of supply and the specific locations of markets in different city centres – and, in particular, the development of major covered markets in some cities and not others[1] – might have an important impact on local patterns of uses, and also cultural definitions, of that city. In reminding ourselves of the importance of these markets for the people of the North of England, we also recall the dual role of the marketplace – the agora – in Greek democracies. The agora operated as an open space for the selling of fish, meat, bread and other foodstuffs, but also as a place for banking and trading, as well as a 'place of assembly' in which conversation was encouraged, and sometimes purposively organised, on matters of shared public interest and concern (Harvey 1957).

In the late nineteenth century, another important development in patterns of shopping in the North of England was the emergence of 'the Co-op', with its origins in the general store opened (with a capital of £28) by the collectively minded workers of Rochdale, near Manchester, in 1844. The Industrial and Provident Societies Act of 1862 allowed the range of small societies that had sprung up to federate, thus making possible a national network of cheap retail stores owned by its customers – the Cooperative Wholesale Society – formed in 1863. Membership of these 'Co-ops' in Lancashire rose from 40,000 in 1865 to 400,000 in 1910 (82.5 people for every thousand in the country) (Walton 1995: 118). By 1914, membership of the Cooperative Wholesale Society (CWS) nationally totalled well over 3 million people, with sales over £88 million, with a continually strong presence in the North (Read 1979: 258).[2] There is also an important sense in which the continuing expansion of the CWS headquarters in central Manchester, in the period between 1860 and 1930 (when Manchester was establishing itself as the biggest distribution centre for foodstuffs in the North of England) (Kidd 1993: 191), was a major factor in the mobilisation of the idea of Manchester as the headquarters of the North. So also, much later, did the opening of the CIS (Cooperative Insurance Society) building in 1962 (at that time, with 17 floors, 'the tallest office building in Britain') serve to confirm that metropolitan definition of Manchester.

Whilst the daily shopping of the mass of the population of the North of England in the first half of this century might primarily have involved the recursive use of the corner store or the neighbourhood Co-op, the bank, and other necessary local shops, this does not mean that there was never any departure from such routinised activity. Housewives would certainly make regular forays into town – for example, 'to the markets' for both the food and clothing needs of the household, and there would be some smaller markets in particular neighbourhoods and smaller towns. There was also the long-established tradition of travelling salespeople coming regularly into the neighbourhood – for example, the 'fish van' from places like Fleetwood (for the North-west), Grimsby (for South and West Yorkshire) and South Shields (for the North-east and North Yorkshire), selling fresh fish, kippers and other specialities. In many suburban areas and council estates of the North of England, the local patronage of the market and the fish van retains some considerable significance.[3]

It is important, however, to avoid an account of the history of shopping in the North of England as a product only of a strong and autonomous industrial class culture, with a division of labour restricting the working-class wife in the domestic sphere. The development of major 'department stores' in England in the middle years of the nineteenth century[4] (Read 1979: 251) certainly catered primarily to the wives of the new commercial and industrial middle-class. These department stores quite specifically targeted wealthy women, providing under one roof services normally provided by different shops, and so avoiding the necessity for wealthy women to venture out into the streets outside (Cahill 1994: 104). Rudi Laermans argues that the nineteenth-century department store was a kind of equivalent of 'male downtown club and bar', allowing middle-class women 'a certain, albeit limited, kind of public freedom' (Laermans 1993: 87). In addition, as John Urry has observed, they were a place in which middle-class women could legitimately expect to be served: the department stores were: 'a temple to woman, making a legion of shop assistants burn incense before her.' (Urry 1990: 152).

The major department stores established in Manchester (Kendals – originally Kendal Milne[5] - Marshall and Snelgrove, and Lewis's)[6] and in Sheffield (Coles)[7] had (or have) this specific market in mind.[8] But in each of our two Northern cities, it is noticeable how a range of other department stores opened up, primarily in the latter half of the nineteenth century, catering to a section of the local public in what now would be called a 'different market segment' – the lower middle class and upper working class of the time. The importance of these large, usually locally owned, department stores to the local city into the post-war period – in Manchester, Affleck and Brown's, Baxendales', Finnigan's, Henry's and Pauldens',[9] and in Sheffield, Cockayne's (later called Schofield's),[10] Walsh's,[11] and Banner's outside the city centre, in Attercliffe – cannot be exaggerated. We must also refer to the national development in the 1890s of 'multiple chain stores' on the new High Streets emerging in different urban areas (Freeman, Hardy and Willis for footwear; Burton's for men's clothing; W.H. Smith for books; Boots the Chemists and Lipton's for imported food) – initially, in the South, in suburban High Streets, but latterly, in the North and elsewhere, in city centres themselves and the developing shopping centres of smaller towns.

The redeployment of shopping into smaller established centres across the larger urban region of Manchester – outside city-centre Manchester itself – actively helped to transform the historically given significance of small towns in the region, such as Altrincham and Bolton, reconstituting them as what are now called, in the language of the local growth coalition, 'satellite' or 'secondary retail towns'. So the everyday shopping of the citizen in the Manchester region, henceforth, might involve the neighbourhood and the city centre, but it could also encompass (as in Greater London) the nearest town within the conurbation and its particular shopping centre. This process was far less marked in a city the size of Sheffield in the first half of this century: like most cities of the North of England, Sheffield remained a city that was lived and understood by its citizens in terms of the one neighbourhood of residence and the city centre.

The post-war history of shopping in Britain as a whole spans the period of 'rationing' and 'the retail revolution' of the 1950s and 1960s (particularly the emergence and spread of the supermarket from the early 1950s and the demise of the local grocery store), and finds contemporary expression in the struggle between the High Street and the out-of-town shopping mall. Each of these developments has left traces on the shape and form of the city centre (transforming, though never eradicating, the original form of the nineteenth-century centre) and on the kinds of mental map of the city constructed by different publics in the larger conurbation.

Importantly for our times, the story is one of entrepreneurial success and some planning failures, especially in the 1960s. Perhaps the best-known failure, locally, was the new Piccadilly Plaza building in Manchester, finally erected in 1963. The Plaza was a scheme of the Colman Group in the late 1950s, designed with the intention of locating an international hotel and shopping complex next to the main city bus station and Piccadilly Gardens (*Manchester Guardian* 16 April 1959). Constructed at speed, like many other city-centre buildings at the time, the Plaza has been unpopular from its inception. The ground-floor 'take-away' cafés, next to a string of bus stops, form one of the most widely disliked places in the city, whilst the façade of the Plaza building is suffering serious discolouration from industrial deposits. The highest elevations of the Piccadilly Hotel, atop the Plaza, are crumbling badly and, as property surveys would say, are in need of urgent attention. Like many buildings of this period, it is seen by local residents and visitors alike as an 'eyesore' – part of the material infrastructure of place that is either actively disliked or, at best, ignored if possible.

In Manchester, the failure of Piccadilly is one reason for the move of the city centre 'further down' towards Cross Street and St Ann's Square – a shift that was also encouraged by the opening of the Arndale Centre, unquestionably one of the most important moments in the post-war shopping history of Manchester. The building of this city-centre indoor shopping development began in 1972, 17 years after the site was first acquired, but was not completed until 1978, when the City Council under-wrote loans of over £16 million. The Arndale Centre, at the foot of Market Street, contains 200 shops, 200 fixed (underground) market stalls and a car park for 1,800 cars, the whole development being built over a street-level bus station (Bridges and Lodwick 1980). The building of the Arndale Centre had a major effect on the city-centre core of Manchester, not only in introducing a massive 'modern' enclosed concrete 'box' into what previously had been a largely Victorian area,[12] but also in moving the centre of gravity of shopping away from Market Street itself and from other streets which had a central significance for shoppers:

> The effect of this is vividly displayed in Oldham Street, where a multitude of 'For Sale and 'To Let' boards bear silent witness to what once was a prime shopping street. Letting problems in Piccadilly Plaza, a rather poorly designed shopping development that has struggled to succeed almost since the day it opened, have been exacerbated.
>
> (Bridges and Lodwick 1980: 200)

For all the unpopularity of the architecture of the Arndale, however, it is a very heavily used space. In the early 1990s, according to its current owners, P and O Shopping Centres, it continued to attract some 800,000 visitors a week, and there was clearly some expectation that the popularity of the Centre could be sustained and expanded by a programme of modernisation and refurbishment,[13] undertaken in 1991–3 – particularly by the addition of a North American-style food court reached by an escalator from the centre of Market Street. In 1994, P and O Shopping Centres were at the forefront of the campaign for Sunday shopping in the city centre, and had positioned themselves for this innovation by adding a Warner Brothers Studio Store and children's entertainment in the Voyagers restaurant area, extra car parking, and free wheelchairs for those with restricted mobility (under the so-called *Shopmobility* scheme).

Constantly in the background of all such discussion on the part of city-centre companies and the shop owners was an anxiety about the continuing effects on trade of shopping-centre development in the secondary retail towns throughout Greater Manchester and the suburban areas, and also an awareness of the trade being lost across the Pennines to Meadowhall. City-centre commercial interest was also concerned at the projected development by the Manchester Ship Canal Company of the £200-million Trafford Centre at Dumplington, near Urmston in south Manchester. These plans had been nine years in gestation and were going ahead until July 1994, when a legal action by an *ad hoc* consortium of retailers, property holders and local authorities (the North West Group) successfully went to the Court of Appeal to oppose the go-ahead given by the Minister of the Environment. A report released to the local press by the North West Group suggested that the opening of this major out-of-town shopping centre would have devastating effects on the economies of the secondary retail towns of Greater Manchester – on a par, it was always argued, with the effects which the opening of Meadowhall had on the centre of Sheffield.[14] Prior to this decision, and subsequently, a series of reports was released by different interest groups to the local press and local television on the relative health and viability of Manchester's city centre and the threat from Dumplington and other new shopping malls in the secondary retail centres and in the city itself,[15] though it has to be said that discussion of the merits and demerits of these various schemes seems to have been almost entirely confined to the various direct interests or commercial 'stakeholders', with some periodic intervention by the local councils. As with the debates on the expansion of Manchester Airport, there was some sense of important differences of view (rather than automatic unity) within the local growth coalitions, most notably around the contradiction between the short-term profitability of out-of-town centres and the long-term economic catastrophe for city-centre business (with the implications of that for 'city image' and inward investment).[16] There was also some recognition that developers and local politicians in North America – the originating home of the mall – were now seriously concentrating on the rescue of the depopulated and fearful inner-city core and, indeed, in some quarters, the 'de-malling of America' (cf. Mathews 1994).

SHOPPING IN MANCHESTER: PHYSICAL FORM AND SYMBOLIC BOUNDARIES

When Northern people speak about Manchester as a mecca for shopping, they are referring to the city centre, rather than to Greater Manchester as a whole, though for many locals the use of the 'secondary retail towns' and shopping centres in Bolton, Stockport and elsewhere have become the preferred shopping locale. In the city centre itself, the 'end product' of the 200 years of development, including the so-called Retail Revolution, are three distinct urban territories, all situated within a single square mile but each with its own distinct social character: Deansgate and St Ann's Square, Market Street and the Arndale Centre, and Oldham Street and the Barrows, each with a distinct physical presence and different social character. The boundaries between these three urban territories are well understood in a taken-for-granted way by nearly all the different publics making use of the city centre. We suspect, in fact, that this kind of understanding of the physical form of a city centre and the bounded character of particular areas is a given feature of all cities: what may be particularly important about Northern cities first developed in the nineteenth century is the way that post-war commercial development has overlain a locally familiar industrial and commercial heritage (the warehouses, offices and factories) of those cities.[17]

We are saying here that there was a recognition and an understanding, shared by the public making use of each area of what architects call the 'form' of the city. The three areas also played a significant role in the mental map of the city described to us by its users, but with a different evaluation of the relevance of these areas from the perspective of individuals in different social groups. We want to provide a brief description of each of these locations, attending, where we can, to some important features of their historical evolution and significance and their present role in the recursive use of the city.

Deansgate and St Ann's Square

Deansgate, the original main thoroughfare of eighteenth-century Manchester, is the western edge of the centre of the city in the 1990s, and functions as a major traffic route or node carrying traffic to the north and south. But it has a curious character, a product precisely of its long history. It bears absolutely no resemblance to a modern, planned retail strip in North America or, for that matter, to the boulevards of Paris or Vienna. At its southern end, opposite what once was a railway goods yard, it is the location, primarily, for a number of outdoor pursuits and camping shops, as well as comprising the entrance point for the Castlefield heritage and development area. Its central stretch is dominated by the famous Kendals' store (now owned by the House of Fraser chain), a large Waterstones bookshop, and a number of middle-market chain eateries. At its northern end, there is a cluster of wine bars, computer stores, expensive clothing stores, and one of the entries into the up-market Barton Arcade. The street can be 'read' – using Michel Foucault's archaeological method – for the traces or sediments it retains from different moments in the urban and commercial history of the city; or, alternatively, it can be read as a commentary on the internal fracturing of the consumer markets of the middle class, from the healthy outdoor pursuits (of the non-commercial middle class?) to the power dressing, wine bars, clothing shops, and high-tech computer stores frequented by the new urban professionals. The new guidebooks to Manchester all comment, in a rather befuddled fashion, that the 'tone' and character of Deansgate changes markedly from one end to the other.

St Ann's Square, just to the east of Deansgate near its northern end, was first established in 1709 as a residential square alongside arable land, with St Ann's Church, consecrated in 1712, as a boundary marker. Over the years, it has reproduced itself in different ways as a fashionable and elegant central urban square. For many years it was home to a famous coffee house, Ravalds, and also functioned as the station where hansom cabs could be hired. In 1761, it was the site on which many local feuds were ended with a mass celebration of the coronation of George III, with three barrels of beer consumed 'at the King's expense'. Throughout the late nineteenth century it was very much the place for casual urban perambulation (*Free Lance* 29 May 1874: 171). The Barton Arcade, which connects the Square to Deansgate, is a classic Victorian glass-covered shopping arcade and emporium, first opened in the 1870s by John Hope Barton, a local urban property owner with ambitious architectural interests. The square is one place in Manchester in which there is an unmistakable and powerful sense of the nineteenth century, though this is deceptive in certain respects. St Ann's Square was pedestrianised with cobblestones only in 1984, whilst the Stock Exchange building itself, which contributes to the sense of grandeur in the square, was originally opened as the city's Cotton Exchange as recently as 1921 (replacing an earlier building on Market Street and operating as a cotton-trade centre only until 1968). The theatre which now occupies the massive Exchange floor, the Royal Exchange, was opened in 1976. The Square shares with Market Street the fact of having been under constant renovation and reconstruction over the last 10 years: in the case of St Ann's Square, however, with a view to reproducing itself, precisely, as the most fashionable centre. This project may have been helped in recent years by the addition of expensive clothing stores (Ouiset, Betty Barclay) and a large wine bar and bistro, but it is not clear that the addition of a Disney Store in 1992 will not contradict the taken-for-granted segregation of different peoples across the territory of city-centre Manchester.

Market Street and the Arndale Centre

Market Street, now also pedestrianised (but with concrete slabs rather than cobblestones), has always been one of the busiest shopping streets in the centre of Manchester. Dyos and Wolff, writing about 'the Victorian city' of Manchester in the 1970s, describe it as 'the aorta of Manchester' (Dyos and Wolff 1973). According to some older long-term residents of the city and its surrounds, Market Street was the location of the first Chinese restaurant in the city, the Ping Hong, of the Cinephone (the first cinema to show 'continental films'),[18] of Lister's Music Hall, as well as of UCP (purveyors of traditional meats with a 'sit-down' restaurant), a Kardomah's coffee shop, a gentlemen's finery shop and Henry's department store. None of these institutions remains today. In the middle years of this century, the continuing presence of the restaurants meant that the street was a place of leisure, particularly in the evenings, for the adult population of Manchester. It is no longer anything like this: beginning with the opening of the first phase of the Arndale Centre in 1976 and the pedestrianisation of Market Street itself, the area has been fundamentally transformed, in a little over a decade and half, into one of the prime sites of youthful activity and colonisation in central Manchester. The opening of branches of McDonald's, Burger King, and an HMV and Virgin megastore has cemented Market Street's significance as a location of youthful occupation (perhaps *the* central location of the so-called 'townie' population we discuss in Chapter 11).

The 'top end' of Market Street is clearly marked in the mental maps of most Mancunians by Lewis's department store, mentioned earlier, now operating as the boundary between Market Street and Piccadilly. But large numbers of adult Mancunians who suspended use of Market Street during the construction of the Arndale have never resumed their familiar patterns of use since: many have constructed shopping routes and itineraries which avoid Market Street (or the city centre) altogether, or make use of the street only as an access route to the Arndale Centre. Several people we spoke to from Stockport referred to the building of the Arndale, and the accompanying increase in private car traffic believed to have been caused by it, as being synonymous with the demise of Manchester city centre, which they now only visit under duress. It is widely believed that the disruption brought about by the Arndale Centre and the absence of any significant out-of-town shopping mall in the Greater Manchester region have helped the nine regional town centres, including Altrincham, Bolton and Stockport, all three of which have survived and even flourished by retaining their local clientele and adding new customers from elsewhere within the conurbation (Tym and Partners 1986). In 1995, indeed, Lewis's were in the process of building a new department store, with a connected Sainsbury's, in Cheadle, one of south Manchester's affluent suburbs, and questions are posed about the future of their city-centre store.

The gentrification of the Royal Exchange and St Ann's Square in the late 1970s and early 1980s did push up retail values in the city centre, and more people were attracted there in that period to shop. Much development has occurred in King Street or on the northern end of Deansgate, but – in part through lack of alternative – some consumer chains, including Littlewood's and Debenhams in the 1970s, and more recently the fashion shops aimed at teenagers and people in their twenties (Next, Oasis and Wallis), have located themselves in premises on Market Street. At some point in the 1980s, the street was in that sense a contested space, routinely occupied by very different groups of shoppers. But there is no question that the street in the 1990s has taken on a specific character as a street dominated by young people, involved either in 'legitimate' shopping or consumption or in a variety of more ambiguous youthful presentations of self (playing music, 'hanging around', selling political newspapers, begging or simply colonising the space). Throughout the early 1990s, Market Street was the focus of a number of different campaigns of refurbishment – in 1992, a consortium including the City Council, Government and P and O Shopping Centres indicated it had funds to transform Market Street into 'a sophisticated boulevard' (*Manchester Evening News* 28 August 1992) – but we shall see later that the constant changes in Market Street since have been a matter of considerable and varied local agitation and dispute.

Oldham Street and 'the Barrows'

The character of Oldham Street has altered significantly compared with the earlier post-war period and especially since the opening of the Arndale Centre. Whereas it is remembered by the older residents of the city as being a 'respectable' shopping street, centring on Afflecks and Browns general department store, it is now no longer so regarded. The department store building – a product of the widespread development of such stores in the middle of the last century – has been converted into what once would have been called a 'counter-cultural' clothing store (Afflecks Palace) exclusively for young people. On three floors, the complex now consists of a large number of small stalls selling second-hand or low-cost handmade-cum-designer clothes for fashion aficionados as well as clubbers and ravers. Other outlets on Oldham Street include an independent record store, a mountain bike shop, a continental-style café bar and a 'trendy' hair stylists, and reflect the successful colonisation of this area by businesses catering to a youth market. The City Council has even tendered a £700,000 contract for an 'artist in residence' to 'rejuvenate' the image of Oldham Street in collaboration with local young people as consultants and advisors (*Manchester Evening News* 15 January 1993). Many of the older buildings in this area are the smaller warehouses and workshops of the cotton trade, all now looking for a new social and cultural purpose.

Towards Piccadilly Gardens, however, this street assumes a different character altogether, as the location of a number of mass-market entertainment pubs, patrolled by bouncers and, according to popular belief, the regular site of violence on Friday and Saturday nights. There are stores selling cheap clothing and other household items and an amusement arcade. Nearby, 'the Barrows' is the only outdoor market in central Manchester. It sells almost exclusively fruit and vegetables, though there is always one stall selling records and tapes, but is a significant destination or 'stopping place' for many poorer Mancunians whilst shopping in town.[19] Just as the character of Deansgate can be read as an expression of changes in the consumption practices and interests of middle-class Manchester, so can the transformation of the Oldham Street area be read, first, as an expression of the disappearance of the city-centre cotton trade and many of the public houses serving the workers in this trade, and, secondly, as a measure of the rather desperate 'modernisation' of some public houses, looking for daytime and evening custom from urban transients.

We have already indicated that the negotiation of Manchester city centre routinely involves the use of mental maps of the area, distilled into what individuals may refer to as 'their routes'. What is also quite obvious is that people of different social backgrounds (young people in groups, subsistence shoppers looking for a bargain, young professionals en route to a wine bar, unemployed men of different ages looking for company to pass the time of day) routinely make more or less heavy use of quite different parts of the city centre, and that each of these different social groups learns how the centre of the city is geographically and spatially divided up for the use of each, and where the boundaries lie. On the map of contemporary Manchester, the key markers differentiating areas from each other are Lewis's corner, at the intersection of Market Street and Piccadilly Gardens (defining the boundary between a youthfully dominated streetscape and the 'poor people's Manchester' on Oldham Road and the markets); the junction of Market Street and St Ann's Square (the entry point to a space dominated by young professionals); and the feeder-streets between St Ann's Square, Deansgate and King Street (given over to serious family and middle-class shoppers). So each of these three areas has a markedly different social character, as in some instances is clear from the architecture and material surroundings in it, and each produces a distinct response from the people making use of these spaces. In contrast to an architecturally deterministic account of the relationship between individual sense of fear or well-being and urban space, we argue that the responses which these spaces evoke in others are more a matter of the type of people who are predictably to be found in these particular spaces or territories; and that the overall feel of the centre of this large conurbation is also a product of the mix of people that can routinely be found across the whole central area.

SHOPPING IN SHEFFIELD: PHYSICAL FORM AND SYMBOLIC BOUNDARIES

The pattern of shopping in Sheffield, we want to argue, is much more homogeneous than in Manchester: the bulk of the local population, of different social backgrounds, will have been accustomed over the years to basic shopping in their own neighbourhood, with frequent 'visits to town' for most other types of shopping. There are few 'secondary retail centres' (other than the Ecclesall Road corridor) and certainly no secondary retail towns within the city. The arrival of Meadowhall in 1990, which we discuss later, is the major transformation to these patterns. Sheffield's city centre itself, the focal point of 'visits to town' by different sections of the population of Sheffield, comprises three identifiable shopping locales: Fargate/Orchard Square, The Moor with its street market, and the Markets proper;[20] but there is evidence that a greater proportion of central urban space (especially Fargate and the Moor) is 'shared' by a broad cross-section of the Sheffield population than is most urban space in Manchester, outside the Arndale Centre.

Fargate and Orchard Square

Where Sheffield's long central thoroughfare reaches the Town Hall (at an intersection with the three side streets of Barker's Pool, Leopold Street and Surrey Street) it becomes known as Fargate. This street has always had a certain ceremonial and iconic significance. In the early post-war period, it was a well-established street for shopping and the taking of morning coffee, largely because of the presence of Davy's provisions store (attracting customers into the store with a particularly powerful aroma of roasting coffee) and Coles highly fashionable department store at the bottom of the street – as locals would say, 'where it becomes High Street'. It was also one of few streets in central Sheffield in the first half of this century to avoid carrying motor cars and trams together: the trams were routed around West Street and Leopold Street, away from Fargate itself. The more recent history of this street, beginning in the 1960s, has seen it closed to motor traffic altogether and pedestrianised, becoming home, rather later than other major cities, to the main national stores (British Home Stores, W.H. Smith, Thomas Cook, Marks and Spencer, and Boots, followed by Next in the 1980s). The pedestrian stretch is generally well maintained by the Council (though recently there have been complaints about the continual presence of litter in the Sir Stuart Goodwin fountain at the top of the street) and is depicted in local publicity as a kind of continental boulevard or piazza. Coles department store – which, as we indicated earlier, has an iconic status in the local history of shopping – is just 150 yards away, on Barker's Pool opposite the City Hall (Sheffield's main venue for orchestral and other concerts). For very many Sheffielders, as we indicated earlier, any decision by Cole Brothers to move to Meadowhall would signal the final demise of the city centre.

For some commentators, however, this demise was at least postponed by the opening at the top of Fargate, in 1987, of Orchard Square, a gentrified 'shopping yard' with balconies, specialist and gift shops, delicatessens, a downstairs food court and a novelty horloge. Despite the recent addition of a Virgin music store by the entrance to the yard, Orchard Square is clearly targeted primarily at the middle-aged and elderly shopper and young families, rather than young people as such. It was clear in our enquiries that the proximity of the Square to Coles and to the national chain stores on Fargate, with the Crucible Theatre behind it (with its facilities for morning coffee), offers a well-structured shopping route for up-market shoppers in Sheffield city centre, albeit without the 'quality' of Manchester's King Street or the range of Meadowhall itself. There is a definite sense, however, in which everyone in Sheffield uses Fargate, albeit on different routes and for slightly different purposes: it is seen locally as a 'commonly owned' urban territory.

The Moor

The character of shops on The Moor, the section of the same long thoroughfare stretching 'down from' the Town Hall to the south, is altogether different. There are two long-established department stores (Debenhams and Atkinsons), but more importantly, since the 'trial' pedestrianisation of 1978, the street has become the site of a large street market, concentrating entirely on cheap merchandise. This reconstruction of The Moor as a kind of poor people's market coincided historically with the rapidly developing crisis of the steel industry and the local economy generally. Out in the open air, The Moor street market has become a place in which popular market trading occurs on a regular basis, and many bargains can be found. In the face of some criticism of the 'tone' and appearance of this new poor people's market, the Moor Traders' Association has felt the need to upgrade the street's image and to enhance its visibility. A number of brightly painted metal arches announce 'Welcome to the Moor', and signs erected by the Council designate the discrete identity of the area as a precinct.

Castle Market

Throughout its history, Sheffield has been home to a number of covered markets, but only two currently remain: Castle Market, opened in its current form in 1959, and Sheaf Market, opened in 1973. Both of these are at the extreme north end of the city's extended central thoroughfare, and therefore nearest of all the city-centre locales to the large numbers of poorer Sheffield citizens living to the north and east of the centre. Despite the improvements being made to one of these markets, including the introduction of CCTV into what is thought of as the city centre's crime blackspot, the future of the Council-owned 'covered markets' is currently uncertain, and there are rumours of their possible sale at £20 million. The markets retain an importance to a great number of Sheffield shoppers from all over the city, and perform a critical social function for many elderly residents, although the opening up of The Moor as a street market has created competition. Perhaps in recognition of this truth, in December 1992, the City Council in conjunction with the Sheffield Development Corporation (SDC) announced proposals for two open-air markets in the East End of Sheffield, in Attercliffe and Zion Lane as part of a regeneration policy for this area.

Meadowhall

The defining moment in the post-war history of shopping in this city was without question, however, the opening of the Meadowhall Shopping Centre in September 1990. Meadowhall is built directly on the site of a major local steelworks (Hadfield's), which in 1980 had been the site of the biggest mass picket in the steel strike of that year (Kahn *et al.* 1983: 97–9), but which closed three years later. The site is directly adjacent to the M1 motorway, to the north-east of the city, convenient in the past for deliveries to and from the works, and now for the car-travelling shoppers of the North of England. On opening, it was proclaimed as 'the largest shopping mall in Europe'. The brainchild of the local entrepreneur E.D. Healey and what is now known (given its more recent activities in the Don Valley) as the Stadium Group, Meadowhall houses 223 stores on two levels in 1.5 million square feet of consumer space and provides free parking and its own rail and bus station. In 1994, Meadowhall was connected directly with the city centre and the council estates to the east by light rapid transit link, the South Yorkshire Supertram. As the publicity produced by Meadowhall's own management company proclaims, the mall is located in one of the most densely populated areas of England, with fully 9 million people living within one hour's drive of its car parks. 'Average weekly patronage' at Meadowhall in 1994 was measured at 480,000 people.[21] Apart from its massive collection of shops, Meadowhall also features a giant 'videowall' constantly playing in front of the 'Oasis' eating zone, where there is an array of take-away options with foods 'from all over the world'. A further leisure development is planned in the form of a 'Tivoli Gardens' pleasure park and cinema on a site immediately adjacent to the mall.

There is no question that the effect of Meadowhall on the city centre of Sheffield has been devastating, with an estimated 20 per cent reduction in city-centre trade at the end of the second year of Meadowhall's trading,[22] although the effects of the national recession may also have contributed to declining trade figures in the city centre. We discuss some of the social effects of the emergence of the Meadowhall mall, and also the different publics' concerns about travel and transport in respect of this out-of-town development and the shops in Sheffield city centre, in the substantive analysis of our discussions with local residents in the remainder of this chapter.

'I'VE GOT MY ROUTE': NORTHERN SHOPPERS IN MANCHESTER AND SHEFFIELD

The brief description we have provided of the spatial distribution and social character of shopping locations in cities (themselves the product of commercial enterprise, architectural styles and preference, and levels of investment at different historical moments) is one key step in an account of the use of a city. But it important, as writers such as de Certeau, Giddens and Hägerstrand all argue, to understand the use of these physical spaces and configurations as a personal accomplishment, heavily informed by patterns of custom and social difference. The street survey we completed in our two cities in 1992 gave us a detailed picture of who makes use of the different urban territories, at what time of day or week and why. The more in-depth discussion of places which we encouraged in focus groups helped us to delve in more detail into how local people actively situate themselves in a materially given 'consumer space' and, more or less actively, appropriate it for their own purposes. In our two Northern cities, this practical negotiation and use of the city centre was particularly discussed, as we have already suggested, by reference to individual department stores in the city – many of which, it should be added, no longer exist or have changed location or form or are under considerable threat. Contrary to expectations, perhaps, this 'mapping' of the city in terms of major departmental stores was not just engaged in by the middle-aged or retired, but also by young people, who would often articulate their feelings about the city and their place there, with reference to department stores that they perhaps once knew when small or even those which had closed before they were born.[23]

Whilst the heyday of the downtown department store is past, the social hierarchy of consumers that these stores both produced and fed remains. In some senses, and for some sections of the public, the supermarket has taken over as the department store's inheritor – 'we're living in the age of the supermarket' (Gardner and Sheppard, 1989: 152) – and some people talk about supermarket use (for example, in terms of the price and quality of goods or the amiability of the staff), in ways which were once reserved for department stores. To some degree, unquestionably, this is a matter of age, with the more elderly being more accustomed to this attribution of distinction to different shopping locales (department stores, supermarkets, High Street stores, etc.), but there is also a sense of a similar taxonomy operating among young people in terms of their different use of various consumer outlets, including food outlets and clothing stores.[24]

One of the key principles used by shoppers on both an everyday and an occasional basis is the construction of an itinerary or route. These personal routes have often been developed at an early stage in people's lives and are 'second nature' to them, as a result of which it frequently becomes difficult to accommodate their forced disruption. The reasons people gave for their development of and adherence to particular routes appear to be a mixture of: (i) practicality ('Which shops do I need to go to? Which parts of town am I unable to visit due to access problems because I have a disability? Which route from A to B brings me out near my return bus stop?'); (ii) strategic calculations as to how to minimise feelings of insecurity or anxiety ('How do I get to where I need to be to fulfil my practical objectives without having to use that dark underpass, or walk through that garden where the drunks congregate?[25] How do I get the goods I need without going into that claustrophobic shopping centre?'); (iii) economic considerations ('How do I get what I need as cheaply as possible; and (iv) avoiding temptation in the form of more up-market shops?') and aesthetic or idiosyncratic sentiment ('I always like to feed the birds near the Cathedral; I like to take in the peaceful atmosphere of that particular square'). In each of our two cities, considerations such as these determined a number of different preferred individual routes, but there was also a definite social patterning to different types of use.

Earlier in this chapter, for example, we identified the main artery running through Sheffield city centre: male teenagers at a school in the city routinely referred to the route they would take through the city centre of a Saturday morning as 'going up Fargate and down t'Moor'. It seems essential to them to pursue this particular path through the city, not only to check out the key sports and computer shops on the route, but also to be present in this space at that particular time. A sighting of a fancied girl, a group of lads from another school or an amusing incident along the way provides endless further hours of speculation or amusement during the following week back at school. The repeated construction of this kind of encounter, on The Moor in Sheffield and, perhaps, on Market Street or (more likely) a local neighbourhood High Street in Manchester, seems to have been a vital aspect of adolescence in these two cities.

We also spoke, by contrast, to a group of elderly Chinese people who lived in Manchester's Chinatown; they also placed great importance on their walk around the city centre, which for many of them served as their daily exercise, a reason to leave their flats. A typical walk would take in Market Street; the Arndale Centre, where they might call in to buy some fresh fish from the underground market or some groceries from Little-woods; Macdonalds, where they would stop off for a cup of tea; the fruit and vegetable Barrows behind Oldham Street; and finish up in Piccadilly Gardens for a rest.

'YOU GET TWO CUPS OF TEA THERE, FOR THE PRICE OF ONE'

For those who can afford it, the morning coffee or afternoon tea, taken at leisure in comfortable surroundings, is integral to the shopping trip. Although there were differences between the way in which those people we have called 'up-market shoppers' in both cities discussed this practice, there was some debate over the particular advantages and disadvantages of coffee shops in each city. The meaning of this activity appeared to be rather different in the two cities and contingent upon (or productive of) the 'cosmopolitan' versus the 'traditional' local ambience of Manchester's and Sheffield's city centres respectively. In one of our focus groups in Manchester, we asked:

Penny Fraser:	What about going for cups of coffee, anything like that, a place to sit and relax?
Dan Smithson:	Royal Exchange.
Phillipa Franks:	The Italian coffee places, San Marco and San Giorgio.
Dan:	It's off the beaten track.
Phillipa:	I'm not adventurous, the only place I know is Kendals.
Dan:	San Marco does all this Italian ice cream, but it's all tucked away in the middle of nowhere.
Sandra Collins:	It's a downstairs one. Those are the only two places for a proper cup of coffee. Even the Royal Exchange, you're not guaranteed one.
Dan:	The best place for coffee is probably Piccadilly Station, they've got one down there.
Sandra:	It's quite good, isn't it.
Phillipa:	That's a real detour.

What is interesting about this exchange is how it demonstrates that even such specialist and non-essential knowledge can be shared in some detail between a group of strangers in a city the size of Manchester. Certainly we had gathered this group together because of some similarities in their shopping patterns (they admitted in our street survey to regular shopping in up-market areas in central Manchester), but in many other respects, they were very dissimilar from each other. But the level of detailed, shared knowledge was definitive of a kind of shared social universe, itself defined in terms of the use of this particular 'part of town'. These same Italian coffee shops were not referred to by any other of our discussion groups, despite our asking them all to tell us where they would go for a cup of tea or coffee whilst in town. We have clear evidence, here, of the heavily socially patterned character of this use of the city.

In the discussions we held with shoppers making use of 'up-market shops' in Sheffield, however, there was a rather different and quite marked interest, focusing on 'value for money' rather more than on what we might call the 'authentic consumer shopping experience', and it was clear that these essentially economic considerations had enormous influence over patronage of particular outlets and also on the routes taken through the city. This question of cost provoked animated discussion amongst a group of 'up-market' shoppers in Sheffield:

Janet Howson:	I go to Atkinsons. You get two cups of tea or coffee for the price of one.
Angela Brewster:	Coles is very expensive. I've stopped going to have tea in there. The tea isn't very good. But they are far too expensive.
Daphne Palmer:	I used to like Rackhams. That's very nice.
Angela:	That's too expensive.
Muriel Bentley:	I go to Rackhams if I want to treat myself.
Daphne:	It's £1.50 for a scone and tea, it's too dear.
Geoffrey Bundy:	I found the nicest cup of coffee in the central library. The café on the top floor.
Reg Jessop:	It's a bit dear.
Geoffrey:	Sixty pence. It's seventy five pence in Coles.
Daphne:	Cole Brothers is very expensive.
Angela:	We go in because it happens to be convenient, but we never really enjoy it.

The continuing search for 'value for money' was a feature of the forays made into town by shoppers in both our cities. But there was a definite sense in 1993 that this pattern of shopping was becoming ever more dominant in Sheffield city centre, as 'the recession' continued in the local economy and the long-term impact of the loss of manufacturing wages coming into households began to be felt. In Manchester city centre – visited by a vast cross-section of the population of the larger urban region – shopping was less obviously restricted to this particular, strategic form – although, even here, it would be simple to identify locations where this kind of shopping predominated.

THE DEPARTMENT STORE AND 'THE CRISIS OF THE CITY CENTRE'

Earlier in this chapter, we identified the nineteenth-century department store as constructing a particular place of safety and also of status endowment for middle-class women. There is absolutely no question that the city-centre department store, for all that its existence is under threat from the out-of-town shopping mall, continues to play this role, however contingently, in our two Northern cities – though rather more precariously in Sheffield than Manchester.

Rackhams in Sheffield (the store now owned by the House of Fraser, originally established by John Walsh) is referenced as a symbolic feature (and also as a boundary) of the Sheffield downtown landscape by middle-class women in that city, providing a particularly clear illustration of the delimitation of safe and appropriate physical space. Discussing her children's independent excursions into town, Jacquie Partridge stressed:

They go as far as the House of Fraser and that is their limit. That's as far as they are safe.

Figure 5.1 The department store as local icon: Kendals, Deansgate, Manchester
Source: photo by Jenny Young

Figure 5.2 The department store as local icon: Cole Brothers, Sheffield
Source: photo by Ian Taylor

Delimiting where she would feel happy going and where not, Sue Blake commented:

> I like Fargate. Rackhams up to Debenhams. I would always shop in that area.

Monica Fletcher clarified why the geographical location of Rackhams is significant:

> Across the road from Rackhams and down, it really is appalling. *That part of town is finished completely.* [Our emphasis]

Rackhams (or 'the House of Fraser') is seen by many women as the boundary between respectable and disreputable parts of town, although this has not necessarily always been the case, as Sue Blake added:

> I'm reasonably young, but I remember shopping with my mum when I was younger. All the market area and what was Schofields, C&A, British Home Stores [i.e. the area 'down' from Rackhams] . . . That was where everyone wanted to go. I've seen that change from my teens.

Nat Feingold, an unemployed Sheffielder, took the argument one step further, whilst also echoing Monica Fletcher's exact phraseology about the northern end of the city centre:

> Obviously from Rackhams . . . *that part of town is finished completely* . . . The IRA can't bomb Sheffield, it's done it itself. [Our emphasis]

In Manchester, it was clear that a key boundary between 'respectable' and 'disreputable' parts of town was Lewis's department store at the corner of Market Street and Piccadilly Gardens, given the negative sentiments which were widely associated for nearly all our different publics with the Gardens, its Piccadilly Plaza 'eyesore' and its bus station (one of the main resorts of 'winos' and other 'vagrants' in the city). As in Sheffield, however, the store and the location had not always had this significance. As Mohammed Ramsahai, a middle-aged professional worker from Oldham, told us:

> In 1961 when I came here [from Pakistan], the most attractive thing in Manchester was Piccadilly centre, Piccadilly Gardens, and then the other well-known building was Lewis's. If anybody who came to Manchester and had never been to Piccadilly Gardens and Lewis's, we used to say 'You haven't been to Manchester'.

The decline of Piccadilly and neighbouring Oldham Street was mentioned in some form or another by nearly everyone we spoke to, although the perceived cause of this decline was not always articulated. For some of the younger people or newcomers to the city, it was not so much the specific sense of loss (of the aura of Lewis's or a safe city-centre garden) as what it represents now: a location that is thought to be threatening or 'out of bounds' because of 'the drunks', homeless people or 'undesirable types' that 'hang around' there. A group of middle-aged and elderly Mancunian women, however, discussed the cause of the change to this area in some detail, clearly identifying Lewis's as a mental boundary:

Pamela Reiss:	I think Piccadilly itself, the area of Piccadilly, since they built the Arndale, has lost its character. It was a really central part that brought the whole city together. Now, with Marks and Spencers being down the other end, and the Arndale being down there, it stops at Lewis's. *It stops there.*
Ingrid Harrison:	There's no atmosphere at all along Oldham Street and *that end of Piccadilly. It's dead.*
Amy Hardcastle:	*It's just been cut off* . . . It's took a lot of the atmosphere away from the city centre. People used to like to go and look in the shop windows. Now all the shops have moved away. Littlewoods, and all these, were in the centre of Piccadilly. They've all moved away to the Arndale.

This sensitivity to the injury that has been inflicted upon Piccadilly is heightened by resentment at what has happened to the fountain in the centre of the Gardens area:

Amy Hardcastle:	But it's a sin about the fountain. Henry's Stores family donated that fountain, and it's been neglected.

The impact that department stores have on the urban landscape is not confined to the presence of the shops themselves: family department store businesses such as Henry's often made a charitable contribution to the non-retail urban environment. The anxiety being expressed about the demise of the city-centre store was in this sense a lament not just for the personal services and a sense of status which these stores delivered to 'bourgeois women', but also for a certain vision of the city – ordered, in particular, around a pleasurable day-time visit to the 'nice shops' and a restaurant, in a city space characterised by some signs of public and private benefaction and aesthetic care.

The department stores of our two Northern cities are not, however, the exclusive preserve of generations who recall their heyday before their gradual supersession by 'niche retailers' on the one hand and superstores on the other.[26] An office worker in her twenties from Sheffield told us how:

We always used to meet at Rackham's, the House of Fraser. Then we'd go up the High Street, onto Campo Lane, the bottom of West Street.

Another older woman, a committed and loyal Coles Brothers customer, described how this loyalty had been passed down to her family, so that her four married children have the same meticulous way of shopping there:

> start[ing] at the bottom, and work[ing] up to each department, then back down. They love Coles.

The demise of the department store is often used as a metaphor for undesirable social or cultural change in the city.[27] One Sheffield-born young woman, Kirstin Lloyd, wondered about the first impressions that visitors must have on coming into Sheffield for the first time:

> I think it just says that Sheffield has lost its direction. I remember Schofields and Cockaynes, they were a brilliant place. Ever since it's been shut they haven't reopened it, it's just stuck in the centre. They've just forgotten it, let it run down, let all the area round there run down. Then they go and invest in areas like Meadowhall.[28]

Danny Haughton looked at a photo on the wall of boarded-up shops in Sheffield city centre and sighed:

> That used to be Cockaynes . . . that has been empty, to my knowledge, for twenty years. That used to be a wonderful shop.

Such expressions of regret in relation to city-centre department stores are also evident in relation to neighbourhood stores. Banners department store in Attercliffe, Sheffield's old industrial East End, was facing final closure during the course of our research. This store was well known locally for giving change to its customers in the form of 'Banners Checks', a coinage which could only be used in Banners store – a measure of the centrality of the place which Banners occupied in local people's lives (East End Publishing 1990). The attempt to keep Banners open by transforming it into a 'small business centre' was eventually rejected by the local Council, who classified the indoor market that emerged as equivalent to a 'car boot sale' (*Star*, 10 October 1992). This may have been acceptable to the remaining residents of the Attercliffe area, but clearly was inconsistent with the reconstruction of the Don Valley as the access route into Meadowhall and the central focus of the new City of Sport, a strategy for the regeneration of Sheffield.

IN SEARCH OF THE BIG BREAKFAST: RETIRED MEN IN THE NORTHERN CITY

A key issue for retired men in Manchester was the question of where one could find a 'decent breakfast' in town, above all one involving 'value for money' and the friendliness of the staff. The absence of a good, friendly café in the city centre was remarked upon, and Littlewoods emerged as a popular substitute:

Walter Harper: From my point of view, I think Littlewoods. If you want a meal there, you can get a meal.

Mr Hill: Don't they do a breakfast?

Walter: That's 99p. Anyone who wants a meal.

Mr Smith: I have one if I come out of the house without breakfast before going into town.

Derek Halstead: I had one when I was in Littlewoods in Preston the other week. I found myself at a bit of a loose end and I had a job to do early on in the morning. It was swimming in fat. In a sort of way, it was a good buy.

Walter: They're very reasonable. I remember when I went in with the wife, you scratched a card off, one, two, three and you got free tea.

John Rollinson: At Stockport, if you go on the Underbank, you can get a meal, fish, chips and bread and butter and that. You've got to show your Senior Citizens Card.

Walter: If you walk down Market Street . . . there's a sign there, as big as me, 75p for a breakfast.

Derek then proceeded to discuss the merits of cafés in the market hall in Blackburn in similar terms:

> It doesn't matter which day you go, it's full of people having a really good meal. Not a pre-processed thing, you're getting a real good steak and kidney pie, chips, peas and so on . . . it's very competitive in price. It's waitress service, they know you, they recognise you, they speak to you, you speak to them by name. It's a marvellous atmosphere. They almost work at the double, but because the people who run the place are all right with them, you get a congenial effect. There is not anywhere in a big city like Manchester, there is absolutely nowhere that all that is on a par with that. If I go into Littlewoods, (a) I don't think the food is that good; (b) I don't actually think it's that cheap; (c) you shuffle along with your tray. You find an anonymous table in a mass of characterless surroundings. Like as not you'll have to clear it . . . if I need or want a meal in Manchester, like as not I will use Littlewoods. I don't find it agreeable, but if needs must.

It may not be stretching the point too far to suggest that for large numbers of elderly Northern men, as well as for many other identifiable social groups in the North (the long-term unemployed and some of the youthful populations), it is precisely these aspects of the consumer outlet (the café or restaurant) which are important. There may also be a sense in which these kinds of criteria are becoming more rather than less important for more and more groups in the larger public of the North of England, as the economic inequalities of the area continue to intensify.

DISABLED PEOPLE AND THE SHOPPING ROUND

Perhaps the most important of all 'subaltern counter-publics' in the shopping sphere are people with some form of physical disability. These variously disabled people are marginalised, by virtue of not being fully 'able-bodied', from the dominant culture – for example, in consumer advertising – and also marginalised historically in terms of specific provisions in public and private buildings, transport and other urban facilities. Our focus group discussions with disabled people in the Disability Forums of Manchester and Sheffield illuminated not only the general problems which people of physical ability experience in most cities, but also some of the key differences for disabled people between these two cities. Like most citizens in Manchester and Sheffield, the disabled people faced the problem of regular, if not daily, shopping, but they also entertained some interest in the idea of shopping for pleasure in the city centre, in shopping malls or in other areas of the city. However, for these citizens, the problems of travel and transportation we identified in Chapter 4, as well as the material infrastructure of the city, took on a specific and more focused character. Particularly in Sheffield, where the hilly terrain creates a particular set of challenges for some people with a physical handicap, and where Meadowhall opened as a major shopping location some distance away from the city centre itself (accessible at the time of our research only by car or bus), the close relationship between shopping and transport provision was inescapable.

The three connected issues of accessibility, integration of routes and timetable restrictions in transport were to the fore in both cities. In Sheffield, however, disabled people were particularly quick to identify the contradiction between their needs for accessible bus transport and the deregulation of municipal bus services in 1986. James Myers recalled how:

> Before deregulation, Sheffield City Transport – they experimented with what they call a Leyland bus. It was a flat entrance bus, and when it pulled up to the kerb, the driver pulled a switch and pneumatic jacks dropped the entrance to the level of the pavement. It was going to be the bus of the future. Then this terrible government brought in deregulation and every Tom, Dick and Harry that had a pound in their pocket that could afford to buy a clapped-out fifteen-year-old bus and put it on the road, did so. You had five or six buses vying for one passenger on every bus stop. The transport – South Yorkshire Transport – who'd been subsidised by the Council, suddenly decided they couldn't go for these accessible buses. They had to buy the cheapest buses they could get so they could compete with these other companies. They got ones with four steps.

Associated with this deregulation of local buses was a breakdown in the idea of an integrated system of routes across the city ('local bus knowledge') on which the disabled, like many elderly people and young mothers, very much depended. There seemed little awareness on the part of private companies of the time that it would take for the disabled to undertake a visit to relatives at some far-flung point in the conurbation, or even a shopping trip. There was some resentment in Sheffield at the local Transport Executive's identification of a 'two-hours' mid-morning period as the recommended time for the disabled to go shopping and make use of their concessionary ticket entitlement, especially as many disabled people wanted to combine these periodic (and personally demanding) visits to town with visits to relatives or friends. The absence of 'public transport' in the evenings, especially in outlying estates and other areas, severely limited possibilities.

For many of the disabled people we met, the 'deregulation' of the city was not just a matter of the competition between transport firms. It was also seen as a breakdown of urban planning, especially with a view to allowing and encouraging the use of space (including shopping space) by people in wheelchairs or otherwise 'encumbered'. The 'redevelopment' of Sheffield's East End, with the opening of Meadowhall at one end and the subsequent development of new sports facilities at the other, was seen as a clear example of such a 'lack of coordination' and planning. Greg Francis thought there was:

> Total fragmentation. Each little bit does its planning in total isolation from all the other bits around it. We could have a beautiful little walkway round that Sheaf Valley that would connect everything to everything, away from the traffic. It would save them money. It would bring them customers and passengers. But do they look at it that way? No, they don't. They look at it from their own point of view. Because the planning is so weak these days, no one can force them to consult with anyone else.

Richie Leigh in Manchester pointed to a similar lack of coordination between the City Council and the local Development Corporations in that city, insisting that 'a lot of the buildings that have been refurbished' by the Corporations had not met the criterion of making all new buildings accessible. The Arndale Shopping Centre in Manchester was praised for efforts it had made, individually, in this respect, in its provision of its own wheelchairs for the disabled in a facility near the underground car park, but the general lack of integration and overall planning of the city by private and public partnerships was a pressing source of concern. On the one hand, the newer shops in Manchester city centre, in particular, were praised for their introduction of electric doors and use of textured surfaces (which were particularly helpful to those walking with a stick), as were the new Metrolink vehicles for their accessibility and the provision of dedicated seats by the entrance of each vehicle; but on the other hand, the lack of attention to the safety of the disabled or the infirm actually on the street, in crowded, congested streets and at particular intersections (the corner of Market Street and Piccadilly Gardens), was a major area of anxiety.

We shall see later, in Chapter 9, how many of these concerns are also shared by mothers with young children, and in Chapter 10 by the elderly. For these 'subaltern counter-publics', indeed, interested as they are in shopping in the city, there is a kind of shared, cultural knowledge of the city as a set of places containing particular hazards and difficulties, largely unapprehended in the 'dominant culture' and unevenly recognised by those private companies with a commercial interest in encouraging their patronage, or by public authorities who are formally responsible for their safety and well-being. We have a specific, situated sense of the routine risks and hazards, as well as the pleasures, of consumption and shopping.

MALL LIFE IN THE NORTH OF ENGLAND: MEADOWHALL

The focus of contemporary writing on the city, by architects and cultural theorists alike, is the shopping mall, particularly the large, out-of-town shopping malls like the MetroCentre in Gateshead (cf. Chaney 1990) and Meadowhall in Sheffield. In this writing, the mood is either one of uncritical celebration of the new sphere of freedom these malls are seen to produce, or of warning as to the new forms of social discipline the malls encourage. Rob Shields's analysis of the mammoth South Edmonton Mall in Edmonton, Canada, tries to dissect some contradictory aspects of the 'spatial performance' of users. In particular, he argues that: 'although the promoted image is one of freedom, unfettered buying and liminality, the reality is one of control, new forms of discipline and surveillance' (Shields 1989: 160). For Shields, following Foucault, the ordered mall with its closed circuit television and central observation chamber is, above all, a contemporary panopticon, involving 'at once surveillance and observation, security and knowledge, individualization and totalization, isolation and transparency' (Foucault 1977: 249). However, in a situation where the 'undisputed aim' of such shopping centres is to encourage spending, there are many who simply 'play at being shoppers' in the mall – the ultimate subversion of the planners' and owners' objectives:

> The users, both young and old, are not just resigned victims, but actively subvert the ambitions of the mall developers by developing the insulation value of the stance of the jaded world-weary flâneur; asserting their independence in a multitude of ways apart from consuming. It is this practice, as opposed to the only too modern centralising ambitions of the mall builder, which is the heart of post-modern experience of the mall.
>
> (Shields 1989: 160)

Meaghan Morris, reacting to both Australian and American exemplars, notes how malls are presented to us, in their own promotional literature, in a very idealised, static and abstract fashion. She also observes that those who develop plans eventually have to confront the social composition of their local customer population. At the same time, malls must attempt to evolve over time, particularly in respect of how they position themselves in the local consumption markets (Morris 1988). Some new-build malls in the 1980s attempted to reflect directly the social composition of their immediate environment. Crystal Peaks in South Sheffield was a local instance of this type of mall:[29] indeed Meadowhall itself commissioned a statue, 'Teeming' (albeit cast in an artist's studio in Tuscany), for its main mall, depicting three Sheffield forge workers pouring molten steel into a crucible.

Morris's commentary is helpful in encouraging our recognition of the kind of local-spatial and temporal considerations that some writing about the mall ignores. Simply because the malls are ready-made shopping and socialising environments without any history, unlike the traditional High Street, this does not preclude the possibility of their being endowed with particular kinds of local meaning – as the sites of culturally specific practices which, we have argued, are a feature of the department store and which, we will argue later, are also put to use in individual shops in neighbourhoods.

Research in Southampton in the early 1990s suggested that the opening of a new shopping mall involved no necessary or final disturbance to established patterns of use of local city centres. Individual use of the mall did not automatically indicate approval of it, especially of its impact on the local economy or city centre, but did indicate that the range of goods in the mall was an improvement on the city centre and that the mall was convenient to use (Whitehead 1992: 7).

The striking feature of Meadowhall, of course, and of the MetroCentre in Gateshead, is the fact of their location in an old industrial area of the North of England, on the edge of cities (Newcastle and Sheffield) that have not defined themselves as metropolitan centres of consumption. Meadowhall itself, as we have already indicated, is built directly on the site of a major Sheffield steelworks, closed in the early 1980s, on the outer edge of a city which has historically seen itself as decidedly non-metropolitan, and even as 'cut off' geographically and culturally from mainstream metropolitan practices in culture and trade. The response of Sheffielders to Meadowhall in that sense is a measure not just abstractly of shoppers' aesthetic response to a new building or even of their psychological appreciation of the convenience of its facilities: it is also a measure of the response of local citizens to a specifically metropolitan icon, a 'temple of consumption'. The majority of Sheffield people we met seemed, at first blush, to exhibit very similar, mixed responses to Meadowhall to the responses of people in Southampton to their new mall. Fear of the mall's effects on the city centre, set against an appreciation of its convenience, were very much apparent, although there was also a range of other reactions. We identified five principal arguments, amongst which one, that of 'principled objection', was the most resonant of a local, Sheffield, reaction. We can illustrate each of these responses in turn.

Discourse of convenience

The convenience of malls such as Meadowhall for many people is undisputable: the parking is free, the opening hours are later than most shops in the city centre, there is the possibility of hiring an electric scooter or wheelchair for those with restricted mobility, and it provides a widely praised crèche. Furthermore, the atmosphere is clean and dry, any litter is swept up immediately and there is a sophisticated surveillance system in operation. The 'Videowall' and the Oasis eatery further extend the concept of the mall as an ideal day out for all the family.

A group of disabled Sheffielders were generally quite enthusiastic about Meadowhall, although some voiced criticism about the slipperiness of the floors, which was perceived to be a product of constant brushing up of litter and polishing, making it dangerous for those who are unsteady on their feet. Other groups also referred to the mall's convenience. Two unemployed people from Sheffield, Hazel Lowe and Steve O'Donnell, agreed on its attractions:

> It's pleasant and everything is in the one area. If it's raining then you're sheltered from the rain.

> Meadowhall, it's laid out nicely, I'll agree with that. They've done a good job with it.

Claire Moran, a clerical worker from Sheffield enthused:

> It's comfortable to shop in . . . there's plenty of eating places.

Jacqui Partridge, an 'up-market shopper' thought that:

> If you're disabled or if you've got babies, then the answer really is to go to Meadowhall. Everything is laid on for you.

Principled objection

Many Sheffield residents expressed concern that Meadowhall was killing city-centre trade and atmosphere, and indicated that they would tend not to visit it on principle. Nat Feingold told us:

> I don't go there. We don't go there on principle. I want to support the shops in the centre of town. We don't want to go because we feel that it's unenvironmental and it's just killing the city centre . . . The chains [stores] that are in Meadowhall are now putting more lines on. Say Marks and Spencers will have far more out there than in the city centre. With the result that nobody shops in M&S in the city

centre. If you go in there wanting a suit or something, people say 'It's not here, you'll have to go to Meadowhall.'

Scott Trueman explained:

> I lived in North America for three years, I saw what happened to the city centres there. As soon as shopping malls came on the scene, on the outskirts of town, the city centre became unsafe at night, unstable. All the shopping was finished. You only went down town for work . . . Houston, New Orleans. New Orleans not so much because it's got a tourist quarter. Where you get shopping malls ringing the town, the shopping dies in the centre of town. Take the small shops away, take the town centre shops away and you've got nothing but a dead American city. This is what's happening in Sheffield.

Sheffield and Meadowhall are two different places

A significant number of our Sheffielders, who we sensed were typical of a large body of local opinion, felt quite strongly that Meadowhall and Sheffield were two separate places. Kirstin Lloyd worked in a Sheffield hotel and found herself directing visitors to Meadowhall. She told us:

> [I tell them that] it's two miles down that road. Then they'll ask where the city centre is and I'll tell them that it's just down that way. It's then when it hits you that you really are directing people out of the city centre . . . they always ask if they can walk to Meadowhall. You can see them looking and thinking why's that there in that area? It just brings them [visitors] to Meadowhall. It doesn't bring them to the city centre. It doesn't bring them to the things that we've got to offer, like the theatres, the cultural parts. It just brings them to Meadowhall.

This feeling is reinforced by the findings of our survey of Meadowhall users. Of 184 people surveyed there over one week, 58 per cent came from towns or cities outside Sheffield, and most of these people claimed not to know the city centre at all. Others were concerned that Meadowhall had done little for Sheffield people. Some Sheffield police officers were among them:

> It's done nothing for the local population at all. It causes traffic problems.

> When you consider how many Edgar Allen's [steelworks on whose derelict site Meadowhall was built] employed. The majority of people who use it are probably not even from Sheffield.

However, its appeal remains insidious: Josephine Armitage, a young woman not originally from Sheffield, explained:

There's things that I sort of like about it. I go to the cinema. But it's quite frightening, the way it's like America. What's sort of weird about it is that there's almost sort of nothing to buy. Everything is exactly the same . . . what's frightening about it is that it overtakes. It's frightening how much you can get sucked into that feeling of . . . I don't know, it's just . . . nothingness. It's like watching television that you know is not very good. You sort of enjoy it at the time, but you know that it's not good for you. That it's not stimulating your brain.

Non-plussed by Meadowhall

Many Sheffielders simply seemed non-plussed by Meadowhall, and had perhaps been once or twice, just to have a look, or not at all. Imran Akbar had never been:

I've not been but I've heard about it. They say everything's dear.

Helen-Anne Goode was also unenthusiastic about Meadowhall:

We went once and had a look around and that was it. I just don't shop there.

Heather Moody visited it primarily for its restaurants:

I've been to Meadowhall, not to shop, because I'm the sort of person who'll shop in town. I've been down there on my birthday.

The celebration of Meadowhall

There are those, however, who expressed unreserved admiration for Meadowhall, and interestingly these often tended, in our research, to be older residents who had lived through many changes in the city already. Geoff Helliwell and Geoffrey Bundy opined:

I think it's a marvellous structure. I know it's done a lot of harm to the city centre, but it was derelict steel works land. It has improved the environment round there . . . most of the work was done by Italians. It's great. The marble floors and the pillars. It's all come from Italy, a lot of this. It's really a superb building, there's no question about that. The building itself is absolutely marvellous – the structure and everything about it – it's a palace.

I just wanted to say, in my opinion, for anyone with a car, Meadow-hall is the best thing since sliced bread.

Edith Boardman was delighted with Meadowhall:

There's lots of forms to sit down on . . . there's a lot of seats, it's lovely. . . you go down these little side streets – there's all shops, then you get into the Oasis where all the food is . . . it's the best thing that's ever come to Sheffield.

The prevailing local folk wisdom in Sheffield, however, was that goods at Meadowhall are more expensive than they are in town. For many, this was deterrence enough, particularly on the part of those who have never been or been only once or twice. The group of retired men and women in the Afro-Caribbean Centre in Sheffield told us they considered it 'too dear', as did members of our group of unemployed and retired manual workers. The Oasis eating area, particularly, was considered 'a bit on the expensive side' by many. What a focus group conversation does not reveal, however, in and of itself, is the extent to which these kinds of account (discourses of cost and economy) are also an expression of the antipathy to metropolitan growth and 'development' which is an important defining element in the 'structure of local feeling' in old industrial enclave cities like Sheffield.

A group of mainly unemployed Pakistani women from the Nether Edge area of Sheffield were nevertheless very keen on Meadowhall, principally because they could go there with their husbands and families during the evening and parking was free. They were also impressed by the fact that there was now a Pakistani restaurant in the mall. Mabuba Razhar indicated he would like to see a fresh produce market there:

The only thing I miss is having a market. If they had that then I would never go to town.

However, a 'real' street market would, of course, contradict the principles of ordered, sedate consumption on which the new malls claim to be founded. Certainly, the only market in Meadowhall at present is a simulated Mediterranean street market with stalls of pre-packaged trinkets. In the imagination of the Meadowhall management, a 'real' market would risk attracting precisely the sorts of people associated with the unruly city-centre markets whom a significant number of 'up-market' mall shoppers go to Meadowhall to avoid.

Meadowhall had been in existence for some five years, at the time of writing, and had established itself as the leading shopping centre in the UK in terms of overall turnover, ahead of the MetroCentre in Gateshead and Merry Hill outside Dudley in Warwickshire (*Manchester Evening News* 24 January 1995). The Meadowhall management and the Sheffield Development Corporation have been at pains to emphasise the importance of Meadowhall in bringing visitors and 'spending power' to Sheffield: in the summer of 1993, they gave great publicity to a study from Sheffield Hallam University showing that 20.2 million people had visited the city in 1992, with 16.9 million aiming for Meadowhall. The local paper's coverage of this report argued that this made Meadowhall a more popular destination than Blackpool (Whitehouse 1993). In the meantime, the city centre of Sheffield continued to show evidence of decline.

It may be more accurate, in fact, to identify the emergence of what Dr Gwyn Rowley (in the *Independent* 22 February 1992) calls a 'geographic dichotomy', or what we would want to see as a new and fundamental social division in the city – between those who can afford to shop at Meadowhall and come to feel a sense of belonging in the mall, and those who cannot, at least with any degree of regularity, and do not feel any such sense of belonging. For the latter population, we should remember, the city centre was often a necessary destination for other reasons (the Social Security Offices, the Town Hall), but the personal commitment to the city centre, albeit in its dilapidated state in the early 1990s, was often also underwritten by protests of local pride and loyalty. What has yet to be seen is whether the arrival of the Supertram in Sheffield, bringing passengers from outlying estates directly into the city centre and also into Meadowhall, further reconstructs the recently reorganised local stratification of the shopping population.

SHOPPING TO SURVIVE IN SHEFFIELD

Whilst we must pay attention to changes in consumption patterns brought about by the arrival of Meadowhall in Sheffield, we should not be deluded into thinking that the core shopping of North of England people as a whole is carried out in malls. In the United States there were in October 1990 some 25,000 out-of-town malls, and the bulk of the family shopping would be completed at stores located inside these complexes (*Guardian* 26 October 1990). In Britain in 1995 there were only five such major out-of-town shopping malls. The bulk of the family shopping in Britain was done in supermarkets, in the city centre (including 'the markets'), the neighbourhood High Street or, in some localities, still, indeed, 'in the Co-op'. In amongst the shoppers patronising these locations, particularly in the city centres, are those for whom 'going shopping' is about the collection of the pension or the dole cheque, picking up bargains at the market or at the 'Lo-Cost' supermarket, going to the Electricity Board shop to add credits to their meter card, having a cheap lunch of fish and chips, then coming home again, making sure that the bus taken is from the same company as that which was used coming into town in order that the return ticket will be valid. We refer to this shopping public as 'subsistence shoppers'.

THE LOCAL SHOPPING OF THE POOR

Despite often being considerably more costly, local shops are often relied upon very heavily by subsistence shoppers. Lack of access to private transport means that shopping will be carried out several times a week, and it may be more convenient to purchase heavier items nearer to home, to save having to carry them on the bus or long distances, perhaps with children in tow as well. Purchasing basic items from shops near to home cuts a person off from 'temptation' to buy 'non-essential'

Figure 5.3 The local shopping of the poor: Asian corner store, Cheetham Hill, Manchester
Source: photo by Karen Evans

items that cannot be afforded. Local shops can also serve an ethnic minority community with specialist foodstuffs and other items that are not found in the city centre. The elderly Chinese people living in sheltered accommodation in Chinatown relied on the Chinese super-market and bakery located in the heart of their local area, that is, in the heart of Manchester city centre itself. The Asian women from Nether Edge did much of their shopping in the Asian goods shops near where they live.

Traditional neighbourhood shopping areas, having felt the first wave of the retail revolution (the opening of supermarkets) and now confront-ing the out-of-town centre, continue to be in decline. Spital Hill in Pitsmoor, Sheffield, is a prime example of such a down-market district centre, serving as a marked contrast in that city to Ecclesall Road in the West End. Spital Hill now has many boarded-up shops, causing the overall atmosphere to be one of neglect, 'dead space' and poverty, yet several people remembered it in its heyday, when it was a thriving shopping street. Heather Moody:

> I used to live quite close to there and when I was quite small it was such a lovely area. We used to shopping round there. You didn't have to go into town. Going into town was a treat. These days it's a place I wouldn't go to on my own at night . . . there's some really shady characters about.

The following discussion arose among a group of women of different ages:

Penny Fraser:	Are there any places that we haven't mentioned, that you would consider to be the worst parts of Sheffield?
Monica Fletcher:	This area here [pointing to photograph of Spital Hill] is quite bad. That used to be really nice. Now it's all boarded-up shops.
Margaret Godfrey:	Spital Hill, years ago that was a nice area.
Avril Hetherington:	Spital Hill is grotty.
Maureen Gilmour:	It used to be a lovely shopping centre.
Karen Evans:	What sort of shops did they used to have there?
Margaret:	Everything.
Maureen:	I used to shop there when I lived in Pitsmoor. I used to walk from where I lived. I used to have a great big coach-built pram. I'd got to walk up a big hill to get back home. Often I'd have my three-year-old son underneath on the shopping basket, he were fast asleep. I'd be panting with a pile of shopping.
Avril:	You could get everything on Spital Hill.
Monica:	You'd get a pork butchers, then a general butchers. You'd get little specialist shops, for such a small area.

Folk memories of Spital Hill are strong and affectionate. The women quoted above no longer go there for shopping, but many other local residents still use the depleted shopping facilities (a mini-market and another small grocery chain) and the post office, 'for convenience'. A neighbourhood occasional broadsheet, the *Pitsmoor People's Press*, first published in the summer of 1992, features a piece in its November edition on the apparent betrayal of local interests by the Council, which had designated Spital Hill an 'improvement area'. As the news sheet puts it, this was taken as a sign that local people were 'finally being taken seriously'. However, it transpired that the Council's promises of an 'improved shopping area' were misleading and that they would only meet half of the improvement costs. Then came news that a government grant for the improvement work was to be reduced, following which the scheme collapsed entirely and traders lost money that they had already put into it.

OUT-OF-TOWN SHOPPING: RACE, CITY, COUNTRY

A striking feature of the practices of many Mancunians and Sheffielders of Afro-Caribbean and Asian background was the strong links maintained with London and other major conurbations such as Birmingham, Leeds, Leicester, Bradford and even Manchester (in the case of many Sheffielders). Links to these places seem to be initiated and established through visits to members of the extended family, followed by exploration of local specialist food stores. Generally, references to London in

Manchester and Sheffield were negative, but Asian and Afro-Caribbean people talked enthusiastically about inner-city London's fresh produce markets – Southall and the East End for Asian people and Brixton and Hackney for Afro-Caribbeans. According to Ray Watkins, from a retired persons' Lunch Club in Sheffield:

> The market's all right. The only problem, if you can call it a problem, is that food in Sheffield is always more expensive than, like, London. Fruit's a lot cheaper than Sheffield . . . it gets delivered there so doesn't have to travel so far. But from London to Sheffield!!! Fruits like yam, banana, things like that, are a lot dearer than London . . . Hackney, Brixton, any part of London there's more markets, more varieties.

It seems clear that the use of the city by Sheffielders of Asian background, especially the city centre, is much more cautious and sparing than for many other identifiable groups of the local public, but, as we discuss more fully in Chapter 8, it was actually a more extensive and engaged use of the city than was that by young Afro-Caribbeans, for whom the city was very clearly a hostile, white environment.

THE MARKETS

The existence of two types of market in Sheffield, located at either end of the city centre, and the personal alignment of individual Sheffield shoppers with either one of these markets or the rejection of both, has provided an additional (and unexpected) dimension to our social taxonomy of public space. In Sheffield, the 'real' markets are located in the run-down northernmost segment of the city centre, beyond the Rackhams watershed. But, as we indicated earlier, there is now a street market at the other end of the city centre on The Moor, a product of developments since 1980. However, when most Sheffielders talk about 'the markets' they are not referring to the one on The Moor, although it is now sufficiently well established to be a permanent feature of that area. A Sheffield police constable with responsibility for patrolling the central area summed up the social composition of these markets in the following way:

> I think the true Sheffielders live in Crookes, Hillsborough, what have you. They travel into town by bus. Rough, working-class, honest upstanding people who use the markets. It's the poorer people who use the markets. They are a bit coarser . . . I'm ashamed to say almost, they're a different social class from me . . . I don't look down on them, I like them and it's one of the reasons I call them true Sheffielders . . . you get pushed and shoved about a bit at the market, they don't say please and thank you.

These markets have a readily accessible mental image for this officer: that of a particular social class, indeed a particular strand within that class – the 'honest' or 'respectable' working class or 'true Sheffielders'. Our own conversations with users of these markets revealed a pattern of use that can be clearly distinguished from that of the market on The Moor. However, even among users of these 'real' markets, an interesting distinction appears between those who visit them routinely and those who use them more sporadically, and this distinction comes across strongly in the way in which they express their relationship to the markets.

First and foremost, the markets are visited unselfconsciously by many older people for whom a trip to the market is an integral part of their weekly routine, Fridays emerging as the most popular day for visits:

Geoff Helliwell:	White fish can only be had down the market . . . then into Sheaf Market for vegetables for the week-end . . .
Scott Trueman:	I'm within walking distance to the market, so anything I need . . . there's no fresh fish stall in Burngreave [where he lives] . . . I wouldn't stray more than a mile from the house. I've no reason to . . . There is everything in that community. I'm close enough to the markets.
Alf Webb:	Monday dinner I do my shopping – Castle Market.

The following discussion emerged from another group of shoppers:

Penny Fraser:	Which part of town would you go to?
Rita Peasgood:	'Round the market and High Street.
Penny:	Would you go to the market for specific things? . . .
Rita:	I go for specific things. I do a lot of sewing for my family. I go for lining and curtaining.
Henry Hemsworth:	I go to the market . . . on a Friday . . . My friend, she goes round the market better than me. We always go together.
Penny:	Does anybody else use the markets?
Edith Boardman:	Yes, I do. I use it Fridays.
Danny Haughton:	I've found most of the fish market and what I call the vegetable market, the prices are so low you cannot compete anywhere . . . I got three pounds of minced beef, it cost me one pound in money . . . for us that's three main-course meals.

These people visit the markets because the goods there are cheap and for some they are on the right side of town for where they live. A visit to the market can also be a social occasion (as distinct from a leisure occasion, which might be a way of describing a visit to Meadowhall). Danny Haughton, looking for bargains in the market, had noticed how:

Women always seem to stand in a group in the middle of the road. Especially at the fish market, it's crowded. They're always standing in the middle of the path. They either chat or they are looking at the counters, they don't know what they're buying.

Parveen, a young Pakistani woman, reflected:

> When I got married I came from London [to Sheffield]. Six brothers-in-law. I was mixed with girls. Suddenly you come to a family where it's all boys. I had nothing in common with them . . . My neighbours were old people. I'd go to the market, meet people. I realised it was like Coronation Street, everyone tells you their problems.

Angela McRobbie, writing primarily about the appeal of the street market for youthful consumerism and fashion identity, emphasises that:

> The popularity of these urban markets also resides in their celebration of what seem to be pre-modern modes of exchange. They offer an oasis of cheapness where every market day is a 'sale'. They point back in time to an economy unaffected by cheque cards, credit cards and even set prices.
>
> (McRobbie 1989: 29–30)

> [The street market] lacked the impersonality of the department store and thrived instead on the values of familiarity, community and personal exchange. This remains the case today.
>
> (*ibid.*: 31)

There is also what we consider to be a more 'self-conscious' and occasional use of the 'real' markets. These users of the market are probably more at ease in a department store or in some other, more impersonal High Street store, but have some use for the markets, and would not consider them as places to avoid. Within this category there are Sheffielders and tourists or newcomers, who regard markets with some curiosity. Those Sheffielders, primarily involved in what, with no conscious irony, we have called 'up-market shopping', talked of the markets in the following terms:

Angela Brewster: I'm not a market person. I will go down to the market and have a walk through, specially for the small things that I need, but I don't like the crowding and the pushing. I'm not awfully keen on the market.

Monica Fletcher: I'm having to collect [my mother's] pension and see to everything, so obviously I'm in the market area a lot, at least three times a week, which depresses me. It's not very nice. It doesn't look attractive, it's dirty, smelly . . . it really has gone down. It's terrible . . . the only time I go in the market is to have my shoes heeled. Although it's the same company it's cheaper in the market. It's only 99 pence whereas everywhere else is two pound something. Or if I want any dress material. That is about the only time I will go in that area.

Tourists or newcomers to the city cast a very different gaze over the bustling market scene. They can sample the social diversity, the cheap wares and the 'pre-modern' quality of social relations benevolently, because it is not somewhere to which they will return. Indeed, if anyone can be considered as having a leisure usage of these markets it is these people. Josephine Armitage, a young woman from the south of England who had lived in Sheffield for a few years, explained her position to older women in the group:

> It's interesting what you say about the market area. I've hardly been down those areas, I wouldn't know . . . where I'm from, you just didn't have markets, things like that, so it was really quite an interesting place to go. With everything so cheap, it was great.

Angela Brewster, a regular user of the 'up-market' shops in Sheffield, remembered how:

> About three years ago I had two young Russians come to stay with me. They thought Sheffield was absolutely fantastic . . . when they'd admired everything, they wanted to go to the market. They bought all sorts there. I remember thinking that I don't know my own city. I saw a different side of the city when they were with me.

Figure 5.4 Poor people's street markets in the 1990s: The Moor, Sheffield, August 1995
Source: photo by Sarah King

The street market at the other end of town, on The Moor, is attractive to some people who might not consider visiting the 'real' (covered) markets, but who enjoy the search for a bargain, the haggling and the quick sale that have been institutionalised on the poor people's street market on The Moor (the pleasures of this particular kind of 'free market'). There are also those for whom the whole market concept is repellent. Returning to the policeman's original formulation of market users, these people are of 'a different class' and the predominant image of the markets for these people is that they are the preserve of:

> [the] vagrants down there. It's not their fault that they're homeless, drunks, what have you. You don't feel very happy about having to associate with them.

Two women, unprompted, told us how they would be unhappy about their children going to the markets and also how they set boundaries for their children, who were negotiating for greater independence:

Greta Drabble: From the point of view of pickpockets I'd hope that she wouldn't go to the market. She's got no security sense about purses.

Alison Morrison: They [the children] are not allowed to go any further than the Hole in the Road. I won't have them under the Hole in the Road. That's the whole of the Sheaf Market, they're not allowed to go there at all.

Markets have always been associated with the troublesome, unruly sections of the working class and lumpenproletariat (already, in the popular imagination, predisposed to crime and delinquency). Phil Cohen echoes the commentaries of Charles Dickens in writing about the increasing regulatory and punitive authority meted out by the London police in late Victorian inner-city Islington, North London, against street traders ('costers'), and the retreat of the 'labour aristocracy' and the middle classes from these sites of the irregular economy (Cohen 1979). It is perhaps no coincidence, therefore, that the markets in Sheffield have been chosen as the first site in Sheffield city centre to be placed under the surveillance of closed circuit television (*Sheffield Star* 31 August 1992).

Several people carefully distinguished between the 'proper' markets, which they would avoid, and The Moor street market, which has a different feel to it:

Alison Morrison: The proper market . . . I go in for, I knit dolls and sometimes go for toy filling, and I can't get out quick enough. I look around and see them, they're coughing all over the chicken portions, I think 'God, how can people'. I feel so depressed round the market. I never go unless I have to. Down The Moor, I like the market affair that's down The Moor.

Monica Fletcher: I like that part of The Moor. You get the market part, yet you're not in the dirty Sheffield Castle Market, or Sheaf Market. It's a different type of atmosphere. They may be the same traders, but it feels better.

'GETTING IN THE RATIONS': SOCIAL INEQUALITY AND DISCOUNT SUPERMARKETS

The relocation of many supermarkets into the outer suburbs has hit hardest at people living in the inner city who have no access to cars (Gardner and Sheppard 1989). This can leave many without adequate grocery facilities in their neighbourhood at all. Local residents may have to rely only on corner stores which stay open late in the evening, with a 'mark-up' price on all goods, even daily 'essentials'. Alternatively, there may be access to one or other of the cheap discount stores or mini-markets which have emerged, especially in poorer and inner-city areas, to service the so-called 'giro economy'.

Nearly every group of people that we spoke to discussed the tendency for supermarkets to move out into the suburbs, some with regret, others with approval. Walter Harper, retired manual worker from Manchester, regretted the fact that:

> They're putting these shopping centres outside the town, where it means you have got to have transport to get to them. How they are having them now in these outlying districts, it's terrible. You've got to have transport. They'll do away with all these shops. Big projects they are; Sainsburys and all them people.

Whereas Doreen Dart, also living in Manchester and retired, welcomed these facilities:

> I of course have been going a great deal to the hypermarket, Sainsburys at Heaton Park, that's very pleasant to go and shop there. It's convenient for me, I've just got to go a short distance on the bus. It's very pleasant, there's a coffee shop there, toilets, all the facilities. I think that what is good are these hypermarkets that are being built on the outskirts of the cities, they are going to draw people out of the cities.

For most of the poorer shoppers we met during our research, however, 'Sainsbury's' and the other supermarkets were too difficult to reach without a car or else the basic essentials on which they depend were too costly there. The first of the discussions below is from Sheffield and the second from Manchester:

Rita Peasgood: Morrisons [supermarket]. I don't think I have come across one that hasn't had a nice assistant. They're friendly.

Penny Fraser: Do other people go to Morrisons?

Katherine Brooks: Not every week. When I'm a bit down on my tea,

	things like that, then I go and build it up again . . . it's cheaper than all the other supermarkets.
Danny Haughton:	I think Lo-Cost is cheaper.
Kath:	I think you've got to shop around. Asda is usually cheap.
Danny:	*That's out of the way for me.*
Kath:	I think Sainsburys is about the dearest for food.
Walter Harper:	Sainsburys and all them people. They're the most expensive that there is. Sainsburys, you buy stuff there, the prices are terrible . . . if you go to Kwiksave, they're ten times cheaper.
Geoff Greenhalgh:	When I'm going round, I'm looking for bargains. Kwiksave is the cheapest for sugar. But I've found that Rusholme Kwiksave is cheaper than Wythenshawe . . . [I] shop for other people. There's one lady, she likes the tea from Tesco's.
Albert Swan:	When you go to Tesco's do you buy other things? It's notorious for being expensive.
Geoff:	It depends. Sometimes the margarine is cheaper.

The growth of the discount mini-markets (like Kwiksave or Discount Shopper) is one of the more under-researched aspects of life in the North of England, and we would not claim to have researched it systematically ourselves. We have not, for example, analysed the relationship between a discount mini-market that is part of a national chain and a corner store, along, say, dimensions of personal trust. What our research does make clear is the importance of these shopping sites in the recursive shopping of the poor.

FLÂNEURS IN THE HIGH STREET

It has not been our concern to deny the presence in these cities of the kinds of casual and pleasurable shopping described in so much of the contemporary writing of commentators on the post-modern city, but it has been our concern to situate this particular shopping style in amongst a mix of other shopping publics. There is no question, in the meantime, that the more 'well-off', suburban residents of North of England cities engage in very different shopping practices to those of the 'subsistence' bargain hunters. So, far from staying away from temptation – in the shape of goods which cannot ever be afforded (one tactic of the unemployed or less well-off), 'up-market' shoppers do treat themselves to the aesthetic experience of browsing the expensive stores. Shoppers we spoke to in Manchester routinely shopped in the city for 'non-essential' items, above all in the department store, which holds a 'visual fascination' for them (Laermans 1993: 92): it is more than just a 'site for consumption [being also] a *sight* of consumption' (*ibid.*, citing Ewen and Ewen 1982, emphasis in original). But this does not mean that our suburban *flâneurs* and *flâneuses* in the North of England never engage themselves in routine shopping – 'for the groceries'[30] or for bargains – in the markets or subsistence stores.

In response to a question about her shopping routines, Phillipa Franks responded immediately:

> I've got two patterns . . . I get my rations at Kwiksave, basics . . . Any pleasure shopping, or shopping that involves choice, the nearest proper bakers I know of is Kendals. I get all my bread at Kendals, because it's from a Jewish bakery and it's absolutely delicious. Marks and Spencers for fancy food . . . it's usually a pleasure expedition, things that I need, then a little look round the clothes shops.

It is remarkable how often Ms Franks and other 'up-market' shoppers referred to this routine shopping as a sphere, particularly, of pleasure. The conversation continued:

Sandra Collins:	I tend to do my shopping in Manchester if I'm going, say, to the Royal Exchange to a play or a lunchtime talk. I never come into Manchester without going into Kendals and getting some of their ham on the bone.
Pauline Scott:	I do that as well.
Esther Atwood:	I've a neighbour, an old man who's 70-odd, and I get him ham from Kendals.
Pauline:	I would think that I come to Manchester about once a fortnight. That is what I call pleasure shopping. That's the clothes or make-up or present shopping. I think, like you, I always go to Kendals and Marks and Spencers. Those are never missed. Sometimes I'll go to Lewis's, sometimes I may go to Debenhams, but Kendals and Marks I always go to . . . that's why I come, for the department stores and for the nice shops around King Street and St Ann's Square.
Sandra:	It's nice to come and look, isn't it? Look at all the things you can't *really* afford . . . that's the pleasure. You go in Marks and you know that you can afford those things. But if you go in Kendals, you can't.
Penny Fraser:	But you still like to have a look?
Sandra:	Oh, yes. It's so beautifully laid out. There's the window dressing and everything. It's just beautiful.
Pauline:	The other thing that's really just pure pleasure is the bookshops that are open late.

We noted earlier how the more up-market or exclusive shops in Sheffield, on the other hand, are found outside the city centre, on Ecclesall Road, cutting through the middle-class suburbs of Hunters Bar, and in Crookes. The ordinariness of Sheffield city centre's shopping facilities is lamented:

Jacquie Partridge: I just feel that if I want ordinary things, then Sheffield is ideal . . . but if you want something exclusive, forget it in Sheffield.

Angela Brewster: I agree. I wondered why my daughter keeps going to Leeds, York and somewhere else. She's always coming back with different clothes that I've not seen in Sheffield.

The suggestion here is that the idea of being a *flâneur* in Sheffield, even in the last decade of the twentieth century, would present something of a challenge, most probably restricting any determined Sheffielder to the 'Westside' of the city (Broomhill and Ecclesall Road) and a rather selective use of certain outlets in the Meadowhall Shopping Centre. In this last respect, indeed, Sheffield may be quite typical of many cities in the post-industrial North of England (and elsewhere in this 'old country') in the contradictions and obstacles it presents, in terms of both physical fabric and received cultural contexts, to the iconic, leisured consumer of 'High Modernity'. It contrasts, in particular, with the possibilities that are presented in the pedestrianised up-market shopping areas, arcades and wine bars of central Manchester.

CONCLUDING THOUGHTS

We have tried in this lengthy chapter to present a taxonomy of different kinds of shopping practice that appear to be current in Manchester and Sheffield, grounded in the accounts of the different people who identified themselves as heavy or regular shoppers in our street survey and subsequently accepted our invitation to attend a focus group discussion. Our objective has been to produce a grounded sociological account of the variety of shopping practices that are engaged in, on a daily or weekly basis, in these two cities. Along with writers in the cultural studies field, we are very much convinced of the importance of the daily and weekly shopping in structuring the personal lives and cultural world of citizens, but, along with writers in other traditions (for example in economic history) we recognise that the practices of many citizen-shoppers are heavily influenced by 'the sphere of economic necessity'. Always cutting across both these different realms – the culture of consumption and the realm of economic necessity, as it impinges directly on different sections of the public – in these two long-established industrial cities, is a locally well-known mental map of the city as a set of shopping locations. It comprises, as we have tried to show, the neighbourhood corner store, the Co-op, or the local High Street or shopping centre for 'necessities', but also the city-centre department store, youth outlets, the markets old and new, and the mall.

Local awareness of these locations and the territories they occupy, and the boundaries to these territories, is very widespread, but there is a marked social pattern to the actual use and patronage of these spaces.

Table 5.1 A taxonomy of shopping in the North of England

Shopping locale	Social and spatial attributes			
	Declared individual motivation	Cultural resonance	Geographical purchase	Primary user 'public'
Corner store	Convenience*	Neighbourliness	Neighbourhood	Neighbours
High Street/ local shops	Convenience, necessity	Everyday routine	Neighbourhood/ locality	Locals
Discount supermarket	Essential supplies, economy, cash payment only	Poverty	Locality	New Poor
The Co-op	Saving**, convenience, necessities	Co-operation	The North	Old working class
Covered markets***	Cost, ethnic and fresh food	Personal service, sociability (the agora); risk	Town/city	Working-class wives, ethnic minorities
New markets	Bargains, haggling	Pleasures of the market	Town/city	New poor, transient middle class
Secondary shopping town centre	Avoidance of the big city, crowds, accessibility	Small town/ tradition/ friendliness	Small towns/ conurbation	The town
Department store	High consumption	Distinction	Region	Old money, suburbia
City-centre, youth outlets	Style/'being seen'	'Teenager' as a social category	Region	Teenage consumers
Malls	Efficiency, ease of use, safety, cleanliness, parking	Global consumption	Region	New *flâneurs*
Fashion corridors	Power dressing	The edge of style, power	Mobile populations	New business class
Garden centres	Gardening stuff	Weekend leisure	City	First-time buyers, other homeowners

Notes:
* Key defining aspects of the corner store include the availability of credit ('tick') and also personal trust relationships between the customer and corner store owner.
** Cooperative societies in the North (and elsewhere) continue to offer membership of the society and annual dividends to members.
*** Manchester as an exception in the North of England (see n. 1).

Some of these shopping facilities will be seen, especially by protagonists of the shopping mall and other contemporary consumerist outlets, to be dated relics of the past. Local Co-op shops in the North of England no longer deal with 'dividend books', and the Cooperative wing of the Labour Party is no longer an obviously powerful force in national politics, but, given the increasing inequalities involved in continuing free market developments, it is not clear that the kind of local shopping represented by the Co-op, with its emphasis on cheap daily necessities, is about to be transcended. The same logic of increasing inequality will underwrite the continuing growth of new clusters of expensive 'high fashion', leisure goods and sportswear both in the city centre and in the more affluent suburbs of our cities (Wilmslow and Alderley Edge just south of Greater Manchester) or along certain urban corridors (Ecclesall Road in Sheffield). The mistake that can be made, by cultural theorists and sociologists alike, is to miss out on the complexity and contradictions involved in shopping, and what Raymond Williams would have seen as the dynamic mix of emergent and 'residual' social forms. We are now in a position to present a basic taxonomy of shopping practices in these two cities in tabular form (Table 5.1).

Shopping is a vital human activity in the 1990s, conducted in the spheres of both necessity and pleasure. The ways in which that shopping is undertaken through these different urban spaces is a key element in the construction of a personal sense of the city for citizens; or, perhaps more accurately, a sense of the local city as it is available for the use of citizens with different levels of social and economic resource. It is also centrally implicated in the sense of well-being, fear or anxiety which people experience in their city. Our overall argument is, indeed, that it is important to understand local fears and pleasures in the city in such specific sociological terms, focusing on actual patterns of urban routine, rather than to speak in abstractions (as do so many cultural commentators, on the one hand, and technical writers on urban fear, say, in applied criminology, on the other) as if there is only one – essentially leisured and consumerist – sensibility involved in shopping in the city. These are issues to which we return in some detail in Chapter 10. So also, finally, it is important to recognise the routine and recursive character of much of the people's shopping in old industrial cities (like Manchester and Sheffield), and to understand, as we have tried to do here, the coexistence of shopping to survive with shopping for pleasure.

Part III

IT TAKES ALL FOLKS: DIFFERENT PUBLICS IN MANCHESTER AND SHEFFIELD

6

ON OUR UPPERS

Poverty and Homelessness in Manchester and Sheffield

THE POVERTY OF ENGLAND AND WALES, MANCHESTER AND SHEFFIELD IN THE MID-1990S

Despite many protestations to the contrary by apologists of free market economics, experience in Britain (as well as in the United States) since 1979 suggests that increases in poverty and social inequality are a given feature of free market societies – a logical consequence of the adoption of free market policies at national level. A large number of studies now document, in considerable quantitative detail, the scale of the 'social revolution' that has taken place in Britain in the 1980s and early 1990s, which has put into fast reverse the slow movement which had been taking place through the earlier post-war period towards a more equal distribution of wealth in Britain (cf. for example, Walker 1990).[1] Official Department of Social Security figures, released in July 1994, showed that the poorest tenth of the population of England and Wales suffered a 17 per cent fall in real income after housing costs between 1979 and 1991–2, compared to an average income increase of 36 per cent: the richest tenth of the population enjoyed an increase of 62 per cent.[2] These figures almost certainly underestimate the scale of the social revolution in question, since they rely so heavily on the numbers of people registered for work or willing to answer the Census and other survey enquiries. It is now widely accepted that very large numbers of people in 'the inner city' and other deprived areas do not so register.[3] In November 1994, it was estimated that almost a third of full-time workers in Britain (about 5.5 million in total) were earning less than the 'threshold of decency' set by the Council of Europe – in other words, that their wages were actually the 'wages of poverty' (*Guardian* 22 November 1994, reporting a survey by the House of Commons Library). This increase in levels of poverty is the subject of some essentially rather cold-blooded academic and political debate, particularly as to whether the poverty in question is 'absolute' or merely relative (i.e. by comparison to what were celebrated as increasing levels of 'comfort' elsewhere within the same society). So also there is some interest in both academic and political circles as to the unevenness of the general increase in poverty – however measured – and inequality.

Even within quite small regions of the country, there is evidence of considerable concentration of poverty within particular neighbourhoods or towns and, therefore, of a very local form of income inequality: particular towns or rural areas within the same region may be relatively prosperous by virtue of some helpful local economic development, where other towns or urban areas may seem to be locked into a spiral of decline, and to have become what Massey and Meegan, in their pioneering work on the unevenness of de-industrialisation and its effects, called 'sinks of unemployment' (Massey and Meegan 1982).

This unevenness is, in one sense, at the very heart of our comparative examination of the cities of Manchester and Sheffield. But it is important also to register, or re-emphasise, that poverty and inequality are no new social phenomena or experiences for the North of England as a whole. The unevenness of fate and fortune within England has been discussed for most of this century in terms of the idea of the 'North–South Divide' and was a topic of public discussion even during the heyday of mass manufacturing and full employment. In 1979, after some 34 years of post-war social reconstruction, the three North of England Census regions (the North, the North-west, and Yorkshire and Humberside) – the heartlands of mass unemployment and outright poverty during the inter-war depression – were once again experiencing significantly more poverty than every other region of England and Wales. The average weekly household income in 1979–80 in the North (Cumbria, North Yorkshire, Tyneside and Teesside, including Newcastle and Sunderland) was £119.30, and in the Yorkshire and Humberside region only £116.70. The North-west household income was £128.00. In the South-east, by comparison, the figure was £153.20, making this by some distance the most affluent region of the country (Winyard 1987: Table 6). In the South-east region, in 1979–80, only 9.4 per cent of the population were dependent on social security benefits, by comparison with some 14 per cent in the North-west, 15.1 per cent in Yorkshire and Humberside, and 15.7 per cent in the Northern region (Winyard 1987: Table 5). Unemployment across the regions followed a similar pattern: indeed, Adrian Sinfield, in his authoritative retrospective analysis of post-war unemployment succinctly concluded that:

> Practically every year for the last thirty, the North, Wales, Scotland and the North West have suffered the highest rates throughout Britain.
>
> (Sinfield 1981: 23)

He also provides data on the impact of the first year of the Thatcher government on regional unemployment rates, as measured at that time (Table 6.1).

It is important to emphasise, however, that the development of inequalities across the country is not simply a matter of unemployment. One important dimension in the current situation in the North of England, in common with many newly 'residualised' or de-industria-

Table 6.1 Unemployment by region (November 1979 and 1980)

Region	1979	1980
Northern Ireland	10.5	14.9
Wales	7.2	11.4
North	7.9	11.3
Scotland	7.5	10.6
North West	6.6	10.3
West Midlands	5.2	9.4
Yorkshire and Humberside	5.2	9.4
South West	5.2	8.8
East Midlands	4.5	7.6
East Anglia	4.0	6.7
South East	3.4	5.7

Source: Sinfield (1981) Figure 2, p. 24

lised regions in continental Europe (the Ruhr Valley, the Pas de Calais) or in the United States (the Northern Rust Belt), is the prevalence of very low levels of pay earned by those in work. There are therefore large numbers of people within the region who are best classified as 'the working poor', people who are fully employed but still only living with the barest necessities of life.[4] There is clear evidence, in the statistics on unemployment and on poverty, of a persistent tendency towards inequality of income and wealth for citizens of the North of England as a whole (along with Scotland, Wales and Northern Ireland) by comparison with the South and South-east, such that we might want to speak of an organic pattern of regional inequality within England. Crucially for our purposes, the statistics on such inequality provide confirmation of what, throughout most of this century, has been a taken-for-granted feature of the 'common sense' or the 'structure of feeling' of the whole North of England. But there is also a first indication in the figures provided by Sinfield of a new unevenness and inequality, specifically resulting from the de-industrialisation and 'freeing of the market' initiated in 1979, which further exacerbated the 'North–South divide' throughout the 1980s and early 1990s. By December 1993, studies were showing that the worst effects of the de-industrialisation of the 1980s in England, in terms both of job losses and also of local 'gross domestic product', were concentrated precisely in the North. In respect of the measure of gross domestic product, the biggest losers during this period were, indeed, South Yorkshire (and, therefore, the City of Sheffield), which was already below national average (measured as 100) in 1979, at 95.7, but which in 1993 was down to 76.1. Meanwhile the biggest winners were Cambridgeshire, Surrey and Buckinghamshire (House of Commons Library research, reported in the *Guardian* 20 December 1993).

We would argue that popular, commonsense understanding of this more recent escalation of poverty and inequality in the North as a whole involves a reaffirmation and reformulation of the taken-for-granted resentment felt in the North at the injustice of its regional 'treatment', at the hands of the government, the South or simply 'London'. The particular form of this would depend on an individual's age, job position and personal prospects in the current transformation, and also on the kinds of option actually available in particular localities. We would also argue that the responses of local populations to the widening inequalities are mediated to a degree by a local consciousness – we think at the level of individual cities – which informs local people, in general terms, about the prospects of some improvement in the local post-industrial, post-Fordist economy. Underlying many of these adaptations in the North of England, however, there will always be recognition of the unjust fate or destiny of the Northern region as a whole by comparison with the rest of England – a feeling that the 'odds are rigged'.

In the meantime, popular experience of the new poverty and of social inequality in the North of England in the mid-1990s can be approached, we would argue, along two other key dimensions, which, we believe, help to organise individual and community responses in particular localities: the individual or household-based fear of poverty and its personal implications, on the one hand, and the concerns that are produced by the fact of living in a city in which there are large numbers of increasingly poor fellow citizens, on the other.

'THERE BUT FOR FORTUNE': FEAR OF FALLING IN THE NORTH OF ENGLAND

We have already suggested that the fear of poverty is by no means unfamiliar to large numbers of citizens in the North of England, though there are generations of Northerners, brought up during the 1950s and 1960s, who may have felt until the 1980s that the uncertainties and hardships reported to them by their parental generation for the 1930s were abolished 'for all time' by the post-war settlement. The return of popular anxiety in regard to poverty in the 1980s was clearly associated, in particular, with the fear of job loss (either one's own or that of a crucial household 'breadwinner') consequent on the accelerating loss of manufacturing work in the locality. This 'fear of falling' amongst working people, of course, was not just a question, we would argue, of the fear of redundancy: particularly amongst the unskilled and semi-skilled male workers who were losing jobs in their thousands in the 1980s, there was a fear, based on local knowledge, that the only alternatives available locally to personal long-term unemployment might be a variety of 'unmanly' or demeaning alternatives (for example, delivery driving or packing tins in a supermarket). Other than the loss of masculinity involved, there was clear anxiety over the loss of salary income, and the implications of this loss for personal lifestyle. 'Fear of falling' is, of course, a definitive feature for everyone of the contemporary experience of competitive free market societies: Barbara Ehrenreich has brilliantly examined how this anxiety now plays into the inner world of the professional middle class in America (Ehrenreich 1984).[5] Our own work, and that of other observers, also shows these fears to be definitive of the lives of 'working-class families' in the rapidly de-industrialising North of England, but in particular and specific ways.[6]

The wholesale loss of 'traditional' full-time paid employment in manufacturing industries across the North, alongside the increase in the number of part-time or temporary jobs in the service industries, has posed a fundamental challenge to the taken-for-granted division of domestic labour in the typical Northern household. In Greater Manchester, in 1989, women held 47.2 per cent of the jobs, as against only 43.9 per cent in 1981, an increase in women's share of the total employment market of 7.5 per cent (Peck and Emmerich 1992a: Table 16). National research would suggest that this general move towards a 'feminisation of the labour force', which has already been very marked in the growth of the service industries in the country as a whole, will accelerate in the North.[7] It immediately needs to be said, of course, that very large numbers of the jobs being taken up by women are part-time (about 85 per cent of part-time employment in Britain is of women), and there is certainly very scant evidence of any major opening up of the professional and well-salaried labour market in England to women, outside of London. In the meantime, for all the increase in the numbers of women in part-time or full-time work across the North, there is little evidence of any really widespread or fundamental change in the familiar divisions of household labour in either the 'working-class' or typical middle-class Manchester or Sheffield household.[8] The adaptations which were made in the 1980s have been subject to severe strain in the 1990s, as more and more service industries have laid off workers, reduced the starting salaries on offer for 'job seekers', or replaced full-time positions with part-time ones or short-term contractual work.[9] In December 1994, for example, a survey by the Low Pay Unit in the Greater Manchester area revealed that three out of ten jobs advertised in the city's job centres paid less than the National Insurance threshold of £57 per week, and that one in two paid less than £100 per week. The report drew the important conclusion that 'the majority of the jobs on offer would not lift a family above benefit levels' (*Manchester Metropolitan News* 2 December 1994). In Manchester in the early 1990s there was widespread popular recognition that the local labour market was evolving along the lines described by the Greater Manchester Research and Information Planning Unit (1992–3):

> The local economy is becoming increasingly divided. Development booms in parts of Greater Manchester are going hand in hand with some of Europe's worst poverty levels in inner city areas.

In September 1993, Sheffield's evening paper, the *Star*, carried a major feature on a report from the City Council's Directorate of Planning and Economic Development which identified 12 different, small areas of the city as being 'in acute poverty'.[10] The list included areas of the city which in the earlier post-war period had never been affluent but which would never have been identified as the site of any serious human problem.[11] Newspaper reports like these gave expression, we would argue, to fears and anxieties felt by many sections of the population about the personal threat of redundancy as well as the danger of a real material and symbolic decline in the character, and sense of well-being, of one's own immediate neighbourhood. There was a barely half-suppressed fear of a personal 'downward mobility' and also of what, in the literature on the 'problem estate', is sometimes called the 'tipping' or downward spiral of the whole area, leaving the area prey to the activities of angry and disorganised young men operating on the fringe of the local hidden economy of crime.

Very closely associated with these fears of the domestic economic impact of job loss was a palpable fear as to the implications for one's ability to make full use of the 'facilities' of the local city. This often took a highly gendered form. For working-class men, particularly, the threat was to their capacity to continue to make recursive use of the pub, the football, betting shops and other sites of male sociability. Scott Trueman, a steelworker redundant now for three years, still tried to stretch his 'dole' to a couple of pints, but of necessity had attempted to establish an alternative contact point with other unemployed workers in the Burngreave Library. He commented:

> There's several pubs around. I often go in one of them. The price of
> beer these days, I don't have much chance for socialising.

Scott's personal use of the city now extended 'no more than a mile from the house' and never into town (which he could not afford), except en route to the Peak District 'for a trip out'. At other times, he was to be found in the library 'hearing about work'. Not far below the surface in Scott's comments in our discussion group was a simmering anger at his inability to participate routinely in social bonding in the local pub or in the sphere of consumption – shopping 'in town' or at Meadowhall.

Given the established divisions of domestic responsibility in these households, however, the concern of women over job loss 'in the family' focused on their ability to manage household budgets, notably in respect of the daily or weekly shopping but also to handle the costs of domestic heating and fuel.[12] Associated with this was an anxiety about being forced into the kind of careful, strategic 'subsistence shopping' they knew, from personal observation or local gossip, to be necessary in poor households within the urban region (and which we discussed in Chapter 5). There was a clear recognition that any such experience of personal downward mobility would involve the strategic modification of personal use of city shopping facilities, the transport system[13] and, indeed, the city as a whole. Implicit in these fears was a sense of becoming corralled, in terms of area of residence and the parameters of one's everyday experience and consumption, within the 'poor people's city' that is embedded within the larger urban environment.

The most publicly intrusive expression of this poverty in Manchester is the number of beggars and others presenting themselves as homeless who occupy public space in the city centre. The methods in use for counting the numbers of people begging on city streets are controversial, although no serious commentator, even in the present British government, denies that the return of street begging and homelessness are connected phenomena of the 1980s and early 1990s.[14] In just one three-month period (April–June 1994) in Greater Manchester, according to the Department of the Environment, some 2,970 households were accepted for rehousing by local authorities and a further 1,710 households were in temporary accommodation awaiting rehousing, suggesting a total population of homeless people over a period of a year at somewhere between 10,000 and 15,000. The local Shelter office, however, was quoted at the end of 1994 as claiming that the real number of 'acceptances' of people as 'officially homeless' in Greater Manchester in 1994 as a whole was about 39,000 (*Manchester Evening News* 23 December 1994). According to the Department of the Environment, the numbers of people registered as homeless in Sheffield in the first and second quarter of 1994 were 630 and 420 respectively; but other reports suggested that the local Council, given its financial crisis (discussed in Chapter 3) – once it had offered accommodation, as it is required to do under the Housing Act of 1977, to 'vulnerable' families with children and to single parents – then only had the resources to house claimants under 18 years old as 'officially homeless'. Single people over 18 had to struggle in 'the private sector' (Department of the Environment 1994). Most of these homeless people go unrecorded by any official agency and mostly do not intrude into public consciousness, except when they use the streets to beg, drink, socialise or sell the *Big Issue* (the weekly magazine sold for the support of the homeless), thus displaying their status as a homeless person in a particularly public way.

In December 1993, the Sheffield *Star* reported the local branch of Shelter's estimate that some 60 people were sleeping on the streets of the city on any one night ('Christmas on the Streets' *Star* 16 December 1993). In the city of Manchester in 1991, a Shelter survey found 200 people 'sleeping out'. However, estimates of the number of beggars in central Manchester ran to some 1,000 people, primarily young men aged 18–25 years old, with visible concentrations at key city-centre locations such as Piccadilly Gardens.[15] Popular perceptions of Manchester's city centre as being home, in the mid-1990s, to an army of beggars and homeless people were ironically confirmed by the launch in December 1992 of a separate, self-financing North-west edition of the *Big Issue*. In November 1994, the North-west *Big Issue* was sold by between 60 and 120 active sellers based in Manchester, achieving sales of over 12,000 in that city alone. By early 1995, the local press was suggesting that Manchester had become 'the beggars' capital' of the North of England, and a variety of initiatives was being launched to try to manage the scale of begging taking place and especially to remove it from the streets.[16] Our own impression that Sheffield has not become a centre for beggars and homeless people on the street was generally confirmed in our focus group discussions, although there was certainly concern in that city over the way in which the Peace Gardens, outside the Town Hall, and the nearby Goodwin fountain had apparently been colonised by public drinkers ('winos').

There was also an only partly suppressed sense in which the dramatic and significant presence of the poor on the streets is in theory a signification of the fate which might await unlucky local citizens.[17] Fear of unemployment was certainly quite evident in our focus group discussions. The local newspaper and television media of both our cities, in the early 1990s, were continuing in the practice – firmly institutionalised at some point in the early 1980s – of giving prominent feature coverage to the closure of local industrial plants and the number of redundancies involved. The fear of personal redundancy and its consequences is predictably related, as well, to reports in the local press about continuing haemorrhaging of 'real jobs' from the local economy. One way of putting this point is to record that at the end of 1994, even on the very restricted measures adopted by the Department of Employment, there were officially some 109,852 people unemployed in Greater Manchester as a whole and 31,463 in the City of Manchester itself – a proportion of whom, at any time, are 'killing time' in the public spaces of the city[18] – and some 25,171 in Sheffield.[19] Only very small proportions of these unemployed people were reduced to begging or actually made homeless: and there is clearly a sense, as we have said, in which Manchester is more of a centre for begging (and the selling of the *Big Issue*) than is Sheffield. But the figures surely suggest that these two cities were home to very large numbers of very poor people, whose presence on the street (which is dramatically signified for some people by the presence of people in cheap clothing or with a generally unhealthy appearance and demeanour) is a defining aspect of the experience of these cities for others.

SHARING THE CITY WITH THE POOR: MANCHESTER AND SHEFFIELD IN THE 1990S

We take it as self-evident, then, that one important effect of the de-industrialisation resulting from global economic change and the unleashing of the free market in Britain since 1979 has been a significant increase in poverty and inequality, and that some of this poverty and inequality finds clear visible expression in the appearance of large numbers of poor people and particularly those who are publicly declaring their personal destitution or homelessness by begging on the streets.

This co-presence of the 'new poor' on some streets and other public places in the centres of major cities is a feature of urban experience in all free market societies, coalescing in the United States in the late 1980s around an anxious public discussion about 'bag ladies' on the streets of major cities in that country, and also in Russia in the 1990s in an equally anxious moral panic about the harassment allegedly utilised by 'Gypsies' or other identifiably 'different' peoples begging on the street.[20] However, not all cities sustain the same extent of begging and visible homelessness. The project of 'going to town' (for example, to work or to shop) in Manchester in the mid-1990s routinely involves an encounter with the new poor as beggars, whereas in Sheffield beggars are far less frequently seen or directly encountered. A report in a national newspaper in 1993 suggested that the characterisation of Manchester made by Canon Richard Parkinson in 1840, that 'There is no town in the world where the difference between rich and poor is so great', was true once again.[21] The contrast between 'affluent locales' of city-centre consumption and the presence and appearance of the new poor in Manchester is stark. Certainly by comparison with Sheffield, the city contains a number of major conspicuous-consumption sites, like its up-market shopping streets and theatres, which have increasingly been targeted by young beggars. In addition, the city's success in promoting itself as a place for tourism and also its lively night-time economy may have made it a more attractive place in which to make a living on the streets, thus drawing in young people from outlying districts.

Members of the larger public in Greater Manchester employ a number of strategies of avoidance and/or accommodation to deal with the new poor, and especially beggars, including a variety of strategies in terms of giving or not giving money, and of the organisation of personal routes through the centre (cf. Evans and Fraser 1995), many of which involved changing long-established habits. As Khalid Saddiqui regretted:

> I used to like walking and I used to walk from the University to Piccadilly station every day, and I never met anyone asking for money, begging for money. It used to be really nice, just walking down. But now, for about five or six months, things have changed dramatically. . . This is one of the changes which I have noticed, and which has made me stop walking from my place of work to the city centre, which I used to enjoy.

There is, however, a suggestion that the presence of the new poor in most city centres in the North – whilst certainly felt as a potential source of unpleasantness or harassment – also produces a certain kind of fascination. 'Poverty' is no longer hidden from view, 'in its place' on the estates or in the inner city to which citizens of the larger conurbation would rarely pay a visit. It has intruded into central public spaces of the city to become a key element of the urban spectacle.[22] We found clear evidence in our focus group discussions of the development of suburban and other 'inventories of city-centre peoples', used by different members of the public to make sense of, and categorise, the different types of poor or 'problematic social type' in the city centre. This lay 'inventory' is a kind of discursive repertoire associating certain signifying features of urban space and/or 'urban others' as a source of fear or reassurance, rather than a logical analysis of the social structure of the street. Though by no means confined to the young, these inventories were particularly developed on the part of young people who paid frequent visits to town.

In the pilot survey of bus users in Manchester city centre conducted by one of these authors (with Christine Peacock) in 1991, for example, Ann Elland, a 16-year-old from Poynton, Cheshire, observed how she felt unsafe around Church Street:

> it is a bit grotty and that. You don't feel safe because there is not many people round and also because there are tramps and strange people around.

The terminology used to describe those 'other people' provoking unease or anxiety varied very widely amongst our respondents. It ranged from 'beggars' and 'tramps' through to 'lager louts' and 'hooligans', with some very specific references, especially in Manchester, to 'convicts' (thought to have been released from Strangeways Prison, less than one mile from the city centre), 'mental patients' and 'football fans', 'especially on Saturdays and on Derby days'. Particular anxieties seemed to be provoked for some other publics in the city, especially up-market shoppers, not only by the young men and women to be seen on Market Street, Manchester (variously known as 'crusties' and/or 'travellers'), accompanied by dogs on a string lead, but also, more generally, by people selling on the street. Brian Middleton, a professional worker in the city, grumbled that:

> It's all traffic, isn't it ? Noise and traffic. Anywhere you go in town. Market Street to a certain extent because of all the fast-food people and people flogging lighters, toys and all that. They shouldn't be allowed there.

Observers were unsure about identifying particular groups of young people on Market Street (or elsewhere) in Manchester as 'drug users' or 'junkies', though they were happy to allude to the prominence of such people, in an abstract sense, in the city. One elderly lady, hypothesising that some of the young people on Market Street, Manchester, might be drug users awaiting their prescriptions at Boots, immediately added that she was not so much frightened as saddened by this prospect.

MENTAL MAPS, MAPS OF POVERTY AND URBAN SPECTATORSHIP

The inventory of 'Others' identified in different group discussions was, precisely, a discursive list of people whose presence in particular places provoked unease for different groups of observers of the urban spectacle. There was always a strong sense that the particular form assumed by these typifications, especially in Greater Manchester with its broad concentric circles of inner-city and residential areas, was a particular effect of the social and cultural segregation in that city. The representations of urban Others advanced by people living in Manchester's southern suburbs (nine or ten miles from the centre of the city) tended to have a 'fantastic' and stereotypical quality, whilst the typifications produced from residents of the inner-city ring itself or of 'mixed residential areas' (Stretford, Chorlton, Sale, Eccles), had a more pragmatic, naturalistic and sometimes even sympathetic quality. Professional people working in the city centre and also regular up-market shoppers, in the meantime, tended to have developed quite elaborate personal strategies, especially involving use of back-street routes to avoid regular confrontations with 'the poor'. In the smaller city of Sheffield, by contrast ('the biggest village in the world'), with its central urban spaces and facilities more frequently shared by a mixed local population, and, indeed, with the relative absence of beggars, we heard far fewer negative denotations of the fearful urban other – though they were by no means absent.[23] There are surely some larger questions here, not least the possibility that Manchester's long history as the centre for a large 'industrial region' has engendered a local cultural familiarity with the facts of poverty, a product of the region's long and restless involvement with free trade and commerce and the boom and slump of the business cycle.

It is impossible to ignore the parallels between this suburban inventory of the new poor encountered in public space in the city centre and the set of social commentaries produced about the poor by urban missionaries and social reformers like Charles Booth, Edwin Chadwick and Henry Mayhew in the mid-nineteenth century.[24] Judith Walkowitz discusses this literature as:

> a literature of urban exploration . . . emulat[ing] the privileged gaze of anthropology in constituting the poor as a race apart, outside the national community.
>
> (Walkowitz 1992: 19)

and detects a very specific kind of Darwinian anthropology at work, particularly in Mayhew's exhaustive ethnographic studies of the street people of London in the 1860s and, most especially, in the extensive but entirely idiosyncratic taxonomy which Mayhew advances of the urban poor. Mayhew offers a study of the 'wandering tribes' of the city, theorised in part in terms of the seasonality of the casual labour market but very largely organised around an account of the different moral strengths and weaknesses associated with particular tribal species ('the costermonger', the 'nomad', etc.). The descriptions so provided of the urban topography of London in mid-century carry with them an implicit evolutionary mapping of the moral value and personal strengths of different types of the poor who are likely to be encountered on the street by other middle-class observers. This moral mapping of the poor into a complex anthropological taxonomy is often reduced in more blatantly political discourse into a dichotomous discussion of the 'undeserving' and 'deserving' poor, and Mayhew himself was keen to situate his different urban species dichotomously in different halves of the metropolis – specifically, in a city divided between the West and East 'Ends':

> In passing from the skilled operative of the West-End to the unskilled workman of the Eastern quarter, the moral and intellectual change is so great, that it seems as if we were in a new land and among another race.
> (Mayhew 1861: vol. 3, p. 233, quoted in Stedman-Jones 1971: 30 and in Walkowitz 1992: 19)

We have already indicated, earlier in this book, how the development of the conurbation of Greater Manchester over some two centuries has involved the segregation of a wealthier middle class to the south of the City and the concentration of very large lower middle-class and respectable working-class populations to the north of the city centre (Prestwich, Whitefield, Bury), with the outer and inner zones of these residential areas coming down into the commercial centre through a massive 'girdle' of inner-city areas. Where geographers and transport professionals may see a city divided, after the manner of Chicago, into a series of concentric zones, the majority of the local population, whether of recent vintage or long-established residence, clearly understand that this is a city primarily divided between north and south, albeit that this overall shape of the larger city has also included a number of smaller town centres (Altrincham, Bolton, Bury, Oldham, Stockport, Ashton, etc.) within the conurbation as a whole. Sheffield, by contrast, is a city divided along the same west–east dimension as London itself, in the sense that the historical centre of industry, and of the associated 'workmen's dwellings' (built some 100–150 years ago), are 'down-wind' of the suburbs and, therefore, to the east (Attercliffe, Darnall, Tinsley and beyond). The material (industrial and architectural) evolution of these two cities along these two geographical divisions provides the condition of existence of a stubborn set of 'images of the city' which have developed over the last two centuries, which help to inform local citizens' understanding of the ways in which 'poverty', 'crime' and personal danger are distributed spatially across the city as a whole. The importance of such long-standing 'images of the city' in popular common sense is the subject of a considerable literature in human geography and in applied social and cognitive psychology (cf. Lowenthal 1961, 1975; Lowenthal and Bowden 1976), and is also the resource upon which the American geographer Kevin Lynch based his very influential work on the idea of shared and different, research-identifiable 'mental maps' utilised more or less subconsciously by residents of cities (Lynch 1960, 1972; Tuan 1975).[25]

The commonsense conception of our two cities is partly dictated by this major north–south or east–west 'axis', with its connotations of class and status, but it is also determined by the presence and recognition of a number of recognised key 'paths' (the city user's 'movement channels'), 'edges' (boundaries), 'nodes' (strategic foci to the citizen's movement through the city), 'districts' and 'landmarks' (Lynch 1960). There is no question that these elements of a mental map can be configured in very different ways by different individuals in our two cities – for example, in respect of the active and purposive organisation of a journey or, more passively, simply as a familiar background to one's movement through the city (Pocock 1972). The maps are also clearly important, alongside a 'sense of direction', in directing others, or in guiding oneself, through a major city. There is no question, either, that the continuing presence of certain 'landmarks' and 'paths' is important to the kind of local knowledge that is used, by large numbers of ordinary Mancunians and Sheffielders, in making sense of their cities – for example, as discussed in Chapter 4, in 'getting about' on the buses (their 'local bus knowledge'). We also spoke, in Chapter 2, of the important role of public houses as symbolic institutions in local communities and in respect of the local gender order: it is clear that pubs continue to have a significant role in many men's use and knowledge (their mental maps and their general conception) of Northern cities. So too, it must be said, was this true for some women, especially younger women in Sheffield, whose Friday and Saturday evenings might begin in the Stone House (a large, Georgian-fronted pub on Church Street) and continue 'up the street' later (the well-established and locally well-known 'West Street run'). In city-centre Manchester, we will see in Chapter 11, a similar role is played by the new wine-bars around the northern end of Deansgate.

What is perhaps of most interest to us here, however, is the way in which these 'mental maps' have originated in a mix of personal and class experience and local myth, and the ways in which these maps now organise use of the city, and the continuing reproduction (and distribution across the territory of the city) of the city's social and class inequalities. With Stallybrass and White (1986), we can decipher a particular, obsessive preoccupation in the talk of most local citizens (but especially, as suggested earlier, of suburban residents on the farthest fringes of the cities) with the precise location of 'the poor areas' of the city. Associated with this concern to know where this poor area is precisely situated, primarily for reasons of avoidance but in some cases as a preparation for a visit of exploration, is an inventory of the kinds of person and behaviour which are to be encountered there. It is fascinating to observe how much energy and commitment is fed into these descriptions of the 'poor areas' by people who do not live in them, and also the degree of personal knowledge that is somehow claimed.[26] It is important as well to see how the representation of these areas in the popular imagination, like the interpretation of the city-centre poor, feeds on a set of stereotypes, drawn from sources ranging from Darwinian social anthropology through to the latest popular, sometimes racial, theory of crime in the English tabloid press, as well as on a set of more specific rhetorics about the quality of life, for example, in high-rise flats (the Kelvin flats in Sheffield) or on outlying council estates (Wythenshawe in Manchester).

The sources of these powerful popular theories of the 'poor areas', and the way in which these 'poor areas' are identified across the mental map of the city or conurbation, are complex and do not simply depend on a binary opposition of the 'tranquil' suburb and the 'disorderly' estate or high-rise. Some 'poor areas' come and go: we will discuss the role of 'race' in reorganising the mental maps of the majority of Mancunians and Sheffielders in Chapter 8, constructing Moss Side and Burngreave as territories colonised by a racialised Other. In Sheffield, Burngreave has more or less successfully replaced The Manor (a major post-war estate to the north-east) in the local imagination as the home territory of the threatening Other; The Manor in its turn had replaced Attercliffe and Scotland Street (the feared territories of the 1920s and 1930s) (Bean 1981; Sillitoe 1953) at some time in the early post-war period, as the hypothetical venue of both 'criminal activity' and generalised conditions of poverty and destitution. Other areas seem rather more fixed in the dominant mental maps of the city: the troubles of the Ordsall Estate in Salford, Greater Manchester, during 1992 occurred almost precisely in the same place (near Liverpool Street) as some of the most serious gang troubles in that district in the 1920s, reported by Andrew Davies (1992).

We are not arguing that local urban myth is closely attentive to the different sets of circumstances which might account for the presumed character of particular local areas, but we are saying that the use of these 'mental maps' of the city by our Manchester and Sheffield correspondents betrayed a kind of intuitive knowledge both of continuities in the urban area (the chequered history of the Ordsall Estate in Manchester) and changes (for example, specific incidents of crime and social disorder in particular areas). The mental maps of our Northern respondents were not merely dependent on the continued presence of familiar urban landmarks and continuity in the general physical form, especially 'the paths', of the city.[27] We also want to suggest that the construction of particular areas and districts of cities, for example, in local press coverage and in local talk, as being either 'areas of acute poverty' or 'high-crime areas' is an ongoing and continual process, which certainly involves the active work of the imagination on the part of the suburban and other 'publics' outside these areas, and which may, in part, have to do with what Stallybrass and White (1986) see as a kind of 'eroticization' of the underclass, or what Walkowitz (1992) describes as an obsessive fascination in respect of the 'poor area' – constructing these areas, in the imagination, as a modern-day equivalent of the 'rookeries' of the Victorian city.

We should not be misunderstood. It is in no sense our concern here simply to identify an unproblematic process of reproduction of mental maps of the city from generation to generation, assigning moral qualities, or their absence, to the local population of those places (attributing areas a 'reputation') and also constructing, in the process, a fearful and forbidden spatial 'Other'. To do this would be to ignore the sense in which particular activities or subcultural developments in particular areas, like the use of firearms in crime, might distinguish these areas in certain, significant ways from others within the conurbation.[28] Perhaps more importantly, at the other extreme, it might also leave unaddressed the extent to which the 'dominant' definition of the city is challenged by significant numbers of people living in these same localities. We shall see, in Chapter 8, how the local and national reputation of Moss Side is challenged by a very wide cross-section of the local population. In Sheffield, the negative reputation attaching to particular blocks of high-rise flats (Park Hill, on the hill above Midland Station, or 'the Kelvin' on Middlewood Road) succeeded eventually in persuading the Council to redeploy Park Hill and decant its existing tenants, and then, in 1993, to close the Kelvin. We none the less found significant evidence, during our research, of a quite considerable attachment to both these 'communities' on the part of their tenants, and we were attentive to the troubled coverage in the local press of their final closure – as if there was some recognition that these flats had been a kind of social community, at a certain level of civil society where 'community' was very obviously needed.

The struggle over the continuing presence of 'poor areas' is, we suspect, a feature of the local consciousness of most de-industrialised urban areas in the North of England. But we do not believe that this struggle can simply be understood as a kind of play of the fantasy and imagination between the propertied residents of the suburbs and a subordinate, fascinating poor, mediated by local journalists in their never-ending search for a headline, and thus, to be interpreted as a struggle over 'text'. Much more fundamentally it is a matter of struggle over the distribution of public resource available in particular conurbations at the end of the twentieth century, and the moral and social arguments as to who 'deserves' particular attention and provision. That struggle is played out in the North of England – unlike in North America, Germany, Northern Italy or many conurbations in France – against the background of a particular post-war history of economic failure and political traditions which allow for only restricted and uneven programmes of public provision, in both housing and the physical infrastructure of place.

THE MATERIAL CHARACTER OF URBAN SPACE IN THE NORTH OF ENGLAND

There was little question, as we have suggested, that the overwhelming source of fear and anxiety identified by people making use of the city centres of Manchester and Sheffield was the presence of a particular kind of person – 'an Other'.[29] In these old industrial cities, with much of their 'modern' architecture constructed of concrete or other functional materials, erected cheaply during the 1950s and 1960s, and now showing the effects of 30 years of industrial pollution and the local climate, these places and buildings were still, by and large, not so much feared as simply disliked, ignored or tolerated. One of the insights in this research (especially clear to one of the researchers who had lived seven years in North America) was the very low level of expectation held by these North of England publics, especially in Sheffield, with respect to the aesthetics or convenience of public buildings and facilities or urban spaces.[30] In the meantime, the presence of these 'strange' Others in particular places in the city (groups of threatening young men in base-ball caps and sports clothing on the balconies outside the markets on Castle Street in Sheffield) was widely known amongst nearly all pedes-trian users of these city spaces. There is no question that it was this colonisation of particular, usually already 'unpleasant' places, for many users of the city, which precipitated active dislike or fear of these physical locales and the various strategies of avoidance by significant numbers of local citizens and city users. In Manchester, in particular, we found evidence of very long detours, made especially by professional men and women and by elderly men, to avoid the use of Market Street, in part because of the young people to be encountered (but also, it should be said, because of its general ambience, in particular the litter). Edward Clarke, a professional person working in central Manchester, indicated he would never 'get to Deansgate down Market Street':

> I would prefer to walk down King Street . . . I don't think they could dispute Market Street's a midden. It's filthy, muck everywhere. That is indisputable.[31]

In Sheffield, we found evidence of many frustrated attempts to negotiate the city centre without making use of Castle Square, the 'Hole in the Road', and its immediate surroundings. Mary Green, who made use of the city only in the day-time, commented sadly on how:

> The people look a lot drabber. It's very obvious in that part of town.

We need to clarify our argument here, however, not least because of the wider emphasis which is placed by both academic and practising specialists in the field of crime prevention on the utility of such strategies of avoidance by individuals, and also on the idea of architectural renovation of urban space as part of a strategy of personal and commu-nity safety. The juxtaposition of 'unpleasant locales', or what Yi-Fu Tuan (1979) calls 'landscapes of fear', with the presence on a predictable basis of unpleasant or threatening groups in particular urban-centre sites (pedestrian underpasses, bus stations, cheap and 'tatty' shops, whole areas covered with litter or graffiti)[32] does not necessarily mean that these sites are, or can be, avoided altogether, or that they become emptied of human traffic. The survey work we undertook on the density of use of city-centre sites in Manchester and Sheffield revealed, precisely, that these disliked sites (Market Street and the bus stations in central Manchester, and 'the Hole in the Road' and Flat Street in Sheffield) were amongst the most heavily used of all the different locales investi-gated in our two cities (cf. Evans *et al.* 1995). In part, this is because the sites were unavoidable: they had been colonised precisely because they were located at what Giddens and Hägerstrand would recognise as 'stopping places' dictated by the physical layout of the two cities, Market Street being one of a small number of pedestrianised streets in Manchester city centre; because they were the only route to the central bus station; because they were one central walking route in any local city user's daily exploration of different 'nodes' in the city (the bus or rail station, the shop, the offices, the cinemas, pubs and clubs), like 'the Hole in the Road' in Sheffield or Piccadilly Gardens in Manchester; or because they were part of the access approach to cheap shopping facilities necessarily used by very large numbers of the local population. Prime examples of this were the Markets (the Barrows) in central Manchester, the infamous Bury New Road in north Manchester (identified by the national press as in 1990 the 'most littered street in Britain' but also the location of a number of bargain clothes stores and of a street market on Sundays), and the Flat Street 'balcony' above the Sheffield Transport Interchange – the only route to the Lo-Cost supermarket. Large numbers of people of different social backgrounds – though not everyone[33] – had to use these places willy-nilly and adapt to their messy, slightly threatening character,[34] until such time as these spaces should be subject to some radical improvement in local civic architecture and public provision or until such time as the city in question, as a social and economic institution, stopped producing such a range of problematic or threatening Others. This was clearly not thought by any of our respondents in either North of England city to be an immediate prospect or pressing possibility. Such a utopian and, indeed, 'post-modern', consumerist vision of a clean, 'user-friendly' and risk-free environment for the poor did not in this sense intrude into the 'local structure of feeling' and there was no real sense that it ever would.

7

OUT ON THE TOWN
Manchester's Gay Village

One of the more striking features of the rapid changes taking place in Manchester's city centre in the late 1980s and early 1990s was the transformation of an old warehouse area by the city-centre canal into a series of wine bars and restaurants dedicated to the use of the gay and lesbian populations – the so-called 'Gay Village'. In early 1995, in what was still a rapidly developing and changing area, there were 15 gay or mixed pubs and clubs, three cafés, a hair-dresser, a taxi service and a shop in the core of the Village, and a number of other venues on its fringe. The development of the Village and, more recently, the production of a 'gay supplement' in Manchester's *City Life* magazine have identified Manchester as a mecca for gay people from elsewhere in the North of England, and has also distinguished Manchester from other cities in the North, like Sheffield. Few of these have witnessed any successful claiming of urban facilities specifically for the use of gay people.[1]

In this chapter, we want to provide an account of the emergence of the Village as an identifiable urban enclave and also to hear the voices of gay men living in Manchester speaking about the impact of the Village on their lives and on their use of the city. Primarily, we want to utilise the accounts we were given by eight regular users of the Village (all gay men) to offer commentary on the issue of gay people's use and non-use of this city and other old Northern industrial cities – all of which, as we have insisted throughout this book, are dominated, culturally, by powerful social myths regarding the power of heterosexual men, whether of the industrial working class (the Little Mesters and steel forgeworkers of Sheffield and the cotton weavers of Greater Manchester) or, indeed, of the industrial and commercial classes ('the steelmasters' and 'the Men who Made Manchester'). We are concerned, in so doing, to try to grasp the 'specificity' of the subordinate life lived by gay people in these northern cities, always against the inescapable background of the hegemonic masculinist mythology of the old industrial North, and, in particular, the contrast between Manchester, which now has its own 'gay Mecca' (Bell 1991), and Sheffield and other Northern cities, which do not.

An article in the *Guardian* in 1993 described the recent expansion of gay bars and clubs in London, especially around Soho, and saw this expansion as being driven by 'the recession', turning erstwhile 'straight' venues into provisions targeted at gay people, in the pursuit of what had come to be known as the 'pink pound'. According to its author, Lynn Wallis:

> the accelerated growth of gay venues began at the start of the recession in the South East in late 1989, when desperate business-men recognised that the average punter no longer had ready cash for nights out on the town, but gays did.
>
> (*Guardian* 25 August 1993)

The article argued that these developments could be expected to be quite general, and that a 'market opportunity' for entrepreneurial provision for gay people existed everywhere. But it also recognised that some cities were ahead of others – notably, Manchester, which 'has had a gay village for about three years now'. Wallis was recognising the delayed impact in Britain of developments that occurred 15–20 years earlier in North America, in cities as geographically dispersed as San Francisco, Portland, New Orleans and Toronto.

This particular journalistic piece was clearly guilty of some metro-politan generalisation, simply assuming that the London situation was common to all other British cities.[2] In fact our research into the North-ern cities of Sheffield and Manchester very strongly suggests that these cities have exhibited quite different responses to their gay and lesbian populations, and each of these is different again to that London experi-ence. The discussion we held with eight gay men living in Manchester soon highlighted the difference between the gay scene in Manchester, which they saw as relatively intimate and friendly, and in London, which was seen as much more impersonal and also dangerous. Sebastian, a solicitor working for a practice in Manchester which advertises itself as a lesbian, gay, and woman-friendly service, told us:

> I've got friends that come up from London. They come, and they love Manchester. They are used to the gay scene in London [but] there's a different atmosphere here I think.

This was confirmed by Bill, originally from east Sussex, who had lived in Manchester for eighteen months, working in the Gay Village around safer sex issues. He saw the main difference between the two cities as being the compact nature of the Manchester gay scene as opposed to that in London. His comment was echoed by Harold, who had lived around Manchester all his life:

Bill: You do travel miles . . . from Brixton all the way through to Kensington . . . whilst here you have a concentration of centres . . .

Harold: It gives you confidence doesn't it? . . . It's an area for us.

Bill: It's like San Francisco.

The contrast was very often with the 'oppressive' atmosphere of other Northern cities. Sebastian had himself always lived around Manchester. He claimed:

> I think the reason that you do feel so positive about yourself is because you do live in Manchester, or major cities. You go out to places like Huddersfield, Bradford, and Leeds – smaller cities. You find that the people aren't quite so positive about their own sexuality, they are not able to express it like you can in Manchester. You can go out in Manchester often. I used to go out in Manchester a lot, now I don't really bother as much as I used to do. The novelty wore off. The thing is, though, *it's there*, you can go to it.

In part, it can be argued that the public confidence of the 'gay population' of Greater Manchester is a function of the greater numerical mass of the population who may identify themselves as having a gay sexual preference or who feel affinity with the gay identity and lifestyle. We recognise the problems with any such attempt to estimate the size of the gay population, especially given the way in which popular fears of AIDS have resulted in some disavowal of public gay identification, and also given the significant blurring, on the edge of popular culture, of fixed sexual identities (Hindle 1994). However, if we were to hypostasize the findings of the Kinsey Report of 1949 on male sexual behaviour and preference, where it was asserted that 1 in 10 of the adult population were homosexual in sexual preference, then the suggestion would be that there must be some 180,000 people of gay sexual preference resident in the Greater Manchester conurbation,[3] where the City of Sheffield would only be home to some 35,000 people with a gay sexual preference.

THE HISTORY OF MANCHESTER'S GAY VILLAGE

The history of the Gay Village within Manchester has not yet been comprehensively explored. What follows here is an impression of its development gathered from people's own tales and experiences of having lived in the city and used the facilities for lesbians and gays which have been on offer. There is a general agreement that the Village, as it is also known, grew up around a small number of pubs in a generally forgotten part of the city centre. This space was well known as the location of the long-distance bus and coach station (Chorlton Street) and also as an area of prostitution. Prior to 1968, when gay lives were led very much in the private sphere, 'homosexuals' – the term used before the rise of the Gay Liberation Front – were drawn to places where they could meet anonymously, particularly in public houses. They were especially concerned to avoid walking out of a pub known as a meeting place for homosexual men and directly into places where they might meet people they knew. For this reason pubs used by gay men were often situated in out-of-the-way places. The Manchester pubs most often mentioned as attracting a gay clientele at this time, the Rembrandt and the Union, are still a part of the Village today, the former, it is widely acknowledged, having had a gay clientele since the 1940s. The licensee of the Union was imprisoned as late as 1965 for 'outraging public decency' by running a public house in which gay men were welcome. The same pub assumed the name of the New Union after his release.

The opening of clubs and bars specifically for gay men was first made possible by the Sexual Offences Act of 1967, with the clear distinction in that legislation (derived from the Wolfenden Report a decade before) between the legalisation of activity between consenting adults conducted in private and the continuing penalisation of sexual activity obtruding into the public sphere. The early 1970s witnessed an explosion in the number of gay clubs and discothèques in Britain, with entry to these facilities by ticket through unmarked doorways, and advertising of them very largely by word of mouth. Later in the decade, however, there was increasing identification with some aspects of a 'gay lifestyle' and also, across the whole North of England, an intense popular and youthful interest in the Northern Soul dance scene, centred particularly on Manchester. In Manchester itself, a small number of disc jockeys, prominent in the Northern Soul circuits, doubled up their work between the Soul clubs and the small number of gay clubs that had opened up since 1967 . The coincidence of the rise of identification of gay lifestyle and 'club culture' in a city which was beginning at the time to rival Liverpool in the production of popular music and, particularly, of new bands was a particularly dynamic moment; and there is no question that the emergence of the Gay Village has, in part, to be traced to this combination of influences.

In this period – from the early 1970s to the early 1980s – gay venues were actually dispersed throughout the city centre as a whole, although some of the clubs and pubs were in the area which was subsequently to be developed as the Village. This area was growing in size, with the addition of Napoleon's in the 1970s, which became the 'headquarters' of the gay scene. Other clubs were still opening up in different parts of the city: John Dalton Street, on the other side of the city centre, had two popular gay venues, whilst another opened on Deansgate very near to Bootle Street Police station. Whittle and Jones note how:

> Before 1967, there were various 'cottages' [public toilets] which were popularly known as cruising areas where men could go to meet other men for sex, or to meet. It would seem appropriate that when the 1967 law reforms enabled the first openly gay clubs in the city to open that they would be sited near the main cruising areas.
>
> (Whittle and Jones 1993: 4)

The reconfiguration and renovation of buildings in the Village area actually occurred in the mid to late 1980s, with only one club maintaining a viable presence outside the enclave. This closed down as a gay venue in 1990 at the height of a clamp-down on clubs throughout the city inspired by Chief Constable James Anderton,[4] but re-established itself as a gay facility in 1993.

The public identity of the area as a 'Gay Village' began to be asserted, for the first time, in the mid-1980s – ironically at a time when the then prime minister, Margaret Thatcher, was leading an ideological offensive to reinstate a particular, Victorian idea of 'family values'. This highly visible campaign was readily turned towards criticism of gay lifestyles, especially when the first reports began to emerge of the HIV virus and subsequent deaths from AIDS in America. Gay politics and lifestyles were quickly coming to terms with this new threat, but anti-gay feeling was generally whipped up by the popular press. Many gay men talk of this time as one of 'withdrawal into the [gay] community', and this general feeling may have contributed to the withdrawal of gay venues into their 'own' space, geographically separate from areas of the city where homophobic encounters or even assaults were feared. The late 1980s was the time of the so-called 'Lawson boom', with considerably increased competition for city space and higher rentals, as entrepreneurs in the city moved to cater for the new leisure interests of a young professional class with money to spend. In Manchester, the 130 pubs in the city centre began to feel some competition, for the first time, from the spread of the wine bar and also from a rapid expansion in the number and range of city-centre restaurants. The Village itself, however, close to Chorlton Street bus station and the established locale for prostitution, was not immediately recognised as ripe for development and improvement by mainstream development agencies: arguably, full recognition of its potential was delayed until the establishment of the Central Manchester Development Corporation in 1988. Given the cheap rents and property prices in the area, a clear market opportunity existed for gay entrepreneurs to take part in the process of gentrification of the city centre, but within a distinct urban territory and space.

The topography of the area colonised by the Gay Village undoubtedly aided its identification with this minority club scene. The area is one which sits among old, disused warehouses left over from the industrial heyday of Manchester, but it is also close to Piccadilly rail station (the main station from London), Chinatown (the largest such area outside London) and the main building of UMIST (the University of Manchester Institute of Science and Technology). It is by no means simply a residual wasteland, and, as in many North American developments – for example, the Marigny neighbourhood of New Orleans discussed by Lawrence Knopp (1990) – its close relationship to significant other civic, educational and leisure sites has been influential in its recent renaissance. The old warehouses which have been the material resource for the 'gentrification' of the Village area were located alongside the city's canal system and have proven to be easy conversion projects. The historical links of some streets in the area, especially around the Chorlton Street bus station, with prostitution – another socially censured activity, but one which presumably was widely patronised by many local men – may also have given some cachet to the area as a site of forbidden pleasures. Rather than acceding to an urban tradition in which 'forbidden sexualities' are only to be pursued in seedy and sordid surroundings, however, gay businessmen proceeded to brighten up the area and publicly identify its existence. They also tried to bring a sense of humour and defiance to the images which they emblazoned in lights on clubs (witness the limp-wristed Statue of Liberty on the side of the New York, New York public house), and certainly they have repopulated its dark, narrow streets and waterways. The Village has become a place in which gay sexuality is affirmed and supported. The canals and buildings, which had long been recognised as important symbols of Manchester's industrial heritage but were suffering from neglect, have been 'rescued' and given over to another use (in the language of the Marxist political economy adopted by Castells and others, given a new 'use value'). Certainly, the rescue of the canals and warehouses in the Village area has met with the wholehearted approval of key figures and agencies in the local 'growth coalition'. The Central Manchester Development Corporation's area of geographic responsibility shares a boundary with the Village along Canal Street and has launched projects opening up, repaving and lighting the walkways alongside the waterways. The CMDC has also provided grants for the cleaning of buildings on Canal Street. As in the Marigny neighbourhood of New Orleans, there is in effect an alliance of the agencies in the local political and commercial institutions that have the responsibility for the project of urban development and 'renaissance' with the interests of leading entrepreneurs from the local gay population.

The facilities and events in the Gay Village are currently widely advertised in the gay and student press which circulates in Manchester, but also throughout other cities and towns in the North and the Midlands, and the Village is increasingly successful in bringing people into Manchester city centre at night from these surrounding areas. The opportunity for further commercial development that this increased level of patronage produces is clear, and many new gay venues are currently in the process of development. There is criticism within the gay community in the mid-1990s that some of these are not owned by gays but by 'imposters' exploiting 'the scene', but these continue, nevertheless, to be heavily used by a gay clientele. There is also a sign that gay venues are once more opening up outside the Village's boundaries, in areas which have been seen as more 'mainstream'. Within the larger 'development community' in Manchester, there is a recognition that there may soon be competition for prime sites and space between the Gay Village and developers wanting to open more night clubs or other facilities (in the gambling industry, in apartment building construction and in other fields).

The development of the Village has occurred against the background of what seems to be a 'liberalisation' of police attitudes towards Manchester's gays and night-time economy,[5] which has had a profound effect,

making many expressions of youth culture possible which were previously denied. This included the relaxation of licensing laws, which
allowed clubs to open until 4 a.m. during the Manchester Festival in
1993. The analytical issue is whether this 'liberalisation' is in some sense
contingent on the 'withdrawal' and sequestration of gay leisure activity
within a well-defined enclave and at night and the weekends, some
distance from other 'mainstream' commercial outlets, and therefore
accepting of an implicit cultural geography of leisure use of different
space and territories by different publics at different times of the day and
night in Manchester city centre.

URBAN SPACE AND SEXUAL PREFERENCE

The reconfigured urban space and upgraded buildings that comprise the
Gay Village – an enclave in the central city area where gay people can
feel relatively secure – is a product of the initiative and energy of
individuals and groups within the lesbian and gay 'community' in
Manchester, imaginatively reappropriating that city-centre area of warehouses and canals as a centre of clubs, bars and restaurants. But this
public colonisation of a central city space in Manchester is itself, of
course, a product, of the more general 'coming out' of homosexual
and lesbian people over the last 30 years. We want to retrace some of
this history here very briefly. But our overall argument is that the public
affirmation of 'gay sexuality' which is so often proclaimed, in essentially
Whig-historical a fashion, as the result of this process of liberalisation is
actually much more apparent and straightforward in some localities (or
'urban enclaves') and cities than others, and that the public expression of
this particular sexual preference in the industrial North of England
generally is especially problematic.

Gay sexuality emerged from 'the dark days' prior to 1968 into a heady
combination of Gay Liberation in the 1970s, the subsequent celebration
of gay lifestyles in the early 1980s, and the emergence of the pink
economy that followed. The move from identification with 'homosexu-
ality', which always promoted a pathological definition of this sexuality,
denoting disease and abnormality of character, to one in which 'gayness'
could be declared, and a recognition that same-sex preferences and
desires existed and were discussable, marked a turning point. The
subsequent emergence of the more public gay 'scene' – particularly in
San Francisco and some sections of other North American cities – is seen
by many commentators as an alternative home to that provided by the
family household in mainstream society, and a spatial alternative to the
mainstream neighbourhood. Initially, the rhetoric of gay magazines
insisted that these areas would become a kind of haven for the many
thousands of people in each city of 'different' or diverse sexuality. This is
not a promise we have been able to explore in depth in this research, but
the work we have done suggests that whilst the culture of Manchester's
Gay Village is accepting of the many 'badges' which lesbians and gay

men have chosen to adopt to express their personalities and tolerates a mix of styles and ages in its clubs, it nevertheless caters, primarily, for males with money who like to drink. As our focus group respondent Bill remarked:

> Economics actually empower people in lots of ways. It's actually brought us together through having clubs and pubs, and people are actually aware that having a gay night brings a lot of people in. There is meant to be the pink elusive pound, but it's worth a lot of money. It's thrown around a lot, it's like gay men don't have families, supposedly. I feel quite frustrated when I do go out sometimes. I think this is it really. You do have pubs where you drink, and you have to spend money, or take drugs. There are clubs where you have to drink, and you spend money.

In some respects, however, little has changed for those who do not have the economic power to participate in the pink economy. Bill is unemployed at present and felt this restriction more than most:

> There's a lot on the scene if you can afford to go out there. That's one issue, money. If you've got enough money to buy drinks . . .

Karen Evans: What if you can't afford to go out, what do you do then?
Bill: Well you go cottaging . . . if you're looking for sex.

As if to underline the fact of economic inequality of means with respect to gay people's use of the Village, a 'cottage' has recently developed in a disused warehouse just to the south of the Gay Village. The co-presence of this hidden sexual economy alongside the Village itself is an important gloss on the Village's own self-confident descriptions. There is no question, however, that the Village 'scene' is a liberating experience for many, particularly those who must routinely hide their sexuality at work, in their day-to-day relationships or in other public places. At the same time, it is clear that the 'scene' itself brings a pressure to bear on individuals, demanding conformity to its particular image of gay sexuality, and it is arguable that this neutralises some of the diversity which exists within this expression of sexuality. There is an unmistakable sense, in particular, in which the Gay Village is another overwhelmingly 'male space' within the city, albeit in a territory where gay men do not feel the pressure of 'compulsory heterosexism'. Commentators on the growth of gay neighbourhoods and leisure facilities in North America confirm that a similar process of hegemonisation of the alternative space by gay men of the entrepreneurial class is at work. Castells (1983) argues that this process is an expression of an 'innate male territorial approach', whilst Adler and Brenner (1992) have argued that attention must be paid to the differential material resources available to men as against women, as well as recognising that lesbian women, confronting the larger dominant culture of masculinity and the danger of male violence against them, may opt for a less transparent culture built around networks and trusting relationships rather than wanting to colonise space and territory. The main identity of the Gay Village is in this sense as a leisure space for gay men, and whilst lesbians do sometimes make use of its facilities, it is not their space.

So also, it should be said, the use of the Village by gay men themselves is strategic and selective. There is little evidence of widespread routinised use of the Gay Village's facilities for business as well as pleasure ('working lunches' or office meetings) – a use which is made of the wine bars of Deansgate and the range of mainstream city-centre restaurants – except by entirely gay organisations. There is very little sense of mainstream organisations coming regularly into the Village for their various business and social events.

In the last two decades, of course, the threat of AIDS has meant that gay men, more than many other groups, have had to come to terms with death amongst their community; it has also necessitated changes in lifestyle and a collective need for support arrangements for individuals through difficult times. Under these circumstances the idea of gay 'community' has taken on an added significance. In addition, the gay community in Britain has faced overtly political attacks, as with Clause 28 of the Local Government Bill (now Section 28 of the Local Government Act of 1988) which prohibits the promotion of 'gay lifestyles' by local authorities. The struggle against this legislation helped to forge a sense of collective interest amongst gay and lesbian people throughout the country. Manchester was chosen as the national focus of resistance to 'Clause 28', hosting national demonstrations which attracted 20,000 protesters on one occasion, underlining the significance of Manchester for the rest of Britain's lesbian and gay population.

The ultimate failure of the campaign against Clause 28 has resulted in a reconstruction of the sense of 'gay community' in its 'pink economy' formulation, defined, primarily, by shared lifestyle and leisure interests. This has led some commentators, like Shepherd and Wallis (1989: 40) to argue that: 'a ghetto political consciousness exists, but it is no longer the dominant consciousness among self-defining gays'.

The claim is often made that gay sexuality and the gay community are inherently progressive, as a consequence of the experience of oppression at the hands of the dominant culture. So, for example, Michael Bronski comments on how: 'Gay liberationists called for the elimination of prohibitions against different forms of sexual behaviour which challenged restrictive gender roles. They were concerned with creating a society and culture which would celebrate sexual expression' (Bronski 1984: 193). By implication, the creation of gay enclaves within cities was to be the vehicle for institutionalising diverse sexualities in a tolerant and pluralistic set of alternative spaces and networks. We have already suggested, however, that there seems to be a very specific hierarchy within Manchester's Gay Village: the gay men who spoke to us were mostly quite aware that the 'Village scene' did not 'liberate' lesbians to anything like an equal extent. Bill argued that the Village was beginning to encompass other uses than those specifically aimed at club goers. He suggested, too, in his comments that the Village was less focused on 'cruising' than it had been previously and that this heralded a change in attitudes.

> Nowadays I think there's development within the gay culture. You've got shops and things actually opening up. I think that's quite a positive thing. I think that's a change in the gay psyche. It's changed from the 1960s to nowadays. I think that's the evidence.

Not everyone agreed that this change had already taken place: Samuel, a gay Christian active in the Village, wanted to see it occur. Conversations which he had had with older men through his church work had led him to believe that there was a pressing need for a wider range of facilities within the Village:

> I think there's a need to move, not to destroy what already exists, but to move towards non-club and pub-related places, coffee houses maybe.

Harold: Manto's is a coffee house.

Samuel: Yes, but not everybody likes it . . . The majority of people that I know wouldn't go into Manto's, because they don't feel they fit into the set that would go there.

There was some hope in the group with whom we were in discussion, who ranged from early twenties to early forties in age, that the gay community in Manchester would adapt and change, in line with their own changing, developing biography and the ageing process:

Harold: By the time we're 50 there's going to be a huge group of people that'll all be 50 and all want somewhere to go.

Bill thought this was already beginning to happen:

> I think in the end people will get pissed off with it . . . going to the clubs for years and years . . . I even get that at my age . . . There will be an organic change within the gay scene and that's happening anyway.

Others were not so sure, and saw the Village as catering primarily for young gay people, including those who had never experienced the constraints of a 'closeted life' before the opening of the Village, and certainly before the impact of the legislation of 1967. There was some awareness that the priority placed on the idea of 'a scene' directed at younger, high-spending gay consumers was, in some senses, a form of discrimination, driven by commercial or political and interest-group considerations. Some of the gay men taking part in our discussion felt ironically that heterosexual society was in fact more accepting of a wide age-range of people, at least in its pub culture. There was some sense of a *ressentiment* here, with the more middle-aged gay men feeling they had

had to suppress their sexuality, perhaps getting married and never feeling able to 'come out' as gay people at all, and resenting the freedom of young gay men.

There was energetic disagreement as to the extent to which older people were accepted on the gay scene at the present time. Pete, an employee of the National Health Service, who also stressed that his experience as a 'working-class' gay man might be different from that of middle-class users of the Village, pointed out:

> You look around the pubs in the Gay Village and they are not all the same. Each pub has got its own character. The Union and the Rembrandt do attract quite a lot of older men . . . they feel comfortable in there. Those kind of pubs were there a long time before 1968.

Sebastian felt that it was more acceptable within the gay 'scene' to go out in a mixed age-group than in heterosexual society:

> It's the only community where you can go for a meal with somebody twenty years older than you and still be acceptable.

Others felt strongly that this did not change the fundamental orientation of the Village towards a youthful clientele. Matt, a man in his twenties, agreed:

> It's just for young people . . . what happens when you're 50 and you can't be going out, or you've got a gammy leg and you can't be dancing all night?

It was also agreed that lesbian women did not play a large part in the life of the Village. To some of our discussants (all of whom were male) this was because lesbians were excluded by gay men; to others it was due to the preferred lifestyles of lesbians being incompatible with those of gay men. It was admitted that men dominate the Village and that the women's 'scene' is relegated to occasional women-only nights in otherwise mixed or predominantly gay clubs. In a similar way the 'scene' was recognised to be heavily dominated by white men. In many ways the Village does not cater for minority tastes within its boundaries: it has grown up around a specific (white, male and middle-class) culture and it is in the interest of the gay, white, male entrepreneurs who have opened up the Village that their facilities continue to be heavily patronised by gay men who feel comfortable within that culture and who have 'discrètionary income' to spend.

THE GAY VILLAGE IN THE LARGER MANCHESTER

Our research in Manchester included a survey, carried out in different sites around the city, eliciting information on responses to different parts of the city and to the city in general. One of our interview sites was directly adjacent to the Gay Village, and the people we spoke to there –

many of whom had not ventured directly into the Village area itself – still associated the area with dereliction and unattractive buildings and had an image (a memory) of it as a depressing area. But at the same time, nearly all the people we interviewed thought they knew their way around the area and where the boundaries lay: it scored highly in terms of its 'readability'. Also, quite strikingly, it scored highest of all the six places in Manchester where we chose to carry out interviews in terms of its perceived sense of safety. Ironically enough, four people interviewed in Manchester during our survey had had some experience of crime or 'trouble' in that area, but even these did not see the area as a particularly fearful place. The upgrading and gentrification of the area by gay entrepreneurs ostensibly catering for a minority lifestyle has created in the process an area of the city which is generally seen as one which it is safe for all to frequent, despite the continuing association of the general vicinity with female and male prostitution. It is widely acknowledged that heterosexual use of the area is quite high, as women in particular take advantage of an area which they can walk through without being harassed and pubs which they can use to meet up with friends (cf. Evans and Fraser 1995).

Where such gay enclaves have not developed within cities, as in Sheffield, the lesbian and gay lifestyle has remained much more hidden from public view. It is of some significance in this respect that, whilst none of the people we interviewed during our street survey in Sheffield spontaneously referred to their own sexuality or volunteered a definition of themselves as 'gay' or 'lesbian', a small minority of the people we interviewed on the streets of Manchester were confident enough so to do.

The few gay venues in Sheffield are scattered throughout the city. A pub used by lesbians and gays is situated near the railway station (prior to 1967, Manchester's gay pubs were also found near what are now called transport interchanges) and the remaining two are in sparsely populated areas, one being in Attercliffe, which has been heavily depopulated since the demise of Sheffield's steel industry. The pubs, like the areas in which they are found, are run down and unmodernised. The overwhelming impression is of a subordinated sexual minority in hiding, shirking the gaze of the larger public, and reticent about its own difference and diversity. Joseph Bristow, a gay man from Sheffield, writing in a recent collection of essays on gay life in Britain, comments on how:

> If one thing strikes me about the gay pubs in my own city, Sheffield, it is the *ordinariness* of many of the clientele – they could be drinking and smoking almost anywhere.
>
> (Bristow 1989: 59)

The Gay Village in Manchester is confident of its own difference from the dominant culture and is committed, at least rhetorically, to a diversity of sexual identities. The local equivalent of San Franscisco's Gay Pride parade is an annual carnival, complete with street floats, which ventures out through the city streets on August Bank Holday weekend, returning into the Village for a weekend-long celebration. At other times of the year, on Friday and Saturday evenings, there are periodic, informal, showy displays in the Village area by transvestites and others, promenading along the canal sides in front of the various pubs and clubs.

Sheffield City Council, dominated as it has been historically by trade union representatives from the steel trades, has not supported lesbian and gay rights to the same extent as has the City Council of Manchester. But the fact of City Council support alone cannot explain the growth and confidence in gay lifestyles in Manchester. Evidence shows that there was a thriving 'gay scene' in the city for some time before the election of the 'left Labour' council in 1981. Gay activists had already organised themselves politically and had eventually won support for the opening of a Gay Centre from the new Council, very soon after its election. Furthermore, the Council employed two gay men as equal opportunities officers in 1985. Many of our respondents in the gay community insisted that the Council's support was really just a confirmation of the ground that had already been won in Manchester in earlier years.

It is important for our argument in this book on difference in local culture to note how many of the gay people who participated in our focus group discussions had been attracted into Manchester as a result of positive exploratory visits from other cities (with frequent references to the tolerant atmosphere, especially in the city centre). Samuel was originally from Cardiff but moved to Manchester to be with a friend. He was well aware of Manchester's gay scene before he moved, and had already made comparisons with his own city:

> The biggest thing that has come over to me is, you go to Cardiff and there's an extremely, almost nonexistent, gay scene. It's, like, two pubs, if they can be bothered to call themselves gay, and one club. It's like again, if you haven't got a strong circle of friends, you've had it. You might as well go and live in Outer Mongolia, there's a better gay scene there!

This gay person's shameful critique of his town of origin was accompanied by the assertion that Manchester is inherently different, in some way, to other cities. The gay men in our discussion group found this 'sense of difference' hard to articulate. However, there was some feeling that what is usually referred to as the 'local culture' of Manchester, although definitely resonant with the culture of work and manufacturing, was not as 'macho' as in other cities. Words like 'cosmopolitan' and 'European' were used to sum up its atmosphere. It is generally seen as a tolerant city, open to different ideas and different ways of living. As Sebastian explained:

> You can take straight friends, you can go with whoever you like. If you go to a club in Bradford, you've got to knock on the door, you can't take a girlfriend, platonic girlfriend, in with you, because it's men only. You get asked 'Are you straight?' Where in Manchester, straight couples can go in the pub anyway, because it's quite accep-

table. The general feeling is that people's minds are broader, *because it is Manchester,* and because of the Gay Village, because of the general outlook on life anyway.

This was echoed by Samuel's experience of moving to Manchester from Cardiff:

> But again, the attitudes to other cultures, and other types of people, are so different in Cardiff. There's still this narrow minded sort of 'you can't do that, you've got to have a husband, you've got to have a wife, you've got to have two kids'.

The existence of the Gay Village plays an important part in the shaping of a culture of toleration for them, as gay men. But a part of the 'elective affinity' displayed for Manchester involved references to the welcome, it was believed, the city extends to other minority groups, symbolised (in a characteristically 'consumerist' perspective) by the existence of areas like Chinatown in the city centre and the cluster of nearly 50 Indian restaurants and food shops on one stretch of the Wilmslow Road in Rusholme: physical areas-cum-'social spaces' that were read as evidence of Manchester people's toleration and celebration of minority cultures. Harold grew up within the Jewish community in Prestwich. He pointed out that the gay community is one of many different 'communities' within the Greater Manchester area:

> We're not the only minority. There's loads, and loads of ghettoes. It all helps I think, like a flavour of everything.

Samuel added:

> Something that came home to me just a few weeks ago. It was Chinese New Year, and Chinatown was packed with all these people celebrating something that is so important to their culture. I was thinking, would I ever see this in Cardiff? Would I ever see a strange celebration of a different culture in another English or Welsh city? I think I'd be quite honest and say no, not for like the next 20, 30 years, because the attitudes are so different.

Sean's job meant that he travelled all over the country, settling in different places as required. When we met him he was working in Liverpool but had chosen to remain a resident of his 'adopted' city of Manchester, which he described as 'the gay capital of the UK'. He added his voice to this discussion:

> The Chinese thing, it's quite interesting because I work in Liverpool, and there's supposed to be the largest Chinese community in the country in Liverpool, or so I'm told, I don't know whether that's right or not. But there doesn't seem to be the same sense of togetherness in Liverpool as you get here. Manchester seems to want to do things, it's done wonders in the three or four years that I've been here.

David, originally from Vienna, had moved to Manchester from London only six months previously, having lived in many major European cities, including Zurich, Paris and Brussels. He was surprised to discover that the gay scene in Manchester compared favourably to these places. He was also impressed by the diversity of cultures which he found in this city 'in the middle of nowhere':

> I remember my boss, I work in a restaurant, my boss told me one day 'Oh, I've been yesterday to Chinatown for the New Year, it was really great. I've taken my child there.' I think that's really unique, that a person can take part in somebody else's cultural celebration like that, as if it's just like they've been to the cinema or something. I found it really positive. The thing of concentrating different communities, so called ghettoes, it's not really a bad idea, and I think that's what the City Council seems to be doing, rather than trying to suppress minorities, and not give them any rights, they think 'well there they are, let's give them a place to live, a place to be in'. If you look, you've got Wilmslow Road for the Indian community, Chinatown, the gay village, I think it's the most positive city in this country when it comes to the issues of minorities. The people seem to be educated to turn out quite broad-minded.[6]

This atmosphere of toleration was usually grounded by reference to a small number of symbolic locations colonised by different cultures (Chinatown, Rusholme or Prestwich, an area of concentrated Jewish settlement), but heavy users of the Village also pointed to the frequent arrival of gay tourists from Europe and North America, and the relative absence of 'gay bashing'. David worked as a volunteer at the Gay Centre and Lesbian and Gay Switchboard and felt that he was in touch with any developments in the Village. He told us:

> At the Gay Centre recently, we had somebody come in from Germany, he asked us 'have you got any groups that are doing things against gay bashing, anti-gay bashing groups', I was thinking 'no, not really'. He said 'How come? In Germany we've got this, we've got that', but I suddenly said 'actually it doesn't happen so much in Manchester'. That's when I actually understood what kind of a place Manchester is. Actually, you are accepted here. The Gay Village is there for the gays. People in Manchester, I feel, think that is *our* Gay Village, it's not *their* Gay Village. '*We* have got a Gay Village in Manchester', I feel that that often comes across, it's not us and them.

Matt added:

> I'm not saying that it doesn't happen, because I've heard about it, but none of my close friends, and myself, in all my years of going to Manchester have ever seen it. I have never experienced any negative views towards me. Perhaps I'm extremely lucky . . . we go shopping,

we can have a laugh, we can go anywhere . . . We've gone screaming [behaving in a camp manner] round Manchester before.

The gay men taking part in our focus group all stressed, however, that not all parts of the city are so positive towards minority lifestyles. The inner-city areas directly to the south of Manchester city centre, including Moss Side and Whalley Range, and much of north Manchester are identified as areas where attitudes are generally felt to be less tolerant. Matt lived in Stockport and did not feel confident in that town. He told us:

[In] Stockport, I've always been conscious about my sexuality.

Harold, another participant who lived just outside Manchester city boundaries, agreed that there was a difference in the way he could act within Manchester and in his own city of residence, Salford, close by Manchester city centre:

In town I feel okay, as soon as I get back to Salford, I'm, like, closeted.

Matt continued:

There seems to be a ring around the city, but if you take any city, isn't it the same?

Outside of Manchester city centre the majority of our participants modified their behaviour. Matt chose to drive rather than take public transport:

I drive, I always drive. I don't use public transport. A lot of gay people have cars, but a lot of people don't. A lot of students don't. But that's probably the reason why I've never come across any homophobia.

Harold tried to appear as 'straight' as he could when in Salford and had had experiences of gay baiting while in that area:

If I go down to the pub for a carry-out, I make sure it's my most ordinary, macho voice, not the occasional squeak! We were walking through the Salford Precinct the other day, it's a very, very straight area, we were just walking past, it can happen anywhere, and we didn't rise to the bait either. It doesn't happen so much in town, once you're out of it.

He insisted that this sense of oppressiveness in Salford extended to Moston, to the north of Manchester city centre, which Pete chose to characterise, to the general approval of the group, as essentially very 'English'. Pete also lived in Salford, on the same estate as Harold, though he did not feel under any pressure to change his behaviour:

I live in Salford, and I regularly walk into Manchester late at night, walk home late at night. I go to a lot of straight pubs, have a lot of straight friends, never get any trouble at all. I don't modify my dress, I don't change the way I look, the way I talk, or anything.

Our discussants were very interested as to why Manchester – or at least certain parts of the city – has developed an atmosphere of acceptance which they had not encountered in other cities. The question as to why the Gay Village has grown up in Manchester rather than London or any other Northern city provoked considerable discussion. Manchester was seen as the 'gay capital' of Britain despite the prominence given to London in so many other ways. The explanations put forward during our focus group discussion were varied: the size of the city is thought to be important, Manchester being large enough to include numerous minority cultures, while small enough to retain a friendly atmosphere. Two of our discussants pointed to the prehistory of strong working-class communities in Manchester (the home of *Coronation Street*) as the source of its reputation as a friendly city, and argued that this friendliness had positive effects for the gay people who have 'come out' here or moved into the city. Bill, not himself from Manchester, felt that the history of the city's development had added a 'community feel' to the place:

> I think it's the history. . . in terms of industry. . . with the communities that were here, it was very much factory-orientated . . . The communities have lasted longer up here, you've got the coal communities, you've got all those kind of industries.

Harold made the same point about 'community' but with an entirely different reference:

> The ghettoes are still here aren't they? . . . I live in Prestwich, which is very traditionally Jewish . . . When I was a kid I could walk down the streets and people . . . would walk up to me and say 'How's your mum and dad?' I'd tell my parents that this lady stopped me in the street and said 'Give my best regards' to them. It carries through with you the rest of your life. I'm sure every other ghettoised person, anyone that's lived in those sort of communities, would carry that through with them.

The political support provided by the City Council and Greater Manchester County Council in the early 1980s was also seen as having helped the gay community at one stage of its development, but it was felt that this support was no longer forthcoming. Both Bill and David were active in organisations which receive funding from the local Labour-controlled authority: they felt that, in the atmosphere of local government cutbacks, the council was less likely to continue giving financial support to groups working with gay men and lesbians. They both felt that the local Council was concerned that open support for such groups might lose them votes and that its officials were therefore looking for ways to withdraw funding. Both felt that the support work carried out with individuals and groups in the Village would suffer as a result, but they did not believe that the existence of the Village itself would be at risk if the Council withdrew its political support.

It is important, in drawing this chapter to a close, to recognise both the value and the limitations of the narrative accounts given us by our gay respondents in Manchester. The voices we heard certainly registered the real sense of pride and achievement that has resulted from the establishment of the Gay Village as a distinct urban space and a set of leisure provisions. There was also a clear sense of the transformation of the moral character and feel of the area into one that 'felt' safe and friendly, rather than threatening and exclusionary – a sense that extended to other users of the area or its vicinity. But the accounts we were given must also be understood as a particular kind of discourse, just as powerfully driven by self-interest and wish-fulfilment as those of an aggressively heterosexual proletarian in the inner city or a local captain of industry living in the suburbs. In particular, as we have noted throughout, the Village is dominated by gay men, and the voices we have presented in this chapter are those of gay men only: they do not speak directly to the experience of the Village by lesbians or other specific sexual minorities. In addition, the discourses we heard in the Village involved a very clear emotional investment in the idea that Manchester, having become the location of the Gay Village, was essentially a 'progressive' place, and specifically, a kind of vanguard European city unlike, therefore, other irretrievably 'English' cities in the North. This kind of definition of Manchester is very much shared by the local Council and Development Corporation (the 'growth coalition'), although where members of these agencies would refer to commercial development, the Metrolink and mainstream entertainment provision such as the new Opera House, these gay men would think, instead, of Chinatown and the strip of Indian restaurants in Rusholme as evidence of Manchester's multicultural character. There is no denying the key important aspects of the city of Manchester: what is at issue, of course, is whether this discursive narrative description can suffice as an account of the city as a whole. The gay men who spoke in such terms certainly also seemed to operate with a rather more pessimistic mental map of the larger conurbation as a whole, identifying, with some considerable level of consensus, a number of urban territories and neighbourhoods that were thought unsafe for gays. The larger city was 'mapped in the mind' in terms of the continuing, residual existence of some very 'straight' and threatening areas, identified in terms of a 'high modern', international discourse as being unreconstructed, irretrievably 'English' and reactionary places. Nearly all our discussants had their own strategies of avoidance, only going through these areas, perhaps, by private car, or for 'passing' in them (adopting an appropriate, aggressive, heterosexual façade). 'The gaze' adopted by these gay men *vis-à-vis* the larger city, in practice, like the gaze of so many of our different publics in the same city, was one of caution and strategic calculation, where the declared public discourse spoke, pleasurably, of toleration and diversity.

8

'WHITE CITY'

Ethnicity and racial difference in Manchester and Sheffield

IMMIGRANTS IN THE INDUSTRIAL NORTH

The classic local study of immigrants in individual English cities in the post-war period, *Race, Community and Conflict*, conducted by John Rex and Robert Moore in Birmingham in the late 1960s, focused its analysis on the struggle faced both by recent immigrants and by other non-white populations in the private and public housing markets of that Midlands city – a 'class struggle for housing' conducted against the institutionalised racism of the private housing market and Council housing departments alike (Rex and Moore 1967). Subsequent commentators have advanced detailed empirical and analytic accounts of the more or less forced concentration of black British people that has arisen, mainly in the 'inner-city' areas of our major cities, and also of the way in which these areas are subsequently demonised as 'black ghettoes' or symbolic locations of crime (Smith 1989). The thrust of these well-known accounts, more or less following on from the work of the famous Chicago School of Sociology in the 1920s, is to argue that this process of demonisation of the inner city (or what the Chicagoans called 'the zone of transition') is a more or less inevitable effect of the process of 'invasion, succession and domination' (cf. Taylor *et al.* 1973: Ch. 4) that characterises the ongoing immigration of distinct groups into large cities, especially in the post-colonial and post-war period when black migrant groups settled in the colonial heartlands (Rex 1973, 1988).

The pattern of immigration and subsequent residential segregation in Manchester and Sheffield over the last 200 or more years was not the specific focus of our study in these two cities, but the research we undertook in no way fundamentally contradicted the general picture painted by John Rex, Susan Smith and others. It will be a matter of comment, however, that the pattern of residential segregation of different migrant or ethnic groups in Manchester has, unmistakably, had to take account of the received physical form of the city, more or less reflecting as it does the Chicagoans' model of concentric or zonal development, and that the development of the 'black ghetto' in Moss Side (the site of riots in the summer of 1981, and further anxious public and political discussion in the mid-1990s) has occurred within an already established transitional zone situated on the flat plain near to the city centre – not far from the major areas of Irish immigrant settlement during the nineteenth century (Little Ireland).

The urban form of Sheffield, by contrast, which was determined by a topography of valleys and hills, but also evolved according to the necessary imperative of building a mass of residential areas well to the west of the city's smoky industrial East End, did not result in the creation of a recognisable inner-city concentric circle or 'zone of transition'. The major area of settlement and ghettoisation in Sheffield in the 1980s and 1990s, Burngreave and Pitsmoor, in its first incarnation was a well-established inner area of Victorian housing, which, on account of its proximity to two major hospitals, was home to many practising doctors and their families. The initial migration of a West Indian population into this area in the late 1940s and through the 1950s, indeed, was a result of a recruitment drive by the Northern General and Fir Vale hospitals, facing a shortage of nursing and auxiliary medical staff. This in-migration was accompanied by a search conducted by local steel firms for semi-skilled labour, with some West Indian workers setting up house in Pitsmoor, as neighbours of other migrants from the islands already established in the medical service. Several other areas of the city, however (Sharrow, Crookesmoor, Nether Edge, Broomhall and Park), were also settled, and, even though Pitsmoor in a local Council survey in 1988 was reported as having the highest proportion of black residents (at about 16 per cent of Burngreave ward) of any area in Sheffield (Sheffield City Council, Department of Land and Planning 1988: Figure 3), it was in no sense a ghetto into which were crowded the bulk of the local black Sheffield population. Nor, importantly, was the area of Pitsmoor/Burngreave historically an area of poverty (its solid Victorian houses being bought up by families working in secure jobs in the local hospitals) and/or an archetypal 'zone of transition', the first 'port of call' of all new migrants in the last two centuries looking to find a home in their new society. It is not clear that the city of Sheffield has ever contained such an area. In 1991, more than 62 per cent of all houses in Burngreave ward were owner-occupied and only 7 per cent were without a car. A survey in a national Sunday newspaper of forty 'dreadful' ('no-go') estates and inner-city areas across the country in 1994 identified the presence of such areas in many major cities, including Manchester, Bradford, Leeds, Liverpool and Newcastle, but not in Sheffield (*Independent on Sunday* 17 April 1994).

Earlier patterns of migration into Sheffield – for example, in the nineteenth century – resulted in the establishment of a small Irish presence in the Scotland Street and West Bar area of the city. In the 1950s, some 3,000–4,000 Pakistani workers, recruited by the steel industry, set up homes in the Attercliffe and Darnall areas, which were later also settled by a smaller number of Indian and Bangladeshi workers. None of these areas (old terraced areas close to the outer edge of Sheffield's industrial East End) approximates the kind of central inner-city transitional zone described in the literature of the Chicago School. The construction of Pitsmoor and Burngreave in the local imagination as a feared symbolic location, and the discursive representation of this fearfulness as a matter of race, is a specific late-developing local instance of the 'pollution' metaphor, applied to migrant areas, as described by Goldberg (1993): the idea that specific urban locations have, in some generalised sense, become 'polluted' in ways which racist commentary works remorselessly to connect to the presence of ethnic minority peoples. Pitsmoor and Burngreave are, of course, home to hundreds of unemployed men, made redundant by the steel industry in the 1980s, and 'their' families. These include large numbers of mostly unemployable young men, whose assumed destiny as future 'Little Mesters' in the steel and cutlery economy, for which they were prepared by local Sheffield culture, is now quite literally impossible.[1] So far from being a racialised ghetto, the area (which as recently as the 1970s was home to a vigorous local history group and other local pressure groups, like the Pitsmoor Action Group, committed to a variety of local civic campaigns) has suddenly become a residualised area with the specific and distinctive set of local problems associated with rapid de-industrialisation (and 'neighbourhood decline') magnified by the fact of two now well-established ethnic claims to ownership of some local space and facilities.

The interest of social researchers and commentators in the 'processes of production' of racialised ghettoes has more recently been succeeded, in the absence of economic affluence and the abolition of the racial ghetto, by a developing interest in a series of other issues and concerns. Not least is an interest in the way in which 'racialised areas' of a different character can grow up within ostensibly similar, geographically proximate territories, 'colonised' by different ethnic groups or by different ethnic mixes, but all sharing an experience of a generalised subordination to the white 'host society' of England. In larger cities such as Manchester whole areas can take on a local reputation, having been 'colonised' (ironically enough for the colonial 'host society') by a particular ethnic or migrant group: West Indian (Moss Side), Asian (Cheetham Hill), Jewish (Prestwich) or Irish (Chorlton). There is a concern that this process of residential dispersal and domination results in a kind of *de facto* apartheid of different ethnic groups, inimical to the liberal conception of a multicultural mix of peoples all making use of the same resources and spaces of the city.

A reanalysis of the 1991 Census data by the Office of Population, Censuses and Surveys produced an 'ethnic map' of Britain which confirmed such a process of *de facto* 'ethnic isolation', using a statistical technique developed in the United States. This study calculated the probability of a member of any one minority group having a neighbour from the same ethnic group, and produced some very high probabilities, overwhelmingly in the old industrial North. In Blackburn, Lancashire, there was a 44.9 per cent probability of a shared ethnic minority identity between neighbours (in a town where 85 per cent of the overall population was white), in Oldham 42.3 per cent, Bradford 39.6, Rochdale 38.7 and Calderdale, West Yorkshire, 36.9 (*Population Trends 78*, quoted in Brindle 1994). By and large, these heavy concentrations of non-white minorities interacting primarily 'in their own communities' occurred in cities in which there was still a massive predominance of a white population across the city as a whole. Table 8.1, for example, shows the ethnic composition of the Greater Manchester region, the City of Manchester and the city of Sheffield: it is only in the smaller city of Manchester that there is a non-white population higher than the national average. The non-white population in England and Wales in 1991 was some 5.9 per cent of the total population, compared to 12.6 per cent in the City of Manchester. Sheffield's non-white population was slightly smaller than the national average, at 5 per cent.

A different approach to the process of racial segregation is that which recognises that a significant number of these areas, at any one time, are in the process of being constructed more or less permanently as 'ethnic ghettoes', rather than simply as preferred enclaves of cultural diversity and pluralism. In this perspective, influenced by the analysis of similar processes of segregation and civic neglect in the United States, whole areas of the city are being systematically forgotten or residualised and left to their own devices in the struggle for survival in the larger free market society. In the American case, these new 'ghettoes of poverty' are overwhelmingly concentrated in areas of black, Mexican and Puerto-Rican residence, and there is unmistakable evidence of massive increases in poverty (measured both absolutely and relatively) in these areas,

Table 8.1 Ethnic groups of residents: Greater Manchester, the City of Manchester and Sheffield (1991)

Ethnic Group	Greater Manchester		Manchester		Sheffield	
	Number	%	Number	%	Number	%
White	2,351,239	94.1	353,678	87.4	475,977	95.0
Black						
Caribbean	17,095	0.7	10,395	2.6	5,007	1.0
Black African	5,240	0.2	3,418	0.8	1,092	0.2
Black other	9,202	0.4	5,045	1.2	1,873	0.4
Indian	29,741	1.2	4,432	1.1	1,415	0.3
Pakistani	49,370	2.0	15,371	3.8	8,880	1.8
Bangladeshi	11,445	0.5	1,997	0.5	1,082	0.2
Chinese	8,323	0.3	3,100	0.8	1,330	0.3
Other: Asian	4,931	0.2	1,990	0.5	948	0.2
Other	12,855	0.5	5,525	1.4	3,598	0.7
(Persons born in Ireland)	(51,044)		(18,465)		(3,437)	
Total	2,499,441	100	404,861	100	501,202	100

Note: 'Persons born in Ireland' are included in the 'White' group, but are separated out in the Census for other purposes in the analysis of the ethnic group make-up of the cities
Source: 1991 Census, County Reports, Greater Manchester and South Yorkshire: Tables J and 6

particularly in the older industrial areas of the North-east and North Central regions during the 1970s and 1980s (Wilson 1991). We do not have any equivalent detailed social research into the historical dynamics of poverty in the old industrial centres of the North of England, but there are numerous local studies of the concentration of poverty – for example, by local authority research units – which suggest that many of the areas which are spoken of by criminologists and police as 'crime areas' and by cultural studies scholars as areas of 'pluralism' and 'difference' are also, quite vitally, centres of the new poverty. This has been produced by de-industrialisation, especially during the 1980s, as well as by the withdrawal of government subsidy and support (for example, of housing and other benefits), under the influence of the free market assault on the idea of 'state dependency'.

Talk of the 'domination' of particular areas by single ethnic groups has itself been superseded in much recent discussion of racial presence in the city by an interest in the ways different ethnic groups, almost by definition attributed a subordinate social standing by the white English as a whole, can begin to coexist within cities. Much of this kind of analysis arises out of the growth of interest in 'identity politics', especially in the context of what is said to be a 'post-modern' or globalising reality (cf. Bauman 1992; Benhabib 1992) – a perspective that is associated, we would argue, with a degree of resignation with respect to the contemporary potential of reformist political or economic policies in individual 'national societies', but also often with a pronounced lack of 'empirical' interest in local voices, local utopias and local histories, in all of their specific and contested forms. This kind of writing on the contemporary importance of learning 'to live with difference' is a vital response to the growth of nationalism and racism across Europe, as well as to the growth of the insular and exclusionary forms of tribalism, which are entirely explicable responses to the decline of local and national economies. But it is still important to understand that generalised moral disquisitions about 'cultural difference' and 'the pluralism of different cultures' in cities like Sheffield can, and often do, suppress the fact that areas of ethnic settlement in English cities are nearly always areas of systemic social exclusion (particularly in respect of the job market) and also of poor housing, poverty and a struggle for economic survival. The considerable anxiety we encountered in Sheffield in the mid-1990s about the presence of a very small group of Somali refugee families on The Manor and Upperthorpe estates is a measure of a generalised insecurity about local labour and housing markets, as well as about the capacity of 'local citizens' to prosper or survive, obtaining in the aftermath of the collapse of the steel and cutlery trades (cf. Taylor and Jamieson 1996b).

In Greater Manchester, by contrast, there are indeed some areas of what we might call 'residential coexistence' of peoples of different ethnic backgrounds (Cheetham Hill, Old Trafford, Whalley Range), akin in some ways to multiracial locales in the United States, though rarely displaying the self-confidence and zest associated with the prize cities of the American Rainbow Coalition. There are also a significant number of shopping areas (zones of consumption, in cultural studies terms) which are heavily used by peoples of different ethnic and cultural backgrounds. This pluralism at the point of consumption was particularly apparent to the white majority population in Manchester's Chinatown and on the Rusholme 'curry mile', whose restaurants and food and clothing shops are heavily used by white Mancunians as well as by people from very different ethnic backgrounds. In Sheffield, the visible evidence of difference, in respect of Indian (as well as Italian and French) restaurants and some Indian and other ethnic foodstores is apparent in the south-western suburbs and along one arterial road (London Road). But the main area of contact between West Indian and Asian peoples is Burngreave, especially on Sunday lunchtimes, when it takes on a distinctly multicultural feel – albeit exemplifying a subordinate, not to say disadvantaged, ambience. Then the area's West Indian and Asian restaurants, and the square of green grass in front of the City Library, are taken over by families from different ethnic backgrounds, primarily from 'poor areas' of the city, constructing a lively and playful Sunday family entertainment.

The conditions which give rise to single ethnic group domination of urban areas, on the one hand, or to the coexistence of different ethnic minority publics in areas that have been relinquished and residualised by the dominant society and then defined as criminal areas, on the other, are an important topic of research in their own right, and are not specific to the North of England. Our own investigations into routine patterns of use of Manchester and Sheffield by different publics certainly touched on, and hopefully illuminated, these concerns. But the main themes to emerge out of the focus groups which we conducted in these two Northern cities, with six different discussion groups of 'ethnic minority' (non-white) people in the cities,[2] had to do with these groups' own experience of the broader, white, city itself and of the specific infrastructure of those cities (their shops, transport systems and other facilities: theatres, leisure centres, sports facilities, parks and open country and, in Sheffield, the Meadowhall shopping centre). Closely connected to these sets of concerns were a range of other areas of anxiety or preoccupations, which had to do, in particular, with the struggle by ethnic minority peoples to find a place for themselves (in a cultural as well as a physical or territorial sense) within these two old Northern industrial cities, each with its very long-established local social structure and associated, usually very firmly articulated, 'local structure of feeling'. Putting the point more directly, our interest here lies in the ways in which migrant peoples, defined in part by the colour of their skins as 'different', were able, first, to establish some kind of home and sense of well-being and security in the industrial North of England *per se* (thus doing battle with 'Northern, non-metropolitan industrial culture' in all its general attributes) and, secondly, to come to terms with the specific local urban

Figure 8.1 White City: Market Street, Manchester
Source: photo by Jenny Young

region and local labour market, as well as various local traditions and the 'local structure of feeling', of Manchester or Sheffield.

Entry into the industrial region and city of Manchester, one may hypothesise, is a very different project for immigrants from Asia or the West Indies from entry into Sheffield or other Northern cities. Greater Manchester's history as a city of commerce and trade has connected it over many years to 'foreign culture' and also given it its long history as a centre of immigration. Sheffield's limited experience with immigration in the post-war period is an expression of the autonomy exemplified over the years by the local dual economy of cutlery and steel. Across the industrial North of England as a whole, there is considerable unevenness in respect of the local experience of immigration and racial difference. Some cities, like Bradford, and towns, like Blackburn, by virtue of the recruitment of thousands of workers from Asia into the local textile trades in the early post-war period, have developed a distinctive, additional (racially coded rather than multiracial) local identity over this period. Others, including Sheffield itself, but also Newcastle, Middlesbrough, Sunderland and Hull, each with its own industrial enclave culture, have not. We also recognise, of course, that there is a particular class dimension to the strategic problems facing new migrants: and that the local social structure of these cities presents a different mix of opportunities and problems for new immigrants into these cities of different class backgrounds (members of professional social classes from India, for example, as against workers from an agrarian area in Bangladesh or one of the poorer West Indian islands). The dynamics are complicated and were not the subject of our particular study.[3]

In the case of Manchester, at the risk of complicating issues further, we would also want to argue, against the somewhat one-dimensional approach of some commentators on racialisation, that the significant presence of a racial Other is not only a signifier of local crime problems and fears ('Moss Side') or of 'pollution', as the racist discourse avers. It is also ironically an important marker, for the rest of the North of England, of Manchester's metropolitan and cosmopolitan status as an international city, the 'capital of the North'. There is a powerful sense that the presence of what is thought to be a significant non-white population, and the visibility of non-white people in local media and retail outlets, in football and in other public roles, in Manchester is a declaration of its headquarter city status.[4]

MOSS SIDE: IN MANCHESTER, IN THE NORTH AND IN ENGLAND

Long before the 1990s – not least because of the participation of about a thousand people in that area in a particularly violent confrontation with police during the summer riots of 1981 – the area of Moss Side in Manchester was already well established in the national imagination as *the* locale in the whole of the North of England which most closely approximated the mythologised black ghettos of the United States. In the late 1980s and early 1990s, a series of some six 'tit-for-tat' killings, universally attributed by police spokespeople in the local press to a feud between gangs involved in the drug trade, further underlined and confirmed the reputation of the area. In May 1991 the Greater Manchester Police issued body armour for officers on patrol in the area, and there was continued discussion of increased use of firearms in other crimes (eventually reaching a peak in 1993, when Greater Manchester Police reported 1048 firearms offences across the conurbation, over double the number reported in 1991) (Greater Manchester Police 1993: 18) and also of the idea that guns have become a kind of 'fashion accessory', especially for stylish young black young men on Manchester's night-time scene [5]. The development which really provoked most national attention, however, was the shooting down of 14-year-old Benji Stanley in a Jamaican pasty and fish and chip shop in Moss Side in January 1992. For some weeks after this killing, the national press was full of reports in which the comparison, always and inescapably, was between Moss Side and South Central Los Angeles, the scene of the riots, murders and lootings of 29 April 1992.

Local charities began to organise trips between Moss Side and Los Angeles for young people from both 'communities', and a number of celebrities, including the boxer Chris Eubank, gave their spare time to working with projects with the young people of the area. A series of new initiatives and public events emanated from the Nia Centre, the established centre of entertainment and social life for black Mancunians. The area has become an icon in various different ways, for various different professional groups and organised associations at national level. It is a symbol primarily of deprivation and disadvantage for some, and of threat and danger for others, with considerable crossover between the two. Locally, it had become a no-go area for many, into which taxi drivers, for example, and many public services (e.g. refuse collectors) were reluctant to venture. There was widespread anecdotal discussion of Moss Side as a centre of activity of full-time Jamaican gangsterism, associated with the idea of the 'Yardie' gang (a form of lay, popular criminological explanation which was quickly taken up, both locally and nationally, by fiction writers attempting to trade on the developing sense of danger and threat).[6] The anxiety, articulated especially by journalists on the crime desks of local newspapers, constantly developing their own lay criminologies for the times, was that Moss Side was some kind of regional centre for drug trading and other heavy crime across the North of England as a whole.

By the early 1990s, Manchester's Moss Side (which, as we will see later, was already in the 1930s a declining rooming-house area into which poor West Indians and Africans had first moved in the light of its cheap accommodation possibilities and the availability of jobs nearby) had been massively redefined as a powerful area; inescapably exerting its irresistible criminal influence on what local common sense wants to see as a relatively non-criminal city. The presence of Moss Side was symbolic in a very contemporary sense; that is, in symbolising the presence not just of a racial Other (in 1991 some 30.5 per cent of the Moss Side population were of Afro-Caribbean or African background, 5.9 per cent of Asian background, and another 5.3 per cent of other non-white background), but also of a specific kind of violent criminality, signified in particular by discussion of the 'Yardie', implicitly linked into the 'international drugs and firearms trade'. The continuing and fretful reproduction of this symbolic discourse had several discrete elements, not least, in general terms, its suppression of the continuing problem of white racism in Northern England and the now routine, interminable containment of black Mancunians and Sheffielders themselves 'within their own areas'. It was connected too, in an important way, to the idea of Manchester as the 'main place' in the North of England, a self-evidently 'post-modern', 'post-industrial city', because it was seen to be having the kinds of problem which post-modern commentators argue must inevitably attach to such cities (violent crime, a black underclass crossing over into the hidden economy, racialised ghettoes, etc.). It was also presented in journalistic reports as having its own local equivalent of South Central Los Angeles's Bloods and the Cripps, in the form of the Doddington and Gooch Close 'gangs', named after two short cul-de-sacs on the Alexandra Park estate. It is precisely this kind of image of Moss Side and Manchester that is received and reworked in other localities across the North of England, with Moss Side and Manchester as a kind of corrupting Other, which, unless checked, may spread its influence across the North, usually (according to this mythology) via the motorway system. A piece by Chris Benfield in the *Yorkshire Post* (published in Leeds), for example, averred in 1991 that:

> Yorkshire Police are well aware that nasty behaviour and the drugs which account for a lot of it, are only too easily transmitted up and down the M62, linking Leeds, Liverpool, Manchester and Hull. Det Insp Peter Cromack of West Yorkshire Police was joking, but joking ruefully, yesterday when he commented 'We sometimes wish we could close it.'
>
> (Benfield 1991)

In the discursive reworking of this kind of modern urban myth, it goes without saying that the empirical 'realities' of the situation within Moss Side, and the actual experience of the place itself, can quickly recede. In 1993, at the height of the panic over murders in Moss Side and firearms use across Greater Manchester as a whole, there were only 34 reported murders across the whole of the Greater Manchester Police area (covering a city of 2.6 million people) and only four in C Division, the area covering Moss Side and adjacent neighbourhoods. There was some suggestion that the finding of firearms by police making searches of private houses was more frequent in Moss Side and adjacent areas, but the numbers were small: actual use of firearms in the course of other offences seems to be dispersed over the entire conurbation. Nationally, there was certainly a marked increase in the number of offences involving firearms in one way or another, but the total number both of reported firearms offences in 1993 (13,951) and of fatal or serious injuries from violent crime (just over 500) was a fraction of that in the United States, where 16,000 people die annually from the use of guns.[7] It is obviously a very crude measure, since police divisions vary so markedly in the size of population covered but in 1993 the total number of offences reported in C Division was actually one of the lowest of all 13 divisions in the city. The highest overall number of woundings, for example, occurred in Salford (a primarily poor white city adjoining Manchester centre) and the outlying towns of Bolton and Wigan.

The development of the particular myths about Moss Side, and especially the comparisons with South Central Los Angeles (where 53 people died during the riots of April 1992), involves a more specific fantasy about the size and influence of this 'Other place' and the powerful and malign influence it is felt to exercise across the rest of the conurbation and, additionally, across the North of England. According to the 1991 Census, Moss Side proper was home to only 13,109 people (only 9,588 of whom were over 16), whilst the city of Compton, a core part of South Central Los Angeles, was home to over 100,000 in 1992.[8] Moss Side is 1.84 square kilometres where the city of Compton covers some 120 square kilometres (*Time* magazine 11 May 1992). If Moss Side was being conceived in the imagination as containing an occupying army of dangerous Others, as Cross and Keith discuss in relation to 'blackness' in English cities generally, it comprised in reality little more than a single company (Cross and Keith, 1993). Sweeping comparisons between the violent situation in English cities, especially perhaps in the North of England as a whole, and post-modern America were not only empirically undisciplined: they were also, we would argue, in an important sense fantastic, involving, that is, a fantasy about the post-modernity of place, on the one hand, and about scale, on the other.

Physically and spatially, Moss Side 'presents itself' most immediately to a public passing in buses or cars along the main arterial road running between the city centre (about one mile away to the north) and the airport and Manchester's southern suburbs as the 'front line' of a decaying area of working-class terraced houses. In fact, the two areas of built-up housing on each side of this main road comprise very different types of housing stock. To the east is a cluster of very traditional working-class back-to-back houses, built around the Manchester City Football Ground. To the west, behind a stretch of older terraces and alongside Alexandra Park (a leafy public park of 60 acres first opened in 1868 on land purchased from Lord Egerton) is a neat, modern council estate of the same name, with some solid housing stock that has not been noticeably subject to criticism either from other architects or from the residents themselves, but whose frontage is dominated by a row of houses built on energy-efficient principles, with very few and very small windows in the 1960s. There is also a significant amount of larger housing, especially to the south, now nearly all in multiple-rented occupation. The area itself over the years has been home to the de Quincey family[9] as well as to political exiles of some considerable importance, like Cecil Padmore and Jomo Kenyatta, a founder of the Mau Mau movement in Kenya and latterly the prime minister of that country.[10] In the last three decades of the last century and the first three decades of this, these larger houses in Moss Side and adjacent inner-ring areas of Manchester were the home to the commercial middle class of the city, which, as we indicated in Chapter 2, had grown a lot faster than the equivalent commercial population in other major cities. Robin Ward's exhaustive and careful analysis shows how the continuing growth of Manchester, especially in the early years of this century, gave rise – exactly as has been described by the Chicago School – to a push of the commercial middle class outwards into the suburbs or beyond, putting distance between themselves and their places of work and employees, and making use of the developing bus, tram and train systems to commute into the centre. Moss Side lost the prestige it had gained in the 1870s, and the suburbs to the south began to exercise a powerful pull. According to Robin Ward, one way of amassing capital and buying oneself into the southern suburbs was to 'farm' or rent out property in the inner city: certainly, it was during the 1920s and 1930s that many thousands of properties around the inner ring of Manchester, especially to the immediate south and east of the centre, were broken up and rented out as apartment houses (Ward 1975: Ch. 7). By the late 1930s, an area in which there were very few black immigrants had already become 'stigmatised', in Ward's words, as a declining rooming-house area, dominated by rack-renting and absentee landlords. A host of associated problems, including the development of prostitution on an organised scale, were developing. The area was, however, cheap; there was a considerable range of properties; and in the 1940s and 1950s, new migrants, including African and West Indian migrants (including some intellectuals and political activists from both sets of countries), moving from elsewhere in Britain where housing was not so plentiful, found Moss Side an attractive location. Though housing was the major attraction, so also did Manchester's reputation as being a friendly trading and commercial city 'with no colour bar' have an influence, especially on migrants from the Midlands.

A third influential point was the availability of work in the nearby Manchester Docks and also in the skilled engineering and other trades: in 1962 only 18 per cent of black workers employed in Manchester were employed in unskilled work (Ward 1975: 310). It is self-evident that the particular problems experienced in Moss Side from the late 1980s into the mid-1990s are framed, in a broad sense, by the collapse of this local manufacturing economy in Manchester, discussed in Chapter 3 of this book; but it is also clear, from the discussions we conducted in the ethnically mixed area of Cheetham Hill and from other local sources, that the particular set of circumstances confronting Moss Side include its transformation from a 'zone of transition' for ambitious new immigrants (its presumed status in the 1950s) into what looks like a permanently residualised territory. In the late 1980s and early 1990s Moss Side appeared as a kind of holding camp or laager for a racially segregated part of the broader underclass, excluded from the waged labour force, with no obvious prospects of moving out of the area, in the manner described for Chicago in the 1920s by Chicago sociologists. In the meantime, we want to argue, Manchester has had attributed to it, in the imaginations of national journalists, politicians and others, its own particular, fearful ethnic ghetto, whose presence in the city is an inescapable marker of Manchester's national and regional status, as a restless and difficult headquarter 'free market' city – a place where money is made, even in these new times, but within the illegitimate hidden economy.

OUR RESEARCH SITES

The research conversations we organised with non-white ethnic minority peoples in Manchester were held not in Moss Side, however, but in Cheetham Hill and in Chinatown. In Sheffield, our discussions were organised primarily around Burngreave and Pitsmoor in Sheffield, but also in social clubs of local Afro-Caribbean and Asian people.

Cheetham Hill is a little-researched area to the north of Manchester city centre. It contains many of the components which go to make up what some writers call the 'cautionary Other', a perception which is unquestionably attached to Moss Side. Unemployment in Cheetham Hill was measured by the 1991 Census at 22.3 per cent for everyone but at 24.4 per cent for young people, with long-term unemployment running at 39.8 per cent. The area as a whole was thought by local police and the press to be home to 'the Cheetham Hill gang', associated with high rates of burglary and muggings and regularly featured in news items detailing gang activity and shootings in the area. In January 1991, the area's growing reputation for criminality was signalled by the murder of a man, reputed to be 'a major drug dealer', outside a public house on Cheetham Hill Road (a killing which sparked a series of revenge attacks in Cheetham Hill and Moss Side through the remainder of that winter), and in May 1991 a police car on routine patrol on the Fairy Lane estate was firebombed by groups of local young men (*Manchester Evening News* 8 May 1991). Its ethnic population is mixed: though the largest settlement is Asian,[11] it has been the site of a succession of migrations by Irish, Jewish and Pakistani migrant labour and also contains African, Vietnamese and Chinese households.

Cheetham Hill was chosen in preference to Moss Side itself as the location for our focus group discussions for a number of pragmatic and other reasons. The area itself, like Moss Side, is associated with gangs, criminality and black settlement, but its reputation as a 'zone of fear' is less well established than that of Moss Side. There was some sense in which Cheetham Hill's emerging reputation within the city was still open to discussion and negotiation, especially amongst long-established local residents. More pragmatically, it was an easier area in which to contact residents and various community organisations. The area's shopping precinct and main shopping street are contiguous and are well used by all the populations in the neighbourhood. In contrast, Moss Side's shopping precinct, now demolished, at the time of our fieldwork was situated alongside a busy dual carriageway on its east side and a main road to the south, some distance from the area's residential streets.

Manchester's Chinatown is an area of half a square mile in Manchester's city centre, bordered by four classic streets (York, Mosley, Portland and Princess Streets). Prior to the last world war, the area was home to the Jewish garment trade. In the early post-war period, however, patronage of bespoke tailors declined, and the area went into a steep decline, with many buildings abandoned and becoming derelict. In the 1970s and 1980s, these cheap buildings were bought up by enterprising Chinese immigrant families, who transformed the area into the largest Chinatown in England outside London, with over 25 restaurants and a number of foodstores, bakers and other Chinese outlets. In 1985, the redevelopment of the area was symbolised by the construction of a large Chinese Arch, jointly financed, at the cost of £350,000, by the Chinese Embassy, Manchester City Council and the local Chinese community (*City Life* 246, 26 Jan.–10 Feb. 1994: 53–4). Chinese people of both Cantonese and Hakka backgrounds began to move into the city from elsewhere in the UK as well as from China itself, with some 8,000 Chinese people resident in Greater Manchester in 1995[12] and a further 50,000 in the North-west area, with Chinatown operating as a kind of magnet (Frank 1994: 80).[13]

We have already outlined the emergence of Burngreave in Sheffield as a racialised area and, more recently, a 'landscape of fear' and a symbolic location for crime. In October 1991, an article in *Westside*, a lifestyle and advertising magazine directed at Sheffield's affluent professional middle class in the south-western suburbs, condensed many of the local urban fears and myths:

> Burngreave is a lively sort of place. A murder here, a fight there, cars squealing round corners on two wheels, youths leaping out of the way. *Just* the place for a quiet stroll. [Emphasis in original]
> ('Walk of Life' *Westside* October 1991)

Our earlier discussion confirmed that Burngreave has the highest number of non-white people of any area in Sheffield, but this does not in and of itself explain the kind of smugly cynical and fearful representation of the area in the pages of magazines like *Westside*. Nor either is it very persuasive to attribute the new-found demonic image of Burngreave to 'biased' coverage of the area in the *Star*, Sheffield's local evening paper, although there seems little doubt that the coverage given to the area by local journalists – for example, of various community events and regeneration initiatives aimed at 'the black community' – may confirm an image of the area (which is actually three-quarters white) specifically and exclusively in racial terms. Photographs illustrating police carrying out raids for illegal drugs in the area which accompanied the *Star*'s front-page story in September 1993, showing predominantly black (Afro-Caribbean) youth under arrest, are typical of many reports given prominence in the area.

SETTING UP THE DISCUSSIONS

Of our survey interviews in Manchester, 12.65 per cent were with non-white respondents. This compares with 12.6 per cent of Manchester's population who were non-white according to the 1991 Census. A higher number of non-white Sheffielders – 13.9 per cent – made up our interviews in Sheffield, compared to the 5 per cent of the Sheffield population who were categorised as being of non-white background in the city in 1991. We had spoken to few people of Chinese origin, despite one of our survey sites in Manchester being close to Chinatown, and very few black and Asian women. We had spoken to a disproportionate number of Afro-Caribbean and Indian or Pakistani men between the ages of 18 and 35. A small number of adult black and Asian men and women attended our focus group discussions, but, in the meantime, the contact we had established with schools enabled us to speak with children of school age in both cities from different ethnic minority backgrounds. However, we were aware that the voices of many ethnic minority adults were missing. We therefore set out to contact those people we had not been able to contact through our street surveys. To this end we arranged focus group discussions with Asian women from Cheetham Hill, Manchester, and Sharrow in Sheffield, with Chinese elderly in Manchester and with Afro-Caribbean elderly and young Afro-Caribbean men in Burngreave, Sheffield.

The Asian women we met in both cities were participating in community education classes and were contacted by their tutors. As such they had already achieved a level of confidence and outside contacts that meant they were able to attend these gatherings outside the home. The Chinese people to whom we spoke were residents of a housing scheme for Chinese elderly people, situated in Manchester's Chinatown. As such they lived very close to the main shopping area and other facilities in city-centre Manchester. They were all over pension age, the eldest being 88, and so their age generally prevented their involvement in many aspects of the city's night life. The casinos situated in Chinatown were seldom mentioned in these discussions although they had probably been frequented by the participants in the past. The Afro-Caribbean focus group took place in Sheffield in a community centre, which organised lunch-time social gatherings, and supplied a meal, whilst outings to the Sheffield countryside and further afield were also occasionally arranged. The people we spoke to in what was a lunch-time meeting were mainly unemployed or over pensionable age. We also spoke to a group of young black men in Sheffield who were regular users of a local community centre.

We are aware that the conversations which we held with these groups cannot adequately reflect the differences which exist within these communities and between the cities. However, they allowed some common themes and different adaptations and strategies to emerge. In contrast to many other studies which have concentrated on the residential segregation of ethnic minorities, we should reiterate that our primary interest was in these groups' use of public space and any constraints which they might feel impinged on their use of public spaces.

Conversation in these groups focused on the mundane daily activities in which the individuals engaged, moving on to an exploration of feelings of security or anxiety which these routines generated. One of the most striking features of non-white ethnic minority group use of the city (at least as discussed in our sessions) was the extent to which daily routines were conducted exclusively within their residential locality. Many of these patterns of city use were also common amongst all economically marginalised people, including poor whites; but we want to focus here on those aspects of the day-to-day negotiation of city spaces which differ from the majority white experience, in an attempt to identify those constraints which are peculiar to these groups of city users and the specific isolation and segregation which they face.

SHOPPING AROUND

It was very clear from our survey work that proportionately far more black Mancunians and Sheffielders were regularly involved in what we called, in Chapter 5, 'subsistence shopping'. Recursive use of cheap discount stores in the neighbourhood was much more frequent than any family shopping trip 'into town'. There was also a heavy use of outlying shopping areas which catered for the particular needs of different ethnic groups in respect of food, clothing and other items that might be spoken of as 'our stuff'. Whilst going to 'town' on a weekly basis is an important part of growing up and away from the parental home for many young people of school age, the black and Asian children we spoke to indicated a much stronger identification with their local area, some never visiting town at all.

City centres often do not include the shops which minority groups would find most useful for their everyday needs, such as food and clothing. Neither Manchester nor Sheffield city centres held much interest for Asian women. Much of their shopping time was spent in Asian food stores or in clothes shops. In Sheffield we were told:

> We don't go there [into Sheffield city centre] because it hasn't got any of those things, we just go there to have a look.

Asian women in Manchester told us that they did use city-centre stores like British Home Stores or Marks and Spencer for their children's clothes but that they would only go into town when accompanied by their husbands, as it would be unacceptable 'in their community' for them to go alone. For the residents of Manchester's Chinatown, however, negotiating the city centre was part of their daily routine, for they live in it and must pass through it to get to other places. Most of their shopping took place in the Chinese supermarkets and shops which, together with restaurants and casinos, make up the Chinatown area. Their 'local area' was in the centre of the city, but, apart from excursions to the markets in the Arndale Centre and the Barrows, little use was actually made of other facilities. The Afro-Caribbean elders to whom we spoke were also concerned to save money, and rarely found 'value for money' within city-centre shops.

Buying fresh produce and visiting market stalls featured highly in the shopping patterns of all our ethnic minority adults. As mentioned earlier,

Manchester has a small city-centre street market and some covered stalls below the Arndale shopping centre, but most of its renowned market areas lie outside the city centre, either in inner-city areas or in outlying towns such as Bury and Oldham. Sheffield, on the other hand, has two popular market locations. Some people from ethnic minorities would travel into these city-centre locations to get the goods they wanted, whilst also maintaining strong links with other towns and cities where relatives live, often stocking up on halal meat, vegetables or herbs which were difficult to obtain in their own area each time they visit. As one Asian woman from Sheffield told us:

> East End [in London] is the cheapest. It's funny to say, but I buy my chicken from London. I buy twenty chickens, it costs me a pound, or one pound ten pence . . . Coriander is cheaper there, you buy four for a pound, here it's fifty pence for one bunch. Some time it goes up to one pound.

The idea of travelling to a city as far afield as London in order to buy goods at an affordable price would, of course, be anathema to the majority population of Manchester or Sheffield. Their expectation would be that 'their own city' should be able to provide all the basic items of shopping for them. Ethnic minority groups cannot routinely claim that of the cities in which they live.

Young black men in Sheffield saw Meadowhall as a place where a black person could not feel comfortable, and where a group of black youth, in particular, might well be asked to leave by security guards. The lack of any shops catering specifically for Afro-Caribbean tastes signalled a rejection of black people in that shopping space:

> Meadowhall – they've never set aside any one of the shops, anything like that, to try and attract black young businesses. You can see straight away the disassociation from black people. It's like separatist. Us, we feel that we are from South Africa, so to speak. Yeh . . . they're showing you straight away that you're not wanted . . . If you're talking about clothes shops, we have none. If you're talking about paper shops, we have none.

In contrast, Meadowhall was visited by Asian school-age children of both sexes. Meadowhall is situated in Sheffield's East End, not far from Attercliffe and Darnall, the areas settled by Indians and Bangladeshis in the 1960s. It offers Asian children a safe, secure environment which they could visit at weekends or after school in order to meet other children of their own age and create their own entertainment without parental supervision. Their parents would allow them to go to the Mall unaccompanied, since they distinguished it in their minds from an entertainment site *per se* (like a city-centre amusement arcade, for example, with what was thought to be its corrupting influence), and also because of its reputation as a safe and controlled environment.

Overall, however, the shopping of all the different ethnic groups was centred in local neighbourhoods. The shopping centres of these cities and their 'palaces of consumption' like Meadowhall – heavily used by many of the city's majority population – were not, routinely, the preferred shopping choice.

TIME OUT

The concept of 'leisure' which dominates the discourse of the Census office and the 'leisure industry' is, we think, quite inappropriate for understanding the preoccupations and actual practices of these non-white Mancunians and Sheffielders. The overwhelming defining dimension of their 'leisure' activity was the attempt to maintain a sense of belonging within a community and an identity in cities which were clearly felt in many ways not to be 'theirs', and which were also associated with different levels of cultural and personal threat. Overwhelmingly this meant that people very much stayed in their local areas.[14] There are some social clubs for Chinese, West Indian and Asian people in Manchester and Sheffield, to which some people would travel during the day. By and large, however, as Parveen, an Asian woman in Sheffield, told us:

> There's virtually nothing for Asian women to do, and that's a problem. The only place you can go here is the pub and we don't go to pubs anyway.

Activities such as watching television, going to the cinema or getting in a video raised problems of their own, as the women felt obliged to censor programmes so they and their children would not see anything which would transgress the cultural and religious norms of 'the community'. Rather than staying in the house all the time, they would often go driving at night with their husbands and their children. The destinations might be particular places in the countryside, the homes of friends in other cities, or, in several instances, Manchester Airport, where they would sit and watch the planes take off and land.[15] These highly segregated and group-protective practices functioned to shelter children in part, and to a lesser extent women, from problems they might encounter in public space. Some young Asian people also exhibited concern that their spending of time in public space might risk problems within their own community. In Manchester one young Pakistani woman, dressed in the traditional *shalwar kameez* but with a very western attitude and air (she was wearing platform shoes, which were highly fashionable in Manchester at that time), told us of problems that could be encountered on the street. She recounted how she had been walking along a busy road in her neighbourhood and had been wolf-whistled and shouted at by four young, white men in a passing car. Her concern was that other members of her community might have seen this incident, that she would have been 'marked' in some way, and that this could have impinged on her standing in the community. Although internally she felt strong enough to cope with this personal intrusion, the other possible consequences of it in her own ethnic community lay outside her control.[16]

Manchester's Chinatown was very much the preferred location for Chinese people of Manchester, and was also heavily visited by the 80,000 Chinese who live in the North-west of England, Cheshire, Staffordshire and North Wales. On Sundays whole families would gather for *dim sum* in the massive restaurants in the area, and the use of Chinatown during the week was also very significant. The one place in Chinatown which was avoided was the Pagoda, which was built as part of improvements to the area in the late 1980s, but has been colonised in the early 1990s by homeless people as a place to sleep. In the day, their bedding was often left under the benches.

The Afro-Caribbean young males in Sheffield felt their race impinged much more acutely on their access to certain areas of the city than any of the other groups to whom we spoke. These young black Sheffielders spoke with great anger about the reception they received from white Sheffielders, as well as other non-white groups, particularly when they tried to make use of the city centre:

> [We] can't go to Fargate, or down the Moor, because, being Afro-Caribbean, you're seen straight away as being vagrant, or in that manner, because it's pure negative connotations.

Very few places in the city centre in Sheffield were seen as catering for their particular lifestyle and interests. The few young black people who did actually use the city centre were therefore more likely to be noticed, remarked upon and seen as likely trouble-makers.

The young black Sheffielders also insisted that they were in effect being denied the opportunity to 'go out' into the city centre at night. There was a feeling that night clubs which catered solely for black music were denied licences in city-centre areas and other clubs were discouraged from accentuating Afro-Caribbean music and culture. This policing of a black cultural presence that was perceived to obtain in the city centre itself meant that the young black Sheffielders, looking to socialise or for entertainment, felt forced back into local areas, in the Ellesmere Youth Centre in Burngreave, sometimes in illegal 'Blues' clubs, or just within their own home. As one participant stated:

> they keep us concentrated in certain areas.

We were told that the door policy at one city-centre night club worked to prevent all-black nights, by allowing only a certain number of black people into the venue. It was felt that the same sorts of policy worked to keep black people out of pubs as well. Similar concerns were expressed in Manchester.[17]

Much of the time spent in these local neighbourhoods involved sitting around in private homes or just hanging around on street corners. In this respect, there was little difference from youthful practices in other poor areas of the city dominated by a white population: in all such areas, young people spoke of 'there being nothing to do', 'nothing for them', etc. The key difference for these young black Sheffielders was the way they felt themselves to be perceived when they moved outside of their own locality, especially in the city centre, and, even more so, when they were seen to enter into what were naturally and unproblematically seen to be 'white' areas. Joseph observed how:

> The youths are all over the place, not only at the centres but they may congregate at a friend's house or on certain street corners, so on. But it would be within their immediate area, trying outside of that, you're seeing people who are not familiar [with] your features. Then they get the wrong idea, the wrong impression. It may be because of your dress or it may be because you have dreadlocks and the negative connotation that is around that [particular style].

Joseph, a young black Sheffielder, himself in full dreadlocks, gave particularly clear expression to the uneasiness his use of places outside the local area engendered in him:

Joseph:	I don't venture far outside. I stay in the community. I feel safer there as well.
Ian Taylor:	You feel unsafe outside?
Joseph:	Not unsafe, but we know our sort of danger. Do you understand?
Karen Evans:	Is that through your own experience?
Joseph:	Through your own experience.
Ian Taylor:	So how far will you go? When do you start to feel unsafe?
Joseph:	Town. Just going as far as town. Walking from the Wicker to the centre, you can get stopped by the police, you understand? Or you get store detectives coming out of a shop, calling you into a shop. So you pick it up, you're being watched all the time. It's uncomfortable, you know what I mean?

Later, Joseph revealed that he did in fact use these spaces, but he then outlined how, in doing so, he had to employ certain strategies to deal with his anxiety:

> Certainly in the day [I use the town centre], but I have to be in the right mood. It's not good vibes, it's not bad vibes. It's just you have to make the right decision.

Or again:

> If you feel like a walk, you wouldn't normally do something like that, understand? You have to have a cause to go somewhere.

And on going further afield to white areas such as The Manor estate, other tactics are employed. For example:

> It's all right if you know some people. You just keep to your own

thing, don't interfere with anyone's business. You go to your friends' house, meet there, that's it.

One of the methods used by young people to manage their sense of security in public space was to move around in groups. But our young black Sheffielders indicated, with some anger, that even this strategy was problematic for them. Groups of young black men moving around the urban spaces were clearly thought threatening by other users of the city, and also by police.[18] So when a group of young black Sheffielders met up in one place to go somewhere, they knew they would have to split up into smaller groups and travel separately, rather than risk antagonising the police and receiving unwanted attention from other people in the Sheffield public. In this way one of the pleasurable experiences indulged in by many groups of young people – that of being in a 'gang', out in the open, away from parental or adult authority – is denied black youth, in ways which they angrily resent. Once again, on the evidence of the work we did in Manchester and Sheffield, this would appear to be a more significant issue for young blacks in Sheffield, though there is also a sense that many young black Mancunians do still prefer to stay within their own enclaves in Cheetham Hill, Moss Side, Whalley Range or elsewhere.

HAVING 'A PLACE' IN WHITE NORTHERN CITIES

The young black Sheffielders certainly felt they were restricted, in their use of Sheffield, to particular territories where they were, in effect, expected to be seen. Other ethnic minority adults to whom we spoke also underlined their recursive use of the same, quite restricted areas, although for different reasons. They tended not to advance a fear of surveillance or harassment by others as an account of their movements being so restricted, but spoke instead of the familiarity of local places and the security accruing from their personal close knowledge of the area. As the interpreter of our focus group in Chinatown explained:

> If they've never been to [a] place, then they won't go. They only go when they are accompanied by guides.

Stories based on personal experience of what can happen to individuals when they stray outside known areas were related to the groups. One Chinese woman, Mrs Tang, told us:

> One day my husband and I, we had got on the wrong bus on the way to his son's takeaway and we were so frightened. This Western woman, she was so kind, she took us back to the bus stop and then she even helped us to find a phone box to call the relatives.

Once out of an area which they knew this couple had to rely completely on a passer-by to help them get on to the right route. Many Chinese and Asian people we met would not have felt confident that such help would be at hand, and felt especially vulnerable in places which were strange to them.

Those who did not have a confident grasp of the English language felt less able to cope with the people and situations which must necessarily be encountered in public space. For Asian women in Sheffield, lack of fluency in English caused difficulties in dealing with racist abuse or other difficult interactions. In Manchester, both Asian women and the Chinese elderly people we spoke to found their boundaries foreshortened because they were unable to ask for fares or to read street signs. This gave the idea of using tried and trusted routes through the city added importance. One Asian woman in Manchester, who had little English, had recently moved from Cheetham Hill to Prestwich – a move to a more suburban location approximately three miles away. Whilst happy with the move and seeing it as an opportunity to escape some of the problems of inner-city Cheetham Hill, she nevertheless felt isolated in her new environment and still identified strongly with Cheetham Hill. She had learned to drive, memorised the route from Prestwich down to Cheetham Hill and drove it almost on a daily basis, but she was not confident enough to attempt to drive anywhere else.

Often very detailed and circumscribed routes were related to us and functioned as strategies for coping with city space, allowing it to become well known and familiar. One characteristic, and very detailed, response to our questioning around typical patterns of use of the city was given by one man, via the interpreter, who told us;

> Mr Chi understands quite a bit of English. He says that a typical day starts at 9 o'clock. He has a bath and then will prepare his clothes for washing later . . . He will walk from here to Longsight – to the Asda supermarket. There he will buy all his vegetables, red meat and other necessary things. Then he will eat fish and chips there. It's only £1.99, it's very good value. Then he will take a bus back with his shopping, come back, have a cup of tea and listen to Chinese opera music on cassettes. And then he will go out again, for a walk. He will go to the Arndale Market, get some fresh fish, anything he can't get at Asda. On the way home he will get a paper. When he gets home he will again have a rest, a cup of tea. Then, to kill time he will walk to the casino and socialise with people there . . . Saturday he supports Manchester United . . . he goes by bus – Old Trafford – a long way away.

This not only reflects the routine which many older people who are not working will adopt to fill their days and bring some kind of organisation into their lives, but also mirrors the bounded experience of many of the elderly Chinese people and other minority groups with whom we spoke.[19] These boundaries are both geographically and culturally patterned. For first-generation immigrants at least, what is available in England is utilised to mirror as closely as possible the life they may have known in their country of origin. Subsequently, as our discussions with schoolchildren revealed, these patterns of use of the city are communicated to children and may form the basis for their later exploration of public spaces.

FEARS OF THE WHITE CITY

The fear of crime can have a significant impact on use of city-centre spaces. There was less spontaneous discussion of the impact of crime on the lives of our Sheffield focus group participants, however, than occurred in Manchester. In Manchester, Asian women in particular discussed in some detail how crime affected their day-to-day lives. They felt that, in Cheetham Hill, Asian households had become specific targets for burglary – and this had a special significance for Asian people, who often keep their wealth as domestic items and especially jewellery. Some women had taken to carrying their jewellery around with them at all times so as to keep it safe from being burgled. However, they also felt that 'local gangs' had become wise to this strategy and observed that Asian women had been mugged in the street, with their handbags snatched and the jewellery they had been wearing stolen. What most concerned Asian women in Manchester and Sheffield was the ever-present possibility that their own children were being introduced to a culture of gangs and criminality. In Sheffield the women had heard that gangs had formed amongst the different ethnic groups in the area where they lived and that each gang had a role to play, with Jamaican youth getting involved in actual breaking and entering, they argued, and Asian youth involved in receiving and 'fencing' the stolen goods. In Manchester the women felt that Asian youth were involved in passing information about the homes of Asian elders and others to groups of white youth, who would then burgle these houses, knowing where valuable jewellery was likely to be hidden.

The Chinese people in our discussion groups generally felt untroubled by crime in the areas of the city which they knew and would use. One group, however, commented that they were wary of the groups of young people they often saw in the city centre at night. Their contact with such groups was unsurprising given that their place of residence is close to night clubs, casinos and restaurants which are heavily used during the evenings. Mr Sing, an elderly Chinese male, told us of the young people who promote some anxiety for him:

> You can tell they just look like mobs [this word was used by the interpreter to sum up the group's descriptions, saying that there was no equivalent word in Chinese]. When they're together in a group, they just look like mobs. There's a look about them to show that they are trouble-makers. We avoid them.

and another, Mr Chi:

> Late in the evening, Friday night, Saturday night, you get a group of

youngsters. You can tell they are out for trouble. They don't dress in suits, they are not the type . . . Sometimes you see a car parked in the middle of the road – a whole group of youngsters go to the car and surround it.

A study of race relations in Sheffield commissioned by the City Council in the late 1980s also highlighted the routine harassment of owners of 'Chinese take-aways' in the city, especially by young white men at the end of an evening's drinking:

[Chinese take-away owners] have come to see racial harassment as being 'as British as the weather'. . . on Saturday nights, the takeaway staff say, 'British boy use take-away as a toilet'. When challenged, the boys answer 'This is my country and I will do as I please'.
(Sheffield City Council, Department of Employment and Economic Development 1989, quoted in Wainwright 1989)[20]

This report did not include discussion of the ritualised confrontations between young white Sheffielders and owners and workers in Indian restaurants, though these have been a feature of weekend life in some parts of the city, and many other Northern cities as well, for some considerable time. Though we were not able to investigate the prevalence of such confrontations systematically in either Manchester or Sheffield, there is a definite sense that these incidents are less frequent in Manchester, not least because of the dominant presence in the city of China-town itself and the 'curry mile' in Rusholme, and the lengthier history of the multicultural presence in Manchester, the city of commerce and trade. In no sense, however, should this be taken to imply the absence of racial tension and conflict, especially in local neighbourhoods or urban districts that see themselves as 'white'.

AVOIDANCE IN THE WHITE CITY

When we surveyed Mancunians about the areas of their city they would be likely to avoid, Moss Side, Cheetham Hill and Whalley Range were cited with monotonous regularity by all city residents, including people of Asian and Chinese backgrounds. They were universally described as 'bad' areas, a term which requires examination. In large part, it carries an unspoken 'racialised' connotation: all these areas are associated, in the local mind, with an Afro-Caribbean presence, even though this is less true of Cheetham Hill than Moss Side and Whalley Range. Vitally, they were also areas associated with drugs and guns, although again the evidence suggests that burglaries and car theft are much more signifi-cant an intrusion into the everyday life of local people than the drug trade directly or offences involving firearms. In Sheffield, Burngreave, Pitsmoor and Broomhall, also with high levels of ethnic minority popu-lations, were cited as dangerous places, but so too on occasion were predominantly white areas such as The Manor.

In the discussions we held in Cheetham Hill itself, for example, Clive Harrison, a young leisure-centre worker, spoke of a general uneasiness in the area, provoked in particular by some 'real bad kids' who lived on the local estates:

> it's not a very nice area . . . I don't hang around street corners in Cheetham Hill at all.

Local people did speak at some length about the level of crime in the area, in so doing focusing on their personal experience of burglary and theft (in the local shopping precinct), and only secondarily on the mythic aspects of gunmen and drugs runners. Fear of crime was very high, however, fed by an intense local circulation of rumour about the latest incidents, drawing both on local community newspapers and on word-of-mouth exchanges. One tough-minded man in his thirties who lived close to Cheetham Hill, Philip Murray, told us:

> The little Spa shop on Cheetham Hill [over the last nine months] there's been armed robberies there twice. You got the Nat West bank – that had an armed robbery. Victoria Wine has had armed robber-ies. It's quite an interesting place to live. It's a bit off-putting, it's not too much for me, I've got no money anyway, I can't be robbed. But for people who are slightly worried about these things, those streets are getting crazy out there.

Moss Side was generally referred to as the worst area in the city and was linked with violent crime, 'disturbances' and drugs. It was less often visited by our focus group respondents, many saying that, rather than avoiding the area, they had no reason to go there. In Sheffield, Burn-greave was seen as particularly frightening at night, when, we were told, 'it looks like Belfast', due to the elaborate security measures and shutters which are used to keep shops and other buildings secure. It was also variously referred to as 'a good place going out' and as being overtaken by 'ghettoised urban blight'. There were some references to its black population, which was seen to exclude white people from the area – 'a white man can't walk up there on his own'. This kind of crude racial antagonism, it must be emphasised, was not used in any of our Man-chester focus groups, even of Moss Side itself. In Burngreave, we were particularly impressed by the agitated discussion by local white residents as well as by some local police officers of one public house, set well back from the main public highway and almost completely surrounded by blocked-off roads, which was perceived to have become the headquarters of Afro-Caribbean drug trading and crime. The range and depth of local myth about this pub (a 'symbolic location of crime' as well as 'a land-scape of fear' for other local populations) would be the topic of a separate study in itself.

However, the 'dangerous places' of both cities were also portrayed in a positive light in discussion. Cheetham Hill, although seen as a high-crime area, was also referred to as 'cheap and cheerful', accessible to the disabled and possessing some lovely old buildings (a product of its earlier history in the nineteenth century), and the local shops were welcomed for their lower prices and friendly service. Moss Side was seen by some as an exciting place to be, as a place to try out different experiences (such as smoking cannabis in shabeens), and used for its good and generally inexpensive leisure centre. In Sheffield, support for areas perceived to be dangerous was more likely to come from people who had lived in the areas in question, like Henry Hemsworth, a retired, white male, who, despite having suffered two break-ins at his house, felt of Burngreave:

> it is a rough area, don't get me wrong, but they *are* more sociable there than what they are on Cemetery Road way. [Emphasis in original]

These Sheffielders' views of these areas differed markedly from those of people who knew of the areas only through reputation. For people who had not visited, or would not visit, an area, the discourse was predictably stereotypical: 'they're all on crack' or 'I wouldn't even drive through the place, let alone walk.' Local knowledge and familiarity challenged these stereotypes, but also generated a detailed local knowledge (especially about walking routes) helping one to feel, or to keep, safe in each area. Stephen Bates told us:

> There isn't a great deal of trouble on Cheetham Hill Road itself. If you start between Cheetham Hill Road and Salford, then you are going to get into slightly dicier areas.

Focus group respondents in Manchester showed how it was possible to hold very different views of a place simultaneously, whereas in Sheffield, views on places tended to be more polarised and rigid. In both cities the key to continued use of these 'dangerous' places was to know the area and be known. Knowledge of the area meant that an individual could assess the actual risk and compare this with perceived risk. As Richard Barker articulated it:

> People say to avoid Cheetham Hill and Moss Side, but I've never found much trouble in Cheetham Hill. Moss Side, I don't have any reason to go.

People were also likely to 'come to the defence' of these areas. When Moss Side was cited as worse than Cheetham Hill by one member of a focus group discussion, others quickly responded with their differing impressions of the place which cut across its image as a 'dangerous place':

Martin Gulliver: It's a joke that. I've lived in Moss Side all my life, I've only just moved to Miles Platting. What they say about Moss Side is a load of rubbish. I've walked around there at 4 o'clock in the morning and I've

Daniel Cashman: never seen anything, but I'd still say all of your little districts were just the same. It's the silly tag 'Bronx of Britain' according to the media. Younger kids tend to possibly cross over to that sort of thing, [they] think it's cool.

Troubled debate about Moss Side is likely to be a feature of public discussion about Manchester for the foreseeable future, with the most likely influence on the area arising from the redevelopment of nearby Hulme, with a massive amount of City Challenge money. The 'rescue' of labour markets in ethnic ghettoes by inward investment on the part of private business is certainly high on the agenda of the 'growth coalitions' involved in local Development Corporations and regeneration initiatives. We discuss these questions in more detail in Chapter 12, but, for the moment, we simply venture the observation that these radical changes in the opportunities facing ethnic minorities in general, and Afro-Caribbean people in particular, seem less likely in enclave cities like Sheffield, caught up with the effects of a late-developing crisis in a local labour market so dependent on a long-standing dual economy and unattuned to the flexibilities demanded in a global market. The Pitsmoor 'demon' is here to stay, as a kind of signifying and fearful Other, for a Sheffield dreaming of the return of Steel.

9

MEN'S TOWNS

Women's adaptive strategies in Manchester and Sheffield

Recent scholarly writing and other social commentaries on 'women and the city' fall into three discrete categories.

There is, first, a body of literature which is concerned with the impact of the city as a material structure on women (cf. for example Bowlby 1984; Holcomb 1984; McDowell 1983). This literature focuses particularly on ways in which buildings, street layout or other facilities – nearly always designed and constructed by male architects and male engineers – have been more or less attentive to what in England and other western societies have been defined as 'women's needs', like the problems faced by mothers of small children trying to obtain access to a building with a pram (cf. Green *et al.* 1987; Little *et al.* 1988; Pickup 1988). This particular approach also includes, however, an ongoing critique, well known to women over many years, of the design and location of what in Britain are called, rather coyly, 'public conveniences' for women (McKie and Edwards 1995).

Closely paralleling this literature is another body of writing, more often of a criminological character, concerned with the city as a set of 'symbolic locations for crime' or spaces which more or less routinely induce a sense of well-being or a sense of fear or anxiety (Brooks-Gardner 1989, 1990; Pain 1991; Stanko 1987, 1990; Valentine 1989, 1992). This literature focuses in part on the physical infrastructure of cities (in the English case, for example, on the dreaded urban 'underpass') and on the current condition of that infrastructure (for example, the fear produced by graffiti, litter and other signifiers of neglect); but it also deals with more cultural issues in respect of individual cities, particularly the fearful reputation of individual neighbourhoods or particular urban spaces, such as the public park (cf. Skogan 1990). In this last respect, the analytical focus is often as much on the coverage of incidents of crime in particular neighbourhoods reported in the local press and then recycled in local rumour,[1] or on spectacular crimes reported in the national newspaper press or on television, as it is actually on the physical or material fabric of place.[2]

A third, equally extensive, body of writing focuses particularly on women as consumers (Bowlby 1985; McRobbie and Nava 1984; Morris 1988), with particular concern for the significance and pattern of shopping in different urban regions and environments. More recently developing out of this interest is a committed enquiry into cities as a site of exploration or adventure for women of all ages (Vance 1984; Wilson 1991; Wolff 1990). With that there is a recognition that generalized discussion of women's experience and use of the city, of the kind that is to be found, for example, in much criminological writing on urban fears, is in danger of suppressing key differences in the use made of cities by women of different ages (adolescent and young adult women actively making very different use of the city to that of the middle-aged or the elderly), as well of different class, ethnic or even regional background (Nava 1992).

Nearly all these themes were raised and elaborated in our investigations of the routine patterns of use of Manchester and Sheffield, though always in terms of their particular local expression. We were given a clear picture of the way in which the routine use of these cities is heavily patterned (or, to use the term recommended in Bob Connell's well-known analyses of masculinity, 'ordered') in gender terms along the dimensions of time and space. Some of these matters we have already discussed extensively in our lengthy analysis of shopping practices in Chapter 5, along with a series of other observations in respect of women and public transport, such as the importance of bus knowledge in the construction of a mental map of the city. Our analytical focus in this particular chapter, however, is not restricted to women's discussion of shopping locations, but extends to Mancunian and Sheffield women's discussion of other aspects of their cities as physical or material places undergoing significant change and restructuring.

One of the most striking features of these two cities in the North of England – certainly to one of the present authors, having lived for seven years in the capital city of Canada – was their irredeemably male-dominated local power structures. By contrast with North American cities, that is, there was a quite astonishing absence of women in any positions of power and influence either in public institutions (the local authorities, schools, hospitals, universities or transport organisations) or in the private sector (local law firms, banks and financial services, construction industries, or even, as in Manchester, the new cultural industries). Even within the subordinate local labour markets employing semi- or unskilled workers, where there was evidence of a marked shift towards part-time service industry work and also of a massive decline in full-time work in manufacturing industry, there was little evidence of any major shift in the taken-for-granted local gender order in the workplace. In Manchester, energetically redefining itself as on the cutting edge of change, the occasional sighting of a woman Metrolink driver did not contradict the apparently unchallenged domination of men within the local labour market, dominating management positions for example, in local supermarkets, banks, shopping malls, the bus and rail stations, and other parts of the local service industry. Our survey work had already underlined the fact that the public spaces of these two Northern cities are overwhelmingly male places, in the sense that they are dominated, numerically, in more or less taken-for-granted, routine fashion, by men.[3] This in itself should not be a matter for surprise, especially given the character of their heavy industrial history. Local reference in Greater Manchester to the history of the City of Cotton speaks either of the male cotton weaver,[4] on the one hand, or 'The Men who Made Manchester' (the captains of local industry and trade), on the other, where the written history of Sheffield's dual economy of cutlery and steel is very much that of the Little Mesters and the steelmasters.

What was a surprise in our discussion groups was that this masculinist conception of the city, and the routinised gender ordering of local cultural practices, so far from being a 'contested terrain' (to use over-worked sociological jargon) was not even an item for discussion, except only in the indirect sense that the discussion focused on strategies taken to deal with the harassment that could routinely be expected from men in certain locations and at certain times of the day or night. We are aware, of course, that the domination of men over North of England life has been critically identified directly and discussed in fiction (for exam-ple, in the novels of Pat Barker about the Durham coalfield, notably *Union Street*) and in drama (for example, in the plays of Jim Cartwright, notably *Road* (1986)), as well as being the subject of autobiographical asides by women journalists and academics from the North.[5] Our focus group discussions did not generate critical discussion of these taken-for-granted features of everyday life in Northern cities – in this instance, the gender order – even amongst those groups which consisted entirely of women. In part, this may be because conversation, as ethnomethodolo-gists have long argued, is a form of naturally occurring practical action and does not itself allow for the suspension (or 'problematising') of the social order. What these women of the North of England discussed was their particular routines for 'dealing with' the already established (naturalised) social order. In line with this understanding, our analysis in this chapter will follow the logic of the discussions we held, and only later try to tackle the implicit question of Northern masculinism as a taken-for-granted structure, problematising the life of these women in a specific, additional way.

The street survey we completed in August and October 1992 had already highlighted a key feature of the routine uses of the city centres, and public spaces generally, in the two cities – the overwhelming pattern-ing of the use of space in terms of gender. Overall, some 53 per cent of all users of public space in both cities with whom we made contact in this survey (1825 people in all) were men. However, in the evening hours (after 6.30 p.m.), the proportion of women to men in public space very quickly and fundamentally changed: in Manchester, only some 29 per cent of users of the city after 6.30 were women and in Sheffield (excluding Meadowhall) 32 per cent.[6] We are aware that these findings might have been slightly different in Manchester, if we had surveyed the youthful population making use of the night clubs in city-centre Manchester later in the evening; and also that there would be certain areas of Sheffield in the centre (West Street) or in other specific locales (Broomhill near the university student residences) where other survey results might have emerged. But the general impact of gender on use of city space is clear, and would probably be more marked in the winter months than in this survey, initially conducted as it was on warm evenings in August and in a mild October.

The responses given to our survey questionnaire confirmed that a fear for personal safety was an influential factor in women's avoidance of certain places in the city, particularly at night, in ways which were not apparent amongst men.[7] So two focus discussion groups were organised with women from both cities who had indicated in the survey that they used public space only during the daytime and avoided it at night.[8] We were also determined to raise the issue of personal safety in the city in our other discussions, for example with women for whom avoidance was not specified as an overarching feature of their routine.

Overwhelmingly, however, this chapter primarily echoes the accounts given by women who, when initially responding to our questionnaire, claimed that they would go into the city and use its facilities during the daytime but would never go there 'at night', and were invited to our discussions on that basis. Subsequent discussion in our focus groups in fact qualified these earlier firm statements made in response to the questionnaire survey about personal practices, as women talked with each other about how they would occasionally approach the use of the city at night, but elaborated on the fears they experienced, and the situations and locations that made them fearful. These discussions very quickly elided into detailed, comparative exchanges about the strategies adopted to minimise these feelings of fear or danger, and the assessment they made of the risks they felt they were taking in each strategy. Personal safety was always a primary concern, but there was also in many cases a kind of moral and aesthetic content to the critique of the physical condition or appearance of the places or the people evoking this sense of threat and danger, and a sense of regret at the restrictions this places on everyone's use of the city.

The first part of our discussion here will focus on three connected dimensions to women's sense of well-being in public space. First, in an attempt to ground the comments expressed by the women we met in these two cities, it will address itself to the question 'What is the city for these women?', 'What parts of the urban landscape feature most promi-nently?' and 'What activities are engaged in by the women we spoke to?' Secondly, it will look at these women's responses to different manifesta-tions of 'change and decline' in the two cities. Finally, we will briefly return to the issue of how women in these cities respond to official campaigns about personal safety but also make other adaptations to the rapidly changing, different cities in which they live.

Figure 9.1 Landscape of fear: urban underpass, Sheffield, August 1995
Source: photo by Sarah King

A WOMAN'S CITY?

We have already mentioned the male domination of central city space in Manchester and Sheffield, as revealed by our survey. The total number of men occupying the public spaces of our survey in Manchester and Sheffield was consistently greater than the total number of women at all times of the day and night. There are grounds for believing that this finding might be general for most large cities in England, though our argument here suggests that this may be more pronounced an aspect of use of cities in the North than elsewhere in England. As a survey finding, this tends to contradict some recent findings about use of cities in the United States, where women's use of urban facilities is reported to have been increasing significantly, as a result of women's proportionate advance in the waged and professional labour market. Some cities in North America have been very active in taking on the lessons of the 'Take Back the Night' initiatives of the Women's Movement in the late 1970s (Lederer 1980), as well as in recognising the commercial advantages of reconstituting the city at night as a potential destination for professional women in search of pleasure and entertainment. Some commentators in the early 1980s, indeed, went so far as to argue that in America:

> urban spaces are women's places. American cities have consistently higher sex ratios than do suburban or rural areas.
>
> (Holcomb 1984: 18)

Journalistic writing on patterns of urban use in France and Italy have also pointed to the different 'gender mix' that is observable on the streets of major cities in those two countries, even after dark, especially in the summer months.

The survey we conducted in Manchester and Sheffield, and subsequent focus group discussion, produced a rather different picture of the routine use of these two cities by women. There was, for example, a clear understanding amongst these Mancunian and Sheffield women that some parts of the city were generally more male-dominated than others and also that the degree of male domination varied according to the time of day or night. There was also, therefore, a clear sense in which women sought out 'other places' – most obviously, as we discussed in Chapter 5, particular shops or shopping areas, but also cafés (especially those located inside department stores, art galleries and theatre foyers) and secluded but safe-feeling parks and gardens.[9] As Trudy Mellor, talking about cafés, remarked:

> I can assure you that single ladies go to the Crucible regularly. The City Hall as well.
>
> The Crucible bar is ideal to go to. You can go in and nobody thinks that it's odd that you're on your own.

The Crucible bar being referred to is a coffee bar adjoining the main bar used during theatrical performances: it is decidedly not a bar in a public house, which women in general would still not enter casually in these North of England cities. The theatre bar at the Crucible in Sheffield, like that at the Royal Exchange Theatre in Manchester, is an accepted destination or 'stopping place' for women – a well-established part of the 'women's city' that is contained or submerged within the otherwise male-dominated public spaces and territories of the city.

Other 'stopping places' in the city have a much more ambiguous, and less reassuring, provenance for women. Public transport termini, for example, played a large part in the routine of 'going to town' for most women. From the evidence of these discussions, conducted in Sheffield only very soon after the opening of the new Interchange but before the arrival of the South Yorkshire Supertram and in Manchester only weeks after the opening of the Metrolink, these sites were heavily disliked by women and could indeed be seen as constituting the most important, archetypal 'landscape of fear' in each of these two cities. As we saw in Chapter 4, bus stations, which continue to be heavily used even in the aftermath of recent changes in transport provision evoke an enormous amount of anxiety and concern. Doreen Dart, a Manchester woman who only used the city during the day, indicated to others in her discussion group, with considerable force, that:

> I've been told that there is a very pretty route to Bolton, which takes the same time without having to go to that dreadful, dreadful Arndale Bus Station, which *I think* requires more lighting . . . Someone passed me an old coin there, it's that dark. That is a place I avoid *like the plague.*
>
> [Emphasis in the original]

Women in Sheffield, especially young mothers, were equally forthright about the continuing congestion of the High Street, crowded with buses from different deregulated companies all competing for custom, and Paulette Timms, like the mothers of Manchester discussed in Chapter 4, anxiously commented on the speed at which the competing drivers manoeuvred their buses into position at the bus stops:

| *Paulette Timms*: | The bus drivers can't see you. If a kid's going to cross, run . . . you're going to get knocked over. And it does happen. |
| *Helen Ann Goode*: | Or they just corner. If you're on the pavement . . . they take your feet off. A child could get sucked underneath. A child got dragged by their toggles and killed. I cut toggles off . . . There are so many buses in Sheffield, I think that is the real problem. |

Consistently with other research enquiries, our work suggested that very few women were in town for what they themselves would refer to as 'leisure' (cf. Green *et al.* 1987).[10] Far more men than women explained their use of urban space in these terms, and, in some cases, the difference was extreme. For instance, in Burngreave, Sheffield, 21 men (25 per cent of all those interviewed) said they were there for 'leisure' purposes compared with only two women (5 per cent). Though the differences were less extreme in the three other sites in Sheffield, they were nonetheless marked. In Manchester the pattern was slightly different, with a greater proportion of total 'leisure users' at most sites being women than in Sheffield, at about a 2:3 ratio of women to men at three of our Manchester sites. In only one (Cheetham Hill) did the proportion drop lower than one in four. We would be reluctant to make too much of these crude statistical findings, except to say that the changes that were occurring in Manchester's city centre at the time of our research (and which have been continuing since) may have been increasing the number and range of pleasurable sites of stopping places available in what we have called the subordinated 'women's city', contained within the larger, male-colonised ensemble of urban places that is the dominant city.

GENDERED PERCEPTIONS OF URBAN CHANGE AND DECLINE

Another quite noticeable difference between the discussions held with women in Manchester and Sheffield lay in the way contemporary changes in the city, and the idea of urban decline in particular, were articulated. In Sheffield, the idea of the 'decline of the city' was a very dominant theme. This was not, it must be emphasised, a reference to the demise of the steel industry. Nor either was it simply a reference to ideas of decay and neglect of the physical fabric of the city, though in 1992 and 1993 the general condition of the city centre, with boarded-up shops suffering their fate from competition from Meadowhall, and street excavations and traffic diversions involved in the construction of the Supertram, was a massive topic of local anxiety and anger. These primarily or apparently aesthetic responses to the condition of the city as a physical place, however, were inseparable from a local feeling particularly widespread amongst women, that those with responsibility for the well-being of the city (especially, in their perception, the local Council, other public and private bodies to some degree) were now somehow neglecting or failing to meet the needs of the city, which was in danger of losing its particular character. The following comments are typical:

Monica Fletcher: Years ago it used to be nice to just wander around Sheffield. Just to go from one end of town to the other, then back. It was interesting, the Peace Gardens and everything. But now, you just want to get on with your business and get back home.

Josephine Armitage: I find West Street very depressing. Things seem to be shutting down. A lot of West Street seems to be totally deserted. This is the main road into town, but there's no one there. It's really weird. You wouldn't think that it's so close to the city centre. There's no one there. There's a few shops shut and boarded up, they get vandalised.

Monica Fletcher: I'm in the market area a lot. At least three times a week – which depresses me. It's not very nice. It doesn't look very attractive, it's very dirty, smelly. . . it really has gone down, it's terrible . . . It's really got bad that Hole-in-the-Road, it's appalling now . . . obviously from Rackhams . . . that part of town is finished completely . . . the IRA can't bomb Sheffield, it's already done it itself.

In Manchester (a city which continues to be associated in the popular imagination with *the* television soap opera, *Coronation Street*, the ultimate signifier of Northern working-class community and a set of important connected Northern myths), regret and frustration at change and decline were expressed more specifically in terms of perceived declines in every-day civility, as well as, sometimes, in public services in the city. The problem was most often identified in terms of the impossibility of a pleasant social encounter on the city streets with 'a stranger' – someone you did not know, but with whom you could 'banter', probably on the basis of a shared local knowledge and whom one could trust. It is not that these issues had no relevance to the women to whom we spoke in Sheffield. It is rather that there appeared still to be some debate in Sheffield, at least in our focus group discussions, as to whether public civility and trust between individuals had or had not fundamentally deteriorated in that city. In Manchester, routine use of the city and public spaces is understood to involve a certain wariness and, indeed, an avoidance of interpersonal contact, but in Sheffield these issues were still open.

Doreen Dart expressed the strongly felt concern that trust between strangers is now impossible in Manchester:

> I think that even if you want to go and sit there, Manchester is now a city where you are always sort of looking around. You can't go and sit and relax in your lunch hour. You're wondering who is going to come and sit next to you . . . because I've been pestered when I've been in the Gardens on my own. Even at lunch-time.

Pamela Reiss explained how she would rather her son went to the toilet behind a bush in the park than use a particular set of public toilets in Manchester:

> I know I shouldn't have done, but I'd rather him do that and be told off by a policeman, than for him to go into the public toilets, which I think is a dreadful situation. I wouldn't even think to go down those steps . . . you don't know who is going to be sitting on those steps these days.

Dorothy Paxton observed how:

> A few years ago you could have said 'Oh for goodness sake go away' [to someone begging], but you're not quite sure if you can do that these days.

Pamela Reiss added:

> Although we try and resist it, this kind of environment [a fearful one] is thrust upon us. We aren't as cheerful any more. I've driven along and seen somebody at the bus stop, especially in the evening once again, if I've seen an older person at the bus stop. I've thought 'shall I stop and say "Are you going my way, I'll drop you?", but I know that

person would think 'What's she up to?' Even if I tried she wouldn't trust me and I wouldn't do it even to ask directions off somebody now. I find I have to open the door . . . I'm making myself to do that, just winding the window down. People don't want to come to the car. People are wary, even of other women.

and, further, she thought:

we are getting into a situation like it is in London. You mind your own business, you're on the tube or whatever and you don't look at anybody. Nobody looks at anybody else. Locally, if you're going to Bury you go and have a coffee and sit next to someone, then you would have a chat. You wouldn't dream of doing that in London. Manchester is getting like that . . . you wouldn't want anyone to start making conversation with you. I think it's a terrible admission, to say that's how we are going.

In Sheffield, we detected a rather different way of expressing this issue of local trust. There was certainly less agitated discussion of interactions between strangers as inherently dangerous and generally less discussion of 'the decline of civility' thesis we encountered very extensively in Manchester. The tension, locally, appeared to revolve around the issue of whether it was any longer the 'done thing' to talk with people 'like they did in the past' or, indeed, to talk to other people at length, not only given all the advice emanating from national and local authority on best practice in respect of personal safety, but also because of an awareness of the 'speediness' of contemporary life. The following exchange captures this problem quite well:

Margaret Godfrey:	A friend of mine, she organises about thirty people to feed the birds in Sheffield . . . We all have a different walk . . . It gets me out and quite often I talk to people that I meet in town.
Penny Fraser:	Do you see the same people on a regular basis?
Margaret:	No, just anybody. People do tend to strike up conversations much more now than they used to do. At one time it wasn't done to just talk to anybody.
Penny Fraser:	When you say, at one time . . .
Margaret:	When I was younger . . . People didn't go to other people and talk to them the way they do now.
Trudy Mellor:	I've always found that people coming into Sheffield, that's the first thing they say, that people do talk. It's very friendly.
Margaret:	They didn't before.
Mary Green:	I don't know. They used to be very friendly before. Now you're frightened to talk to people.
Margaret:	I think you're always a little bit wary.
Mary:	Yes. I don't think it's as friendly as it used to be.
Monica Fletcher:	Everybody just wants to get on with their business.

PURSUIT OF PERSONAL SAFETY BY THE WOMEN OF MANCHESTER AND SHEFFIELD: PROBLEMS AND CONTRADICTIONS

We have already suggested that women's continuing quest for personal safety in these two cities involved recognition of certain zones or locales of safety (the 'woman's city' comprising certain well-known and celebrated shops, café bars and theatres) and, at the other extreme, certain locales (the Arndale bus station in Manchester, the 'Hole in the Road' in Sheffield) which routinely tended to evoke fear and avoidance, or particular personal precautionary strategies, especially in the many instances where these sites could not be avoided. What we were not able to examine directly in this study, of course, are the ways in which the differences between locations are more or less effectively learnt by each cohort of young women, beginning in childhood and adolescence, under the influence of repeated lessons from parents, teachers and peers with reference to the dangers of rape and sexual assault (and usually condensed in the rhetorics regarding 'stranger danger') and then developing further as they start to make wider use of the city as a whole, and the city centre in particular, in their teenage years. Students of child development have shown how this process of learning involves the exploration by young girls of an expanding series of public spaces outside the home (beginning with the streets of one's own neighbourhood and moving on to the streets of the 'downtown' city centre), whilst Bob Connell has gone on to discuss how the street is routinely understood by women as a more or less dangerous, threatening or troublesome locale – always the potential site of wolf-whistling or intimidation, at the one extreme, and outright harassment and assault, at the other. Some streets, for example, are heavily 'sex-typed' and eroticised, as the location of one or other outlet of the sex industry, newsagents carrying shelves-full of pornography or are simply the site of intrusive sexist billboard advertising – all of this street imagery acting as what Connell calls 'a register of sexual politics' to which hegemonic masculinity demands the 'opportunistic submission' of women (Connell 1987: 132–4).

Our focus group method did not allow for detailed examination of the transparency (reliability of identification) of particular specific locations within the city. There was very uneven knowledge of Manchester's Chorlton Street Bus Station's long-established status as the downtown centre for street-walkers of both sexes. But there was some suggestion, in the discussions we did hold, that Manchester presented problems to women in respect particularly of what Erving Goffman would call its 'frontstage' and 'backstage' areas. Pamela Reiss described the city as 'all front and surface', hiding an 'underbelly' and something that 'lurks beneath':[11]

> You think about the Metrolink and the wonderful shops and things like that and yet just around the corner there's this other side to Manchester, that really pricks at your conscience, and you think, you

know, we should be doing something about it. So what do we do? We either don't go to Manchester so we are not confronted with it in the same way, or just try and ignore it . . . It's a mish-mash of feelings coming into the city . . . you go into the nice shops and things and when you just walk around the back you really see the other side of it. You think it's all front.

The precautionary strategies which most women in most cities build into their daily routines have been well documented by Elizabeth Stanko (1990) and by Carol Brooks-Gardner (1990), both emphasising the restrictions which are placed on women's freedom not just by fear itself, but also by the character of the 'crime-prevention advice' given by police and other public authorities. Brooks-Gardner highlights the kind of denial of self and individuality, the restriction of personal experience and also the investment of time that are involved in adherence to both officially prescribed and idiosyncratic personal safety strategies by women. We get some sense of the pains and pressures experienced in this respect by women in the North of England from these extracts from our focus group discussions:

Dorothy Paxton:	Just recently I was approaching the station. In front of me were six youngsters, youths. I thought 'Oh Lord. You have to think ahead, I'd better get my money out now before I go into the hall, I don't want to bring my purse out in front of them.' They may be all right but . . . you can't live your life in hiding, you've just got to think ahead, just be prepared . . . you have to think it out. It's a terrible life, it's a stressful life, very stressful.
Doreen Dart:	They're looking for a weakling . . . That's when I feel really really vulnerable. When I had my arm in a cast. From the very first day, no way was I going to have a sleeve swinging. I happened to have an old coat that I hadn't thrown out, it had a wide sleeve and was a warm coat. I dug it out and prayed that the cast would go through, and of course it didn't. I wasn't bothered about ripping the lining as it was an old coat so I used it right away . . . It's a dreadful way to live. Not to be able to carry on your life and not worry.
Pamela Reiss:	It's a shame when you think of everything that's going on in Manchester and all the theatres, the shows, the clubs, everything that is here. People perhaps think twice about going, or want to get it together in a group rather than just getting themselves a ticket on their own. I'd never dream of doing that on my own, whereas you should be able to, we should all be able to go out and do whatever we want to do.

The regeneration of city-centre Manchester referred to by Pamela Reiss was a matter of widespread approval and celebration. In Sheffield, however, we had some sense of a more complicated kind of public response. We have already shown in Chapter 5 how the pedestrianised Fargate and Orchard Square precinct were together identified as one of the principal 'zones of safety' for women in that city, and heavily used by women. It was the location at which the greatest percentage of all women who were stopped in the street and asked to participate in our survey did so, as well as being the location where the greatest percentage of men who were stopped, agreed to participate. It was, therefore, a 'stopping-place' in which many people felt comfortable, relaxed and apparently willing to stand to answer a questionnaire. Twelve per cent of our survey respondents overall identified Orchard Square as their 'favourite part of the city'. It was also the only place where our focus group discussants spontaneously mentioned having seen police or private security guards on patrol. Only about 14 per cent of women answering our survey mentioned Fargate as a place they would avoid, as against 25 per cent of women who indicated they would avoid High Street, the northern extension of Fargate, a matter of yards away.

The response of women, and other locals, to Orchard Square, Fargate and High Street in Sheffield, is indeed emblematic of the potential contradiction between consumer gentrification (led by market institutions) and considerations of personal safety and security (particularly on the part of women), which has thousands of similar expressions elsewhere (especially in North America, in the form of the phenomenon known as 'the death of the downtown'). Orchard Square and Fargate are city centre shopping areas, reliant for their custom throughout the week on city centre workers, and on any other consumership that can be generated by campaigns to rescue use of the city centre over the weekend. On most weekday evenings, however, the shops on Fargate and in Orchard Square close at 5.30 and the immediately surrounding area very quickly evacuates of people. Between 7.00 and 7.30 p.m. a number of largely middle-class people from the suburbs, usually in family groups, make hasty use of the streets en route to the two city-centre theatres or to concerts, and later in the evening these same people equally quickly return to their cars or other means of transport home. Other than that, the bulk of the people passing through the area in the evenings are men on their way to pubs. The atmosphere of safety and well-being that the gentrification of Orchard Square is intended to encourage is replaced in the evening by an inescapable sense of a place that has been evacuated not just of other people but also of the custodial gaze of any kind of protective public authority, in the shape of either the public police or private security – a quintessential example of what Richard Sennett, in his recent critique of the post-modern consumerist city in the United States, has called 'dead space' (Sennett 1991).

The celebration on the part of local Sheffield women of the creation of safe, bright, new day-time environments such as Fargate and Orchard

Square is not unqualified, since these same public spaces are quickly transformed in the imagination into no-go areas in the evenings (Evans *et al.* 1995). There is also regret as to what is felt to have been lost in the process. There was widespread critique of the lack of character and the blandness of such consumer locales, and the subtle ways in which they walled people off from each other, by the priority placed on efficient individual consumer purchases rather than the browsing which had been possible in the 'old department store' or the bargain hunting in the market. One of the youngest members of the group, a woman in her mid-20s, expressed this sentiment most forcefully in relation to Sheffield:

Josephine Armitage: I don't like the architecture they use. It's all sort of nothingy . . . it's all so gimmicky but it hasn't even got the shops, if you see what I mean . . . I think I'm the sort of person that doesn't really like change either. Even though I've only been here seven or eight years I actually thought 'They can't open a shopping centre in the middle of Sheffield.

Margaret Godfrey: I'm old-fashioned and I like the old Sheffield. It was homely and now it's all modern and Americanised.

ADAPTIVE FEMINISM IN THE DE-INDUSTRIALISED NORTH

In the nature of the project we conducted in Sheffield, relying in the main on a street survey and a carefully chosen selection of focus group discussions, we were attempting to identify and locate a broad sample of citizens in our two cities, and, through our subsequent, more detailed dialogue and discussion of routine use or avoidance of the public spaces in the city, draw some conclusions about the responses of these various, differentially situated citizens to recent changes in these cities. It may be that our discussions tended to construct an impression of a more homogeneous set of adaptations than would be revealed, for example, in face-to-face interviews. It could also be the case that an unquestioning reliance on such an acquiescent democratic popular forum as the focus group might hide from view the activities and influence of individuals whose responses to the pressures of change are more active than acquiescent, and more pioneering and awkwardly rebellious (at least in their motivation) than merely adaptive. This may be a particularly important limitation in glimpsing and understanding the specific responses of different women 'in the community' to local crises of the labour market, changes in the city, changes in family form, crime and social behaviour generally, and many other vital aspects of everyday life in these masculinist Northern cities.

We were given some sense, as we reported in Chapter 4, for example, of the ways in which women in some parts of these cities had banded together in the provision of women-only transport, especially at night, to deal with the threat of harassment and assault from young men in the city at night. But there are instances of more combative and resistant-response by women in these Northern cities, based not just on a perceived threat to one's self (because of gender) but also on an active engagement in the defence of 'community interest', seen to be being undermined by the loss of 'the work' on which historically it was so dependent. In the course of our work in Manchester and Sheffield, we were to read Beatrix Campbell's celebrated study of the 'angry young men' of Britain's council estates, based on her interviews on the Meadowell Estate in Newcastle upon Tyne and the Blackbird Leys Estate in Oxford (Campbell 1993). Campbell identified the profound crisis on these public housing estates as arising out of the particular way work-ing-class men were responding to the demise of their hitherto taken-for-granted local labour markets. It was not only that the young men who were without, and, in many cases, had never experienced paid employ-ment in heavy industry, could not contain or re-channel their anger in any kind of constructive way: it was also that the *older* men, experiencing unemployment after many years in industry, seemed to be incapable of re-directing their energies into any kind of caring domestic role, parti-cularly in respect of being a father to young men facing an unanticipated new challenge in respect of work and/or self-esteem. The impact of mass unemployment, especially in regions like the North of England, was having a differential impact on men and women, since, as Campbell succinctly puts it: 'We know that unemployment and poverty produce a human and economic crisis for both men and women, but that is perceived as an *economic crisis for a woman* and *an identity crisis, a gender crisis, for a man*' (Campbell 1993: 20; our emphasis). More specifically, Campbell continues: 'the masculine trauma lies not so much with poverty as with its assignment to the world of women' (*ibid.*).

Certainly, the young men on probation in Sheffield, whom we discuss in Chapter 11, feared nothing so much as being assigned to the sphere which Beatrix Campbell calls 'democratic domesticity'. The most com-mon response of both adult and adolescent men of the old industrial working class is seen by Campbell, along with Ehrenreich and other writers, as that of panic and flight. A sympathetic reading of this panic-and-flight reaction would, of course, return to, and interrogate, the 'facts' of male gender socialisation (the learning of hegemonic masculi-nity) particularly as it is expressed in industrial working-class commu-nities as an explanation of the current impasse in male responses to the process of de-industrialisation.

A similar understanding of what in some quarters is seen as the inevitable processes of gender socialisation, and in others as a social process of en-gendering, is also implicit in Campbell's account of the responses of many women to the disasters enveloping public housing estates and other areas of industrial working-class residence during the developing crisis of mass manufacturing in the later 1970s and early 1980s. Campbell argues not only that the Home Office's Community Development Programmes in the 1970s were subverted and transformed into exercises of radical and democratic instances of social mobilisation within each CDP area essentially by local women; she also shows how, more recently, women and especially young mothers have been at the fore of much more informal, inchoate local defensive initiatives on the estates (local social movements) during the assault on the poor since 1979. On Meadowell, one of the important initiatives was the Meadowell Action Group itself, the local 'branch' of the tenants, movements that grew up in opposition to the Housing Act of 1988, which also later helped mobilise the community against the poll tax. The MAG, like the local book centre, the credit union and other community initiatives, was led almost entirely by women 'community activists' – and when the boys of the estate finally rioted in 1991, it was these collective and collaborative institutions in the community that were targeted, burnt out and destroyed.

One of the very few organisations to have arisen in response to the decimation of Sheffield's old industrial East End, the area which used to be know as Attercliffe, is the 'Don Valley Forum', led by 50-year-old Rose Birks. The Forum was started up by Rose and her friends, mainly the wives of local steelworkers and other Attercliffe people, as a response to the demise of the local steel industry and, in particular, the plans to regenerate 'the Valley' commercially, launched by local entrepreneurs like Eddie Healey (the instigator of the Meadowhall Centre) and the Sheffield Development Corporation. Though not a Sheffielder by birth, Rose had lived in Sheffield for forty-one years, marrying a brewery worker employed by Whitbread's (the son of a Sheffield steelworker), and spent much of her married life in the industrial community in Attercliffe. Under her leadership and that of other local women, the Forum conducted a continuing campaign to persuade the Meadowhall Centre (which Rose persists in calling 'the Arcade') to employ local labour;[12] highlighted a variety of serious problems in respect of the industrially polluted and neglected landscape of the Attercliffe area; and argued, in effect, for the repopulation of an area devastated by de-industrialisation.

Despite a variety of setbacks – including the closure of the famous local department store of Banners, a few yards away from the Forum's drop-in centre – the Don Valley Forum has expanded membership and the range of its interests: it claims the affiliation of over twenty different neighbourhood tenants' associations, toddlers' groups, luncheon clubs for the elderly, the Tinsley Islamic Centre and various other groups. It has also been an active, alternative voice and vision, in respect of the redevelopment of Attercliffe, to that of the Sheffield Development Corporation, about a mile away on another main road through the de-industrial wasteland, identifying the limits in terms of reindustrialisation and repopulation to the local strategy of simply repositioning

Sheffield as a City of Sport – even though the best of the new sports stadia were built 'slap-bang in the middle' of the Attercliffe/Don Valley area. Like all such populist social movements, its short history was full of contradiction and from the point of view of orthodox party politics, outright inconsistencies: the Forum has been closely involved in voluntary partnerships with local private industry in the provision of security patrols and community surveillance, and in 1992, was receiving a £30,000 grant from the City Council to support its work and to underwrite its rental of a local shop-front 'drop-in centre'. When we first met Rose Birks in 1992, she was actively engaged in a campaign to reclaim the main road into Sheffield city centre for local people, via a proposal to re-introduce 'allotments' (market gardens) alongside the new Supertram line on Commercial Street. Other inspired populist ideas were very much under discussion: the consistent thread was the attempt to try and re-connect local people, including the desperately disaffiliated working men of the area, into some project of community care and democratic planning. We cannot assess how many Rose Birks there are in Sheffield or Manchester in the mid-1990s, but Beatrix Campbell's work in the North East would suggest that this form of community activism by local women is an important theme throughout the North, developing alongside but autonomously of 'women's organisations', in response to the constant pressures, and the failings and limitations, of Northern hegemonic masculinity. So accounts of women's presence and sense of well-being in cities like Manchester and Sheffield must include discussion not just of the routine fears and anxieties that are evoked in the use of these masculine cities (fears which affect even professional women with some standing in the local business class and growth coalitions): it must also recognise the active caring and attempted reconstruction which many local women bring to the defence and re-invention of 'the community' – albeit that these campaigns are often, necessarily, neither feminist in an exclusionary sense (in their determination to speak to a common interest) nor abstractly utopian, in their practical desire to rescue aspects of the already-existing 'local community', even of the male-dominated local culture, in the name of social continuity and social cohesion.[13] It is in these last, realist respects that women activists of local de-industrialising communities, in cities like Manchester and Sheffield, come directly into conflict with the utopian market-orientated radicalism of the powerful local growth coalitions, based in offices in the centres of the city or the industrial parks, or in far-away suburbs.

10

PENSIONED OFF

The senior citizens of Manchester and Sheffield

At the time of the 1991 Census 18.4 per cent of the people living within the boundaries of the city of Manchester proper (74,505 people) and 20.9 per cent of the people of Sheffield (104,853) were aged 65 or above. Within the ten boroughs of Greater Manchester, according to the same Census, 447,928 people (17.9 per cent of the overall 2.5 million population of the conurbation) were 65 or above. Consistent with national trends, these figures were evidence that the proportion of the local population aged 65 or over was increasing – in Greater Manchester as a whole by some 0.6 per cent since the previous Census, and in South Yorkshire as a whole by some 1.5 per cent.[1] In part because of the loss of younger people through migration, the two old industrial urban regions were ageing demographically. Putting the point colloquially, there were more older people around - about one fifth of the overall population in total in these regions as a whole, as in most of the other regions of the North.[2] It does need to be said, however, that the voice of the elderly is noticeable in much current writing on the city, especially from the academy, primarily for its absence.

This chapter will report on four discussions organised with older residents – 'senior citizens' – in our two cities, but we will also pay attention to comments made by more elderly participants in other sessions. In no sense is it our concern to argue that there is some single, unitary perspective on these cities given by the fact of age. We would not accept for one moment, however, that the idea of perspective being brought to the world as a result of age (for example, as a result of 'experience') has itself been undermined by cultural change. Certain post-modernist commentators, for example, argue that the advance of 'post-modern' media is 'breaking down' age barriers and producing a new, 'youthful' consumerism amongst the elderly.[3] These commentators seem to want to eradicate the sociological category of age from their 'analysis'; this all seems rather sweeping. Studies of the television-watching habits of the elderly show a marked preference towards the viewing of 'old movies' in the afternoon – evidence, surely, of a 'generational consciousness' on the part of the elderly in the field of popular culture – which may coexist with other interests, but is in no way extinguished by them. We are more interested here in trying to understand some of the

common understandings, memories, hopes and desires of elderly Northern people, which we take in part to be a matter of their knowing and
even reflexive experience and contemplation of industrial modernity in
the North and its current transformations. There is a host of interesting
questions to be asked[4] – not least, of course, the way that the gendered
division of rights and obligations in Northern cities extends into old age,
especially in the aftermath of the extension of so-called Community
Care programmes, and that elderly women find themselves carrying
on their responsibilities of caring for 'their men' well past their physical
capacities and, often, without regard for their own entitlement to a
peaceful retirement, free of such responsibilities. We have not been
able to pursue these issues here in detail – even though they have clear
consequences, for example, in respect of the capacity of elderly women
to make use of the city – though we have a strong sense that these
divisions of responsibilities had a taken-for-granted character in our
group discussions. What we do welcome is the renewed interest in the
last few years in the elderly – driven, no doubt, by the ageing of the
academy itself. We also welcome the belated recognition that the urban
experience and the culture of cities are not straightforwardly 'youthful',
even in cities like Manchester where the local growth coalition and some
sections of the local academy heavily emphasise its youthful provision
and appeal to the exclusion, sometimes, of other publics.

We are very aware that the voices heard in this chapter are mainly
male, and that many of the reminiscences reported here are about public
spaces and places, and about changes in the nature of behaviour thought
to obtain in public space. Oral historians and sociologists working with
life-history material have focused more heavily on the voices of elderly
women and their memories, which tend to deal more with private lives
in the household and domesticity, and it may be a feature of focus group
method that it does easily encourage this more personal and private kind
of talk. We introduced some analysis of 'private life' in these two cities in
Chapter 9.

We are also aware that the reminiscences reported here are very much
those of elderly *white* Mancunians and Sheffielders, and that this chapter
does not generate an account of the experience of being subordinate in
ethnic terms within these two 'white cities'. We dealt briefly with some
aspects of non-white experience of Manchester in Chapter 8, but serious
and sympathetic exploration of the memories of black, Asian, Chinese or
other non-white populations in these two cities would be the topic of a
separate research project.

What particularly interested us in the discussions we did have with
elderly residents of these two Northern cities was the way in which
collective and individual memory helped illuminate so many key aspects
of the 'local structure of feeling' – in part, but by no means entirely, in
respect of the material landscape and physical form of the city and its
more recent transformation. During the course of a discussion of Market
Street in Manchester (which, in the mid-1990s, to the consternation of

many, has been colonised by young people, but which had an iconic status for some as Manchester's main shopping street in the earlier post-war period), Walter Harper, an 80-year-old retired bricklayer now living in Cheadle Hulme, interjected with some vigour:

> Market Street! You couldn't *walk* up Market Street. I'm talking about when I was 12. Saturday nights, we used to come up, because it was a tram place through there. There would be people walking on the pavements. We kids – for devilment – we'd kneel down on the kerb and say 'mind the cotton, please, mind the cotton'. It's entirely different now.

Penny Fraser: Why? It's still a busy street.

Walter: Oh it is a busy street. But I'm sure it was busier in those days. There was more people then. You've got a walk-through now, haven't you? There was trams and cars going up in that time. You still had both sides of the pavement absolutely jam packed.

Walter later explained that he was referring here to 'a kids' trick' of causing preoccupied and harassed Market Street pedestrians to step over an imaginary piece of cotton or string stretched across the pavement from the edge of the kerb to the shop frontages – a version of a street game played by youngsters in Salford, where he was brought up (sometimes involving real string being used to entangle police officers on the beat, or other unpopular intruders).[5] Market Street in the 1920s and 1930s provided an ideal opportunity for 'devilment' in a more crowded situation.

The talk engaged in by elderly people in general about their cities of residence has an enormous importance for our study. It is not simply that this talk carries empirical information about particular places in the city, their role within the larger conurbation and the significance of recent changes (what 'these changes did to the city'), and in that sense constitutes a particularly intense and rich discourse of continuities and changes in the spatial configuration or physical form of particular localities, providing a perspective and a check on contemporary generalisations (for example, in popular talk or journalism). That is to say, that the talk can carry a diverse set of cultural messages about particular urban spaces, locales or areas, albeit that these messages need to be carefully 'deconstructed'. But it is also talk that is complicit, in that sense, in the ongoing reproduction or modification of local popular belief about particular areas (especially what is sometimes called, too unenquiringly, their 'reputations'). Again, and perhaps even more importantly for our purposes, the talk engaged in by the elderly about their cities has a very specific 'backward-looking' quality: it highlights, and usually celebrates, some notion of 'the past' (which may or may not be 'accurate' in some factual sense) as a way of speaking about current change and also about the general idea of progress. It is, in that sense, nostalgic.

In one of his last books, Christopher Lasch reminded us how it is essential to distinguish between nostalgia and memory as such – even a memory of earlier happy time:

> The emotional appeal of happy memories does not depend on disparagement of the present, the hallmark of the nostalgic attitude. Nostalgia appeals to the feeling that the past offered delights no longer obtainable. Nostalgic representations of the past evoke a time irretrievably lost and for that reason timeless and unchanging. Strictly speaking, nostalgia does not entail the exercise of memory at all, since the past it idealizes stands outside time, frozen in unchanging perfection. ... Memory draws a hope from the past in order to enrich the present and to face what comes with good cheer. It sees past, present and future as continuous. It is less concerned with loss than with a continuing indebtedness to a past the formative influences of which lives on in our patterns of speech, our gestures, our standards of honour, our expectations, our basic disposition to the world around us.
>
> (Lasch 1991: 82–3)

Nostalgia is in this sense always associated with myth, such as, for example, a body of myth in the late nineteenth and early twentieth centuries (very popular in the exploding urban and metropolitan centres of America and Europe) about 'the pastoral' quality of the rural or the agricultural life. Christopher Lasch discusses a number of other myths that have had enormous influence in the course of the last tumultuous century in America, not least the myths of the West as a wild and untamed territory, populated by pioneer individualists but dominated by the confrontations of the outlaw and the sheriff, and then the early twentieth-century idealisation of the urban metropolis as a centre for stylish and innocent, youthful pleasures – the 'roaring twenties'. Each of these myths can be understood as having a particular historical and social and cultural provenance – that is, as having been a particularly popular source of nostalgic themes in subsequent historical moments and amongst specific sections of the population.

According to Lasch, echoing an argument first advanced by Richard Hofstadter (1948), the United States recovered from the traumas of the Depression and the Second World War through a particularly intense attempt at the level of popular culture and mass media representation to 'recapture the past' of the Jeffersonian era, and to ground the experience of post-war progress in the cloak of the familiar. At the centre of this mythology was the image of the homestead and the farm, and the individual (male) yeoman farmer, conquering nature, tilling and taking over the land, and defending it from predatory others. Once this imagery was constructed in the American imagination, and reproduced in the person of presidents like Eisenhower (and later Ronald Reagan), it operated more or less reliably to give some secure grounding to the ideas of progress and change advanced by commercial interests and reformist commentators in post-war America. The salience and visibility of these myths of the past and the promises of progress, however, did vary considerably at different moments in the post-war period: the 1960s in the United States were arguably a period in which different ideas of progress were in contest with each other, whilst the 1970s witnessed a reactive reversion to themes of continuity and tradition. In the 1980s, a specific mix of nostalgia and progress coalesced in the explosion of interest in the idea of heritage, particularly in respect of the renovation and remarketing of historical buildings and sites (the reclaiming of particular and often mythical notions of the past in respect of particular places).[6] Lasch wondered whether it is possible to speak of individual generations as being more or less embedded in a kind of nostalgic consciousness,[7] and he was certainly very persuaded that an individual culture, in particular historical moments or over longer historical periods, can be characterised as having a collective nostalgia.

If this struggle in the cultural imagination between progress and the past was evident in the United States, we have to say that it was absolutely definitive for the vast majority of the people of the North of England whom we invited in 1993 to come to sessions to discuss 'the condition of their cities'.[8] Though these sessions were never presented as exercises in local or oral history (and, indeed, did not lend themselves to the extended narratives on which oral history depends),[9] many of them quickly focused mainly on the past – or, more accurately, given Lasch's clear distinction, took on an essentially nostalgic quality. Long-time up-market shoppers would talk at length about the glories of Manchester's Market Street 'as it used to be' or, in Sheffield, of the old Coles, with its 'proper' restaurant with waitress service. Other shoppers would talk of the vast range of goods 'you could get' in particular neighbourhood shopping streets. There were frequent references amongst many city-centre users to the pleasures that had been given by Piccadilly Gardens in Manchester or the Peace Gardens in Sheffield – 'but you wouldn't go there *now*'. There were nostalgic references in different sessions to a variety of different other places – Sheffield's parks and markets and Manchester's art galleries and theatres. It is tempting to allude to the existence of a shared image of these cities in the past, but it is clear that the kinds of nostalgic reconstruction being advanced in our discussion sessions were also highly patterned by the facts of class and gender: memories of shops (like Kendals and Coles) tended to be voiced by women, where, in other sessions, memories of pubs, football venues or particular urban transport centres (like the train stations) tended to be voiced by men. The celebration of particular pieces of architecture, where it occurred, tended to be expressed by residents of the suburbs, particularly in Manchester. In nearly all Sheffield discussions and in the bulk of the Manchester groups, however, the buildings and architecture which made up the city tended to take on an altogether taken-for-granted quality.

In Sheffield, in particular, and in Manchester, to a very large degree, the nostalgia was not so much about the couplet of 'people and places' as it was about people in relationship to particular historical periods. Echoing through the discussions was a powerful sense of the world of industrial work and its associated sense of community, now lost to 'progress'. Sometimes this was a matter of bitter lament, as when Scott Trueman, an unemployed Sheffield steelworker, responded to our enquiries about his view of the Meadowhall shopping mall:

> I think they ought to knock it down and build a steelworks. It'll only be twenty years before it's like anywhere else. I'll give it twenty years, not quite that long.

Alf Webb remarked on how Sheffield used to be 'a better place to live': that being when:

> Everything were here. The steelworks, the pits. They're disappearing now. That took the life out of Sheffield. You lose your job, you lose your friends really.

There is no question that one of the most powerful refrains running through our discussions with the elderly was a kind of 'class and regional nostalgia' for the lost world of mass manufacturing and its associated set of social institutions and political and civic assumptions. Most particularly lamented was the sense of community that was universally asserted to have been characteristic of that particular historical experience. But there are at least two important qualifications to our recognition of this sense of loss in our towns and cities.

First, neither Manchester nor Sheffield was simply and straightforwardly a single-industry town or community, in the manner of the outlying colliery villages of South Yorkshire. Our Sheffield discussion groups certainly resonated a strong sense of the city as the city of steel and cutlery, but only a very small number of our discussants had a direct relationship with either of those industries. The cutlery industry is not associated with an heroic sense of working-class struggle, dominated as it was instead by the self-importance of the individual craftsman. Sheffield steelworkers did have some sense of their own history as a section of the organised working class, with some mythology of a relatively recent vintage (notably around the mass picketing of Hadfields steelworks on Valentines Day 1980),[10] and the really heroic mythologies of the coal strike of 1982–4 continue to have some influence, given the major confrontations that occurred at Orgreave colliery (just inside the city boundary to the south-east of the centre) in May 1984. Within Sheffield itself, however, as we have already suggested in the opening chapters of this book, an equally important nostalgic refrain is for 'the best days of the Council', which may variously be located, according to Sheffielders of different age, either in the early post-war period in the 1950s and 1960s (during the rehousing of the population) or in the early 1980s (the heyday of the 'Socialist Republic'). So Geoff Helliwell, a retired engineer, commented to us quite typically and in the most matter-of-fact fashion about the early days of municipal Labourism in Sheffield:

> I was born in Meersbrook Park Road, and I moved to the top of Meersbrook Park when they built the estate at Norton Lees. *Labour* built a housing estate there. We bought a house then when I first married, and I've lived there ever since. [Our emphasis]

Across Greater Manchester, the high point of the cotton trade was some time in the past and dispersed across a large conurbation, particularly strongly felt in some areas (north and east Manchester generally) but not in others. In some areas in Greater Manchester, local myth about cotton had to struggle against other local industrial myths (for example, about the Docks area in Salford). In the inner city and on some estates, there is also a version of the Labourism we encountered in Sheffield, but this seems always to coexist with some sense of Manchester as a city of commerce and indeed of free trade, and a sense of working-class history – like that of the East End of London (cf. Hobbs 1989) – attuned to the exigencies of boom and slump, and the necessity for smart individuals to create their own opportunities in life.

A second qualification to the idea of a shared collective memory of place is the fact that the nostalgic references made by the majority of our elderly to the past were not generally to individual historical events or to individual buildings or places as such.[11] They were references, instead, to what the Italian social historian Alessandro Portelli calls 'syntagmatic' (as distinct from paradigmatic) biographical memories (Portelli 1991: 69).[12]

Syntagmatic events are events which 'parallel one another' in terms of meaning and probably, though not necessarily, in time period. Paradigmatic events are literally simultaneous. This distinction is certainly helpful as a way of thinking about the kind of nostalgia we encountered in our two North of England cities, with its discursive reference to some unspecified lost 'times' of industrial plenty and working-class or civic community. So, for example, the folk memories of many Sheffielders might allude in generalised terms to a time when Coles was still at Coles Corner, when there was a national consensus around full employment and welfare, and when there were still two railway stations in the city, whilst elderly Mancunians might speak of the great days of aircraft construction in post-war Manchester, the best years of the Hallé Orchestra under Sir John Barbirolli, and the glory of the 'Busby Babes' (the Manchester United football teams of the 1950s and 1960s).

By and large, we would want to argue that the nostalgia for 'lost community' was quite generally shared in an abstract sense in both our Northern cities, especially by the more elderly: there were few enthusiastic declarations of preference for the competitive, individualistic life of the 'free market' in the 1990s. But some qualifications are necessary. Most obviously, the mythology of 'steel city' and of 'Cotton-opolis' was very unevenly understood or accepted within different migrant communities in these two cities: it was a mythology of the long-established, white working class. So also, however, was the appeal of working-class industrial community subject to some critical discussion from women, as well as from some men, in ways which are perhaps only now permissible. These were, after all, as we indicated in Chapter 2, 'dirty old towns'. Geoff Helliwell echoed George Orwell's feelings about the dirt and grime of industrial Sheffield in the inter-war period, and then rejoiced in the fact that:

The River Don has been cleaned. There's trees and grass banks.

Other Sheffielders referred to the much-publicised recent discoveries of salmon and other fresh-water fish in a river which in the 1950s would have been one of the most polluted rivers in the country. Similar references were made to the reclaiming of Manchester's city-centre canals by the Central Manchester Development Corporation, and the contrast with city-centre and inner-city areas in the past:

Derek Halstead: I remember, going back, going for my first job .... I was born in Blackburn, the most industrialised part. But I worked with this fellow in Oldham who'd gone for the same job as me twenty years before. He said he got off the train at Victoria, found where the bus was to Oldham, got off at Miles Platting, and said 'My God, I can't stand this. I'm going home.'

Walter Harper observed, however, how:

Now, you can walk outside this door and see how they've improved all this area. The canals, the boats are in there now. You can walk from here to Whitworth Street, you can see all the water there. There's no dirt in it. It's all cleaned up.

'In the olden days', the group concurred, 'they wouldn't have bothered.'

These last references – celebrating the environmental improvements in the old industrial city – are an important corrective to any temptation to speak of the reminiscences of the elderly in our two cities in terms only of loss and regret or of what has been called the 'labour metaphysic' of big industry and working-class male institutions. So also is it important for us to register the sense of attachment which some of our elderly North-erners felt either abstractly to the North itself or to their specific city of residence. In the case of our Sheffield discussants, it has to be said, many of the most positive references were to the city's proximity to the open country of Derbyshire ('beautiful country, there's no getting away from it'), where in Manchester the references tended to focus on the continuing redevelopment of the city centre, with particular mentions of the museums and galleries where time could be spent, cheaply and to good effect.

PRISONERS OF SPACE?

The existing literature on the use of cities by the elderly focuses very heavily on the diminished use of those urban territories by older people, as a result of reduction in physical capacity or financial resources, or perhaps as a result of psychological fears (for example, of assault or predatory crime), thought generally to be more widespread amongst the elderly than the population at large. Amongst some of the people who participated in our discussions, however, there was a determination to appear sanguine about contemporary crime. Geoff Helliwell thought that 'the disturbances' in pubs 'nowadays' weren't 'quite as bad as they used to be':

There was *a lot of fights*. [His emphasis]

The pattern of our discussions did not allow for a detailed excavation or comparative assessment of such use of the city and urban fear, or for the character of such fears in places of home residence but, in enquiring about the routine patterns of use of the city, they did immediately underline three aspects of the lives of the elderly in these two cities which need emphasis here.

Routinisation and change

First, there is no question that the use of landscape and facilities of the larger conurbation does diminish, certainly by comparison with early periods of adolescence and some periods of adult life, and start to focus, in particular, on a predictable and largely unchanging set of routines. In both our Northern cities, the everyday life of the majority of the elderly revolved around various cheap supermarkets and shopping centres, cafés and pubs, and the use of public transport, particularly buses. For many of the elderly people we met, there were also a number of social and community centres or 'friendship clubs' as well as, in some cases, periodic visits to the seaside, the open country, bookshops, libraries and art galleries. We have already discussed some of these patterns of use of the city in our analysis of 'subsistence shopping' in Chapter 5. We were particularly struck, in discussions with many elderly people, by the length of journeys which they would undertake searching for 'bargains'. There was too a pronounced kind of survivalist commitment on the part of many of our elderly Northerners – to 'getting the shopping in' whatever the circumstances, which perhaps invites explanation in terms of this age group's experience of shortages and rationing in the Second World War and the late 1940s. Some other older people, especially (but not exclusively) from Chinese and Asian backgrounds, would travel considerable distances for particular kinds of produce, or simply because they did not like the service they received in one shopping facility (the Barrows in Manchester were not popular with the Chinese elderly) or had developed an attachment to a particular store, perhaps in an area where they had previously lived.

John Rollinson, who lives in Stockport, told us that he is:

> in Manchester quite a lot ... The reason I come to Manchester is that it's cheaper to buy in Manchester than it is where I live. I also economise with a fourteen-day Saver ticket. I save money that way. I also come to Manchester in the evening. It's near the area where I come from, where I went to school. It's changed, but there's still a lot of people that I went to school with. I still see them and we have good nights. We don't actually come into the town centre. I stay in Collyhurst, Miles Platting, around that area. I can't fault it, me.

Return journeys into areas of one's birth or areas where one had a developed social circle were quite common, with the ostensibly depopulated area of Attercliffe in Sheffield and the troubled Ordsall Estate in Salford, Manchester particularly frequently mentioned. These return trips home, and also the long and regular shopping trips, quite clearly performed important social and personal functions, not least in helping to enshrine a routine (or a regular timetable) for the week. In some instances, these routines were quite elaborate:

Ian Taylor:	When you are not on holiday, Geoff, when you're actually in Sheffield, how do you use the city?
Geoff Helliwell:	For one thing, I have a hobby. I have one or two hobbies, as matter of fact. My wife says I've too many. I go to the Art Gallery on a Wednesday, painting watercolours. I go to the Art Gallery at ten o'clock and I usually come away at about one o'clock. Then I can do the shopping.
Ian:	What kind of shopping would you do?
Geoff:	I usually get the heavier stuff, because my wife has wrist trouble. I usually leave there, go down by Crucible, cut down Chapel Walk, and go to the fruit shop. Get the potatoes, greens, whatever. Then I usually get my bus near Saxone.
Ian:	On High Street?
Geoff:	That's the extent of my Wednesday. Monday, we usually go shopping down town – probably to The Moor end, and do whatever is necessary. Sainsburys, that sort of thing. Probably have a bit of lunch while we are down there.
Ian:	Whereabouts?
Geoff:	Atkinsons. That's on the Monday. On Tuesday, we probably go to Crystal Peaks, have a look around there. It's leisure, more than shopping. Thursday is at-home day. We usually do the vac-ing.
Ian:	It sounds like a timetable.

Geoff: It's one of those things. Friday, it's down-town but it's to the market end. We find that's the better time for the market. After, we usually go down to Commercial Street. There's a fish and chip shop there, I don't know if you know it. It's very good. Saturday, it depends. A bit of gardening, which I may occasionally do during the week. But it's more or less gardening day. Whatever is necessary, cutting the grass, hedge, so forth. Sunday, my grand-daughter usually comes with the car, most Sundays. It depends on the weather of course – would we like to go to Chatsworth, a garden centre, whatever.

Geoff's timetable, like many other routines we identified in our discussions, depended to some significant degree, especially in the week, on the availability of bus transport, and in many cases on the availability of concessionary fares to make these kinds of cross-town trip and journey affordable. We have already discussed, in Chapter 4, the importance of what we called the 'bus knowledge' of the city, especially amongst the elderly, and the anxieties that have been provoked by the deregulation of municipal buses, but we should add here the anxiety felt by the elderly as to the future of concessionary fares on buses, the rail system and the Metrolink and Supertram systems. A common sight in both cities at 9.30 in the morning is that of groups of elderly people standing by the ticket machines of the new 'tram stations', waiting for the start of the concessionary period.[13] The provision by the local Passenger Transport Executives of 'little buses' in the city centre, directed in particular at the elderly, is much appreciated, even if they are sometimes driven at speed. Katherine Brooks, an elderly shopper in Sheffield, remarked on how:

> There's the 'Little Beaver' buses. They're all right, provided you've taken your medicine. If you sit on the back seat .... I did once: never, no more.

In general terms, however, the provision of such city-centre transport is helpful to the elderly, and feeds into the construction of personal shopping or walking routes through the city centre, as discussed in Chapter 5, or onwards to other destinations via other buses or trains.[14]

It should not be surprising, therefore, to hear that the lived experience of the elderly in our Northern cities revolved around very well-established routines, timetables and routes – 'recursive' daily activity, *par excellence*, engaged in for utilitarian reasons (to save money) or for other symbolic personal purposes (to pass the time in a familiar fashion). It makes sense to think of these recursive routines as a set of secure and valued routes and practices, from which vantage point elderly Northerners construct a 'gaze' at Others in the city and also at changes in the physical or material environment, but more especially in respect of changes in local culture.

Friendship and community

Analytical writers have been aware for many years of the increased isolation of the elderly, consequent on the decline of the extended family and a larger cultural decline in what some commentators refer to as 'intergenerational solidarity' (Hollander and Becker 1987). Compared with the period immediately after the Second World War, fewer and fewer elderly live 'with their families' and increasing numbers are in various kinds of residential home or live by themselves; but on these dimensions, there were enormous differences between our two cities, at least according to the Census returns. In Manchester, in 1991, 42.4 per cent of all pensioners lived alone and 4.4 per cent were in some form of communal establishment. About 33 per cent of households contained at least one pensioner (Manchester City Council, Planning Studies Group 1993: 2). About 35 per cent of households in Sheffield contained a pensioner, but only 18.1 per cent of pensioners lived alone (Census 1991: County Report, South Yorkshire, Table L).

For elderly people in both these Northern cities, one of the key daily problems (other than the task of subsistence shopping) was the attempt to maintain some kind of connection to their earlier social networks of family and friendships, with a view to combating isolation either in the private household or in the residential home. This clearly presented different degrees of difficulty in the two cities, not least because of their size and layout. We have already mentioned the extended trips made by some Mancunians and Sheffielders from the outer suburban areas and estates back to the areas of old terraced housing or new-build estates where they were born or brought up, in search of a sense of their own social network and community. Other elderly people we met in our two cities had been able to construct a significant network in the neighbourhoods where they were currently living. Henry Hemsworth, whom we met whilst he was looking for cheap shopping bargains, indicated that:

> Where we live we have a little friendship club. Three nights a week. Mondays, Wednesdays and Fridays. Last night we went to a Pea and Pie Supper ... We're going on a trip to Bridlington. Then we have a Christmas dinner. We can't grumble. It makes you friends. Company and friendship are everything now, especially when you are on your own.

There were many mentions of such social facilities for the elderly in Sheffield, and widespread knowledge of them, confirming the Council's own claim to have built up a good network of such facilities in the earlier post-war period, prior to the forced closures of 1993 and 1994.[15] What we cannot judge is whether there were not just as many such facilities across the different neighbourhoods and town centres of Greater Manchester, whose existence and value was known very locally. But there seems every reason to think of the networks of the elderly in Manchester as being much more dispersed, like its shopping centres, on an analogy with a series of archipelagos, across the whole conurbation.

Sheffield's networks of elderly people were also very localised and extremely diverse, but there seemed to be some sense of shared knowledge as to the level and character of local authority provision and support for the elderly population of the city as a whole. In Sheffield, this was an area in which 'the Council' remained very popular in 1993, for the moment, with a population in need of its services, and there seemed to be a strong approval, in all our discussions with the older people of Sheffield, for the idea of a Council providing for the reasonable needs of the local community as a whole. Though the problem of travel across the city was less challenging in Sheffield than in Manchester (because of smaller distances), there was a lament for the era of the cheap bus fares policy operated by a single and unitary South Yorkshire Council – and, as we showed in Chapter 4, a period in which the elderly could make reliable use of the 'bus knowledge' (numbers and frequency of particular routes) they had acquired over the years.

The fears

It is certainly important, in any study of this kind, to pay attention to different patterns of ageing, recognising, with post-modernists and health professionals alike, the youthfulness of many elderly people as well as the early dependency and fragility of others. The onset of old age can be a time of great foreboding and fears, born in particular of the isolation from the company of the workplace and the restricted range of human contact now experienced. Any analysis of the life of the elderly should be open and sensitive to the kinds of 'weakness' some elderly people express (for example, in respect of the speed at which buses are driven in a competitive local market) whilst also being aware of the resilience and knowledge of the elderly, especially in the industrial North. It is also important, we would argue, to understand how the fears and anxieties which are expressed by the elderly can be understood as a kind of reflexive social commentary as to the unintended consequences of social change – in the case of this generation of elderly Northerners, the crisis of the local industrial economies – rather than being only a literal statement of fear. Nowhere is this more apparent than in the popular discussion of crime. The fear of crime is quite clearly to be understood, in part, in literal terms, and we will be examining this fear, for Manchester and Sheffield, in the ensuing discussion. It is also to be understood, however, as a form of 'knowing' social commentary, in which the elderly are offering their wisdom – in metaphorical and heavily nuanced ways which, in other cultures, would be closely heard and apprehended – about 'the ways things are nowadays'.

In the research literature on crime and the elderly that began to develop in the early 1980s (Clarke and Lewis 1982; Hartnagel 1979; Lawton and Yaffe 1980; Yin 1982), a major emphasis is on the way that escalating fears about 'criminal victimisation' result in increased 'avoid-ance of the street' by the elderly and, in many instances, a kind of home imprisonment. Fifteen years later, there is no suggestion in either the North American or the British case of any reduction in such levels of fear (specifically about the probability of victimisation). There is some sugges-tion, indeed, in the wake of a number of reported cases of murder and rape, that the home itself is no longer assumed by the elderly at large to be a safe refuge or sanctuary from violent or predatory crime.

Our research was not designed to investigate these specific issues. What we did hear was the voices of the elderly speaking about their own fears and anxieties which accompany their use of these two cities, particularly their central areas, partly in respect of the chance of general harassment and unpleasantness, but also in respect of the chance of criminal victimisation *per se*. From the limited discussion that arose, in sessions where 'the condition of the city', and not crime, was the focus, four other connected themes emerged.

The unpredictability of crime

We have already indicated the importance for the elderly people in our North of England cities of establishing and maintaining a routine – whether, in the case of everyday shopping, in the immediate neighbour-hood or, on their periodic visits into town, in the pursuit of particular routes. The choice of these routes through city-centre territories is itself subject to some modification from time to time, depending on experi-ences which the elderly may have had – in terms of locating a familiar bus stop, for example, in a deregulated bus market, or of avoiding locations dominated by particularly aggressive beggars. This set of recursive strategies may also take into account especially unpleasant physical locations (underpasses or subways) and places that are simply physically difficult to negotiate. Reginald Walker in Manchester thought subways were the 'the worst thing they ever fetched out' [*sic*]. He would 'walk through them, but would avoid them of a night ... I'd rather walk over the motorway.'

There is a strong sense amongst the elderly we encountered that these features of the urban landscape were matters that had to be 'taken into account' in the planning of a trip to town, and that these difficulties were accepted 'as a part of life': at the individual level, the issue was whether one felt 'up to it' on a particular day. What could not be taken into account, in this strategic, probabilistic sense, was the question of crime – particularly, the chance of some kind of predatory assault. The possibility of such victimisation by crime seemed to be recognised by our discus-sants, ironically, as we will say below, in part because of the cycles of rumours and stories through informal social networks. Some of the fear was identified and 'rationally' appraised in terms of direct experience or observation of incidents in an elderly person's own neighbourhood. But the really unsettling question was that of crime which occurred unpredictably, and, perhaps more unsettlingly, in familiar streets not previously associated with such troubles. Geoff Helliwell, in Sheffield:

> The thing about this mugging business. It happens in various parts of the city. It's actually happened in Fargate.
>
> Ian Taylor: I didn't mention Fargate. You did.
>
> Geoff: No, but it has actually happened in Fargate. If you like, you can put it down to lawlessness. Holding up building societies ... all sorts of things have happened. It happens all over ... Even in the very centre ... but last week, I think it was two in the morning, some yobbos threw bricks through the windows of the pub. The landlord and the landlady were in bed. They smashed all the windows, the Prince of Wales pub. That's on the outskirts, a rather nice area of Sheffield, near Graves Park. I said this thing goes on all over. It's not really confined to one place.

Disruptions to mental maps and personal routes

The anxieties provoked by such unpredictability can in part be understood as a disruption this produces in the viability of the mental maps of the two cities which had been internalised by the elderly, particularly in respect of the places where violent or predatory crime might be expected. Very firm conceptions were held on this particular mapping of the two cities:

> Ian Taylor: Are there particular places in the city that are actually dangerous, more difficult or unpleasant?
>
> Alf Webb: There's one especially. Burngreave. Even the police call it a no-go area at night.
>
> Ian Taylor: Is that right or wrong?
>
> Geoff Helliwell: It is, yes.[16]

Derek Halstead in Manchester was more circuitous:

> I think if you plonked the average person down in Market Street and said 'Walk down there, through St Ann's Square, down Peter Street' ... on the whole, if they were sufficiently open-minded, the people would not sense they were under great threat. I'm not sure what they would feel in Miles Platting.

Other discussants spoke of their fear of Oldham Street in the city centre (the home of 'druggies') and of the shopping centre in inner-city Cheetham Hill. Moss Side was never actually identified by discussants, but there was a sense of its taken-for-granted status as a landscape of fear and crime. Derek Halstead claimed particular knowledge, in the meantime, as a result of his work with a local Labour Party, in saying that some of the small towns on the periphery of Greater Manchester, like Rochdale, were 'rotten ... high rate of incidence of crime that's drugs-related and so on'.

What we seemed to be witnessing in our discussions with the elderly, when the topic turned to crime and their own personal sense of safety in particular areas, was an immediate sharing of information about the present status of a place in terms of a practical, strategic map of the larger conurbation, adjudicating the veracity of local reputations. There was evidence of a very keen interest in any source of reliable information, with which the elderly might strategically renegotiate their use of a city.

Social networks and personal knowledge

We have already alluded to the firmness of the claims made by the elderly to their knowledge of the character of particular places. In some cases, the firmness of these claims was referred to in terms of some personal experience, often in the elderly person's own neighbourhood. George Greenhalgh, who never felt threatened in central Manchester, nonetheless recounted his experiences on Wythenshawe, described by many Mancunians as 'the largest council estate in western Europe':

> What I have found in Wythenshawe, where I live, is young kids running after me. I daren't go in my flat [whilst they're watching] because if they find where my flat is ... It started last September. I'd been refereeing a football match. I always have a bag with spare kit in. I'm a belt and braces chap, I was coming home, and they were playing up some stores near the bus station. I told them off, so they chucked stones at me ... Saturday, I'd been refereeing another match and there was a car on the pavement with no disc on, and there's these kids. I walk past and they start chucking stones at me.

The direct experience of 'threat' and 'danger' by the elderly must never be discounted. But it is clear that the designation of particular places as 'landscapes of fear' or as 'symbolic locations for crime' also arises, in very many instances, much more indirectly from the reading of reports in the local press (the *Manchester Evening News* or the *Sheffield Star*) and also the mushrooming free community newspapers delivered through the front doors of most residents of these two cities (cf. Taylor 1995a). In still other instances, the source of the definitive information was word of mouth through the informal social networks in which the elderly invest so much energy and commitment. Mr Simpson, in Manchester, knew 'quite a lot of people who have been robbed, on the street, in the house' (around Cheetham Hill shopping centre), 'mostly pensioners'. The mechanisms governing the circulation of fearful stories and rumours, and the relationship between local newspaper and television coverage of crime, personal experience and story-telling within the informal networks of the elderly, should be a focus of a separate study, informed by a determination to take seriously the fears of the elderly. It is by no means clear that these fears are well understood from the perspective of a 'theoretical' standpoint in which they are seen primarily as a result of over-dramatized mass media reportage, unrelated to the practical and personal knowledge and experience of the elderly themselves.[17]

It is clear, too, that the size and relative complexity of our two cities was an important factor in the dissemination and circulation of rumour. Each city had whole areas that were widely understood and openly talked about as 'symbolic locations' for crime (in Manchester, Cheetham Hill and Moss Side, and in Sheffield, Burngreave, rapidly displacing 'The Manor'), but, beyond these areas, the fixing of a particular character in respect of crime and personal safety to particular areas was either a contingent issue – an area might be so described in one conversation but not others – or else actively contested. In Manchester, as in London, there was a powerful continuing sense of the circulation of particular bodies of detailed local 'knowledge' about particular incidents of crime within very specific, delimited areas (sometimes equivalent to the areas covered by local community press, though not always), sitting alongside much more abstract and general stereotypes of that area circulating around the metropolitan conurbation.[18] It is not clear that these stereotypes were at all universally accepted, and it is clear that the acceptance of a particular definition of the character of an area was heavily influenced by individual biography (place of birth within the city), longevity of residence, occupational background and class culture, gender, age and ethnicity. In Sheffield, by contrast, there was some continuing sense that 'the city' retained a kind of coherence or unity, and that the distribution or 'mapping' of poverty and crime, as well as the symbolic locations or 'maps' of crime and landscapes of fear, were a matter of 'general knowledge': 'what everyone (of a particular generation) knows' about the place as a whole.

New times and the elderly

To reproduce a description of Manchester as the first city of the Industrial Revolution and Sheffield as one of the main centres in the North of heavy manufacturing and craft industry is also to recognise these two cities' long historical experience of a certain, very familiar, form of social reproduction. These are cities and larger urban districts in which, for generation after generation, the processes of family socialisation and education faithfully accomplished the task of producing more or less the required numbers of young men for entry into apprenticeships in the cotton or steel trades, and also, equally 'magically', more or less the required numbers of young women to marry these young men and take on the responsibilities of management of the domestic sphere (cf. Willis 1977, 1978). The double-edged nature of this familiar process of social reproduction (on the one hand, its enormously important role in the creation of close-knit industrial communities, but, on the other, its consequences for the subordination of women and the reduction of individual ambition) has been the subject of an extensive literature (cf. in particular, Common 1938; Roberts 1973).[19]

Some of those who are now in receipt of pensions in Britain have known of earlier challenges to the gendered aspects of this process – in their youth, when significant numbers of women came into prominence in public life at the time of the General Election of 1929, but also much later, during the Second World War, when women on the home front took on the jobs done by absent men. It is not clear how far these experiences can be said to have influenced the 'consciousness' of these generations, especially over longer periods of time. But it is clear that the imagery connecting industrial work to the strength of local community, via the kinds of socialisation taking place within working-class households (and further on up into the local lower middle class), is the dominant imagery through which the prevalence and character of local crime are understood.

Scott Trueman, an unemployed steelworker old before his time, spoke sadly of the Netherthorpe Estate in Sheffield (originally built in the early 1970s, on the hill below the University of Sheffield):

> You've got your people there living in concrete blocks on top of each other. We all know it leads to bad housing, especially young families, single families ... Where I used to live, it was all family life. There was a man, a woman and two or three kids. Now you'll only find one family like that in every ten. *They're either very old, on their own – or it's young women struggling to bring children up.* [Our emphasis]

Derek Halstead in Manchester and Geoff Helliwell in Sheffield both, independently, connected this dislocation of the family to the negativity and gratuitous violence they associated specifically with young people – 'teenagers' or 'even younger' – in these two cities. The larger context of this crisis of the family was spelt out by Scott Trueman:

> All the young lads up to 24 years of age have never had a job. There's no incentive to get one, anyhow, for what they are going to pay them. It's ridiculous ... All the buildings round here have a steel cage on the window. Even the grocers. They're all shuttered at night. It looks like Belfast. When anyone goes through, they must think 'What happened here?' I remember when it wasn't like that. Round about when we got the Tory government, it happened. Heavy industry went. People who lived here who had money: they went. The place got worse.

Accounts of this kind can be reproduced across the North of England and, following Christopher Lasch, we would argue that they should be understood as operating, like the myths of urban North America with their emphasis on the rural homestead or the small town, as a nostalgic reference 'to a place one can call home'. These urban North of England myths can be censured for their uncritical and nostalgic labour metaphysic and their idealisation of narrow and insular working-class communities, organised, sometimes coercively, around the support of the family wage-earner, oblivious to the needs of working-class women and repressive of healthy relationships between parents and children, as well as between women and men. They can also be identified as involving a reductionist and paranoid account of the crisis in mass manufacturing – a crisis that really does not reduce to the malevolence of the Conservative Party in Britain, since similar levels of deindustrialisation are evident in many other industrial societies. The popular myths also quite clearly ignore, as Beatrix Campbell has argued so powerfully, the different ways in which women and men have reacted to the demise of the taken-for-granted labour markets in the heartland of the industrial revolution (Campbell 1993). But accounts of this kind (of the absence of the discipline of the workplace, the nexus of the working-class household, and the informal controls imposed by the local neighbourhood on pubescent and post-pubescent young men) are nonetheless still the dominant frame through which the elderly generation interpret the current dislocation of neighbourhoods and city centres, and, in particular, the prevalence of theft, burglary and, the new and unpredictable phenomenon of drugs-related crime.

The overwhelming sentiment amongst elderly people from skilled manual working-class backgrounds, in particular, was one of sadness and even bitterness at the condition of the city and, especially, that of its people – at the fact that the promises of the earlier post-war period (an inchoate but firmly felt idea of 'progress and improvement' focusing on an enhancement of job opportunities, specifically, and also 'a better life' in terms of civic and public provision in areas like housing and education) appeared to have been dashed. There was a particular bitterness that the opportunities confronting the next generation of 'our people', so far from being an improvement on the experience of earlier generations, would be more restricted and difficult. It was in this sense, as we suggested earlier in this text, that the attitudes of some of our elderly Northerners to the beggars and other young people on the streets involved some sense of solidarity or pity as well as discomfort or fear. Even among the more economically secure, suburban elderly people, there was some sense that their lifetime investment of personal effort and their individual pursuit of a moral life had not helped the enhancement of the quality of public life in the city (as is evident, in particular, in the everyday experience of the city-centre shopping streets). In both these elderly populations, there was a sense that the advent of individualistic consumption, and the loss of a sense of shared community on the streets, was a kind of devaluation of their own lives – not the legacy they would have wanted for 'their' cities. So, we are suggesting, there was a particular kind of troubled nostalgia in operation here: not just passively for the orderly industrial community and its sustaining social relations (albeit built around the masculinist signifiers) in preference to the Darwinian competition of 'the market', but also for an earlier moment in the lives lived by these elderly North-

erners within such familiar industrial communities when it was legitimate, and certainly very common, for locals to expect some 'better-
ment' in the lives of local people as a whole; meaning here not just the
buildings and the urban spaces but, indeed, the 'quality' of their
working lives and life's other possibilities as well.

11

THE URBAN OTHER
Children and young men in public space in Manchester and Sheffield

At various points in this book, we have alluded to the widespread unease or outright fear that is provoked amongst residents and users of our two cities by the presence of groups of young people (especially young men) in public places, or by the anticipation of their presence. For many people going shopping in the city or looking for some evening leisure, and also for some professional workers en route to and from work, one of the fears was of a disturbing encounter on the street or on public transport with groups of unruly youngsters – once again, particularly young men. The taxonomy of the poor we discussed in Chapter 6 (which is used in reference to young people and adults alike) needs now to be modified to allow in more specific reference to local discussion of 'louts', 'hooligans' and 'yobs', both in abstract terms and also in respect of the practical strategies which are used by other publics in their avoidance of such gatherings.

We would, however, want to stress the *abstract* quality of the unease that is felt about 'yobs'. Local newspapers regularly carry letters, or other reports, complaining about the behaviours of these 'yobs' in public spaces in the city centre, on public transport or in local neighbour-hoods. But the discussion of individual young people in our discussion groups was often surprisingly sympathetic, and did not involve the attribution of these kinds of label. There is a balancing of an awareness of the real difficulties of life being experienced for some young people (a form of social solidarity echoing the long history of Northern experience) with an active dislike of the predatory and uncontrolled yobbery of the lumpenproletariat.[1] In this sense, the anxieties of other publics over young men, when encountered in person on the streets, were similar to the unease provoked by the presence of the poor and the homeless.[2]

In this chapter, we have three connected purposes. We want first to draw on our research discussions in the schools of Manchester and Sheffield to describe the way younger children of both sexes (aged 13 to 15) develop a sense of their neighbourhoods, the larger area (particularly the area between home and school) and then the larger city. There is a learning process here, in terms not just of the physical configuration of buildings and streets, but also, we would argue, of local culture (in this instance, what it means to be a young Mancunian or

Figure 11.1 The urban other: street beggars, Manchester, July 1995
Source: photo by Jenny Young

Sheffielder). This account of the recursive use of the city by the young is intended to follow the example of Anderson *et al.* (1994), in taking seriously the idea that the city both as a geographical space and built form (school and other buildings, shops, roads) and also as a site for a variety of social encounters with other young people and with adults can be a problem for young people themselves. Our interest in this first section is to try and gain some sense of the specific character of the problems which Manchester and Sheffield (as a smaller urban centre) pose for young people, recognising that this query must take account of the influence of gender and ethnicity.

Our second concern is to address the use of these two cities by groups of young people in their late adolescence, in particular, to offer some observations on the differences between Manchester, the 'youth capital' of the North, and Sheffield as a more 'typical', 'average' Northern ex-industrial city. The characterisation of Manchester, with its 42 city-centre clubs (in 1993), as the centre of the popular music industry and the youth scene in the North of England – a site of post-Fordist cultural production and consumption – is widespread, not least in a series of celebratory books by Steve Redhead (Redhead 1990, 1991, 1995) and in some connected 'working papers in popular culture' (O'Connor and Wynne 1993). In its redesignation in the late 1980s as 'Madchester', the city was the subject of some equally effusive journalistic celebration in the locally best-selling 'coffee-table' publication, *And God Created Manchester* (Champion 1990) and in many other journalistic accounts, including some in continental Europe and North America. Much of this writing on Manchester's youth scene in the 1980s, however, has been essentially descriptive, offering a 'reading' of the city and its music and clubs as a particular kind of youthful and consumption text.[3] We want to attempt, briefly, a more contextual analysis of the youth scene in Manchester, and particularly of the socially very patterned and unequal character of that 'scene', and of the vital relation between it and the growth of what may be called a 'survivalist culture' in central Manchester. The emphasis here will be on the close relation between the new local economy of music and cultural consumption, the hidden economy of crime, and the continuing presence of significant numbers of dispossessed young people in public space. The relative absence of a major local alternative economy of music and consumption in Sheffield – with only about nine night clubs in the city centre – is a key factor in the construction of Sheffield as a different type of urban experience for youth, and one which is more focused on the locales of leisure and consumption used by earlier generations (especially pubs).

This will lead us into our third objective in this chapter, which is to offer an analysis of use of the city by the young people which recognises change, especially the continuing rise of an economy based on consumption and the parallel collapse of the secure job markets of the Fordist era,[4] but also continuities, notably the continuing domination of the city centre and other public territories in the suburbs and secondary retail towns, especially certain symbolic locations (for example, in one area, a bandstand on the main street), by young men. It is not our concern to argue that this 'colonisation of public space' by young men is a feature only of the North of England, but it *is* our concern to recognise the very strong 'trace' of masculinist practices and customs in the routine daily experience of these two cities. We will want to relate our observations, in the final section of this chapter, to a particularly suggestive discussion we were able to hold with a group of young men on probation in Sheffield, as well as to some other materials derived from conversations and interviews throughout the course of this research.

What will be obvious is that this chapter gives voice mainly to young men talking about these cities, and, to some lesser extent, to other members of the public in these two cities talking about young men in public space. This is no oversight on our part as we argued in Chapter 9, the public spaces, outside of the restricted configurations of shops and cafés we called 'the woman's city', in these two Northern cities are essentially colonised by men. The commonsense discussion that took place in our focus groups in respect of the problem of young people in public space was almost without exception, and without challenge, about young men, except for the occasional reference to young women beggars or 'crusties' on Market Street in Manchester. Our discussion here, in that sense, is an accurate representation (not an acceptance) of the normal-ised hegemony exercised by young men over public space, and the ways in which the 'problem of young people' in our cities is 'naturally' and commonsensically the problem of young men, without necessarily being represented in popular common sense as a gender issue.

NOWHERE TO GO

Fears and anxieties about the safety and well-being of children in public space in the city are not new (Ward 1975), and even the current level of agitation about the security of children left 'home alone' in North America by 'over-accelerated', or careless parents have a prehistory in the concern over 'latch-key children' during the Second World War and the 1950s (in Britain as well as in the United States). But this fear for children's safety is not a given, unchanging feature of cities in all historical periods, or, indeed, all societies. The definition of the given facts of a city's material or physical presence (for example, as the site of dark underpasses, narrow walkways, etc.) seems to be subject to some cultural variation, as 'threatening' or otherwise; and, even more impor-tantly, the definition of the risk attending social life itself in a city seems to be a function of the availability of custodial staff, informally charged with looking after children's welfare (the bus conductress, the school-crossing attendant, in North America the school bus driver). The anxi-eties of parents about releasing their children into public territories in the city, that is, seems to be influenced by the presence in a city of certain key signifiers of custodianship – that is, of whether a city is 'looked after' or 'attended' – not least, rationally or otherwise, the presence of graffiti, litter and related signs of what James Q. Wilson and George Kelling, in a widely quoted article in the United States, interpret as emblems or traces of 'incivility' (cf. Wilson and Kelling 1982).

There is no question, either, that other, more fundamental influences 'in the culture' of a society are at work here, in defining whether social interaction as such is interpreted as more or less invested with risk and danger. Statistics show that there has been a radical reduction in England and Wales, during the 1980s and early 1990s, in the number of younger children being allowed to return home unescorted from school, especially on dark winter evenings, or indeed allowed out of the private home at all to make use of sporting or other facilities in the local neighbourhood.[5] There seems little question that this increase in cau-tionary use is a response to the increased prevalence of a fear of 'the Other' that has developed in close relationship with the growth of more privatised forms of life during the last two decades, especially in cities – that there is a kind of dialectical relationship, in other words, between fear and what Raymond Williams called the 'mobile privatism' of the market society. The construction of this 'fear of the Other' will be heavily dependent, of course, on very specifically situated ideas of what constitutes the child's own community, neighbourhood or other membership groups, and this process of inclusion and exclusion may vary considerably across cities of different size, class and ethnic mix, and other dimensions of local culture (including the extent to which these cities have embraced 'newcomers' and difference).

What is at issue here, however, is not just the question of personal safety but also the broader issues of acquiring a local identity (in this instance, as we argued in Chapter 2, becoming a Mancunian or Sheffielder) and positioning oneself within the locally available youth cultural formations, initially encountered at school, but also observed on visits into town and on other 'outings'. It is important to emphasise, we think, how much of this 'knowledge' for younger children is conditional and dependent on hearsay rather than on direct experience[6] (for example, in Manchester, about night clubs or concert venues; in Sheffield, more frequently, about pubs) – particularly in the larger urban area of Greater Manchester, where the range and number of myths about place and about 'other people' are more extended. Our own research (like that of Coffield *et al.* (1986) and Loader (1996)) confirmed that the actual urban experience of young children up to the age of 14 or 15 is very much confined to the immediate neighbourhood. Discussion by 13–15-year-olds of their own neighbourhood often involved a quite elaborate and affectionate display of knowledge with respect to local police, local 'characters' and so on, but any discussion of areas of the city beyond the local neighbourhood tended to rely on stereotypes, impressions or particular stories current in the local culture (for example, on local television programming). This stereotyping of other areas was particularly powerful in attributions of a 'class character' to an area. Young children in a suburban area of Stockport, for example, were already familiar with a key suburban theme of Greater Manchester, that of the invasion of young people from the inner city, forcefully claiming that they had been:

> followed home one night by some lads from Longsight. They kept calling round. We had to get the police. They'd come in the house and sit down and smoke cigarettes and smoke draw. Then they'd start asking how much the TV cost, things like that. My dad chucked them out, but they just kept coming around.

This sense of territory was in no way confined to suburban young people. A group of young Asian boys from a school in the Burngreave/Pitsmoor area of Sheffield talked in terms of there being a very local solidarity 'amongst people from different countries' to defend that area, such that if any outsiders came in to the area, calling people racist names or otherwise being threatening, they would band together to 'sort the racists out'.

The theme of race was, if anything, more pronounced in its negative connotations in some Sheffield schools than in Manchester. So the presence of Moss Side in Manchester was a matter not just of fear and dismay to young Mancunians, though few had ever been there, but also of some celebration on account of its national and international reputation. In one discussion in Stockport, conducted entirely without reference to any demonstrable evidence or 'facts' (the allusion might have been to a boxing challenge tournament), two girls recounted the story of how some young people, their own age, went from Moss Side to New York ('the Bronx') for a fight:

First girl:	Like the ones in Moss Side having a fight with the Bronx in America or whatever. Moss Side won as well.
Second girl:	What?
First girl:	Moss Side had a fight with one of the roughest areas in America.
Penny Fraser:	You mean boxers?
First Girl:	No – actual people, gangs.
Second Girl:	Where did they go?
First Girl:	I've no idea. It was ages ago.
Second Girl:	Maybe the Bronx people came over here?
First Girl:	I know they met up.
Third Girl:	Is Moss Side the hardest in England or something?

There was some sense amongst our Manchester younger children of Moss Side's problematic national reputation as being at one with Manchester's generally problematic reputation elsewhere in the country – as an awkward and dynamic 'shock city', doing now what other cities will do themselves later (even 'hard crime'). In Sheffield, the response of young people to Burngreave and Pitsmoor was much more bemused: there was a powerful sense, indeed, that Burngreave and Pitsmoor were simply different from the rest of Sheffield and, in that sense alone, a place to be treated with caution or even fear. In part, we would say with orthodox human geography that these are matters of city size; but we also see in these responses some evidence of the different 'structure of feeling' of the two cities ('cosmopolitan' Manchester, the city of commerce and trade, as against 'village' Sheffield, city of steel and cutlery).

For many young people, this issue of the size, status and general level of excitement or otherwise of their city was also very much played out in the sphere of consumption, in terms not only of their assessment of the range and quality of shops in their cities (and in different areas) but also of how other children, their own age, engaged in the practice of consumption. In both cities, considerable energy went into the denunciation of other children as 'townies'. This particular construction of Other Children does not seem to involve any one fixed clothing preference (though baseball caps, sweatshirts and running shoes were important signifiers), style of speech or patterns of behaviour. It is rather more a general category of Otherness (an early adolescent 'gallery of folk devils') to which feared or disliked other children are allocated in conversational exchanges. One of the powerful undercurrents in some young people's talk about 'townies' or other urban folk devils (like young prostitutes, 'druggies' or beggars) is the fear of recruitment into that kind of life. In one Sheffield discussion, a young girl puzzled over how many of these other young people seemed:

> just normal people. Some, you can tell. Some, you can't. They'll go up to anyone our age, asking if we want to buy drugs, like.

Fear of being targeted by other children selling drugs was accompanied in some instances by fears of other kinds of 'contamination': one 14-year-old schoolgirl in Sheffield, in an aside, commented that she was unhappy about walking through certain areas for fear of being somehow recruited into prostitution there.

The overwhelming anxiety amongst many young children, however, was about violence and harassment from older children. The knowledge of 'bullying' in the school situation seemed to help only partially in understanding the patterns of risk in the city centre, where a series of stereotypes (about 'heavy metal types' and others) were mobilised as an anticipatory device. The city centre was seen, however, not just as a place of fear, but also as a place in which some self-expression might be possible because of the anonymity of the centre. Manchester's city-centre clubs were a great attraction, particularly amongst girls aged 14 to 15 who could sometimes gain admission to these clubs (where the boys could not).

It is not our intention to suggest that these patterns of early youth culture, particularly the struggle to avoid definition of oneself as a 'townie', are markedly or fundamentally different in Manchester and Sheffield, but we do want to suggest that the general cultural script in Manchester is that this is a 'headquarter city' for youth, and that the city itself is 'open' to Others, including, in an ironic fashion, having its own distinctive black Manchester.

TEENAGE CULTURE IN THE NORTH OF ENGLAND IN THE MID-1990S

Most of the classic sociological writing on older youth and adolescence from the earlier post-war 'Fordist' period (up to the late 1970s and early 1980s), with the mass of the youthful male population destined for work in mass manufacturing industry, focuses closely on the social and cultural aspects of this period of transition – notably, in the English case, on the role of youth culture in creating some kind of 'magical resolution' to problems of class inequality and the power struggle between an adult population and each emerging new cohort of adolescents (cf. Hall and Jefferson 1978; Willis 1977, 1978; Robins and Cohen 1978). The 'storm and stress' experienced by young people during adolescence, which is the focus of nearly all psychological writing on youth, is analysed by socio-logical commentators as part of the process wherein young people, particularly young men, having made an attempt in their early years at school to advance themselves in order to escape their destiny in their local labour market, must adapt and adjust to their fates – to prepare themselves, culturally, for entry into that market, bringing with them the appropriate kinds of personal attitude, language and cultural assumption 'for work'. The aspirations held by working-class parents for their sons to 'do well' in school and go on to get a better job than their father, in the majority of cases, encountered the reality of blocked opportunity. Especially in the period from the mid-1950s to the late 1970s, there was limited mobility within the labour market. The persistent 'blockage of opportunity' that was still a feature of the era of Fordism was given pride of place in the accounts offered by social scientists of juvenile crime, committed either for financial gain or (as in the case of vandalism and similar behaviour) for symbolic reasons ('rejecting the rejectors'). In the meantime, as Angela McRobbie's work over the years has shown so effectively, young women in England – especially in the industrial cities and regions – were involved less intrusively and visibly in their own transition from the parental home to their 'own home' (via a 'respectable marriage'), all the while negotiating the perilous divide between the enjoyment of the liberties of adolescence and the necessity of maintaining a personal reputation as a desirable wife, a 'good catch' (McRobbie and Garber 1978; McRobbie 1978, 1980).

'Adolescence' in Fordist economies, dominated by mass manufacturing employment, in this sense involved the parallel and interdependent processes of young men preparing themselves for entry into the labour market and young women preparing themselves for the marriage market, in the meantime recognising that the period between 16 and 19 years of age was a socially licensed period for having fun, prior to the assumption of adult responsibilities in the world of industrial or domestic labour. In the writing of the Birmingham School of Contemporary Cultural Studies, the other crucial issue was that this period was one in which individual life-chances were finally allocated, most often reproducing the destiny implied by the social position of one's parents. It was, therefore, also a time of life in which individuals routinely and predictably invested their personal psyches and identities in the culture of resistance and insubordination (what Paul Willis calls the 'profane culture') (Willis 1977) which has characterised 'working-class communities' and regions in England from the beginnings of the Industrial Revolution – some would argue, deriving its long-term character and strength from peasant cultures in the pre-industrial period, from the 'free-born Englishman' described by E.P. Thompson, occasionally prone to riot, or, as Ralph Miliband once argued, to other, less spectacular, shows of 'routine insubordination' (Thompson 1963; Miliband 1978).

This process of reproduction of the class relations and the sexual division of labour of the Fordist period had an almost invisible, routinised character in England, in the sense that it was rarely grasped openly in political and social discussion as a final and almost irreversible allocation of lifetime inequality. It was also, mostly, a relatively orderly process, in the sense that it had a taken-for-granted character even within this very unequal industrial society: failure to 'do well' at school and to move on up through the system of 'sponsored mobility' (Turner 1960) 'naturally' consigned individuals to working-class careers, to which they would be more or less cheerfully directed by schools career counsellors or their family, friends and 'mates' working in the local labour market itself.

An extensive literature sets out the ways this routine allocation of life-chances to individuals worked as a social process, particularly in schools. Curiously, however, this literature has not paid much attention to the ways in which these processes of sponsorship or exclusion of children in schools connected to the lives those children pursued outside schools, either during early adolescence or around the key point of 16 (for the majority, in the early post-war period, 'school-leaving age'). There is no particular curiosity displayed as to the particular sites or locales in which youthful activity was concentrated, and within which the processes of individual affiliation to career and life-strategy, as well as subcultural formation, occurred. But, as Bob Connell's analysis of the street in *Gender and Power* (1987) so powerfully shows, the processes of social reproduction (of gender relations and of the relations between different categories of young people and adults) are always located in particular spaces or places.[7] The negotiations and struggles over occupancy of the local park, the neighbourhood shopping street and, indeed, the mall are, in this sense, a kind of power struggle, for space, with more general consequences in the process of social reproduction. In the 1950s, when the most spectacular subcultural development competing for the attention of young people was the Teddy Boy, one of the key locations for such a struggle was 'the dance-hall' (Rock and Cohen 1970), and in the case of the Mods in the early 1960s, to a very significant degree, it was the street corner café (the 'caff').

For the bulk of the adolescent cohorts coming of age in the earlier, 'Fordist', post-war period, the main places of resort outside school were, during the day, playing fields and parks, and on weekends and some weekday evenings, cinemas, youth clubs and pubs. The neighbourhood street itself, which had been such an important site in earlier years (for 'hanging around', 'doing nothing') (Corrigan 1978) had usually been left behind – as a territory reserved for younger boys and, particularly in working-class neighbourhoods, as a space in which local housewives and mothers socialised. Though there continued to be some use of the local neighbourhood, for the majority of young people by the age of 16 or 17 the city-centre area, especially city-centre public houses, had become the preferred place of resort. This regular use of the city centre by adolescents involved certain key locations chosen either because of their location (close to youth club or cinema, perhaps, or even just to the bus station and the 'last bus home') or because these pubs had specifically orientated themselves to a youthful clientele. In city-centre Manchester, for example, Oldham Street was for many years a favoured location for young people from the poorer areas of north Manchester, including the Langley estate in Middleton, some 10 miles from the city centre. It was home to a number of large and long-established pubs, like The Merchants, and also close to the bus stops for the routes going back 'up Rochdale Road' at the end of the evening.[8] In Sheffield, pride of place went to the 'West Street Run', beginning at the Stone House (a very large city-centre pub created out of a Georgian town house) and extending 'up West Street' as far as the Hallamshire Hotel. There were alternative routes in both cities, with Sheffielders from the East End preferring one that encompassed the Blue Bell on High Street and extended 'down the hill to the Wicker' and the buses home.

Associated with this recursive use of city centres in the North of England in the earlier post-war period was a definite and patterned set of problems. There was the potential of a clash between different groups of mobile young people circulating through the city: 'locals' versus 'students', for example, or, in particular city districts, between young people, knowingly or otherwise, taking up occupation for an evening of a pub which served as an everyday 'local' for local people, particularly local men.[9] In city centres in the North of England, as elsewhere, there was always also the danger of 'trouble', usually some youthful mischief making, on the 'last bus' (or, in Sheffield's case before 1960, the 'last tram') in the hour up to midnight, or, frequently, that of more serious trouble in the struggle to obtain a late-night taxi at city-centre ranks. It would be relatively straightforward to plot a number of locations onto a plan of these two North of England cities, especially around their central areas, identifying what we might call 'a map of potentially troublesome locations' – particular street corners and pavements, usually around pubs and other places of public resort (the bus station and the taxi rank) – though, as with all such maps, there would always be different patterns of use and also of popular knowledge and interpretation.

The demise of manufacturing industry in the North of England since the mid-1970s, and, with it, the rapid transformation of local labour markets, have coincided with the achievement of hegemony by a consumer culture (and, indeed, a culture industry) specifically targeting young people. The broad outlines of this 'culture industry', organised around fashion and music, had been familiar to earlier students of culture on both sides of the Atlantic, but it is arguable that it was only in the 1970s that the culture and communications industry attained an economic and social significance on a par with the fast-declining industries of production. During the 1980s, the economic and social power of the culture industries was given further encouragement by the 'enterprise culture' mobilised by the Thatcher government, particularly in respect of the support for small businesses working creatively on the 'leading edge' of fashion and music. There is no question that Manchester, city of trade and commerce, was one of the cities to respond most quickly and creatively to this new 'opportunity'.[10]

'MADCHESTER': THE CULTURAL INDUSTRY IN MANCHESTER IN THE 1980s/1990s

The existing accounts of Manchester's new culture industry[11] place most emphasis, in an idealist fashion, on the raw populism of the music and the creative energy of a series of local bands, particularly those playing so-called 'independent' music, which emerged in the city during this period: The Smiths, the Happy Mondays, Inspiral Carpets, the Stone Roses and, most recently, Oasis (cf. Champion 1990; Redhead 1990). But it is clear that the development of the 'Madchester scene' in this city during the period from the late 1970s to the late 1980s[12] was very closely connected, at least at that particular conjuncture, to local urban regeneration initiatives, driven in part by the rescue of city-centre warehouses and other buildings undertaken by the Central Manchester Development Corporation itself and resulting from the enormous tax incentives and grant aid channelled through the CMDC. This was also a moment of opportunity for the fast-developing local subculture of youthful entrepreneurs. One of the most striking features of the areas immediately around Manchester's city centre in the 1980s was the reclaiming of the warehouses and factories, left over from the high point of the cotton industry, for other innovative purposes. The Hacienda on Whitworth Street, first opened in 1982, played a leading role in the development of Manchester's youth cultural 'scene' in the 1980s, but it was only one among many old industrial and other buildings reclaimed for use as night clubs, bars, record stores, cafés and restaurants.[13] Affleck's Palace, which has an iconic status amongst young Mancunians, is the most obvious local example of what Angela McRobbie refers to as 'the ragmarket' for teenage consumers (McRobbie 1994): it occupies the site of the old Affleck and Brown's department store of 1860, discussed in Chapter 5, and comprises four floors of stalls and shops, selling cheap clothing and other prized items in the youth-style market. Elsewhere in the city are some 20–30 small record companies attempting to follow the example of Factory Records, established in 1978 by Tony Wilson, a locally born entrepreneur and TV presenter, and a significant number of other small independent companies involved with the production of programmes for local television and radio.

The size of this local youthful enterprise culture in Manchester is a matter of some sociological interest, not least because of the claims which are sometimes made that this new cultural industry can represent an alternative source of legitimate employment for young people in the city.[14] In the early 1980s, according to Shaun Ryder of the Happy Mondays, no more than 200 or 300 'cool geezers' (owners of record companies, night clubs, fashion outlets and journalists) were involved. In the mid-1990s, the local enterprise culture of youth clearly involves far more people than that, and it also embraces a much more extensive network of businesses, buildings and places. *City Life*, Manchester's entertainment listing magazine, first launched in December 1983, had by April 1994 established for itself a circulation of 20,000 and was claiming 'exposure to 80,000 high-profile, intelligent and affluent people', of whom 57 per cent were under 29 (according to its own reader profile).

THE SURVIVAL CULTURE

City Life magazine may see itself as being read and consumed by large numbers of young professional people and by students. But it is also vital to understand that the youth culture industry in Manchester has a more general purchase on the whole social and economic formation: an expression of the very rapidly changing economic circumstances of the 1980s (the 'New Times' of 'disorganized, global capitalism'). The purchase of Manchester culture industry on local young people presents itself at the levels of ideas in terms of 'style' but also has a material reality in the form of the casualised local labour market.

Youth cultural styles in Manchester have a less fixed, generationally specific character than any of the youth styles of the earlier Fordist period, and are perhaps best understood as different adaptations to dynamic changes in the market rather than as 'a resolution' to the contradictions within that society. The 'youth scene' in Manchester, in particular, is defined, both locally and nationally, by the particular 'attitude' that its enthusiastic adherents express: an 'attitude' informed by a definite class inflection, identifying cohorts of young people with a background in the industrial North, now destined to an even more difficult future. The constituents of 'attitude' include some necessary local knowledge about the perils of the street (drugs, violence, joblessness and homelessness) and are held in a precarious coexistence with the liminal pleasures of music, sexuality, certain specific kinds of soft drug use, coolness and style, cross-cut with an openness to other cultures (Los Angeles, Jamaica and, more recently, Asia). A massive youth scene has grown up around a set of different musical traditions (acid house, techno, house, ragga, jungle, indie and hip-hop), each of which is associated with different presentations of self, but none of which is reducible straightforwardly to class position, ethnicity or gender. Alongside these fast-changing youthful styles, there are also mainstream clubs in Manchester catering to young people with no overt music identification, attracting primarily young office workers – the successor to the Northern Soul club scene of the 1970s – and clubs catering for gay people. Some clubs vary in the way they market themselves through the week, and many of the clubs run so-called student nights in mid-week, with cheaper entry and drink. The relations between these styles, and their relative valorisation, is subject to constant change. There is, however, a more or less permanent residual category of young person, the 'townie', distinguishable by 'casual sportswear' and baseball cap, and very much dismissed by those 'with attitude' as 'a loser' or, in other words, precisely, as a person who does not have the kind of attitude and style with which to prosper in a survival culture.

There are analogies, as always, between some of these emergent forms of youth culture and some of the innovative aspects of the dominant culture itself, but no direct correspondence. So for every successful local youthful entrepreneur sustaining his or her leading position in a dynamic local hierarchy of new businesspeople, there are hundreds of young people employed in part-time and temporary jobs in restaurants and bars, in record and television companies and in fashion outlets, sometimes working extremely long hours for what would have been seen, only a few years ago, as very small salaries indeed. A large, but unknown, proportion of this new casualised 'service class' within the local youth culture industry consists of women: one of the most important offshoots of the transformation of the local labour market being the growth of the all-night café (and, to a lesser extent, the wine bar)[15] as the preferred site of business as well as pleasure in central Manchester – an alternative to the male-dominated world of the pub. For every young person who has a job within this insecure and competitive local labour market, there are many thousands who do not. Of those who were classified as employed, a significant number are actually 'on schemes' or 'on the YTS'; that is, on a government employment training programme of one kind or another. In Greater Manchester, according to the 1991 Census, some 1.1 per cent of all men aged between 16 and 64 (about 79,000 people – the vast majority of them young men) were 'on schemes'.[16] For an unknown number of young people, officially classified as employed, the only experience of work was on what one commentator has called 'the magic roundabout' of one retraining scheme after another, punctuated by periods of unemployment in between (Craine 1994). In Greater Manchester as a whole, according to the same Census, some 62,872 people aged 18 to 24 were officially 'economically inactive'.[17] In some areas of the city and the wider conurbation, official rates of youth unemployment were approaching 45 per cent, and other analyses were suggesting that the amount of very long-term unemployment (over periods of five years or more) was approaching levels for which there were no twentieth-century precedents.

Given the cut-backs throughout the 1980s in the building of public housing, and the restricted size of the local rental housing market, large numbers of young people were confronting the prospect either of having to remain in the parental home or move into cheap multi-occupied accommodation: for large numbers of adolescents in cities like Manchester, the real fear was not so much of the homeless themselves as it was of joining the homeless of their own age already widely visible on the city streets. In a quite agitated discussion of the homeless with some young children in one Greater Manchester high school, the mocking views of two young boys that 'the beggars should be allowed to die of exposure' were challenged by a young girl angrily observing:

> Don't say that. If your parents kicked *you* out on the streets, you'd soon change your tune.

This crisis in local labour markets (polarising between high-income employment and low-income, part-time, temporary employment) is general to the western world, albeit in different and particular ways. Enzo Mingione, for example, has offered a compelling analysis of the different kinds of life-strategy that are available, at different levels of the local labour markets, in Northern and Southern Italy (Mingione 1994), and Gavin Smith has described the different kinds of 'idiosyncratic livelihoods' being constructed by different groups of young people in Pais Valencioano, Spain (Smith 1994). One key sociological issue here is the extent to which the 'strategies' which young people are pursuing in these different localities in the North of England in the mid-1990s are one part of a joint household or family strategy, collaboratively working the 'informal' as well as formal economy, of the kind described for the Isle of Sheppey by Ray Pahl (1984), or to which young people, particularly young men, break free of such family constraint or responsibility in the informal, more or less legal economy in order to branch out into individualistic 'strategies of survival', sometimes in the hidden, illegitimate economy. The research that has been undertaken in Greater Manchester in the early 1990s, particularly in local audits of crime, suggests that in some areas significant numbers of young men (in preference to collective work within their parental families or any successor families of their own) have been attracted into various kinds of apprenticeship in 'craft criminality' – for example, in organised thefts of computers and other valuables from business premises and public buildings.[18]

YOUNG PEOPLE AND LOCAL ANXIETY

The incidence of burglaries of business and domestic premises reported to the police in Greater Manchester in 1992 was 4,022 per 100,000 people – some 51.7 per cent higher than the average incidence of 2,652 per 100,000 across England and Wales (Criminal Statistics, England and Wales, 1992: Table 2.6).[19] Along with car theft, therefore, burglary was the most frequently experienced type of criminal victimisation in the Manchester region. In local discussion – in the 'lay criminology' that is an important element in local fear of crime – these types of crime were almost universally attributed to the growth of the 'drug trade', so constructing a discourse which leads, almost without exception, into a familiar set of calls for stern action against pushers and overseas drug barons – particularly as this drug trade has been seen to involve young people in school.[20] This local awareness of 'drugs' depends on a mix of visual information (the sight of people assumed to be 'junkies' or 'druggies' outside Boots on Market Street in the early morning) with the coverage given to the local youth scene, on the one hand, and violent drugs-related crime, on the other. In the early to mid-1980s, considerable excited coverage was given in the local media to the so-called 'acid house' parties, held in different locations around the city, and, in the late 1980s and early 1990s, a similar kind of press coverage was given to the 'raves' which were being held in mainstream clubs in Manchester (as well in other major cities in the North).[21] There could certainly be no denying the prevalence of such a club life, as the buses and trams on Friday and Saturday evenings were full of young people on their way into the clubs (one estimate suggests that 20,000–30,000 young people attend raves in Manchester every weekend (Pearson et al. 1991: 10)).

The reaction of the larger set of publics in the city to the young ravers seems to have been powerfully informed by a set of agitated fears regarding the kind of liminality involved in such events, and also the 'devilish' effects of the drugs that are thought to be widespread 'in the clubs'.[22] These fears are reinforced by the periodic release through the local press and television of survey results reporting on the presence, if not the actual use, of drugs in the lives of local young people. Amongst the most widely quoted such local surveys was that conducted at the University of Manchester at the end of 1991, suggesting that six out of ten 14–15-year-olds in the North-west had been offered drugs and that some 36 per cent had used them (20 per cent in the last month).[23] The survey also suggested that some 200,000 young people in total (about 40 per cent of all people under 18) had smoked cannabis, sniffed a solvent or taken some kind of psychedelic or stimulant 'dance drug' (Measham et al. 1994). Statistics of this order, from general surveys of 14–15-year-olds, were compounded in the public mind by stories regularly played out in the media and by locally circulating rumours concerning the prevalence of heroin and cocaine use (particularly 'crack' cocaine) on some of the city's estates and in certain specific inner-city areas.

In February 1991, these anxieties took on a much more tangible form when a fatal shooting occurred outside a pub in Cheetham Hill, North Manchester, explained by local police as a product of rivalries between 'organised gangs', allegedly trading in drugs and based in that area and in Moss Side. As we discussed earlier, in Chapter 8, two further murders quickly followed in Moss Side in April, in one instance of a 17-year-old, Frank Stapleton. These murders provoked immediate and intense response in the local media – not least in a Granada Television programme, *Up Front*, screened throughout the North-west, and connecting the rise in firearms use in crime to the local trade in drugs.[24] The London-based Guardian Angels organisation also announced at this point that it was opening up in Manchester, responding to the agitated levels of fear about crime expressed by residents of the Wythenshawe estate in south Manchester. As we explained in Chapter 8, stories about Moss Side and about firearms crime in Manchester ran in all the national press throughout the month of May, always on an analogy with South

Central Los Angeles, coming to a head with the murder of 14-year-old Benji Stanley, gunned down whilst queuing in a 'pattie' (Jamaican fast food) shop in Moss Side. Manchester and Moss Side were now, in effect, confirmed in the national imagination as the centre not only of the illegal drugs trade[25] but – again in a familiar American analogy – also as the home to firearms-using gangs involved in what was assumed to be a mushrooming drug trade. Particular emphasis was placed by senior police officers and local journalists on the so-called Gooch Gang (from Gooch Close) and the Pepper Hill mob (later retitled the Doddington gang) on the Alexandra Estate, so providing local publics with a template through which to understand the incident – as a product of the actions of heartless and amoral gangs struggling for control of territory.[26] A further twist was given to public anxiety by a series of press stories implying that the carrying of guns in Manchester's night clubs and even on the city-centre streets was the latest fashion amongst young people – an allusion that was apparently given support by the wearing of 'Smoking Gun' and marijuana logos and imagery on shell-suits by a small number of young Mancunian 'townies'.[27]

There is no question but that the reputations which were now being elaborated of the Moss Side and Cheetham Hill districts, through the guns-and-drugs couplet, were providing young men from those areas with the kind of recognition and personal status that was not available to them in the legitimate local labour market. There is no question either that the coverage of Moss Side in the early 1990s bore all the familiar trappings of a 'moral panic', with the linguistic and other allusions in press reports out of all proportion to the numbers of murders and firearms offences actually being reported in the area.[28]

We discussed the key issues in Moss Side's elevation to a demonic status in Chapter 8 and, in particular, highlighted the displacement of public concern over increasing social inequality into racialised themes about an urban underclass. Our concern here is to disentangle a little further the local discourses about youth, drugs and violence as a part of our attempt to understand the local dynamics of urban fears in Manchester. *City Life* magazine tried to grapple with the issue in the editorial to its special 'Violence Issue' of 6–21 January 1993:

> We have two main strands to modern Manchester violence. We have casual and random violence associated, usually, with alcohol abuse; and we have serious, targeted violence associated with guns, organised crime and drugs. The former bothers us because we might be the next victim. It is the fear of such violence which bothers us. The remedies are pretty straightforward: increase the price of alcohol, liberalise the licensing laws so pubs and clubs don't turf out drunken customers at 11.30 p.m. and 2.30 a.m. (on Friday and Saturday, the two most violent half-hours of the week) and put people back to work (especially young men).
>
> The latter is a much more daunting problem. If allowed to get out

of hand, we could go the way of the USA ... There is no easy answer, but legalising drugs would destroy a swathe of organised crime (as did the ending of Prohibition in the United States). When Operation China removed 22 drug dealers from Moss Side, the vacuum was filled within days. The reorganisation of the criminal justice system would be a step in the right direction but, failing that, we need a latter-day Elliott Ness and a good taxman.

City Life's analysis of Manchester violence works partly to identify that violence with the drunken behaviours of 'traditional' Northern men, especially at pub closing time. But it also connotes with the threats posed by organised crime in the well-known areas inhabited by the urban underclass. In this way, it works to disconnect crime and violence from the local cultural industry, of which the magazine is itself a part, and, in particular, from the insecure, competitive local labour market (the 'survivalist' culture of part-time and irregular employment) associated with it.

There can be no question that the routinised heavy drinking common amongst Northern men[29] is a source of considerable social anxiety to others, especially in the hour after closing time; and we in no way want to deny the presence of an organised crime structure in Greater Manchester, with its continuing potential for violent confrontations. But the local culture industry and the sites in which it does its business are in no sense 'crime-free zones'. The Hacienda club was closed down in 1990 after discoveries of arms amongst patrons and a series of related incidents in other clubs: it has since reopened with very heavy security measures at the door, and a marked move towards the middle-ground of the music scene, with an emphasis on 'popular house'.[30] In May 1994, 30-year-old Chris Horrox was gunned down in Sackville Street, central Manchester, whilst putting up wall posters advertising a forthcoming concert. It was later revealed that control over such 'fly posting' – estimated as worth £200,000 a year (from one-off fees paid by concert promoters) – had been vigorously disputed by rival free market operators (Manchester Evening News 3 May 1994). There was a recognition in many quarters that similar struggles for control are taking place across the different markets that govern the distribution of part-time work and other perquisites in Manchester, and that, in many areas (computers, office equipment, refreshment supplies, etc.), the distinction between legitimate and illegitimate branches of local enterprise culture is not as clear cut as the City Life editorial would imply. It may be important, in further (potentially dangerous) work in this area, to recognise the ways in which ostensibly legitimate and substantively illegitimate business overlap, and, under the continuingly competitive conditions that obtain (and could worsen) in the local consumer market governing economic survival, spill over into real crime. In these circumstances, it may be that the impressions and stereotypes of the

Manchester scene, connecting up extraordinary images of young people, crime and violence, might have a clearer relationship to 'reality'.

YOUNG PEOPLE'S DAILY AND NIGHTLY STRUGGLE FOR 'THE CITY'

The city by day

One of the limitations of our research in Manchester and Sheffield in 1993 is the fact that we were not able, within the limits of our resources, to carry out any systematic observational, ethnographic study of the use of city-centre and suburban areas at different times of the week. During the completion of our survey work on the streets of these two cities, however, some definite impressions were formed, and, in many cases, underlined in our focus group discussions. So also did our own ongoing use of Manchester, as residents of this city, and Sheffield, as regular visitors, help substantiate or qualify our impressions. We showed in Chapter 9 how the use of these Northern cities by women is massively more prevalent in the daytime hours than in the evenings. In the period between 9 a.m. and 6 p.m., according to our own survey, 46 per cent of all users of the city territories of Manchester were women, but in the period between 6 p.m. and 8.30 p.m. only 26 per cent. In Sheffield (excluding Meadowhall), the corresponding figures were 45 per cent in the day and 32 per cent in the evening (Evans and Fraser 1995). Daytime use of the city centre proper was very much dominated by middle-aged or elderly women, either by themselves or with their husbands, followed by younger women, especially young mothers with toddlers or other young children. Buses and trams going through the concentric zones of the conurbation into central Manchester, after the beginning of the concessionary fares at 9.30 in the morning, sometimes fill up with poor young couples or single men and women from the inner city, no doubt heading into town to escape their areas and wander the Arndale Centre and other locations, filling time and looking for diversion.

On the evidence of our research, the regular daytime use of the city centre (and, indeed, of secondary retail towns) seems to be accomplished without excessive levels of harassment and fear. Regular users of the Metrolink in Manchester, however, derived comfort from the knowledge that the vehicles are all equipped with alarm pulls and direct communication to the driver, as well as by the publicity given to the CCTV systems in operation at all stations. We have already mentioned the high level of satisfaction in Sheffield with the ambience of the Transport Interchange, which has replaced the old bus station, a well-known 'landscape of fear' in the earlier post-war period. There was some sense of unease about travel on buses and trains, for reasons we discussed in Chapter 4, and these concerns were mainly about night-time use, with the major source of worry being the possibility of an encounter with unruly young men, unpoliced by a ticket conductor or other custodian of public authority.

The city at night and on weekends

It is, however, really at night and especially at weekends that the anxieties of other publics are most definitive. We have already mentioned the departure of massive numbers of young people every Friday and Saturday evening, and on 'student nights' at other times in the week, to the clubs of central Manchester. By about 9.00 in the evening, the centre of Manchester has been colonised by several thousand young people, who then share the pavements of the city with middle-class, adult theatre goers, patrons of city-centre restaurants, and groups of young men, or lads, embarked on an evening's drinking. The show of fashion and style – from hennaed hair to baggy trousers – marks out the youthful ravers from the other groups in the city, and declares their increasing influence over, or ownership of, the city-centre space.

In the meantime, however, other publics have different priorities. For a group of young men in a focus group in Manchester, the main problem was finding pubs that sold cheap beer and did not exclude them on the basis of their dress. Michael Brophy, from Salford, complained about the Pig and Porcupine, located on Deansgate (near a group of solicitors' offices):

> you go in there on a daytime and the attitude of the staff is against you if you're dressed wrong. The bar staff are like 'Yes, what do *you* want?' But if you come in wearing a suit and tie, it's different.

Michael used only certain other pubs and areas in the city centre:

> The areas I go to, I could guarantee that actually most – or nearly all – of the people that I know myself will be in that area. They will not, most of them, use the rest of the city centre. It's crap basically. It's rotten.

Richard Barker from Chorlton was more committed to the city's clubs than Michael, but he shared Michael's concerns with the cost of 'a night on the town'. He would go into town if there was a free night at one of the better clubs, but he would only go directly there. He would never stray into King Street or 'those sorts of areas', where, he proclaimed:

> There's nothing there. It's just a load of posh shops.

Stephen Brooks, a young married office worker from Crumpsall, north Manchester, made a clear distinction between his use of the city centre when with his wife and when with 'his mates':

Stephen: Whenever I go to town, it's either with my wife – say, to the cinema, maybe a drink at some of the places Richard

	mentioned. Or it's a social night with people from work. We all meet in town and get drunk, that sort of thing.
Karen Evans:	When you are with your wife, do you go to different places from the ones you go to with your work mates?
Stephen:	Yes. When I'm with my workmates, we tend to end in the middle – really obvious places where people in offices go. Like The Bank, The Crown. All the really trendy – grotty – places. Whereas when I am with my wife, we tend to go somewhere cheap, good beer, or quiet, something like that. Or maybe where there's some music on – like The Flea and Firkin.

One really striking aspect of the use of both Manchester and Sheffield city centres by groups of young men 'out drinking' was its essentially routinised and traditional character, including its choice of routes. The group of young men in Sheffield were all aware of the 'West Street run', which had an identical significance for them to that it had for adolescent males in the 1950s. James Ciccarella, a 22-year-old civil engineering student at Sheffield University, observed how he:

> starts at the top end of West Street, The Hornblower, down to The Washington, The Mechanic. Trippet Lane – I go to The Grapes, The Feather and Partridge, sometimes Fagins.

There was widespread agreement as to the main routes for pub crawls in the city and the character of particular pubs, with only some disagreement over James Cicarella's insistence that different pubs in the city 'belonged' to supporters of the city's two football teams, Sheffield United and Sheffield Wednesday. What was never in dispute is that these city-centre pubs, other than, perhaps, the Stone House, were *their* territories and preserve: places where you would find 'real Sheffield lads'.

In Manchester, there was a widespread recognition of a large number of 'old pubs' in the city centre, with their own established clientele or with a particular kind of landlord regime, which were seen to be friendly, but also some other pubs, including the long-established Merchants, which were quite hostile to casual visitors. This demonisation of the Merchants was a matter of common agreement amongst the young men with whom we discussed these issues in Manchester:

Michael Brophy:	I've been in there on a night, not so long ago. It was a group from work, on a crawl basically. We started at Deansgate and worked our way up, ending up at the Merchants. By the time we got to t'Merchants, people were so worked up about the atmosphere in there, there was a karaoke night as well. People were so worked up, we decided to call the night off ... As soon as we got across Piccadilly Gardens, the tension was gone.

Richard Barker:	It does get really crowded in there. If you started off the evening in there you'd go after an hour.
Michael:	It wasn't very rough as such. It was just that as soon as you walked in ... people just turn around and stare, wait and see what you order to drink, see what money you take out of your pocket, which pocket you put it back in. Then they are watching how fast you drink. You end up feeling really paranoid.
Stephen Brooks:	When you go to the loo, you make sure there's nobody waiting to mug you.

The fear that these young men in Manchester expressed of violent confrontations and thefts in certain pubs in the city could have been an analytic topic in itself, notably in respect of the distribution of these 'fearful' pubs within the city centre and across the wider conurbation of Greater Manchester.[31] Some of these fears could be seen as a response to the transformations that have been forced on pubs during the last 20 years, wherein economic survival has required the transformation of some city-centre pubs into 'entertainment centres' with little fixed clientele and what the breweries believed to be a mass, classless popular appeal. Violence between young men was always a feature of pubs, even in the happier days of mass employment and thriving neighbourhood pubs, but it was often then subjected to the informal control of other locals in the pub. The latest transformations in social provision in Manchester city centre – the development of the wine-bar and coffee-bar culture and the move towards 'a 24-hour city', with clubs staying open into the early hours of the morning, especially during the summer months – have certainly modified the overall ambience of the city centre.[32] This new regime of sociability (which, as we suggested earlier in relation to the Hacienda, is not immune from wider developments in respect of violence) still exists alongside a well-established regime of male 'pub crawls' and the nightly closing-time ritual of male aggravation and confrontation.

The threat and aggravation associated with young men on a pub crawl through the city centre or a suburban area was one element in the fear expressed by others in respect of young men in public space. The reaction of other publics to this kind of potential for trouble (involving avoidance of the young men at the moment of any actual incident, and, possibly, the strategic decision to avoid that area of town in future) was particularly well rehearsed on football match days, which were widely understood as a time when young men felt themselves collectively authorised to colonise both pubs and other places of public resort (in Manchester, the Arndale Centre; in Sheffield, the 'Hole in the Road'). In the aftermath of the publicity given the shootings in Moss Side in 1991–4, there was evidence also of a free-floating fear that use of the city centre might risk encounters with young men specifically engaged in serious crime – making use, indeed, of firearms.

The discussion we were able to hold in Sheffield with a group of young men (all of whom were on probation for various offences of theft, burglary, drug-related offences and joy riding) did, however, illuminate some of these issues. It confirmed the existence in that city of a significant number of young men, resident mainly in high-crime estates or in the racialised enclave of Burngreave, for whom the idea of employment in the legitimate local labour market was understood to be unrealistic and who spent the bulk of their day on the look-out for opportunities to steal or to be otherwise employed in the local hidden economy of crime. As Beatrix Campbell (1993) so powerfully showed in her study of angry young men on the Meadow Well Estate in Newcastle, there was absolutely no question of these young men adapting to the collapse of manufacturing industry work via some kind of personal or collective renunciation of what they took to be a natural and necessary form of hard masculinity. They all referred to their criminal activity insistently, in the argot of the lost steelworkers of the area, as 'grafting', and referred to their groups of friends or co-workers in crime as 'their crew'.[33] There is no inclination whatsoever on the part of these young men to take any responsibility for domestic labour (Campbell 1993). Instead, there is a continuing dependence on mothers and other women to provide for their basic needs in the home, where a lot of time is spent, as well as a commitment to periodic expeditions to engage in opportunistic theft, interspersed with the pleasures of drug use (mostly of 'draw' – marijuana – but with few qualms about chemical drugs). Kit told us that he would normally:

> get up about 10. I call for me mates and that, con some money off my mother, get a draw, drugs, go out and earn some money. I just go walkabouts.

John, by contrast, was less driven:

> I probably get up about 12 or 1. Mope around the house for a bit, go and annoy my social worker. If I had money I'd go to McDonald's.

Ian Taylor:	Which one is that, the one in the city centre?
John:	Yeh, at the bottom of the Moor.
Ian Taylor:	Is there anywhere else you would go?
John:	I'd go to Meadowhall.[34]

At first hearing, the responses of these 'lads' to our questions about the routines of their 'working day' confirmed the worst fears of all other users of the city, including those of the city centres. On asked where they would go 'grafting', and whether there was any preferred pattern, Zeke insisted his crew would go 'anywhere'. Later discussion – which involved some extremely detailed argument about the horsepower and design of particular cars – revealed that the more experienced members of the group would move 'well out of their own areas' and go out to suburbs 'like Bents Green', said Zeke, 'where there's money shining like the sun in the trees'.[35]

Further, determined discussion then revealed that the use of the city by these angry young men had a very definite pattern. Mostly, the lads 'keep moving around different areas', grafting, as Eddie put it, 'depending on where the police are'. In this ongoing 'cat and mouse' game, Steff insisted:

They're only catching the 14–15-year-olds, the ones starting doing it.

They would rarely go grafting in their own area, where they were known, and, as a predominantly poor white group, they were very reluctant to go into Burngreave, especially for burglary: according to Eddie, because of 'the Rasta gangs'. In addition, 'if you don't buy their draw', he insisted, 'they beat your head in.' There was some disagreement on this (one of the young men was himself black, and constantly challenged the routine racism of the rest of the group). Where there was very little disagreement, however, was over the centre of town itself. Steff complained that he could not go into any of the shops any more, because all the store detectives knew him. Zeke indicated that he 'wouldn't go into town with his crew', because they might encounter other crews, and then there would be trouble. Mostly, they worried that going to town in a group – their preferred form of male bonding, akin to the city pub crawls of groups of older and more privileged men – might result in 'aggravation' with the police. Overwhelmingly, these lads confirmed that their daily use of the city was conducted primarily 'on their own patch', except only for their regular 'journeys to work' – stealing cars or doing burglaries in areas which, to them, looked to be rich and rational areas to go grafting, depending on their information about the current priorities of the local police.

Two points need to be made here. There is, first, a sense in which we must recognise the existence, here, of a hard, unpleasant and risky urban existence (and a definition of the city, with its 'local patch' and 'really posh areas') which is the regular daily experience of some generations of disenfranchised young men of these de-industrialised cities across the North of England.[36] The disenfranchisement in question involves the loss of what this fraction of the working class assumed to be its birthright – of a lifetime of hard work (grafting) in the steel industry or other heavy manufacturing (and, of course, the domestic and sexual arrangements and community-based leisure that went with it). The severity of this disenfranchisement, and the availability of alternative futures, may vary across the old industrial North – we are suggesting that Manchester is 'better placed' than Sheffield and most other Northern cities – but the scale of disenfranchisement that has occurred in the relatively short period since the late 1970s is extraordinary, especially by comparison to the period before 1970, when the employment of able-bodied men in the North of England was a taken-for-granted 'fact of life'. For the disenfranchised young men of the Manor estate in Sheffield in 1994, the larger city now comprised a whole series of problems and threats – not least in respect of the absence of funds, but also in respect of a whole number of other truths. There is an important sense in which these young men seemed to realise that the city was no longer, self-evidently, 'theirs'. They complained about the presence on the streets of students (Eddie), immigrants, particularly a group of Somali refugees recently rehoused in Sheffield (Kit) 'who call us white trash' (Eddie), 'women with babbies' (Steff), and the new Supertram which was 'No good to us' (Dave).[37] When it was observed that they seemed to be rather critical of Sheffield, and perhaps they would prefer somewhere else, the overall consensus, in a group with no Afro-Caribbean youngsters, was that they might like to move to Jamaica, for 'the ganja' and 'the buzz'.

The second, connected, observation is that this particular group of 'lads' were very infrequent visitors to the central public areas of the city. Shoplifting expeditions were seen by them as far too risky, not least because of the levels of security obtaining and the fact that they were known.[38] Though they were nearly all passionately interested in football, they could no longer afford the prices charged by the Premier League Sheffield Wednesday, and they would not routinely be found in the city centre on a Saturday looking for confrontations with visiting fans. They did not have the funds for regular crawls through the city-centre pubs like the men of their parents' generation, though, in some individual cases, there was the hope that this situation might change over time.

It is by no means our intention here to suggest that the disenfranchisement of these young men has put some final dampener on their use of city-centre pubs and, therefore, the recruitment of new generations of drinkers to pubs in the North of England. (But the ongoing closure of public houses in the North, in conjunction with the rise of the café and wine bar, does indicate that a significant interruption in the particular process of social reproduction has occurred over the last two decades.) What we do want to suggest, however, is that the widespread fear that city-centre pubs are the specific site of crime by disenfranchised young people must be treated with some scepticism. We are encouraged to argue that the widespread fear of young people in the cities of the North of England – for all that it involves a specific, discursive anxiety over violence and drugs, associated with deprived young men in the underclass – ought to be linked, as we indicated earlier in this chapter, to two main points. The first is the continuing prevalence of an unregulated form of masculinity in city-centre pubs amongst older men with some money in their pockets, to which some of these 'lads' might eventually graduate. The second is the general effect of a competitive survival culture connected to the youth cultural industry, at one extreme, and to the larger, equally competitive and precarious, hidden economy of crime, on the other.

Part IV

CONCLUSION

12

CONTESTED VISIONS OF THE CITY AND DIFFERENT LIFE PROJECTS IN THE DE-INDUSTRIALISED NORTH

Addressing the condition of cities in America in the mid-1980s, Harvey Molotch and John Logan argued, with admirable precision, that:

> there are two distinct sets of urban interests (and local political agendas that follow from them) in any ... urban area. Some people seek wealth through the development, sale or rent of land and buildings; others' primary interest in place is as a setting for daily life and production. These two corresponding sets of purposes, often in direct conflict with one another, correspond to the Marxian description of commodities as providing for both exchange value and use value.
>
> (Molotch and Logan 1985: 144)

Already very dominant in the early 1980s in the redevelopment and gentrification (and the exploitation of the exchange value) of American cities were: 'a set of actors who push for local growth maximization to increase returns from real estate manipulation and other business activities specifically dependent on local growth – collectively making up the "growth machine"'. (*ibid.*). Molotch and Logan's analysis of the activities of 'local growth coalitions' in the United States, in this paper and in their longer text *Urban Fortunes* (Logan and Molotch 1987), emphasises the domination of these coalitions by restless and expansive commercial interests, and it also draws attention to their pursuit of policies that are frequently 'environmentally destructive, fiscally damaging and socially regressive for urban populations' (*ibid.*).

One does not have to accept this fundamentally polarised conception of urban interests to agree that the interests of a commercially dominated urban growth coalition do not naturally coincide with the interests of other people living in an urban locality. These local citizens' interests are primarily 'oriented toward use values of urban space' (*ibid.*), and this orientation may take these local citizens in different directions, emotionally and politically, from that of the growth coalition, though in Molotch and Logan's original conception there will be an inherent tendency towards periodic conflict and divergence between 'users' and exploiters of urban resources. It does need to be said that there is some tension between this polarised conception of growth coalition and citizen interest and the later account which Molotch and Logan provide of the struggle in the United States in the early 1980s between cities, for new positions of influence and wealth in the reorganised national and international economy. There is some evidence that cities which were successful in repositioning themselves as what Molotch and Logan call 'headquarter cities' in the new, post-Fordist, global economy (like Atlanta, Georgia) were also those in which local growth coalitions were attracting considerable local support, not simply within the circles of the commercial entrepreneurial elite.

Part of our purpose in this closing chapter is to use Molotch and Logan's notion of 'the local growth coalition' and their taxonomy of urban futures (particularly the struggle of old industrial cities to escape residualisation as 'module production centres') as a way into an analysis of the focus groups we did with Mancunians and Sheffielders[1] on the 'current situation' of their city, and its immediate and long-term 'prospects'. We had also carried out some direct interviews with representatives of the 'local growth coalitions' about the definitions held in these circles about the future of their cities,[2] and these interviews will be drawn upon in our own discussion here. We are hopeful that this approach will add a certain dynamic – not to say futuristic – quality to the attempt we have been making throughout this book to offer a comparison of the differences between these two, ostensibly similar, neighbouring old industrial cities. It is not only that we want to capture the organic 'local structure of feeling' in Manchester and Sheffield: we also want to capture a sense of what Alan Warde, discussing the limits of statistical data and ordinary community studies, saw as the vital but elusive contemporary 'comparative trajectory of development' in these different localities (Warde 1985: 76).

RESIDUALISATION: THE 'ESTATES'

Even as we approach the end of the twentieth century, these two old industrial cities are home to vast areas of publicly owned and privately rented housing stock of very uneven quality – much of it falling below the building and design standards accepted across the European Community as a whole or in North America. The solidity and design quality of housing in South Central Los Angeles or other demonised North American 'ghettoes' is a matter of surprise to anyone used to English council estates or inner-city areas. A century and a half on from Friedrich Engels's descriptions of the cramped, damp and unhealthy conditions of working people's housing in Manchester – especially in the 'girdle' of working people's dwellings around the central city areas – the problems remain. In areas like Ancoats, Bradford, Beswick, Collyhurst, Harpurhey, Miles Platting and Monsall, and like Pendleton and Lower Broughton in neighbouring Salford and many other locations throughout Greater Manchester, there are vast tracts of poorly built and cheap housing, including the post-war estates and high-rise tower blocks, now exhibiting many of the same sorts of problem attributed in the nine-teenth century to 'rookeries' and in the inter-war period to 'slums', which the hastily erected post-war housing was supposed to eliminate.[3] Sheffield has its notorious Manor Estate, mentioned by several locals during our discussions.[4] But what is salient for our purposes in trying to capture the detailed differences between cities is the fact that the demolition of the notorious Kelvin Flats in 1994 leaves Sheffield with-out anything like the number and variety of 'dreadful enclosures' and 'landscapes of crime and fear' which it had in the period between the wars or, indeed, in the 1940s and 1950s. Official discussion of 'difficult' or 'problematic' areas in Sheffield in reports from the local Council now focuses on about 40 small enclaves of multiple deprivation – clusters of streets or houses occupied by the very poor and disadvantaged.

What is common to both cities, however, we would argue, is a silence or indifference – at least in public, political discussion – as to the lived character of these residualised places and territories. If these areas ever appear in local press reports, either they do so as 'symbolic locations of crime' – as a result of some particularly newsworthy recent criminal incident – or alternatively they may appear in a photo-story about some example of local enterprise, as a group of local councillors or other professional people make a bid, on behalf of the locality, for a share in some 'tranche' of urban regeneration monies made available by national government, through various processes of competitive bidding. The marked contrast, of course, is with the immediate post-war period when the condition and the amount of public and private housing available to the population as a whole was a major national issue: the objectives of both major political parties, competing within the narrow social-democratic boundaries of 'the Peace' through the late 1940s and into the 1950s, was to build 'homes fit for heroes' and to do so, in most instances, as rapidly and effectively as possible. In Sheffield, it has to be said, the decision taken under the influence of the patriarch of the local Labour Party, Alderman Ron Ironmonger, was to pause and take stock (not least of the extent of damage to a city bombed out by the Blitz) and to rehouse its citizens in a carefully planned fashion across the newly landscaped hills and valleys of the city, carefully connected by a reliable system of public transport.[5] In the free market 1990s, even in a context of highly visible homelessness (signified, for example, on a daily basis in Manchester by the colonisation of the city centre by beggars and *Big Issue* sellers), there is evidently no such vision for rehousing the 'subaltern counter-publics' of the underclass, with local and national elites having their faces firmly set against the very idea of 'state dependency' and even, in many instances, the provision of social needs as such by the state (rather than the market).[6] In these conditions, we would argue, the daily problems of inner-city areas, urban public housing areas and tower-block developments tend to be marginalised in local political debate and mass media reportage (though the problem of homelessness ner-vously elides, in popular consciousness, with the fear of disorder and crime): the discursive priority, in respect of local people's interest in that basic human need for housing, being displaced onto either the condition of the suburb or the downtown apartments being opened up for the young professionals.

'HOUSING CHOICE' IN POST-INDUSTRIAL MANCHESTER AND SHEFFIELD

Downtown living and the culture industries

In much of the academic writing on the lived experience of 'post-industrial' societies in cultural studies, the predominant interest is in the emergence of new forms of lifestyle and sensibility, particularly on the part of young professionals who are seen as riding the waves of these changes. There is close analysis, particularly in North America, of the inverted patterns of work and leisure of this new 'class', whose pleasures are focused on their careers, and for whom time spent outside those careers is seen as a chore: family and household structure (the postpone-ment of 'parenting'), patterns of consumption of clothing, music and sexuality, and other forms of individual 'desire'. We have a clear general picture of the cultural and social character of this new class, albeit in abstracted terms (that is, constructed as a kind of ideal-typical text, most often with references to a speedy post-modern sensibility). In Britain, empirical research undertaken into Manchester's emerging class of 'cultural intermediaries' by Mike Featherstone, Justin O'Connor and Derek Wynne is providing some interesting detail about the risk-aware, multiply skilled and flexible pleasure-seekers who make up that new class of young professionals within the city (cf. Wynne and O'Con-nor 1995).

We want to make two main observations about this new literature of cultural enquiry. First, one is aware of a certain lack of reflexivity in the studies of this new class. In part, along with commentators like Christo-pher Lasch, we see these cultural studies commentators engaging in a kind of identification with this new class and buying into the world of 'flexible accumulation' and diversion themselves. Something of the same process of identification is apparent in the work of the radical American economist-turned-Secretary-of-State Robert Reich, and the emphasis he places on making America safe for the work of the people he calls 'symbolic analysts' in the high-technology and communication indus-tries (cf. Reich 1991). This specific kind of identification necessarily has political and other effects in these cultural texts, not least in its dismissal or denial of other ways of life in a society or a particular urban centre. Lasch's particular moral and political objection to this sort of writing is that it constitutes an 'elite discourse', driven by trends in the business world and culture industry, and essentially antagonistic to democratic assumptions (Lasch 1995). We can put Lasch's point in a more conven-tionally sociological fashion, however, by raising the issue of whether these kinds of cultural studies literature, caught in an admiring circle with leading figures in the cultural industries themselves, are in any sense equivalent to an exploration of the 'structures of feeling' and social behaviours across the social formation as whole.[7] There is very little attention in these literatures to the continued presence in post-industrial societies or post-industrial cities of publics, including, indeed, the 'silent majority' itself (the suburban middle class). It is not trivial to recognise that whilst these kinds of analysis may have a very direct purchase in cities like Atlanta, headquarters of CNN International and many other major multinational corporations of the media and cultural industries, they may have less direct application in cities which have not attained this kind of headquarter status, and which constitute what Molotch and Logan called 'module production cities'. The total number of young professional people who have so far taken up residence in Manchester's 'Whitworth Street corridor' and in other lifestyle apartments in city-centre Manchester is currently estimated at about 3,000, in a conurbation of 2.6 million.

Figure 12.1 Young professionals 'downtown': a lunchtime exchange,
Manchester, August 1995
Source: photo by Jenny Young

The rise of the new professional classes on the edge of business and the cultural industry is, however, an important feature of post-industrial cities, not only in the way in which people in this class tend to drive the process of urban regeneration, which we will discuss in more detail later in this chapter, but also because they are making choices about where to live in the city.[8] Though the numbers in this class of cultural professionals may be quite small in Manchester,[9] and even smaller in post-industrial Sheffield, their presence is certainly beginning to affect the physical landscape, especially of the central city area. After the American exemplars described by Sharon Zukin (1988), significant numbers of old warehouses and office buildings are being gentrified in Manchester and Sheffield, notably in waterside locations alongside the old canals that cut through the centre of both cities, with the introduction of swimming pools, health clubs and, most importantly, 'dedicated' and 'state-of-the-art' security systems, complete with doormen (Wynne and O'Connor 1995).

We did not make the analysis of these developments, or the decision to move into these new-build downtown apartments, a focus of our own research, but the discussions we held with professional workers in Manchester and Sheffield (invited because their answers to our survey identified them as working 'in the city') did involve significant spontaneous discussion of what people identified as 'the best areas in the city' and also the advantages of actually living in each of our cities. One of the big attractions of being in Manchester, widely referred to by young people, not just from professional middle-class backgrounds, was the sense of being in an exciting and dynamic city 'close to the action' in night clubs, coffee bars and other youth-orientated facilities. This could sometimes take on a powerfully ironic though heart-felt quality, as when, a year after the planting of two IRA bombs in Manchester city centre, James College (originally from Greenock in Scotland, but now living in Sale and a regular user of the city's 'up-market' shops), interjected into a discussion of the excitements of Manchester the comment that:

> I think the thing you were saying about this violence, about being able to plant a bomb ... I think Manchester is quite an exciting place because it *has* got that tension in it.

For gay people across the North of England, as well as from elsewhere in Britain, as we saw in Chapter 7, the presence of the Gay Village acted as a mecca, drawing people into central Manchester. For young professional people, however, a more developed conception was one of actually living in that central area and building a way of life (indeed, 'a lifestyle') there. The decision to move into the centre might involve a decision to buy a 'penthouse' apartment in one of the various redeveloped city-centre blocks, and also to take out private memberships in local health clubs, and to subscribe to various season tickets for the Hallé Orchestra or the city-centre theatres.[10] Other than being informed by the rational calculation of cutting down on the amount of time and stress involved in the daily struggle with public transport or the congestion on the roads, there is no question that the decision to move into the downtown core was in some senses a utopian exploration – a quest for 'a good life' in the 'dirty old town' that once was Manchester. The decision to buy in the centre may have some aesthetic aspects (to buy into the celebrated Victorian architectural surrounds of the city centre) and certainly involved the attempt to identify oneself – to 'distinguish oneself', as the French cultural theorist Pierre Bourdieu would put it – as a member of the fast-moving vanguard of Manchester's cultural professional class.

But it is a decision that makes sense only inasmuch as the cultural professionals living in the city centre can successfully construct and sustain a life in the city in all of its late twentieth-century dimensions. In part, this may imply some very contemporary choices, which may or may not be called 'post-modern' – not least, the decision to postpone being a parent (in the interests of a career, but also because of the various difficulties of bringing up children in a city-centre apartment). It may, indeed, involve precisely the decision to lead the kind of 'autonomous' life where, in the absence of any alternative, individuals choose to take responsibility for their own socialisation and life project – a challenge which Jean-François Lyotard identifies as a central consequence of the collapse of modernist meta-narratives (Lyotard 1984). Living in a new apartment in the city centre is not, in this sense, an attempt to live 'in a community' but rather an attempt to construct a flexible individual life project, surrounded by a range of alternative diversions, pleasures and challenges. Not least of these challenges in the centre of Manchester, in a conurbation with the highest prevalence of recorded crime in England and Wales, is the question of crime.[11] The fear of burglaries or other predatory intrusions into private life may be offset by the presence of doormen and dedicated security systems (these features are certainly prominent in the advertising of these apartments in the local press), but this cannot extinguish the routine sense of fear and risk involved in the regular use of the city centre, constantly underwritten by the presence of beggars and the homeless, and the groups of young men who routinely prowl the centre of the city, apparently in search of 'action'. Nor does living in the city constitute a clear-cut respite from the speedy daily workplace experience of the middle-class professional: the streets echo throughout the night with the noises of the city (police sirens, ambulances, fire engines, burglar and fire alarms, Mancunian men on their pub crawls, and young people coming away from the clubs at all hours of the night, from midnight onwards). It may be that the sound-proofing installed in the apartment buildings suffices to divide the autonomous individuals inside the buildings from the noise-scape outside; what we cannot know is how sustainable the decision to live downtown will be over time, particularly on the part of those professional couples who decide to have children.

Speculations about the viability of 'downtown life' in Manchester must be provisional. In Sheffield, despite considerable publicity being given to waterside apartments at 'Victoria Quays', alongside the South Yorkshire Canal, the process is far less developed. Nor is it clear that a city without an inherited stock of venerable Victorian architecture or cotton warehouses will be able to develop a 'residential area' of apartment-based living to underwrite such a development. It may be that developers interested in such a possibility, in a city with a proud history of municipal housing endeavour, will encounter opposition from political and social interests there that want to reclaim the inner area in whole or in part for residualised populations of Sheffield (42,000 people were registered on the Council's rehousing list in April 1994, of whom 14,000 were urgently 'in need'). The development of the Cultural Industries Quarter in Sheffield, in the valley close to the main railway station, is an important feature of the 'rescue' of Sheffield's city centre, to which we will turn later in this chapter: it is not clear that this quarter can become a residential area of choice in the near future, even for the relatively small number of professionals working in the new industries which are located there.

The English suburb

Even the most cursory examination of the housing markets of Manchester and Sheffield would reveal that the choice to live 'in the city' (that is downtown) is very much a minority one. For the vast majority of the population, the identification of a place to live in the larger city is framed in terms of a utopian desire ('where would I want to live?') and of practical economic possibility. For all the discursive demonisation of the 'council estate' that has occurred in the press and in political culture in recent years, we had a very strong sense in our discussions of a quite finely calibrated taxonomy, in the minds of local Mancunians and Sheffielders, with respect to the differences between individual estates: there was a widespread consensus about the existence and identity of a number of undesirable problem estates in each city, but also an impressive level of agreement about the distinct advantages and qualities of others.[12] Even in the case of the most demonised estates of all, we found some local Northern people, especially women from working-class backgrounds, who wanted to speak well of the strong sense of community and neighbourliness that could be found there.

There is no question, however, but that the overwhelming desire of the vast majority of the people with whom we discussed the issue was to 'live in a nice area' and, in particular, in the suburbs. For many people, currently living in troubled parts of north Manchester or in outer estates in Sheffield, the interest in living in the suburbs had a wistful, not to say markedly fantastic, quality: given the realities of their economic situations, a move into 'a nice area' was literally a fantasy. This escape into the suburbs, however, has a long history in England, and a particular social and cultural resonance. Within the English middle classes, over the last century, the suburb has never been simply an ordered and more or less spacious set of buildings with carefully demarcated gardens and drives: it has also been a signifier of social standing or status, and above all of 'respectability'. The originating exemplar of respectability, the 'big house' or manor house in the village (now so central to the nostalgic television viewing by the English middle class of Agatha Christie's, Ruth Rendell's and P. D. James's detective stories, set *always* in the past), has its urban equivalent in the rows of Georgian and Edwardian 'villas' in the 'best part' of town built in the latter half of the nineteenth century – areas to which upwardly mobile members of the commercial and non-commercial urban middle class have routinely aspired, but which are also the preferred areas of residence in the city of 'private' (inherited) money. Having property in these areas, therefore, locates the owner in the long history of England, evincing a sense of permanence and continuity in what, Patrick Wright reminds us, is 'a very old country' (Wright 1985). The 'peace of mind' that comes from living in these suburbs emanates from a sentimental sense of having attained some 'standing' within 'the nation', as much as from the absence of noise in the neighbourhood or (at least until the mid-1990s) the assurance of having made a secure housing investment.

Lower down the symbolic social hierarchy of England, inextricably signified in the collective mind of the English middle class, by housing, are the suburban areas of the city proper, built in great numbers in the 1920s and 1930s. These massive areas of largely semi-detached houses with separate garages and shared drives are the closest equivalent to the suburban houses of North America, built 'in a big country' on much larger 'lots', with significantly greater separation between neighbours. In a fundamentally egalitarian but privatised culture, the American suburb is, indeed, an 'ideal home' – a private space for gatherings of the extended family, and a convenient base from which to drive to work and to shop in a nearby shopping mall. But it is important to understand that these particular suburban areas are not a signifier of social success *per se* in the way that they are in England: they are a form of housing available, in a more open and egalitarian culture, to many, beyond the rented apartment. In England, suburbs are a 'step up' from the terraced housing of the working class, but their symbolic status is still ambiguous. The utopian aspiration remains that of moving upwards and outwards to the rural village or to the 'really nice area' that is signified by the leafy streets of solid Edwardian and Georgian housing. In part, the anxieties involved in the struggle for better housing are about status and respectability, but also, in part, they are about social segregation: the Edwardian and Georgian villas declared their apartness from the ambiguous class mix of the 1930s semi-detacheds. Local police officers on the beat (the 'village bobby' [*sic*]), performed a crucial symbolic role not only in their learning of the local hierarchies but also by keeping an eye out for intruders into an area – 'those who do not belong'.

The status hierarchies attaching to place and area are well-grasped pieces of local folk knowledge in most English cities, and some of the most socially prestigious village-suburbs are well known nationally (Sutton Coldfield in Birmingham, Gosforth in Newcastle upon Tyne, Roundhay in Leeds): in a taken-for-granted way, they are the areas into which, in an earlier post-war period, successful Englishmen making a career change across the country would move, taking their families with them. It is a matter of some pride and regular remark in Sheffield folk culture that its best-established Georgian suburb, Broomhill – just out from the city beyond the University – was once identified by John Betjeman, when Poet Laureate, as 'the prettiest suburb in England' (Betjeman 1961). It is important to our argument about the importance of such local knowledge in structuring the larger local 'structure of feeling' in a city (and the continuing influence of those feelings) to understand the specific histories and significance of such preferred areas of living. In Sheffield's case, as we have already explained, the location of Broomhill and other aspiring areas of suburban and middle-class residence were well to the west of the city, and therefore upwind of the smoke and effluence of the industrial East End. They also reached out into the open moors, hills and streams at the edge of the Derbyshire Peak District, sentimentally connecting the city with the source of the water power on which the cutlery industry was founded and with 'open country' and nature. Manchester's more affluent suburbs, at some distance from the mills, also adjoin open country (the Cheshire plain), but seem constantly to be struggling, and only partially successfully, to escape the sprawling conurbation of Greater Manchester. Local folk knowledge in northern Cheshire, once again, speaks knowingly of the long nineteenth- and twentieth-century history of 'the flight from Manchester' as involving not simply individuals' aspirations to live outside the spreading industrial city, but also the political desire of jurisdictions to be free of the burden of Manchester, with its considerable demands in terms of local taxation. The journalist and social commentator Graham Turner, writing in the 1960s, speaks of these wealthy commuting areas of northern Cheshire as 'the swell belt', including Bowdon, Hale, Bramhall, Cheadle Hulme and Alderley Edge (with rich parklands 'like those in Oxfordshire'). The 'swell belt', he remarks:

> also takes in the greater part of Wilmslow, although here again the most fastidious feel that Wilmslow is being developed too much, particularly now that it is scheduled to take some Manchester overspill and may soon, indeed, be part of a Greater Manchester.
>
> (Turner 1966: 39)

So the well-publicised contemporary desire to escape Manchester into an old suburb near open country, or better still a classic English village in Cheshire, has a prehistory: it is the origin of the complaints made by Ollerenshaw (1982) as to how few successful individuals lived in Manchester, paid local taxes there and developed a continuous local commitment.[13]

Manchester, in this sense, has shared with many cities in North

America the experience of having an absentee commercial and industrial leadership – that is, a leadership which lives and develops its personal life projects outside the city limits. Sheffield's West End ensures some everyday social segregation from the working masses in the east, but it does not cut its residents off from the city in this emotional and political way. In this sense, the argument of the post-modernist scholar, Christopher Stanley – that Ridley Scott's dystopian film *Blade Runner*, set in a dying Los Angeles where the residents break through in the final frames (of the film company's preferred version) to a dream landscape of mountains and forests, has a specifically or exclusively contemporary resonance – may rest on a superficial reading of local urban folklore and its constant rearticulation over the years of suburban fears of inner-city squalor, crime and disorder (Stanley 1993).

In the case of Sheffield, it may also miss the local significance of the collection of public parks given to the city in the nineteenth century as a result of the municipal benevolence of J.G. Graves and other Victorian industrialists, as well as the taken-for-granted appeal of the city's 'Green Belt', whose existence around the perimeter of the city is a product of 'civic socialism' in Sheffield in the early post-war period. Some 57 people in the street surveys we conducted in Sheffield spontaneously mentioned the city's parks as their preferred places in the city. As Nigel Purcell, an urban professional (originally from Reigate in Surrey but resident in Sheffield for 12 years), explained:

> One thing is the variety ... from the Botanical Gardens, which is horticulturally more interesting, to the linear parks that go up from Hunter's Bar, with moving water and the feeling that you're getting out into the countryside – to somewhere like Graves Park, which is a much bigger open space, children running around playing football, that sort of thing ... You can actually make a positive choice about what sort of park you want to go to in Sheffield.

Katherine Brooks, who bluntly declared that she lived in 'Richmond, Sheffield 13' – as if this was a location she felt we would not know[14] – told us:

> I used to have a photograph album of Sheffield parks. I got it from the library. Every park I went into, I used to stick a star on it.

We noted earlier in this book that Manchester has been less extensively endowed with parks and open spaces than Sheffield and other Northern cities, but the level of local attachment to the parks that does exist was very marked in the early 1990s, as concern mounted about the conditions into which some of the local parks had fallen, and also as local rumour recycled stories of the public park becoming a 'symbolic location' for crime, particularly for the drug trade. The condition of the public park was recognised in the campaign to rescue Heaton Park, which we referred to in Chapter 3, and also in 'Strategic Project No. 27' of the City Pride bid submitted jointly by Manchester, Trafford and

Salford councils in 1994 to the UK and European governments, in which the revival of the park as a public space was seen as critical to the more general regeneration and development of the conurbation.

It would be a very superficial reading of the city that did not recognise that the idea of the suburb as 'a good area', and of the associated space and locations (the Green Belt, the open country, and the parks), is an important, though socially and culturally situated, utopian vision very much connected up to the English idea of a 'good life'. It is, indeed, the English parallel to the kind of suburban middle-class life in America given a sympathetic interpretation by Christopher Lasch in his last two published studies (Lasch 1991, 1995). In the English setting, David Chaney has developed his earlier empirical work on the design (the production) and use (the consumption) of the MetroCentre in Gateshead (Chaney 1990), which he saw as involving a set of encoded assumptions about 'the good life' in a more general theorem about suburban life as a particular form of personal 'authenticity', evoking a complex set of environmentalist and political themes: animal welfare, the rain forests, the search for social and personal peace, and even, he argues, a kind of 'feminist' (or post-feminist) script about the importance of personal identity and care (Chaney 1994, 1995). He also recognises the significance of the essentially privatised form of consumption (for example of the latest pop music on CDs, or computer game software) and the unknown terrors of the inner life of the child brought up in this private suburban 'sub-topia'.

These are not matters we can pursue here. For our present purposes, it is important to establish the suburb as the exemplar of the vision of 'a good area' in England, which carries with it a powerful and continuing set of cultural themes about class, status, nation and the pursuit of 'a good life'. It is important to understand that the bulk of the urban middle class of England (certainly in our two cities) lives in this suburban diaspora, more or less entirely removed in social terms, though not always so clearly separated in physical terms, from the public housing estates, declining inner-city and terraced areas, and high-rise council blocks, but also some geographical and cultural distance from the downtown apartment developments.[15]

MANCHESTER'S AND SHEFFIELD'S 'PROSPECTS': A REPRISE

In Chapter 3, we outlined not only the scale of the economic catastrophe that befell Manchester and Sheffield in the 1980s but also the local responses to the size of the loss of full-time employment in manufacturing and other industries. As in the rest of the country, the responses have been driven in part by the development corporations created by national government in 1987, set up for the express purpose of circumventing 'bureaucratic' local authorities and giving ownership of the challenge of regeneration to 'the market'. The two developed corporations in Manchester, the Central Manchester Development Corporation and the Trafford Park Development Corporation have a considerable presence in the city. The CMDC, in particular, has been given jurisdiction over regeneration in the city's downtown core. By the end of its sixth year of operation (1993–4) The CMDC had reclaimed into use some 29.4 hectares of city-centre land and some 9.4 kilometres of canal, directly built 1,270 new housing units, and opened up nearly 1.4 million square feet of new commercial space. In addition, some 26 kilometres of lighting had been installed, and some 16 kilometres of new walkways, particularly alongside the city-centre canals. In the process, the development Corporation claimed to have brought £340 million worth of capital investment into the city and also to have created 4,677 jobs (Central Manchester Development Corporation 1994: 6). Trafford Park Development Corporation, with responsibility for the regeneration and development of an old, 2,500-acre, working-class residential and industrial area next to the Manchester Ship Canal, (first established by the American Westinghouse Corporation at the turn of the century) was claiming similar success in respect of what the development corporations call 'output achievement'. By the end of 1994, there had been an increase of 8,845 'fulltime equivalents' (FTEs, or jobs) in the Trafford Park development area, contributing to a total of 35,363, and a total of 1,314 companies (722 since 1987), including a number of major American ones, were located in the area. Eighteen kilometres of motorway had been built, 37 kilometres of walkway, and 638,000 trees and shrubs had been planted (Trafford Park Development Corporation 1994). Plans were being formed to redevelop the original village built by Westinghouse, whose houses had been demolished in the 1970s – but which retains its defining grid of streets and avenues – in order 'to put the heart back into the area' (Trafford Park Development Corporaton 1995).[16]

The impact of the activities of these two development corporations on the physical fabric of Manchester city centre and an industrial area of great sentimental significance for the city (alongside the Ship Canal and also very close the Docks, on the Salford side of the canal, now reconstructed by private enterprise as Salford Quays, the North of England's answer to London's Docklands development) is unmistakable. Reference to this massive transformation of urban space does, of course, invite certain curious enquiries, not least with respect to the actual levels of popular patronage of these new spaces. It is unusual, for example, to see any of these waterside walkways of central Manchester actually in use. There is considerable patronage of the much-celebrated Castlefield area (focusing on a reclaimed basin of the old canal system, now rebuilt as a small-open air theatre for concerts and public gatherings) at certain times of the year, especially during the Manchester Summer Festival, but at other times it is a deserted territory. Very few of the regenerated buildings and spaces were spontaneously referred to in our Manchester focus groups in general, except in terms of a discursive but rather abstract approval of 'the improvements they're making' – not least, we suspect, because many of the facilities being opened up in these areas (wine bars, restaurants and health clubs) were of interest only to, and affordable only by, a very specific public in Manchester.

The practical impact of the development corporations on the transformation of material structure and space is important, and in Manchester it has been complemented by a series of parallel initiatives and examples of what is seen, locally, as typical Mancunian enterprise (on the part of today's equivalents of 'the Men who Made Manchester'). The usual inventory of success stories, which we recounted in some detail in Chapter 3, includes reference to the reopening of the Central Station as G-Mex (the Greater Manchester Exhibition and Conference Centre), the opening of the Metrolink system, the arrival from London of the headquarters of the British Council, the opening of the new Terminal at Manchester Airport, recognition of Manchester as City of Drama in 1994, the new International Concert Hall, opening in 1996, and, perhaps most importantly in terms of Manchester's international standing, the two bids to hold the Olympic Games. Though in the end unsuccessful, these campaigns, led by the entrepreneur and adopted Mancunian Sir Bob Scott, did result in the award of government monies and the introduction of other investments which have made possible the building of the new national indoor Cycling Stadium at Meadowlands in east Manchester and the massive multi-sport facility, the Manchester Arena, built into and over the existing Victoria rail station. In November 1995, it was finally confirmed that Manchester would host the Commonwealth Games in 2002. A host of different glossy brochures produced in association with various bids to Brussels and Westminster now speak of Manchester as a major European and international city. A 1993 analysis of Manchester's economic prospects by the City Council pointed to the city as the most important financial centre outside London and the airport as the fastest growing in Europe (ranked 18th in the world), and quoted a survey by DATAR, the French government's agency for regional development, which identified Manchester as 11th out of 165 cities across Europe in terms of economic importance (ahead of Copenhagen, Hamburg, Stuttgart, Rotterdam, Lyon, Turin and Geneva). The City Pride prospectus of 1994, produced by an extensive local consultative process across the three central Manchester local authorities, advanced a cold-blooded SWOT (strengths, weaknesses, opportunities and threats) analysis of the prospects for Greater Manchester establishing itself as 'a peer' city within Europe to Barcelona, Milan, Frankfurt and Lyon (Manchester, Salford and Trafford Councils 1994: 6).

We are neither economists nor futurologists, and are in no position to assess the merits of these or other claims about the strength of Manchester's city and regional economy. One of the key issues in making this kind of assessment is whether an individual urban area contains the particular infrastructure and capacities in respect of production and also innovation that are essential to survival and success in these post-

Fordist 'new times', as well as the kinds of 'lifestyle' facility that will be conducive to international and national companies wanting to relocate in that city.[17] In this respect, the challenge – that of reconstructing older, industrial cities ('dirty old towns') into pleasurable and efficient post-industrial places – will be equivalent to the 'quality of life' questions we identified in Chapter 1. We also assume *a priori* that there are some other key issues about how the post-industrial transformations of an urban region take place either organically, as a logical development of earlier industrial experience, or strategically and entrepreneurially, in response to the new demands of open international competition. Not least of the issues facing cities that are trying to reposition themselves in the global marketplace is the danger of becoming too heavily reliant upon, or orientated towards, the financial services sector as 'the engine' of new growth, and the contradictions between any such developmental strategy and a recovery in the local job market. Robert Fitch's work on New York City shows how a dependence on the so-called FIRE (finance, insurance and real estate) sector has contributed to that city becoming the 'head-quarters' only of job loss, '400,000 payroll jobs having been lost between 1988 and 1993' (Fitch 1994: 17). New York City has the lowest ratio of manufacturing employment to employment in the FIRE sector of any major metropolitan area in the United States (*ibid.*: Table 5). One of the critical questions here would appear to be the optimal balance that can be attained for a locality in present global circumstances, in terms of investment in FIRE, construction, manufacturing, trade and service industries and local and regional government.

For all Manchester's claim to be the centre of financial services outside London – with 111,000 people employed in 'business services' across the region, and a small Stock Exchange still operative in the city's financial district – there really is no sense that the city or the wider region is about to become a major centre of what Fitch refers to as 'fictitious capital'. In 1993, manufacturing industry in the city still employed some 282,699 people, and only 38.3 per cent of the 738,309 people employed in the 'services industry', very broadly defined, were in the FIRE sector. 'Services' in Manchester (and the North of England generally) refers primarily to work in distribution, hotels and catering (220,391 in Manchester in 1993); transport and communication (59,504); construction (53,906) and 'other services' (293,156) (Manchester City Council, Economic Initiatives Group 1993: ii). What may matter enormously in terms of the strategies being pursued by the local growth coalitions of Greater Manchester is whether the delivery of these services, by managers and workers attuned to more local conditions and expectations, can be effectively and profitably developed in the face of competition across the common European market and more globally. There is little question that this challenge is quite well understood amongst those employed in the local high-technology and 'cultural intermediary' professional classes in Manchester, particularly, we think, in the fast-moving media, popular music, leisure and communication sectors (many of which are dominated by youthful and mobile, international entrepreneurs) and, also, the pioneering high-technology companies that have opened up in the Trafford Park Development Area and on other city-edge industrial parks.

In Sheffield, as we began to suggest in Chapter 3, a very different set of circumstances obtains. The physical fabric of the central city area does not bear the imprint of recent changes to the national and international economy to anything like the extent it does in Manchester. The most recent arrival on the city's landscape, the South Yorkshire Supertram, cuts through the city centre to the south-eastern estates, on the one hand, and to the Meadowhall centre, on the other, and is 'shiny', like Sheffield steel, and clean (and hence the source of new local advertising, proclaiming that 'Sheffield Shines'), though the system apparently remains less heavily used than Manchester's Metrolink. Local residents, especially from the suburban middle class, take pride in the development of Tudor Square, a pedestrianised area adjoining the Crucible Theatre and the newly reopened Victorian theatre, the Lyceum. Nearby a new Novotel and one health club have opened up. We have already referred to the Orchard Square development 'at the top end of Fargate', a small shopping development much prized by Sheffielders committed to the idea of 'going to town' to shop. But this really is the extent of the obvious city-centre redevelopment; and it is quite inappropriate in Sheffield, unlike in Manchester, to apply directly the writings of Fredric Jameson or any other radically post-modern critic to the analysis of what really is a series of modifications of familiar and long-established urban spaces over a 15-year period. The impact of the Sheffield Development Corporation on the physical fabric of the city is less obvious and intrusive than in Manchester, but, given its restricted brief (the renovation of the industrial Don Valley), this is not surprising. (It is arguable, in fact, that the most important transformation of physical space in Sheffield is the claiming of The Moor as a poor people's street market during the 1980s (outlined in Chapter 5), a development which sits uneasily with the more consumerist kind of post-modern literature.) The work put in to rescue some areas of the East End from further dereliction has 'enhanced' the immediate physical environs of the Sheffield Arena and the Don Valley Stadium, yet inasmuch as that work was informed by the local strategy to establish Sheffield as the City for Sport, it received a serious setback from the Council and Development Corporation's inability to mount a successful challenge to Manchester's bid for the Commonwealth Games. At the same time, the city was left without any one single focus to its strategy for redevelopment.

In the meantime, the efforts of the Sheffield Development Corporation to bring jobs back into the industrial East End were seen, by the local press and in analyses produced by the City Council's own Department of Employment and Economic Development, to have run up against the phenomenon of 'jobless growth' (*Economic Bulletin*, Fourth Quarter, 1994: 1). Sheffield's unemployment, as measured officially, in

January 1995 was 10.7 per cent: this was an improvement on the 12 per cent of the previous year, but the statistics remained stubbornly above national averages by a gap of some 1.6 and 1.8 per cent. This in itself was a matter of dismay for a city that was always used to 'doing better' than the national average, and local worries were that job availability had 'slowed significantly' and that there was no sign of retrieving anything like the number of jobs lost in steel and the heavy trades in the early 1980s. Employment forecasts for the city 'to the year 2000' were being significantly downgraded in early 1995.[18]

Nonetheless, a series of glossy brochures and leaflets continued to emanate from the offices of the Sheffield Development Corporation, and a series of new themes was articulated as a gloss on the development strategy. The Development Corporation's theme for 1994–5 was that 'Sheffield Shines'; the City Centre Initiative partnership, focusing on the city shopping centre areas, insisted that 'Sheffield's Alive and Kicking' and the Department of Employment and Economic Development itself still tried to speak confidently, in the language of the new era of enterprise and development, of five 'growth networks' (manufacturing, information, leisure, green affairs, and public service). In January 1995, however, the Sheffield City Liaison Group, the Council's partnership with private industry (a product of the Ranmoor Church Forum), issued a consultation document, more soberly entitled 'Sheffield Shaping the Future: Plans for Social Regeneration', highlighting in particular the considerable increase in levels of social inequality in the city and also the much-publicised increases in crime. A series of 'action points' aimed at tackling these issues, and also included was the kind of utopian vision statement that is now apparently mandatory for all urban partnerships, especially perhaps in cities with deep structural problems: in this case, a vision of 'Sheffield as a Working City, a Quality City, a Learning City and a Caring City'. It was unclear what overall theory of job creation, social regeneration and social cohesion really underlay this rhetorical call to action.

In the Sheffield Economic Plan for 1995–6, great emphasis was placed on the continuing redevelopment of what once was Kennings' Garage in the city centre as the headquarters of the new Media and Exhibition Centre, located in the so-called Cultural Industries Quarter; and great play was made of the development of new film and audio-visual facilities in this space and its further potential for growth and development. On the most optimistic possible estimate, however, the number of jobs that would emerge from this development 'eventually' was put at a maximum of 3,500 (Sheffield City Council, Department of Employment and Economic Department 1995: 22). There was an unmistakable sense – which we would argue was well understood in the residualised areas of the city, where the job and poverty crises were most concentrated, and also in the suburbs – that the local coalitions and partnerships were not so much a 'growth coalition' in the Molotch and Logan sense as a kind of 'rescue squad', attempting to minimise the economic and social costs of the late-developing but unmistakable de-industrialisation of the City of Steel. A 'rescue squad', so conceived, is not so much focused on the idea of growth and development (itself, it might be argued, a very bullish, 'American' sentiment) as it is concerned with patching up a badly damaged local economic and social body, perhaps attempting to check the shared apprehension in the locality of an inevitable process of continuing decline, and also to mitigate some of the consequences, already apparent, of this ongoing local process.[19]

We are not suggesting there is no such dimension to the work of the 'growth coalitions' in North American cities, or, indeed, in Manchester, but we would want to insist that the dominant, or hegemonic, local definition placed on the work of the coalitions situated in 'headquarter cities' (working, as in Manchester, in a reference group with Barcelona, Milan and Lyon) is that of expansion and growth, and, importantly, some degree of hope for future economic well-being.[20]

LOCAL ECONOMIC PROSPECTS AND LOCAL CRIME

Across the North of England in general, as indeed in England as a whole, one of the inescapable refrains in local discussions, in the local news-paper press and on radio and television, is the question of crime. In the stressed housing estates we identified early in this chapter as places which the bulk of the population avoids, and prefers not to discuss, the highly visible activities will stretch from burglary and physical harassment through to joy riding in fast cars and drug dealing on street corners, nearly always involving the colonisation of public space by angry and aggressive young men, engaged in various forms of what Bob Connell has recently identified as 'protest masculinity' (Connell 1995). But even in the suburbs of most cities of Northern England in the 1990s there is unmistakable evidence (for example, in the fact that private security services are one of the fastest-growing local labour markets) of an increased level of fear with respect to burglaries of the home, car theft and even the possibility of assault (say, in any attempt which a suburban householder might make to defend himself or herself during the course of a burglary or car theft).

There is no question that this level of anxiety, and the set of local rumours that helps fuel and reproduce it, are in part a function of the amount of coverage which crime, whether in abstract terms or in reference to specific local incidents, now receives from the large number of local newspapers and local advertising tabloids which are delivered, free, to suburban households in these cities. This coverage of local crime incidents has the very important consequence of helping to construct and revise a kind of precautionary mental map of the locality, and a taxon-omy of potential villains, developed by neighbourhood residents, identi-fying particular places in the locality as 'symbolic locations for crime' – notably, as we have already suggested, public parks, but also local public houses and, on occasion, particular late-night take-away restaurants and other places of late-night public (typically, youthful) resort.[21] Incidents in these symbolic locations may then generate the conditions for local neighbours to come together in local Neighbourhood Watch organisations, which emerge and decline precisely in response to these local happenings (Taylor 1995b). There is little doubt that the fears which are articulated in these suburban areas also act as shorthands for, or displacements of, other middle-class fears that are general in free market England, notably in respect of house prices and the security of personal investments, mortgage relief and a cluster of other economic areas, including unemployment. There is a powerful sense in many such English suburban areas in the mid-1990s of what Barbara Ehrenreich, examining the inner life of the American middle-class professional population in the early 1980s, called 'the fear of falling' (Ehrenreich 1989).[22]

But there is also no doubting that the presence and distribution of these anxieties and fears are quite uneven, and different in expression, in different local areas and in different cities. We indicated in Chapter 1 that the City of Manchester has very often been associated in the local and Northern imagination with quite high levels of crime, occasionally changing places in the imaginary representation of 'high-crime cities' with Liverpool. By contrast, at least throughout most of the era of mass manufacturing other than the 1920s, Sheffield was associated in the local imagination (and also in Home Office surveys) with very low levels of reported crime by comparison with other cities and regions in the North and also in relation to the national average. On several occasions in the 1960s, the Home Office misread this as function of good crime-prevention practice. In 1992–3, however, the South Yorkshire police-force area returned the highest level of increase in recorded crime of any of the 43 police forces in England and Wales (an increase of 15 per cent in one year), and did so in a year in which the majority of forces were reporting

Table 12.1 Reported crime: selected police forces, England and Wales (1988 and 1993)

Force	1988	1993	Percentage change
Cheshire	49,044	80,156	+63.4
Cleveland	58,474	78,279	+33.9
Derbyshire	43,204	91,454	+111.7
Durham	44,381	67,180	+51.4
Greater Manchester	293,785	364,858	+24.2
Humberside	85,113	140,988	+65.6
Lancashire	96,500	134,581	+39.5
Merseyside	149,954	142,325	−0.5
Northumbria	160,708	213,936	+33.1
North Yorks	34,686	57,967	+67.1
South Yorks	89,292	157,229	+76.1
West Yorks	175,825	301,838	+71.7

Source: Home Office Statistical Bulletins on notifiable offences 1994, 1995

some reduction in recorded crime, and when there was actually a very slight overall reduction (of 1 per cent) in overall recorded crime.[23] Table 12.1 summarises the trend in recorded crime for the major police forces in the North of England over the six years to 1993.

Raw figures of this kind have to be treated with caution, not least because they are not weighted for population in each police-force area or for any change in the population in these areas over the six years in question. Nonetheless, the unevenness in the picture of crime increases across the North of England (and the decline in Merseyside) is suggestive of the power and influence of some essentially local social processes, and also, perhaps, of the patterns of de-industrialisation in different regions at different points in time. It certainly is remarkable that South Yorkshire, which had hitherto been a low crime-rate area, should have experienced the second strongest increase in recorded crime over this six-year period, after neighbouring Derbyshire, and also that the absolute increase in crime should have exceeded that in both Greater Manchester and Greater London (the increase in crime in the Metropolitan Police area over this same period was only 26.5 per cent, whilst the national average was 49.1 per cent). If we were to read these crime statistics as some kind of (indirect, highly mediated) measure of a collapse in local social cohesion, albeit affected by different recording practices in different police-force areas, we would have some sense of the different contemporary trajectories in the local communities of the North. The actual incidence of crime in Manchester remains very high, but the rate of increase is less marked than in many other areas, whilst the rate of increase in reported crime in Sheffield and South Yorkshire (which has to be assimilated in local radio and press reports, gossip, myth making and rumour, alongside the continuing news of job losses and the 'crisis of the city centre') has been the second highest in England and Wales over a continuing, six-year period.

'Living with crime' in a large conurbation like Manchester, a city of trade, commerce and immigration over many years, may not be quite the same kind of task as it is in other northern cities. It may be identified – like the long daily struggle into work – as one of the costs of living in a 'metropolis' with pretensions to being an alternative capital. So also may the coincidence in the city of a hidden economy of criminal and legitimate activity have something of a history. Like the bombs planted by the IRA, this may be seen, by some, as giving a certain frisson to the city, making it in some senses an 'exciting place', and this sense of Manchester may, indeed, not be entirely new. It may be that Manchester was a city in which a certain kind of anonymity was always available (for example, to women making use of shops and restaurants in the earlier years of this century). Phillipa Franks, for example, told us how:

> I chose to come to Manchester. I lived at the seaside and I'd always lived in nice places – because I had a family. When I become single, I thought 'I know where I want to live, and that's in the middle of

Manchester.' I'd come here first in the middle of the seventies with my eldest child when she went to work at the Manchester Royal Infirmary and I thought 'Oh, I like this place, it's so alive.' I'm interested in theatre and art galleries and politics. As I say, when I became single, I thought 'Hey ho' and I came.

Young men might come into Manchester for the football, pubs and night life, and young women for the shops, clubs and night life. It may be, indeed, that Manchester already exhibited in the 1980s many of the features of the 'risky' post-modern city, the site of legitimate and illegitimate pleasures and desire, in an intrinsically English form long before the implosion of Los Angeles onto the American and international mediascape.

What may have mattered for Mancunians as a whole, in an earlier era of mass manufacturing and trade, in accommodating to this level of crime and other, connected difficulties in everyday life, are the various compensations available in the job market, on the one hand, and culturally, on the other hand, of living in the city, with its bustle, its grand Victorian buildings and architecture, and the sense of being 'at the centre of things' (historically, in Manchester, in music, media or football). What may matter to the suburban Mancunians in their thousands in the 1990s is the sense that the leadership of the city (the local growth coalitions) is more or less successfully positioning the city strategically for the new conditions of international competition. An unmistakable aspect of the lived local culture of the southern Manchester suburbs is the preoccupation of all the various local organisations (the Chambers of Commerce and Trade, the local authorities themselves, the community newspapers) not simply with 'mastering' the intrusive predatory criminality which is seen to be creeping out from the inner city, but quite urgently with debating the commercial necessity of building a second runway to Manchester International Airport.[24] There is some sense, that is, in these southern suburbs, of a sustaining vision of commercial success and development, with immediate and medium-term material effect for the local growth coalition itself and some of its suburban supporters – but also an effect which will powerfully affirm, at a symbolic level, the 'life projects' and daily preoccupations of this commercial, middle-class, Mancunian suburban population.

In Sheffield, where only 20 years ago the future of local steel seemed unchallengeable, and 15 years ago the local political talk was of the creation of a 'Socialist Republic of South Yorkshire' built around a move towards free public transport and local civic provision for need, the two projects of industrial and civic Labourism are dead, and are replaced by ways of talk ('visions' and 'growth networks') that do not naturally resonate the local 'structure of feeling', in a city which had been used to thinking of graft, craft and collective interdependency. Several people in our Sheffield focus groups spoke with some sadness about the loss of this sense of a 'good city'. Helen-Ann Goode, in our group of young mothers in Sheffield, remembered how:

> [My family] had heard very good things about Sheffield ... we thought that it was politically more the kind of city that we would like to live in.

The loss of the 'meta-narrative' about Sheffield as 'a good city', or indeed as the site of the Socialist Republic of South Yorkshire, leaves the citizens of that city confronting what many of them saw as the more limited range of life-options available in any large cities: individualistic career building, money making, lifestyle pursuits, etc. There was, however, still some sense in which the apparently restricted character of an enclave city, dominated by an invincible Labour Council, provided a more substantive 'choice' than the alternative 'lifestyle' of a free market city.

For the poor in both cities, there were very different responses to the current transformations taking place. We found evidence in our en-quiries of routine patterns of use of the city that drew heavily on the 'traditional', familiar cultural practices and rhythms of the mass manu-facturing period – not least, in Sheffield, the insistence of young men engaged in theft and burglary on a routine and recursive basis that they were involved in a form of 'grafting': hard, daily, physical work of the kind that 'a man's gotta do'. Closely associated with this was a desperate and accentuated commitment to a level of misogyny, drinking, drug abuse and profanity which we equated with the emergence of a form of 'protest masculinity' – a vain attempt to reassert the lost local hegemony of the 'Little Mester' and also, in this sense, the life project of 'living the city' in and through working-class patriarchy.

We also found evidence, especially amongst the long-term unemployed and amongst men and women with some considerable experience of poverty, of forms of withdrawal from use of the city, conceived of as a set of well-known shops and routine sites of recursivity, and the active patronage of 'an alternative city' involving the street markets (the Barrows in Manchester, The Moor in Sheffield) and other outlets such as Kwiksave stores where necessary subsistence goods were cheaply available. As Philip Murray, in Manchester, explained:

> You've got all these photographs of the better part of Manchester, which are absolutely fabulous, no question of it. But it's for the elite. Not necessarily for the elite, but those who can afford to use the facilities. Christ, I can't afford to look in the windows.

Philip's own strategy was one of avoidance:

> There's an indoor shopping mall at the bottom of Deansgate. It's only been restored recently ... There's just no point in looking at 'knock out' window displays and wishing the world was bloody pink skies all day. All it's going to do is make you think you'd like it. I'm not going to resort to balaclavas and shotguns to go shopping in a

nice area. So it's best that I don't expose myself to it. It's a sad situation but it's a fact.

This foraging around in the city for places of free or cheap diversion does result in some use of the city by the new poor – in this instance, of the civic facilities constructed in an earlier era, ostensibly for the leisure hours of the middle class – but there was some agitated discussion over the deterrent effects of museum charges on the poor. Manchester's and Sheffield's museums, art galleries and libraries have taken on a key significance in the routes taken through the cities by some sections of the new poor, as they develop strategies for what many called an 'outing' in the city (getting out from their houses); and city-centre gardens, especially in Sheffield, have very visibly taken on a new role. They are, in particular, the preferred 'stopping place' of the poor during the day, even for sections of the new poor who have opted for alcohol as another, mental route 'out of' Manchester or Sheffield.

But perhaps one of the most common responses of the new poor to the larger city was simply to stay in there own areas, never to encounter the 'bright lights' of the central city. Whilst taking part in a focus group held in the Castlefield development area, in central Manchester, Caroline Dutton, a young woman who had been unemployed for some time in Manchester before getting a job, recalled her lack of familiarity with the city on returning to the labour market:

> It's like when I first started work. I'm not thick or anything, but I didn't like to let on that I didn't know Deansgate existed.

Castlefield itself, the centrepiece of the Central Manchester Development Corporation's initiatives and the site of many of our focus groups in Manchester, evinced a range of surprised responses:

> I've lived in Manchester all my life and it's the first time I've been here.

Anthony Middlewich agreed:

> That's what a lot of my friends are like. Not many know what's going on round here. You live in a city and not many people know what it's got. They don't even know it's here. Most people who've got no money and that don't get to these festivals and things.

In 'headquarter cities' and declining 'module production cities' alike, the facts of inequality are inescapable, not just in actual use of the city but also in respect of the capacity of those cities to sustain any notion of a good life and full and active citizenship. In Manchester, there is some sense of an individual solution (in terms of jobs, careers and the pleasures of the suburbs); in Sheffield, as in many other old, de-industrialised cities in the North of England, the prospects are more uncertain.

A FINAL WORD: NORTH OF ENGLAND CITIES AND THE DIRECTION OF SOCIAL AND URBAN THEORY

The discussion of cities and their future is one of the favourite topics of conferences and journalistic reportage in the mid-1990s. Architects, planners and local politicians, speaking for the local growth coalitions, are generally rather bullish about the future of the regenerated cities that are about to be created by some fast-approaching deadline, usually around the time of the Millennium; some journalistic discussion, by contrast, especially in the United States, has given voice to an anxiety about the condition of central cities in that country, especially after dark, by wondering whether the City has a future at all in its present form (cf. Morgantau and McCormick 1991). In academic circles, it is fair to say, discussion of the city has tended to have a less millenarian quality and, indeed, it could be said that some of the urban theories (derivative, on the one hand, from formal Marxism or, on the other, from post-modern fashion) have suffered from an absence of the kind of engagement shown by the urban regeneration coalitions or from the pessimistic concerns of urban retreatists. We have tried in this text to avoid these two extremes, but, as we have indicated earlier, we realise we invite critique on the grounds that we have not worked avowedly from a fully theorised template.

In fact, we would argue that we have advanced a theoretical argument throughout, primarily insisting on the importance of understanding what we call 'the local structure of feeling'. Where Raymond Williams's own reference (1977: 131), however, was to 'the particular quality of social experience and relationship, historically distinct from other particular qualities, which gives a sense of a generation or a period', we were interested in applying the idea of a structure of feeling to two large North of England cities (and their immediate surrounding regions) and the set of affective cultural beliefs and assumptions that was prevalent in them. We have argued, following Urry and the tradition of the localities research of the early 1980s, that these local cultures must be understood in references to the histories of industry in these cities, their form of organisation, especially their dependency on muscular power, the gendered divisions of labour, and their rigid or dynamic character. We have in that sense tried to recognise the existence of local forms of hegemonic masculinity, in Bob Connell's term, expressing themselves in routinised processes of reproduction at the management level and 'on the shop floor'. We have wanted to recognise different forms of resistance or adaptation practice amongst local women: the construction of a 'women's city' within the larger urban configuration, or the involvement in local campaigns in neighbourhoods residualised by social and economic change. So also have we tried to display the ways in which the elderly, children and young people, the new poor and different ethnic minority peoples try to negotiate a space within these essentially male-dominated old industrial cities. Each of these publics, we have argued, has its own, highly routinised, patterns of use of particular parts of the city, which new migrants into the city in each of these social categories necessarily have to learn, but which are internalised without much remark by 'native-born' Mancunians or Sheffielders. This differential distribution of social destiny, gendered risk and *de facto* ethnic segregation in the old industrial city is the source of many different 'mental maps of the city', but the use of these different maps by different publics, we have argued, seems always to be accompanied by some awareness of a larger concept of change occurring in the broader city – the city seen as a series of events, people, and newsworthy themes in its historical present – mobilised by the locally powerful political and development coalitions, especially in local media.

The second major interest in this text has been in the different character of the 'local structures of feeling' in these two Northern cities, and, in particular, the extent to which these long-established local structures of feeling are conducive to the project of regeneration, growth and development, and what some commentators see to be the fateful struggle for old industrial cities anywhere in the world. The challenge being confronted, in this view, is whether these cities can escape a destiny of long-term industrial decline and may – some of them – be able to reposition themselves in the growing productive markets of high technology, media and communications, and the service industry. Our examination of the present conjuncture in Manchester points to the existence of a vibrant local economy of part-time and casual work, on the one hand, and major headquarters-style development, on the other, now focused on the Commonwealth Games in 2002, as an associated culture of 'change' and 'attitude', especially amongst the young. In Sheffield, there is widespread evidence of a very strong nostalgic feeling not just for the lost industrial past but also for the form of community associated with some long-established features of the city: its geographical apartness and topographical character, built along the floor of several valleys, its own special dual economy of cutlery and steel, and also its recent political history (the kinds of Council policy pursued in the recent past). We argued earlier in this chapter that the current activities of the Council and its industrial partners might best be understood less as the activity of a 'growth coalition' than as a kind of 'rescue squad' trying to save that community from its feared alternative, that of urban life built around privatised and competitive individualism. We are convinced that the 'local structure of feeling' of other cities in the North of England can be understood as being located somewhere along this continuum between the new global realities and the specific form of inherited local industrial culture, with different degrees of local provenance and legitimacy in each local, lived community.

The question arises as to whether the kind of account we have tried to develop has any importance in principle for the field of sociology. Our primary argument here, akin to many of the arguments about formal sociology implicit in earlier versions of British cultural studies, is the need to recognise the force of history and culture. The cities of the North of

England are old places, very much still the product of their nineteenth-century origins, and local knowledge and practices are expressions of their lengthy history, both at hegemonic levels and also in terms of what Negt and Kluge would see as the cultural practices of 'subaltern counter-publics'. It follows from this that the forms of what Giddens identifies, in his formulation of rules for sociological enquiry, as 'practical consciousness' – namely, 'recall to which the agent has access in the *durée* of action without being able to express what he or she thereby knows' (Giddens 1984: 49) – are of importance not just in a cognitive sense (for example, 'automatically' following a certain route through the centre of the city). They are also of enormous affective importance, in carrying a set of more emotional scripts with their own significant temporal (historical) and spatial dimensions – for example, long-established memories and beliefs about 'the North', this city, particular buildings and places, and the locally powerful or well-known groups. On another dimension, in both these Northern cities, the patterns of avoidance of city space by women clearly derived from a close knowledge of certain streets or locales as having been colonised by threatening groups of young men, or simply as ugly areas, or alternatively as areas in which there is little or no custodianship of public space. So also did members of different ethnic minorities have an indicative map of the cities in which they lived, identifying particular streets and territories as places of avoidance. The elderly of these two cities, occupying a rather different 'risk position', focused on the different dangers of particular street corners, bus stations or streetscapes, so modifying in their later life their own emotional feeling for the city, reassessing whether the city was friendly to their own needs and those of other elderly citizens. Each of the publics with whom we discussed Manchester and Sheffield, indeed, had its own particular active and emotional sense of the city; that is, as a place that was more or less attentive to that public's needs and well-being.

There is no question but that it would be possible in principle to develop even closer analysis of the routinised use of old industrial cities by different publics in even more detail than we have offered here, after the example of the micro-sociology developed by Michel de Certeau, and that this project would be possible, in principle, in any old industrial city, outside this study's focus on the North of England. We think this kind of project would be a very useful departure point for critical empirical work on cities by sociology, especially in giving some practical grounding to an area of social theory which threatens at present, by default, to become an abstract and second-order celebration of the consumer and enterprise cultures themselves. What is intriguing is whether this recognition of the anxious or threatened, nostalgic or utopian detail of 'practical consciousness' of urban places and spaces, which is in everyday use could not in itself contribute to the process of urban rescue that is the preoccupation of those engaged in practical action in urban redevelopment for the Millennium and beyond.

NOTES

1 RECOGNISING LOCAL DIFFERENCE IN NORTH OF ENGLAND CITIES

1. The recent literature on exile (e.g. Robertson *et al.* 1994) has not yet extended to an analysis of the experiences of return. Taylor's inaugural lecture at the University of Salford was one early attempt to grapple with this experience of return to the North of England (Taylor 1990).
2. The City of Manchester, at the centre of the Greater Manchester conurbation, is consistently very much higher than the national average on nearly all the major variables used to measure ill-health, including deaths around birth and infancy, cancer and HIV/AIDS, though there are considerable variations in incidence on all these measures across the 32 wards of the City, especially on the north–south dimension (Stevens 1993). One dramatic illustration of the scale of Manchester's problems is that the city's premature death rate in 1991 was at a level 'last experienced in the country as a whole over ten years ago' (ibid.: 8). Sheffield, by contrast, has prided itself for many years on the quality of its services for infants and young children, particularly through the local Children's Hospital (which was at the forefront, for many years, of research on cot deaths): the city's record on 'deaths around birth and infancy' remained below national average in the early 1990s, despite a recent increase in the number of babies born with low birth weight. HIV/AIDS is less prevalent in Sheffield than in most cities. There are, however, continuing high levels of respiratory problems in Sheffield, well known to local people as 'the Derbyshire lung', and the lung cancer rate is comparable to that of North Manchester (Sheffield, Director of Public Health 1993).
3. This emphasis on the twin themes of 'craft' and 'graft' in local Sheffield culture is recognised in many writings on the city: most recently, by Burns (1991).
4. Peter Jackson provides a useful programmatic commentary on the utility of Raymond Williams's 'cultural materialism' for urban and social geography (Jackson 1989). He also points to the analogy between Williams's under-developed notion of 'the structure of feeling' and Pierre Bourdieu's concept of the *habitus*, referring to the 'cognitive structure of any group, comprising the sedimented history of particular practices that arise to meet certain objective conditions and which thereby serve to reproduce these conditions' (Jackson 1989: 39).
5. Some might object that Manchester has historically been the site of the long-running Granada Television soap opera, *Coronation Street*, and certainly the idea for this series originated from an author from Greater Manchester, Tony Warren. But this series has very clearly been constructed over the years as a metaphor for North of England 'communities' as a whole; and that

is the secret of its continuing popularity within Britain and abroad. In 1993, towards the completion of the research reported here, Manchester was adopted as the location for *Cracker*, a quite extraordinary (and in many ways post-modern) television series on the personal and professional life of a forensic psychiatrist, working on contract with a thinly disguised Greater Manchester Police, beleaguered by increasingly extreme and bizarre forms of violent crime.

6. One of the issues here is whether the emergence of new social groups in a local labour market (the 'mobile' new professionals) transforms the character of public space, and in what way. The centre of Cambridge is currently an intensely contested territory, struggled over by students, new professionals, the local working class and their children, people from local villages, tourists, and also 'mobile' beggars and the local underclass. The 'hegemony' of the new mobile professional class is very localised to the Science and Business Parks, a few wine bars and restaurants and a number of private clubs. In other parts of this old city, other, more traditional definitions of place are still very dominant.

7. There is a strong sense of region in the United States ('the South'. 'California', the 'Northern Rust Belt') and a connected set of regional characteristics. It is not clear that local cities and towns, however, generate a similar strong sense of identity and difference.

8. For an analysis of the role of the 'community press' in the construction of local fear about crime in the South Manchester suburb of Hale, especially in relation to certain key 'symbolic locations', see Taylor (1995a).

9. Geoff Pearson's study of popular crime fears about youth (Pearson 1983) is attentive to the role of memory in these forms of anxiety, but the theoretical stance adopted ('moral panic theory') results in the devaluation and dismissal of popular memory, rather than a careful examination of the rationales that might underly such memories.

10. The nostalgic representation of the Sheffield 'Little Mester' in these texts is examined in some detail in Taylor and Jamieson (1996a).

11. It is important to compare the migrations of the 1980s and early 1990s from industrial areas with those in earlier periods. The North-east of England, for example, lost 93,000 people in the period from 1904 to 1914, 141,000 between 1914 and 1921, and more than 190,000 between 1921 and 1931 (Robbins 1994: 150). Much of the out-migration from this region was to other industrial regions – and this pattern was repeated in the 1960s when miners from the Durham coalfield moved to jobs in the Kent coalfield. The destinations of emigrants from the industrial North since 1970 have been much more dispersed, including destinations in the broader European Community.

12. On this perception of decline, compare Beauregard's study of the overwhelming, apparently uncontradictory, 'discourse' of disaster and decline he argues characterises local press coverage of cities in the Northern States of the USA (Beauregard 1993).

13. For some examples of the 'quality of life' literature in the United States, exploring and measuring 'residential and community satisfaction', see Campbell *et al.* (1976), Fried (1982) and Marans and Rodgers (1975).

14. These nineteen factors, in order of importance, are:

    1. Violent crime
    2. Non-violent crime
    3. Health provision
    4. Pollution levels
    5. Cost of living
    6. Shopping facilities

7. Access to areas of scenic quality
8. Cost of owner-occupied housing
9. Education provision
10. Employment prospects
11. Wage levels
12. Unemployment levels
13. Climate
14. Sports facilities
15. Travel-to-work times
16. Leisure facilities
17. Quality of council housing
18. Access to council housing
19. Cost of rented accommodation

As the *Sunday Telegraph* reporter, Alex Bellos, observes, it is as important to examine the criteria which Dr Rogerson has introduced into his measures of the quality of life, and the weighting given them, as it is to examine the league tables which emerge from the process (Bellos 1993). What is being presented is an abstract and formal system of evaluation, which clearly involves a series of assumptions about the priorities which 'the population in general' allegedly brings to the assessment of the city in which they live. So it is intriguing to pose the question as to whether this system of evaluation would connect, in any simple sense, to the priorities or the desires of unemployed steel-workers in Sheffield or young black women currently resident in Moss Side and Hulme in Manchester. *Whose* quality of life concerns are being evaluated, and on what justification?

15. The fate of the de-industrialised North of England is fast becoming the focus of an extensive new set of literatures, ranging from novels to analytical social commentary, involving both sympathetic and antagonistic stances. For a brilliant critique of the moralistic fashionable criticism of the North of England as home to an unenterprising, patriarchal and 'dependent', unhealthy and inhuman working class, see Raphael Samuel's view of Mark Hudson's *Coming Back Brackens* (Samuel 1995).

16. We were intrigued to hear in the course of writing this book that the next publication of Sharon Zukin, the urban sociologist working along very similar lines of enquiry to the work we pursued in the North of England, was to be on the role of local culture in different American cities (Zukin 1995).

17. In May 1995, however, the House of Lords finally gave permission to the Manchester Ship Canal Company to proceed with the building of a massive £200 million shopping mall at Dumplington, in Urmston, overturning the appeal against the original planning permission given in 1993 by the eight South Manchester local authorities concerned. (See our discussion in Chapter 5.)

18. The idea of a distinct North of England identity – signalled in language and speech, and in a sense of close local community feeling and friendliness – has a long history in popular discussion and has recently attracted some scholarly curiosity. Frank Musgrove has attempted a definitive history of 'the North', constructed as a narrative on an unending struggle between the North, conceived of as a geographical region, and the centre (London), dominated by powerful individuals and elites (Musgrove 1990). (See the excellent critique by John Walton of the failings of this text as a real social history of Northern peoples (Walton 1992).) Helen Jewell's more recent history is particularly useful on the representation of the North in English literature, and on the 'prehistory' of the Northern regions prior to the Industrial Revolution (Jewell 1994). Philip Waller's work is illuminating on

the relationships between regional dialect in general and the restricted character of a political 'democracy' which places an exclusive value on the 'Queen's' or the 'King's English' (Waller 1987). In the field of sociology and cultural studies, Rob Shields's otherwise highly original investigation of the North of England as one of several 'places on the margin' is helpful on images of the North in post-war British films, especially in the 1960s, but a little less reliable in terms of distinguishing the 'lived experience' – or what we are calling 'the structure of feeling' – of the North of England, which he often equates with the idea of 'Northern Britain' (thus suppressing entirely the distinctive character and feel of Scotland, whether in its dominant or subordinate and popular forms) (Shields 1991). We have ourselves been particularly impressed by the sympathetic and critical curiosity shown by Patrick Joyce into the folk culture of the working class of the North of England in the period from 1848 to 1914 (Joyce 1991).

19. One of the most sophisticated recent studies is the report produced in August 1993 by the School for Advanced Urban Studies at the University of Bristol, *People and Places: A 1991 Census Atlas of England* (Forrest and Gordon 1993). This report carries a series of graphical representations of the standing of various cities and conurbations in respect of social and material deprivation. The City of Manchester is identified in it as the second most deprived 'district' in the UK, after Knowsley on Merseyside.

20. It is possible to argue, after Habermas, that the presentation of reports of this kind by various interest groups is one of the few means left to give voice to a notion of a public interest in free market societies, which have increasingly delegated issues of political and social importance away from Parliament (and the arenas of 'public will formation', like the local authorities) into what Habermas calls the 'neo-corporate grey areas' of local and national inter-agency collaboration. (cf. Habermas 1989: Ch. 2)

21. The Labour Party report proved extremely helpful to many beleaguered chief constables who were arguing that the different clear-up rates of different forces were a function of different workloads, resulting from different overall levels of crime in their jurisdictions. Developments since 1992 have included a considerable debate in local authority and police circles about the 'objective' measurement of crime-related police workloads in different local authority areas.

22. According to the Labour Party report of December 1992, the level of car crime in South Yorkshire amounted to 2,454 offences per 100,000 population, giving the county a ranking of 14th in this national league table. In the neighbouring county of Derbyshire, car crime amounted to 1,718 per 100,000 people, a ranking of 28th out of the 43 police-force areas.

In August 1993, a league table released by the Insurance Service, using official police statistics, identified Greater Manchester as the police-force area with the highest level or risk of car crime as a whole, with 45.6 car crimes per 100,000 population. Cleveland was second, whilst topping the list for outright thefts of and from cars. In respect of the overall car-crime table, South Yorkshire police-force area was 15th out of 43, with 31.2 crimes per 100,000 population (Kirby 1993).

23. We are obviously aware that the annual totals returned by individual police forces to the Home Office and the Chief Inspector of Constabulary, and then used in the chief constables' Annual Reports, often show variation even over one year, and that the figures must in some sense be a function of the criteria for making each annual return. The overall totals on each annual return are also a consequence of the different 'recording practices' adopted in each force, as well as by individual computer-operator officers. Given the increasing standardisation of the criteria used for

recording public requests for help and offence reports on computer, however, there are grounds for believing that there is less idiosyncratic subjectivity in these figures than before computerisation. (But see our discussion of 'cuffing' in n. 26.)

24. The particular caveats involved in the interpretation of the data presented here are, first, that the statistics for Sheffield and Manchester city involved our separating off the crime data for the relevant police divisions in South Yorkshire and Greater Manchester that correspond, more or less accurately, to the Census boundaries of the two cities. Local sources suggest this is not illegitimate, as there is considerable overlap between the divisional and Census boundaries. Comparisons of data for Census ward areas with police subdivisional data on beats is not, however, legitimate, as beat boundaries bear no determinate relationship with Census wards.

Second, there have been changes to beat boundaries in both cities, and, in Manchester, to the boundaries of divisions (with the incorporation in 1989 of what was E Division into a new and larger D Division). This reorganisation of divisional boundaries had 'knock-on' effects with respect to Divisions B and C, meaning that any close comparison of trends in the later 1980s and early 1990s in the Greater Manchester Police area as a whole is rendered more complicated.

25. There was certainly no major disturbance on the riotous scale of the events in Birmingham, Bristol, Liverpool or Manchester, but it is a matter of the historical record that there was a tense confrontation between small groups of West Indian youths and the police in August 1981, on the public balconies above the Haymarket. At the height of this confrontation, some 500 people were involved, and, in the final analysis, some 12 people were arrested on various public order charges. This small local confrontation has been discussed in some detail in Waddington *et al.* (1989: Ch. 7).

26. We are obviously aware that the preceding treatment of the differential rates of reported crime in different police-force areas has been couched in relatively uncritical terms. In particular, we have not examined the particular kinds of recording tradition or practice obtaining in each of the different forces. There are real dangers here. The continuing increase in levels of reported crime in South Yorkshire in the early 1990s may have helped create the impression that Sheffield and its surrounding areas were experiencing a particularly severe and disproportionate problem with crime, especially when the rate of reported crime increased by 12 per cent during 1993, against a reduction of nearly 6 per cent across the 43 police-force areas of England and Wales. In October 1994, however, an investigation by the *Sunday Times* suggested that much of the national reduction in reported crime in 1993 resulted from strategic changes in police recording practices (forced by new league tables imposed on the police by the Home Office to measure 'clear-up rates' as a prelude to the release of resources to local forces). Some of these practices, like 'cuffing' – the straightforward failure to report an incident as a crime – have a long history, but they are now encouraged by the new 'efficiency targets' regime. Significantly for out purposes, the *Sunday Times* report quotes Richard Wells, Chief Constable of South Yorkshire Police, as saying that 'crime has increased in his area compared with most other forces after he instructed all his officers to be totally honest about recording crime' (Leppard 1994).

Mr Wells's comment may best be understood in terms of the history of police recording practices in South Yorkshire over the last decade, as first illuminated by the American criminologist Hal Pepinsky, after his six-month research visit to Sheffield in 1982. Pepinsky was astonished to discover that there had, historically, been a clear-up rate of reported crime in Sheffield of over 50 per cent (considerably higher than the national average in England and Wales, and massively higher than the clear-up rates of comparable American cities). Pepinsky's interviews with local political figures uncovered the considerable sense of dismay which occurred when the 'clear-up rate' fell below 50 per cent in 1980, and the decision of the Council's Police Committee that the police would face funding cuts if they were not able to keep their clear-up rate above 50 per cent (Pepinsky 1987: 67). Pepinsky's analysis of a wide range of statistical data provided by South Yorkshire Police suggested that the main way in which officers were able collectively to get the 'clear-up rate' back over 50 per cent of reported crime in 1981 was to 'no-crime' some 24 per cent more offences reported to them than they had done the previous year (Pepinsky 1987: 68). Interviews conducted at South Yorkshire Police during the early phases of this research in 1992, before Mr Wells had made his presence felt as Chief Constable, suggested that the practice of 'cuffing' and 'no-criming' certain kinds of reported crime was by no means still unknown in South Yorkshire Police.

27. One of the difficulties facing social researchers in Manchester is the specification of the 'object of analysis', and, in particular, the distinction between the City of Manchester (one of ten local authority districts within Greater Manchester) and Greater Manchester as a whole. The relationship between these local authority districts as legal jurisdictions, secondary towns as geographical or cultural entities, and local indentity is complex in a way that it is not in Sheffield. There is a clear distinction in South Yorkshire between Sheffield and the mass of smaller towns and villages that make up the larger county area. We are probably guilty in this text of glossing some issues about 'object of analysis' in the Manchester region (in a legal or constitutional sense) in the interest of capturing the fluid but very influential local idea of Mancunian identity, which is prevalent in *both* the City and the wider conurbation.

28. Coffield *et al.*'s work on young people in the North-east of England explores some of these local myths around particular estates, and also reminds us of the very limited territories which are known and used by residents of such estates. For young people in such estates, 'their city' really is the narrow immediate area of residence and a few, cheaper consumer outlets in the city centre and nothing more. Cf. Coffield *et al.* (1986).

29. We are aware that the City of Leeds, in the wake of the regeneration of its city centre and the development of its 'night life' in the early 1990s, has also been claiming the title, especially in its local boosterism, of 'the capital of the North'. There is an important history to be written of the rivalry between the cities of Leeds and Manchester, dating from their early development as cities of cotton: a recent expression of this rivalry, in another area, being the anger amongst large numbers of men in Leeds which greeted the transfer of the French international footballer, Eric Cantona, from the local club to Manchester United in 1993 (cf. King 1995). In the North of England as a whole, however, there is no sense of Leeds as an alternative capital, especially by comparison to Manchester.

30. In the North-east for example, there is the image of 'the big Hewer' – the rate-busting coalface worker – or in Liverpool that of the docker. Even in post-modern North American cities, the influence of this gendered imagery of the male worker (the steelmen of Pittsburgh or the lumberjacks around Vancouver) has a continuing residual resonance in local cultures.

2 DIRTY OLD TOWNS

1. One of the most common local pub names in South Yorkshire in the twentieth century has been 'The Nailmakers'.

2. According to Alan White, in an unpublished discussion paper (White 1993), the reasons for the renewed interest in the idea of an industrial district, characterised by cooperative relationships between craftspeople operating at different levels of reward and with a flexible approach to product specialisation, have to do with the current crisis in the post-war system of mass manufacture (or 'Fordism'): many commentators see a parallel between the industrial district idea, first used by Marshall in respect of Sheffield in the late eighteenth century, and the business and innovation parks that have grown up throughout the capitalist world in the last decade and a half. In this respect, it is important to pay attention to Charles Sabel and Jonathan Zeitlin's re-examination of Marshall's thesis, arguing that the fact of the power of the trade unions remaining unchallenged within the cutlery trades was one reason for the beginning of the decline of the industry (as a result of lack on innovation) from the middle of the nineteenth century onwards (Sabel and Zeitlin 1985). This interpretation is forcefully challenged by White, who argues that, for all their prominent role in direct action and struggle, the unions in Sheffield remained weak throughout the century, and that wages were always lower than in competitor countries (White 1993).

3. The 'Saint Monday' tradition in Sheffield, wherein workers did not turn out for work after their carousing on Saturday and Sunday or, if they did, worked very slowly, was actually celebrated in a local song ('The Jovial Cutlers') dating from the time of the Napoleonic Wars (Thompson 1968: 73).

4. The importance of the steelworks to wartime production during the Second World War rendered Sheffield a prime target for enemy aircraft. The city was particularly heavily bombed on the evenings of 12 and 15 December 1940 (now known as the nights of the Sheffield Blitz). A total of 668 civilians and 25 servicemen were killed, and a further 589 seriously injured. The physical evidence of the effects of the Blitz (in the form of bomb-sites and great stretches of vacant space generally) persisted in Sheffield well into the 1950s as a reminder of a traumatic event, which continued to define the memories of generations of Sheffielders who lived through it. The subsequent write-up of the Blitz, in the form of a documentary play, *It's a Bit Lively Outside* by Joyce Holliday, tells another story of defiance, symbolised by the statue of Vulcan on top of Sheffield Town Hall, unscathed by the bombers. Cf. the publication of the same title by the Yorkshire Arts Circus in collaboration with the Crucible Theatre and Sheffield City Libraries (1987).

5. Edward Carpenter, the nineteenth-century utopian socialist who moved to Sheffield from Cambridge and spent most of his life in Holmesfield, some ten miles out from the southern edge of the city, observed in his autobiography, how: 'from the very first [he] was taken with the Sheffield people. Rough in the extreme. Twenty or thirty years behind other towns, there is a heartiness about them, not without shrewdness, which attracted [him].' Quoted in Walton (1968: 230).

6. The folk song, 'Rother Sing a Don Song', which circulated the folk clubs of South Yorkshire in the early 1990s, written by Ray Hearne and sung by Roy Bailey, in some ways improbably spoke to the different demands of men and women of shift work in the forges:

> Sons and daughters, dark and light,
> Toilers through the endless night,

Turners all, the world around,
Our heroines your history books ne'er mention,
Rother Sing a Don Song of who we are.

Lads and lasses, workers, grafters,
Mam's on days and Dad's on afters,
Buffers, fettlers, datallers,
Proper little Mesters, rollers, nailers,
Rother Sing a Don Song of who we are.
(Ray Bailey, 'Never Leave a Story Unsung',
Fuse Records CFC 298, 1991)

7. This imagery was copied by Stones Breweries, the Sheffield-based brewery, in a national television advertising campaign in 1994–5 for 'Sheffield Gold' evoking sepia-toned pictures of steelworkers at work in front of burning-hot forges (cf. Taylor and Jamieson 1996a).
8. See our discussion of Meyrowitz in Chapter 1 (p. 9).
9. Patrick Joyce provides a really useful discussion on the continuing influence, in popular song, dialect verse, music-hall tradition and local talk, of specific industrial images of the local worker in each of the industrial regions of the North of England – the 'Keelman' on Tyneside, the 'Big Hewer' in County Durham, and the handloom weaver in Lancashire (Joyce 1991: Ch. 12).
10. Migration into Manchester from these countries has continued to be significant throughout the twentieth century, though never at the same rate as in the 1840s. According to the 1991 Census, some 5,995 of the total population of Greater Manchester (2.5 million people) had been born in Germany, 2,652 in Italy, and 1,067 in France, whilst there were also 30,084 who had been born in Scotland and 37,825 in the Irish Republic. In South Yorkshire, out of a Census population in 1991 of 1.3 million, only 625 had been born in Italy and 307 in France, and there were only 5,086 native-born Irish and 13,988 Scots. There were, however, some 3,413 residents of Sheffield born in Germany.
11. The existing Free Trade Hall on Peter Street is in fact the fourth building to bear the name. The first was a large wooden building opened in January 1840, which was then replaced, in 1843, with an enormous brick-built building, large enough to hold between 7,000 and 8,000 people. This was demolished in 1856 and replaced by a building in St Peter's Fields, now St Peter's Square, on the site of the Peterloo Massacre. This building was destroyed by enemy action in 1940 (cf. Briggs 1963: 125).
12. The account we are providing of Kay-Shuttleworth derives, in part, from the discussion in James Donald's powerful essay on 'The City as Text' (Donald 1992), but departs from his interpretation in important respects.
13. There was also concern in the 1920s as to the effects that the introduction of warehouses into the centre of Manchester was having on particular residential areas, streets and squares. Businessmen were busy building their warehouses in the two centres of Church Street and Cannon Street, whilst moving their own homes out to residential areas of Cheetham Hill and Broughton, which then bordered on open meadows.
14. Some other instances of urban centres that have become the site of a mythology of labour would include the city of Winnipeg in Canada (the site of the 'Winnipeg General Strike' of 1991 ((Palmer 1983: 173–7) and the town of Terni near Rome, the site of a violent lockout in the local steel works in 1920 (Portelli 1991). Portelli's fascinating study of the local folklore of the Terni area shows how the collective memory of the labour movement works, over long periods of time, to underline and elaborate such heroic moments in the struggle of labour – sometimes without too tight a regard for the actual sequence of events or the specific historical context in which they occurred.

3 'THIS RUDDY RECESSION'

1. The crisis of Liverpool is discussed in scholarly terms by Tony Lane (1987) but for most people in Britain was most graphically depicted in Alan Bleasdale's compelling television drama series, *The Boys from the Blackstuff*, originally screened on BBC2 Television in October 1982 but repeated on several subsequent occasions.

2. The North-eastern conurbations of Tyneside and Wearside were very heavily dependent through most of this century on ship building and coal mining, both of which industries were in terminal decline throughout the 1970s and 1980s. In the Durham coalfield, which had employed 166,000 men in more than 130 collieries in 1947, the closure of the last such colliery was announced in December 1993 (Hudson 1993). For a useful collection of essays on the history and present condition of Tyneside, see Collis and Lancaster (1992), and for an excellent study of the fate in the new global economy of the Teeside area (with its heavy dependency on steel and chemical industries), see Beynon *et. al.* (1994).

3. We want to distance ourselves here a little from the account of the World Student Games developed in a number of papers by Maurice Roche (1991, 1994). Roche's argument seems in the end to suggest that the Council was involved in a kind of collective infatuation with the very idea of holding what he calls a 'Mega-Event' in a city not used to such international coverage and recognition. This particular 'reading' of the Sheffield Council's commitment to the Games must be compared with the accounts offered by Seyd (1993: 174–9) and, in particular, by Roy Darke (the ex-chair of the Council's Finance Committee) (Darke 1994), where the emphasis is very much on the Games as a *specific kind of local economic strategy* for a city in severe difficulties in respect of job creation.

4. In his analysis of the World Student Games, Roy Darke estimates that the repayments of bank loans by Sheffield City Council to 1997/8 will be in the region of £20 million (or 5 per cent of the net revenue budget). The debt burden will, however, continue until the year 2001/2, because of new 'profiling' of the Council's debts by the banks, and will then have totalled £45 million. This level of Council debt has to be set against what Darke calls the 'visitor spend' in Sheffield – of people from Sheffield and beyond using the new facilities and engaging in spending which contributes to the local economy and thereby, to job creation. As at the end of 1993, the Council's Department of Recreation was estimating this spend in the new facilities, from 1990, at nearly £19 million (Darke 1994: 21, 22).

5. The reports on the economic situation in the City of Steel – like some of the reports on the Games – written by visiting journalists from London or Manchester had a predictably clichéd character, even down to the choice of headlines. Robert Crampton's feature in *The Times* – 'From Steel City to Brass Farthings' (1992) – provoked an outraged response in the local Sheffield press and Michael Simmons's 'Steel City on a Knife Edge' (1993) was also the subject of critical rejoinders. Patrick Seyd also commented on the jaundiced reports by a reporter from *The Guardian* on the condition of some parts of the city during the World Student Games, and the hurt they caused to local pride (Seyd 1993).

6. John Hambridge was then the Chamber of Commerce Chief Executive.

7. Stuart Dixon, Public Relations Officer, British Coal, Nottingham, personal communication 14 November 1994.

8. In a recent volume of essays on writing about Sheffield 'over the ages', the current Local Studies Librarian for Sheffield, Sylvia Pybus, admits she has been unable to identify the origin of this continuing and powerful piece of local folklore (Pybus 1994).

9. Gurth Wilson, Mall Research Services, and John Weston, Head of Security, Meadowhall, interview, 15 September 1992. By the summer of 1993, fears were being expressed that the city-centre markets themselves, despite their

introduction of cheap car parking, could not cope with the competition from Meadowhall – not least because of the 'grubby' environment they provided compared to that of the new age shopping centre (*Sheffield Telegraph* 17 September 1993).

10. The City Pride bid of 1994 was a political process of great local significance in Manchester, Birmingham and London. These three cities were the only ones allowed to bid for an unspecified, disproportionate share of the new Single Regeneration Budgets to be allocated through the Department of the Environment. The thinly disguised 'subtext' of the City Pride programmes is that only these three cities were deemed to have the potential to be major cities in a restructured, post-industrial, pan-European economic community. The 72-page 'City Pride' document – detailing some 42 specific projects and the means for their achievement – was received very positively by the Environment Ministry ('City Wins Back Pride' *Manchester Evening News* 30 September 1994).

11. Eric Hobsbawm in his recently published *Age of Extremes* (1994) selects the year 1973 (the year of the OPEC oil-price increase) as the end point of what he calls the 'golden age' of post-war peace, growth and consensus. It is also interesting, for our purposes, to see how the political scientist and historian of post-war politics in Sheffield, Patrick Seyd, selects the same year as the culmination of that city's post-war development, and the start of its 'decline':

> In 1973 [Sheffield] was a city with an impressive public fabric, with good public buildings, schools, community health, transport, roads, libraries, art galleries and parks. In 1993, the quality of life, when measured by such indicators as the availability of public transport, the extent of traffic congestion, the fabric of public buildings, and extra-curricular school provision, the number of old people's homes and the opening hours of local library services, had deteriorated.
>
> (Seyd 1993: 184)

12. We are aware that the account we have offered here of 'middle-class Manchester' looks like a summary, in particular, of the preoccupations of the *non-commercial* middle class of Manchester. It is important to be aware, here, of the vigorous debate amongst historians of Victorian England and cultural critics as to the role of the commercial middle class in nineteenth-century cities, especially in Manchester (cf. Seed and Wolff 1988). The commercial class of Manchester made major investments in the aesthetic design, particularly, of city-centre buildings, in art galleries and private libraries. Simon Gunn acknowledges the presence and influence in Manchester in 1851 of a sizeable non-industrial bourgeoisie (about 2,500 lawyers and barristers, physicians, bankers and other merchants), but he also points to the activity of industrial families (like the Heywoods, based at Claremont in Manchester's suburbs) in the development of local education and libraries (Gunn 1988). The taste of this Manchester middle class does not seem to have extended, however, as in Sheffield, to the provision of parks for the citizens at large. See also Kidd (1985), Rose (1985).

13. A recent journalistic investigation of organised crime in Britain (Morton 1994) recounts a story of the Kray twins being 'shown out of Manchester' from the Midland Hotel by local police in 1961. The argument is that, had they been allowed to settle, the organised crime structures of London might have been more apparent in Manchester than they are (cf. Walsh 1994).

14. In 1985, the annual increase in the rate of recorded crime in Greater Manchester was 11 per cent, taking the incidence rate for that year to 11,202 crimes per 100,000 people, the highest in any police-force area in England and Wales (*Guardian* 10 January 1987, quoted in Dickinson 1990: 75). The rate of detection in the same year fell by nearly 5 per cent to 27.6 per cent.

15. It is important not to be misunderstood in the comparison between Manchester and Sheffield (and other cities) in respect of park provision. There is clear evidence of a popular sentiment of attachment to parks in Manchester (cf. Davies 1992: 138–41). Mike Harding, the local comedian and television personality, is a key player in the defence of the city's Heaton Park against developers (cf. Harding 1994). The future of the parks of Manchester was a major issue in the local community in 1994, with a swell of local opinion, led by Alan Ruff, the Head of Landscape Studies at the University of Manchester, arguing for their redevelopment as something other than 'boring municipal spaces for dog walking and footballing' *City Life* 238, 29 September–14 October 1994). To recognise this active debate about parks, and the fervent local attachment to them, is not, however, to argue that Manchester is a 'green city'. This is a description that has been offered of Sheffield, with its massive municipal parks, the Round Walk and Green Belt around the perimeter of the city, and the close presence of the Derbyshire Hills and it also informs the letterheads and logo adopted by the City Council - an image of Sheffield as 'the Welcoming City' nestling between the Derbyshire hills.

16. 'Rambling' had a long history in Manchester, beginning with the formation of the Ramblers' Council at the Clarion Café in 1919 and the creation of the larger Manchester and District Federation in 1922. In 1925, this Federation had 66 affiliated clubs across the region and the North of England. Politically very sympathetic to the Independent Labour Party and the Communist Party and therefore absolutely committed to open access to the countryside, the Federation was to be instrumental in organising the famous 'mass trespass' of Kinder Scout near Edale, Derbyshire, on 24 April 1932 (cf. Jones 1988: 138–46). The objectives of the Kinder trespass were eventually achieved in 1949 with the creation of the National Parks, including the Peak National Park itself. The local presence of this ramblers' movement is still evident on any Sunday morning on Manchester Piccadilly or Sheffield Midland stations.

17. This charity day-trip to Blackpool began in 1949, but is currently threatened by the continuing closure of local authority facilities for children with disabilities and by problems involved in the 1990s in getting staff, other than drivers, to work for nothing (Bernard Andrews, Manchester Taxi Drivers' Association for Handicapped Children, personal communication 23 November 1994).

18. One key expression of the continuing influence of the organisation of the cutlery trade in Sheffield is the continuing influence of the 'Little Mester' mythology: the notion that the significant local industrial activity was in some way dominated by craftsmen who were the really dominating force of the workplace. The continuing influence of this particular masculinist working-class mythology, even during the hegemonic period of a mass-production steel industry in Sheffield, is really important - not least in the ways in which working-class women in Sheffield throughout the twentieth century have had to struggle against characterisation as 'Buffer Girls' – crude, unskilled handmaidens to the cutler, fit only to polish up the finished product of the real craftsman.

19. The 'structure of feeling' of Sheffield as a cohesive working-class city – not primarily organised around the interests of any one section of the population – was reinforced in 1981 by the overwhelming concentration of the professionals identified in that Census in just five electoral wards, all to the south-west of the city (Broomhill, Ecclesall, Hallam, Dore and Nether Edge) (Seyd 1994: 206).

20. The idea of local socialist councils being active agents in the provision of services for local 'social need' (and being better instruments than national governments to identify the patterns of social need at local levels) was sketched out in detail by the then leader of the Sheffield Council, David

Blunkett, with one of his Council officials, in a full-length Fabian Tract, published in 1983 (Blunkett and Green 1983).

21. The inescapable issue here is whether we can take the level of recorded crime in a police-force area as being in any sense a measure or expression of the quality of social cohesion in a particular locality. In 1973, there were 18,862 recorded offences in what was then Sheffield and Rotherham Police area, some 12.7 per cent less than in 1972 (an incidence rate, very roughly, of 3,340 offences per 100,000 people - less than half the current reported incidence of reported crime, and about a third the level reported in Greater Manchester at that time). The City of Sheffield was regularly selected by the Home Office in this period for 'its enthusiastic approach to crime prevention matters' (for example, in the 1967 Crime Cut campaign), but a more appropriate sociological enquiry might have been why there was relatively little crime reported in the first place.

22. Twenty-one years later, there was incredulity locally that Hillsborough – 'of all places' – should have been the site of the worst disaster in the history of English football (cf. the discussion in Taylor 1989).

23. One of the most controversial acts of the Labour Council amongst some sections of the local middle class in the early 1980s was to throw open the two municipal courses (Beauchief and Tinsley Park) to the unemployed, allowing them to play rounds free at certain hours of the day.

24. There were all kinds of minority interests in Sheffield in this period, attracting the attention of more distinctly working-class or middle-class audiences. The Sheffield Speedway was also the location for greyhound racing twice a week – one of the main locales for betting in a city with a long history of betting interest: the 'gang troubles' of the 1920s has been initiated, in part, around the dice games played on Skye Edge, Park Hill and Wadsley Common (cf. Bean 1981: Introduction). There was a significant interest amongst working-class men in fishing, usually on the River Trent in Nottinghamshire, as well as in pigeon-racing, from huts on the hills of Walkley, Sky Edge and elsewhere. There were also very significant subcultures of rock-climbers, hill-walkers and marathon-runners in Sheffield, of mixed social class background – reflections, in some sense, of the 'grittiness' of local industrial culture as well as of the continuing influence of the Derbyshire hills.

PART II INTRODUCTION

1. These four focus groups, and the twenty or so people involved in them, do not form part of the total identified in the Preface, since they were not technically part of this comparative study. This initial project on 'Public Sense of Well-being in Transport and Retail Centres in Manchester' was funded by grants from the University of Salford Research Committee and the Greater Manchester Passenger Transport Executive. We would like to acknowledge the support given by these two bodies, which made possible the subsequent successful application to the Economic and Social Research Council for the support of the major comparative project reported here. The two main publications resulting from this study in Manchester were Taylor (1991a, 1991b).

2. We also conducted five focus group discussions with a total of 32 serving police officers in Manchester and Sheffield. We have decided to present an analysis of this important material, touching on the police's own images and mental maps of these two Northern cities, in a separate publication at a later date.

3. The Sheffield focus groups were as follows: 'Subsistence Shoppers' (n=6); 'Women Only Using Public Space in the Day' (n=7); 'Sheffield South-west

Suburbs' (n=7); 'Retired Manual Workers' (n=4); 'Upmarket Shoppers' (n=7); 'Unemployed' (n=5); 'Sheffield Disability Forum' (n=9); 'Young Mothers' (n=5); 'Professional Workers' (n=10); 'Manual and Clerical Workers' (n=6); 'Young Men' (n=3); 'Young Men' (via South Yorkshire Probation Service) (n=8); 'Retired Members of Sheffield and District Afro-Caribbean Community Association (SADACA) Lunch Club' (n=3); 'Asian Women' (n=9); and 'Young Black Men' (n=6).

The Manchester focus groups comprised: 'Upmarket Shoppers' (n=6); 'Young Men' (n=3); 'Clerical and Manual Workers' (n=8); ' Gay Men' (n=8); 'Unemployed' (n=6); 'Professional Workers' (n=9); 'Manchester Disability Forum' (n=5); 'Subsistence Shoppers' (n=9); 'Women Using Public Space during the Day but Not at Night' (n=10); 'Retired Manual Workers and Other Retired Men' (n=7); 'Elderly Residents, Chinese Housing Association, Chinatown' (n=4); 'Second Elderly Chinese Group, Chinatown' (n=4); and 'Asian Women, Cheetham Hill' (n=7).

4. However, a detailed discussion of our general research strategy, and of the approach we adopted to conducting the initial survey and the focus groups, is contained in a set of methodological appendices which are available on request from the authors at Salford University.

5. The one clear exception to this level of public cooperation was from young male adolescents and men in their early twenties, who showed significant reluctance to attend sessions, whether held in the afternoon or evenings. In Sheffield, we were able to rectify this problem, in part, with the help of the South Yorkshire Probation Service: we held two group discussions with young men in this way - one with young men on probation orders and another with regular attenders at a Community Centre, partly managed by the Probation Service, and frequented mainly by Sheffield's young black population.

6. We were somewhat puzzled, therefore, to encounter Nigel Fielding's assertion in his contribution to a recent text on social research methods that 'the elderly, disabled and members of elites are particularly unlikely to attend group discussion meetings' (Fielding 1993: 142). It is tempting to speculate on whether the attendance at our focus groups was, in some sense, a measure of the qualities of 'friendliness' or 'deference' associated with 'the North' - or even, more straightforwardly, a real interest in the topic.

4 GOING TO WORK

This chapter concentrates, above all, on the recursive daily use of different kinds of transport in Manchester and Sheffield, specifically for journeys to work. We are well aware of the importance of other different uses of buses, trams and cars on the weekends and in the evenings, and we allude to the significance of some aspects of transport ('the last bus') in local experience and knowledge of the city. We would not, however, claim to have carried out comprehensive research for a full-scale sociology of transport in these two cities and have tried not to over-write the enquiries we did make.

1. Steve Cosby, Greater Manchester Passenger Transport Executive, personal communication 1992.

2. In November 1994, local councillors and MPs alike in Bolton were up in arms against the Highways Agency of England and Wales at the news that directions to the town would disappear from signs to be erected on the new M60 motorway. The strength of local identity in Bolton was evident in the protests mounted, in particular, against the idea that the signs on the new motorway would subsume Bolton into what the Conservative MP for North

West Bolton chose to call the 'anonymous mass' of 'North Manchester' (*Guardian* 24 November 1994).

3. The gender imbalance in the availability of a car and the holding of car licences nationally and in the North of England was highlighted in the Women and Transport in West Yorkshire study in the early 1980s. Nationally, in 1981, less than one third of women as a whole held a licence; in West Yorkshire in 1981 only 9 per cent of women of manual working-class background (compared to 47 per cent of men) had a licence and also sole access to a car (Hamilton 1990: 17).

4. It is not clear that this kind of individual calculation is really understood by organisations like the PTEs, staffed as they are by people committed in a moral fashion to the abstract idea of public transport. For example, the Greater Manchester PTE commissioned the Harriss Research Centre to conduct a survey of non-users of buses across the city to investigate whether this non-use was a function of inadequate information as such (i.e. on the assumption that if the public were better informed, they would obviously make more use of the buses). The massive report, submitted in December 1993, is currently still under discussion.

5. One obvious example here is the main thoroughfare taking traffic from Manchester airport to the centre of the city, Princess Parkway. This road passes right through the centre of Moss Side, past three blocks of boarded-up shops and terraced house, presenting themselves like nothing so much as a front-stage Hollywood set for a 'ghetto'. To the west of this road is a mix of more modern housing, of different quality, including some impressive Housing Association property, though the front of this side of the Princess Road consists of some box-like housing built in the 1970s with small windows with a view to economies of fuel consumption. The image of 'Moss Side' in the public imagination is anchored around the boarded-up shop fronts and terraced housing of Princess Road itself, on the one side, and these concrete frontages, on the other.

6. For many years, the only effective connection between the two mainline rail stations was on a Centreline bus.

7. For detail on the South Yorkshire Supertram, see Jackson (1991, 1992, 1994).

8. Nor either was it the purpose of our work, as such, to assess the impact of Metrolink or Supertram on the local market for public transport or on the local environment in these cities. Early reports from an impact study on the Metrolink in Greater Manchester, by our colleagues from the University of Salford Department of Geography, do confirm the massive level of patronage of the new system (13 million passengers journeys in 1993 compared to a previous projected annual rate of 7.5 million) and also the increased use of this system in 'off-peak' periods. Some commentators on these reports, however, insisted that the use of Metrolink is simply replacing use of cars or trains by commuters, and express some scepticism as to Metrolink's effect in solving Greater Manchester's car congestion problems or the transport problems of the mass of the local population (cf. Orlowski 1994 and the first reports from the Metrolink Impact Study, Department of Geography, University of Salford. An initial outline of the aims of this impact study is contained in Knowles and Fairweather 1991).

9. Sheffield's tramway system was initiated in 1872 by the Sheffield Tramway Company: by 1927, under Corporation ownership, the system covered the city and involved a total of 427 passenger trams, one of the largest number of any provincial city (Gandy 1985). The trams were well liked in Sheffield for their ability to conquer the city's hills, even in the most adverse of wintry conditions.

10. Internal studies by the Greater Manchester Passenger Transport Executive

in 1993 and 1994 indicated that most Mancunians in the early 1990s continued to rely on buses and trains, rather than Metrolink, to 'get about' the city.

11. Steve Cosby, Greater Manchester Passenger Transport Executive, personal communication August 1992.

12. In Sheffield, though not in Manchester, we also encountered some folk knowledge as to who, amongst one's friends or neighbours, might be on a particular bus at a particular time of day or in the evening: there was some expectation that one might meet someone one knew.

13. The theory behind the 1985 Act was that there should be a clear separation between the social purposes of local transport, which should be guarded by local Passenger Transport Executives (and therefore responsive to local politicians), and operational considerations. For the effective operation of bus services, the theory argued, buses needed to be subject to the discipline, and competition, of the marketplace. After the enactment of this legislation, most local authorities in Britain did sell off their bus services to private operators or encourage their local bus providers to set themselves up as private companies. Greater Manchester was one of the last local authorities so to do, with a continuing hope that the return of a Labour government might mean the recreation of a 'public service' concept of bus provision. The Greater Manchester bus fleets were eventually sold off, via employee buy-outs, in north Manchester in March 1994 and south Manchester in April 1994.

14. Overt discussion of the decrepit condition of local buses was quite uneven in our focus groups, with the greatest level of criticism stemming from suburban residents. Public knowledge of the condition of buses is a matter of personal experience (for example, of breakdowns and delays), and also of reports in the local press. Spot checks by Greater Manchester Police and the Vehicle Inspectorate Agency of buses in Salford and South Manchester in November 1994, for instance, were reported in the local press as discovering that 50 per cent of all vehicles stopped had defects, and that 5 per cent had such serious defects as to be banned immediately from the road (*Manchester Metropolitan News* 2 December 1994).

15. This 'problem of recognition' had a particular twist in Sheffield, subsequent to the 1986 deregulation, when the company that emerged out of the pre-existing South Yorkshire Transport, South Yorkshire's Transport, experimented with a range of different liveries and 'brand names' (City Clipper, Beaver, etc.), with evidence of serious subsequent confusion on the part of the bus-using public. In November 1993, the same transport provider (the biggest in the city with 800 vehicles) relaunched itself unambiguously as a private company, Mainline, using a uniform livery and a single brand name (Steve Arnold, Public Relations, Mainline, personal communication 1 December 1994).

16. For one instance of the anxious local press coverage of the deregulated bus services, see 'Battle of the Buses: The Gloves are Off' *Sheffield Telegraph* 16 July 1992.

17. The Passenger Transport Executive in Greater Manchester was aware of public disquiet about driver behaviour and commissioned a study by a psychologist working with a private consultancy firm of driver motivations (Boddy 1993). The main factors found to be frustrating drivers, and standing in the way of service to users, were the lack of support and facilities for drivers between shifts at depots, the condition of the buses themselves, and the levels of congestion on the roads, making it impossible to keep to timetable. The findings of this report echo many other such investigations in other local authority transport departments, which are discussed in Gavin Smith (1984: Ch. 1), with the demeanour of the bus

drivers interpreted, in classical Marxist style, as a form of worker alienation. This generalised approach does not encompass all the new features of the drivers' work situation in a free market – for example, the threat of vandalism and attack. In October 1993, there were reports of buses originating from Manchester looking for business in Liverpool being stoned by rival drivers (*Manchester Evening News* 4 October 1993). At a safety conference in Dewsbury in March 1993, delegates heard that vicious attacks on bus staff were on the increase in many parts of the country, although information from South Yorkshire suggested that serious attacks on drivers in that county were down from 45 in 1990 to 36 in 1992 (*Sheffield Star* 18 March 1993).

18. John Hardey, South Yorkshire PTE, personal communication 29 November 1994.

19. Steve Cosby, Greater Manchester Passenger Transport Executive, personal communication 28 November 1994.

20. For a brilliant analysis of these contradictory fears of human interaction and isolation on railway journeys, see Schivelbusch (1986).

21. We are aware that there are similar mechanisms at work in workplaces in Central London regarding the current workings of particular underground lines (the Northern Line, in particular). These informal systems of communication were upgraded during the string of terrorist incidents on the London Underground in the early 1990s.

22. In an interesting analysis of the Tyne and Wear Metro transit system in Newcastle on Tyne, Stephen Gilliatt argues that the management of public transport systems are increasingly dependent on their passengers (customers) making use of this accumulated stock of commonsense knowledge to deal effectively with the mushrooming problems of service failure (for example, cancellation of trains) in a system of scarce resources and rapidly changing technologies (Gilliatt 1992). He also hints at the importance of the cultural trait of long-suffering 'endurance' – which, as we have argued earlier in this book, is a particularly striking aspect of the 'structure of feeling' of the North of England as a whole.

23. The attacks on trains in 1993 followed a series of reports in local community newspapers about the throwing of missiles (including rocks) from bridges at cars on the M56 motorway coming into Manchester from the south. One important consequence of the pattern of 'axiate growth' in Manchester, after the example of Chicago, is the inescapable necessity for transport users from the suburbs going into the city to pass directly through some of the more troubled inner-city areas or council estates. Princess Road, from the airport, passes right through Moss Side, whilst the M56 motorway and the Chester rail line cut directly through the Wythenshawe Estate, one of the largest council estates in Europe.

24. The sense of resignation and the low level of expectation amongst the mass of working-class residents of Northern cities is discussed in relation to the litter problem in Manchester in Taylor (1990). The explanation of this level of expectation must clearly be historical and sociological, connecting, in a precise fashion, to the accustomed patterns of treatment of the lower class in Britain.

25. 'Pond Street' – as the Sheffield bus station was known prior to the opening of the Interchange – was second only to the 'Hole in the Road' in Sheffield in the 1970s and 1980s as a location to be avoided, presumed in the popular imagination to be colonised, variously, by drug pushers, football hooligans or just 'nasty groups of lads'.

26. The opening of the new Interchange has not entirely altered the way in which this urban territory is used, especially at nights. Young pupils at one school in Sheffield reported being harassed by groups of older teenagers –

whom they called 'the Pond Street Potters' – who 'hang around' the Interchange at night.

27. The capital investment programme of South Yorkshire PTE is evidence, however, of the importance for localities of the exercise of creative initiative and intelligence by local authorities (and also 'urban partnerships' generally) in the search for European support – in this instance, an EU scheme designed to ease the restructuring of areas decimated by the collapse of steel. There are larger lessons, here, with respect to the politics of the 'local state' understood in relation to 'Europe' rather than in a relationship of dependency with Whitehall and the nation-state.

28. On this issue, however, we should recognise the importance for many motorists of the cost of city-centre car parking. There is every reason in coming years to expect a variety of innovative shcemes by private businesses on this front, akin to developments that have occurred in the North American 'downtown' areas, attempting to hegemonise greater amounts of space for car parks, creating ever-increasing stretches of what Richard Sennett has described as 'dead space' (Sennett 1991, 1992), with the associated increase in public alienation from the city-centre.

5 SHOP 'TIL YOU DROP

1. Covered markets are important aspect of the urban landscape in many Northern cities (Kirkgate and the John Street markets in Leeds) and are landmarks in most local residents' 'mental maps of the city', as well as being significant symbolic markers of these cities' history as places in which the people as a whole went to market. Leeds's Kirkgate market was also the home of Michael Marks' Penny Bazaar, the precursor of Marks and Spencer (cf. Gardner and Sheppard 1989: 147). Manchester is an exception in the North of England in not retaining a covered market in its city centre.

   'Copies' of these covered markets and arcades are a feature in many contemporary examples of urban regeneration, especially with a 'heritage' theme, though by no means confined to the North of England (cf. the Temple Bar in Dublin).

2. To this day, the Co-op continues to have a major presence in Manchester itself, not least in its occupancy of the tallest building in the city centre, but also in its continuing prominence in local advertising campaigns, 'investing in Manchester'.

3. The fish van is the one obvious remaining legacy of the eighteenth-century tradition of 'travelling packman' – travelling from door to door selling different ranges of goods (especially, though not exclusively, household items). As recently as the 1950s, this was the favoured method for the selling of insurance to the general population, and in the North of England continuing memories amongst older generations of the 'Man from the Pru' are testimony to this tradition.

4. The 'official histories' of the department store in England predictably concentrate on the more famous examples in London, particularly Harrod's, beginning in the 1860s. But the North of England is important in such a history. Whilst there is some debate as to which modern store can lay claim to being the 'first department store in the world', Adburgham's classic study of 1964 disputes the widespread belief that this claim should be awarded to Bon Marché, on Paris's Left Bank (which opened as a department store in 1860), pointing out that Bainbridges, in Newcastle upon Tyne, was a flourishing store in 1841. In the final analysis, however, Adburgham concludes that John Watts's shop, The Bazaar, on Deans-

gate, Manchester (later to become Kendal Milnes), was doing 'brisk business' in 1831 and therefore should be identified as the rightful holder of the crown. This claim is certainly sustained (with a five-year modification) by Kendals itself – for example, in its celebration of 150 years of trading in 1986 (Collinson 1986).

5. The origins of Kendals are to be traced to the opening of a draper's store on the present site on Deansgate by John Watts of Didsbury in 1796 (see also n. 4). Watts had determined to give up farming and to open the shop, originally known as The Bazaar, as an outlet for hand-woven ginghams produced by his wife and six sons. Three of the employees of this shop – Thomas Kendal from Westmorland, and James Milne and Adam Faulkner from Manchester – bought the store in 1836, and in 1862, on the death of Adam Faulkner, the store became known as Kendal Milne. The present department store building dates from 1872, constructed as 'a stately four-story store building with elegantly-appointed windows where ladies of fashion alight from their carriages' (Adburgham 1964: 18–21).

6. Lewis's of Market Street, Manchester, was a branch of the Lewis family business of Liverpool. The store first opened in 1880.

7. The Cole Brothers department store was originally opened on the corner of Church Street and Fargate in 1869 (Olive 1994: 22) – a corner still known to many Sheffielders as Coles Corner, even though the store moved half a mile away to Barkers Pool in 1963. Coles has a long history as the most elegant of Sheffield's department stores: in 1893, for example, it was appointed an agent for Dr Jaeger's new Sanitary Woollen System (the height of underwear fashion) and was also able to boast that it had electric light, had 'a passenger lift on the approved principle' and also was on the phone (five years ahead of Harrod's) (Adburgham 1964: 187). In 1940, the Selfridge Provincial Group, to which Coles then belonged, was sold *en bloc* to the John Lewis Partnership, the current owners. The John Lewis Partnership is distinctive in its adoption of a version of employee share-ownership.

8. The department stores that opened up in city centres in the late nineteenth century always had to compete for the custom of the upper middle-class lady with similar or even more elegant stores which had opened up in nearly county towns – in many ways, a preferred site for this kind of *flâneur*, involving little or no contact with the urban working poor. For many sections of the Manchester middle class in the nineteenth century and later, the preferred store was Brown's of Chester, whilst many Sheffield-based middle-class ladies made the trip to Swallow's in Chesterfield.

9. Finnigan's store quickly anticipated the developing logic of Manchester's post-war suburban growth, with its negative impact on departmental store trading in the city centre, in relocating to Wilmslow, one of the most affluent southern suburbs, in 1956 (Law 1986: 32).

10. Cockayne's was for many years the oldest family-owned store in Sheffield, originally opening as a draper's shop in Angel Street in 1829 and expanding considerably in the late nineteenth century. Having relocated at the top of Snig Hill, it narrowly escaped the blitz in December 1940 and remained on that site throughout the post-war period, being bought by Schofield's, a Leeds-based department store chain, in the early 1960s. Schofield's closed in 1983 to be replaced by a very cheap 'Wingprice' store, which failed, and the shop remained boarded up, creating what locals alway referred to as an 'eyesore' and further contributing to the definition of the 'Hole in the Road' area as a landscape of fear.

11. Walsh's first store in Sheffield, a magnificent glass-fronted building with side arcade, was opened on High Street in 1900. It was the product of 25 years' endeavour by John Walsh, a native of County Limerick. In 1925, Walsh's had some 600 employees covering nearly every sphere of consumption,

including house removal and cabinet making. The building was destroyed in the Blitz, but the business returned to new premises on the same site, and so adjoined the 'Hole in the Road' for many years (Olive 1994: 17). It is now owned by the House of Fraser and, along with Coles, is one of the two major department stores remaining in Sheffield city centre.

12. The design of the Arndale Centre in Manchester has been the subject of continuing disparaging commentary over the years. One commentator spoke of its 'uniform skin . . . under which so many disparate things are gathered' and remarked on its outer walls consisting 'largely of putty and chocolate'. It was not surprising, he continued, that this 'had led . . . to frequent jokes about Britain's largest toilet' (Atkins 1987: 95). In one of our groups, Derek Halstead complained how the Arndale had 'totally transformed the individuality of all the different shops in Market Street'. Similar critical comments have no doubt been made about many of the first wave of shopping malls built in Britain in the 1960s and 1970s (including other Arndale Centres in other northern cities, and the Arndale Centre in Stretford, south Manchester): the Manchester Arndale, however, has been signalled out for particular attention because of the 'prime site' it occupies at the junction of Market Street and Cross Street in central Manchester.

13. It is important to register that the refurbishment of the Arndale was actually opposed by the Manchester Street Traders' Association, fearful that any move 'up-market' by the popular-democratic Arndale might have a knock-on effect on their own trade, as less wealthy shoppers might no longer direct their route along Market Street and the Barrows (*Manchester Evening News* 8 April 1993). The constant 'war of position' for the custom of up-market shoppers by department stores and shopping malls is mirrored, in the North, by a continuing struggle to retain the custom of the poor.

14. The North West Group's financial estimates, as released to the press and put to the Court of Appeal, were that Manchester City Centre would lose £75-million worth of trade in one year, Stockport £26-million, Altrincham £17-million, Stretford £6.5-million and Sale £6-million (*Manchester Metropolitan News* 6 May 1994). The Court of Appeal ruled, in July 1994, that the Environmental Secretary had not considered the effects of Dumplington on nearby shopping centres. Early in 1995, this decision was over-ruled by the House of Lords and the centre of Dumplington is now expected to open in 1997 or 1998.

15. Publicity was given in 1993, for example, to a plan to open a £100-million shopping mall on Shudehill, just next to the Victoria Station in central Manchester (*Manchester Evening News* 28 March 1993).

16. One important sub-text in the debate around the crisis of the city centre in growth coalition circles (advanced, for example, in the annual survey of shopping centres produced by the Property Managers' Association) was the growing recognition that there is no *necessary* relationship between the opening of an out-of-town centre and the demise of local city centres: in the North-east of England, MetroCentre's success as a major shopping development in Gateshead has not undermined the centre of neighbouring Newcastle in the way that Meadowhall has done for Sheffield. In very large part, the continuing health of Newcastle City Centre arises out of its proximity to an already existing, fast and efficient public transport system, the Tyneside Metro (*Manchester Evening News, Business Section* 24 January 1995).

17. One important site of struggle between developers and the defenders of an idea of the 'old' (industrial or pre-industrial) city is the preservation of 'traditional pubs'. Manchester city centre is heavily provided with these public houses – 130 of them within one square mile – many of which carry a particular local folklore and kind of reputation. Only half a dozen new

pubs have been opened in the city centre in the post-war period. The great majority of them are housed in nineteenth-century buildings, with two of them (The Nags Head and The Rising Sun) having been in the same buildings since the 1780s (Richardson 1995). Overwhelmingly, of course, the pubs are male-dominated institutions, and their relationship to the city interpreted, as in this chapter, as a 'set of shops' is indirect at best. What does need to be understood, however, is the relationship between the shopping practices of a certain section of the young professional population working in Manchester and the large number of wine bars and café bars that opened up in Manchester city centre in the 1980s and early 1990s.

18. Local historians confirm that the films shown at the Cinephone in the early post-war period were largely 'sex films'. In Sheffield, this was the role played by the cinema in the Wicker, slightly out of the city centre. We are aware that the account we are providing in this chapter of shopping and consumption is largely an account of 'legitimate' consumption. There is a history to be written of the local history of illegitimate (hetero)sexual consumption and the spaces in which it occurred in respect of prostitution, 'continental films' and even the sale of different kinds of pornography.

19. The Barrows seem to be the only remaining evidence or relic of the original Smithfield covered market, a fish, fruit and vegetable market building, which moved to Openshaw in east Manchester in the 1960s. In the late nineteen century, Manchester city centre was home to two covered markets (the Smithfield Market and the Market Place itself) and two smaller market halls, but there was also a significant local tradition of outdoor street markets (Scola 1975; Davies 1987).

20. Another popular shopping destination, located some distance from the city centre, is the Crystal Peaks shopping mall, owned by London-based Chesterfield Properties. Crystal Peaks, constructed around the theme of the crystal-clear water of the Peak District, was designed principally to meet the shopping requirements of the new townships of Mosborough, Waterthorpe and Hackenthorpe to the south-east of the city centre, but many visitors also come from Chesterfield, given its proximity to the Derbyshire border. It opened in June 1988 and comprises 54 units including an estate agent, a library and a covered market, owned by Sheffield Markets. An estimated 140,000 visit the centre each week.

21. One boost to Meadowhall was the passage of legislation in 1993 deregulating shopping on Sundays, but the centre was also helped by the opening of the Supertram link direct to Meadowhall from the city centre. Attendance at Meadowhall has gone from 20 million in its first year (1991) to 27 million in 1993–4 (*Observer* 16 October 1994).

22. These figures have confirmed predictions made by Dr Gwyn Rowley, a geographer at the University of Sheffield. In February 1992, Dr Rowley predicted a 30 per cent loss in 'shop takings' in Sheffield's city centre as the 'final' first impact of the opening of Meadowhall (*Independent* 22 February 1992).

23. In the *Sheffield Star* of 26 November 1993, a 16-year-old boy was quoted as lamenting the close – 10 years earlier – of Schofields department store.

24. Popular comparisons between supermarkets may also be informed by a reading of the local community newspapers or 'advertising supplements', which regularly carry 'consumer report'-type items on the prices and range of different goods in supermarkets.

25. Both the Peace Gardens in Sheffield and Piccadilly Gardens in Manchester, centrally located areas of greenery and flowers which are natural (logical and easy-for-walking) thoroughfares, are avoided by many people because they have a widespread reputation for being where the homeless and drunks spend time during the day and at night. The source of the unease

associated with passing through these gardens varies from moral disdain or reluctance to confront poverty and donate money when approached, to fear of being mugged or verbally harangued.

26. Gardner and Sheppard consider the 1980s to have been the 'decade of the retail specialist', during which time 'the generalists, the multiple chain stores such as BHS, Debenhams, Woolworths, John Lewis and Littlewoods languished . . . [these] were the Aunt Sallies of the decade' (1989: 85).

27. We are not suggesting that the demise of the inner-city department store as a local landmark is a feature only of the industrial North of England. Considerable national publicity was given in 1990 to the closure of Jones Brothers, a branch of the John Lewis Partnership on the Holloway Road in North London. A huge local campaign was launched and locally resident actor, Bob Hoskins, commented that 'It's the only department store which is like your everyday corner shop' (*Observer* 8 April 1990). As this article points out, the disappearance of such a resource (which was making a profit, but whose image was not up to the contemporary John Lewis standard) has many repercussions for the local community. There are those whose physical mobility is limited, for whom travelling to another department store in central London or out at the margins of Brent Cross or Watford is simply not an option. But there are also those for whom the store is a landmark in their personal biography, a key aspect of their sense of place and community. It may be, however, that the loss of such an 'iconic' departmental store is more of a blow to local pride and self-respect in smaller cities and towns than in major metropolitan conurbations, where there are more alternative shopping provisions and sources of pleasurable diversion.

28. It is worth noting the references in this set of comments to the ubiquitous 'they' who appear with great regularity in conversations about the condition of the city in the North of England. The allusion is to an all-powerful complex of decision makers who are assumed, in some unspecified sense, 'to run things'. The origins of this particular folk wisdom may lie in the heyday of municipal local democracy in the first half of this century, when a large number of decisions about housing, schooling and a host of other public provisions were made locally – by 'the Corporation'. The use of this kind of language is clearly socially patterned (it is less frequently heard amongst professionals, especially those with occupational contact with urban development), but there is a sense that this kind of talk has become a quite general shorthand in discussions of the changes taking place in the city in the North of England.

29. Crystal Peaks is an interesting instance of this 'localisation of the mall', not least because of its opening out of its public display areas to some of the professional and community associations of the local ethnic minority population. In February 1995, for example, Crystal Peaks was the site of the launch of 'the Year of the Pig' by the Sheffield Chinese Communities Association, the Lai Yin Association (*Sheffield Journal* 16 February 1995).

30. Home delivery of groceries by phone-order, of the kind that is extremely common in two-career households in North America, is relatively under-developed in Manchester and Sheffield.

6 ON OUR UPPERS

1. We are aware that the scale of the movement towards greater equality of wealth in Britain during the years of post-war reconstruction can be vastly over-rated and that it often was, particularly in popular and political discussion (cf. Westergaard 1965).

2. *Households Below Average Income* HMSO 1994, reported in the Guardian 15 July 1994.
3. In one recent analysis, some 30 per cent of young men between 20 and 30, and an overall total of 1 million people, have refused many such forms of official registration in the last few years, in particular because of a fear of becoming liable for the 'poll tax' and its successors (Stephen Simpson, paper presented to Institute of British Geographers conference January 1995, reported in the *Guardian* 6 January 1995).
4. Schwartz and Volgy (1994) estimated that the size of the 'working poor' population in the United States (employed but unable to afford 'basic necessities') is now about 23 per cent of the overall population. This is seen by them to result from the failure of the Reagan and Bush administrations to show any interest in minimum-wage legislation.
5. Our focus in this chapter is on the 'poor' of Manchester and Sheffield – the many thousands of citizens outside the paid labour market or caught (without many obvious options) in poorly paying occupations – and also the homeless. But it is in no sense our concern to suggest that the 'fear' of the experience of 'falling' was confined to this sector of the population in our cities. Insecurities over job certainty have continued to be widely experienced throughout the professional middle class and the skilled working class in the 1990s, and are a major element in an 'alarming escalation' in levels of personal stress reported by four-fifths of all doctors surveyed in early 1994 by the British Medical Association, 60 per cent of all such cases being related to financial and employment anxieties (cf. Pope 1994). We deal with some aspects of 'suburban fear', the different patterns which such fears assumed in Manchester and Sheffield, and the strategies adopted to immunise self and neighbourhood from such fears in Chapter 12; and there is an attempt at a close reading of the significance of 'fear of crime' and public space in the south Manchester suburb of Hale, written during the course of the research reported here, in Taylor 1995a.
6. It should be said that this 'fear of falling' amongst working-class respondents did not become a major overt topic in discussion in any of our focus group discussions, though we would argue it was a constant background assumption in those discussions. It may be that the focus group, with its privileging of public talk in a group situation, is not the most appropriate strategic instrument for revelations or confessions of personal fears or individual anxiety. There are two studies of the reactions of Sheffield workers to the demise of the local steel industry during the 1980s, based in one case (Westergaard *et al.* 1989) on extended interviews and surveys, and, in another (Beattie 1986), on ethnography and participant observation, notably amongst male Sheffield workers now working in casinos, night clubs and the mushrooming 'hidden economy'.
7. On his analysis of the figures, Victor Keegan argued that the number of women holding down jobs in Britain would exceed the number of men by the end of 1994. The size of what is known as the 'male labour force' has risen by only about 300,000 in Britain since 1970 (to around 15.4 million), whilst the 'female labour force' has increased by 3.1 million. If self-employed people, people in the armed forces and people on training schemes are excluded, then the number of women 'with jobs' (in December 1993) was 10.53 million compared with 10.58 million men (Keegan 1994).
8. It was not possible, within the scope of the research reported here, to investigate the gendered effects of the changing economic structure and labour market on experience in the South of England, where the prevalence of all-male working environments has traditionally been less of a feature of the labour market than in the North of England. Such an investigation would constitute a separate study in itself.

9. In Greater Manchester, for example, there was a 14.5 per cent increase over the eight years to 1989 in the proportion of part-time jobs to the total labour market, and a reduction of 3.8 per cent in the share of full-time work. Part-time jobs in 1989 constituted 24.1 per cent of total employment in Greater Manchester (Peck and Emmerich 1992a: Table 14). These shifts were very close to the changes occurring in the national labour market.

10. In what it called a 'Dossier of Shame', the *Star* highlighted how these 12 quite small areas, some of them 'enclaves' hidden away in more affluent areas, contained about 72,000 people (about 14 per cent of the total population of the city) who were living 'in acute poverty'. The definition of this poverty was that more than 50 per cent of the adult population were entirely dependent on state support, i.e. 'Income Support', for survival (Neil Fielding 1993).

11. In his series of articles on 'Darkest Britain', Nick Davies featured Pye Bank in Sheffield, an area of council housing on the edge of Burngreave which had emerged in the 1980s and 1990s as one of the most problematic areas of poverty in the city. It was home, for a period, to Nomad, a self-help organisation run by a desperate young single mother, Jackie Day, until she 'burnt out' from the effort. The story Davies presents is a very familiar one for anyone who knows the condition of the poorest urban areas in England in the 1990s, but, as Davies himself points out, it was only 15–20 years ago that Pye Bank was a solid, working-class estate, where most people worked, in steel or associated industries. Now 'the jobs have gone' (76 per cent of the 2,500 adults on the estate are unemployed) and the local infrastructure of banks, shops, working-men's and youth clubs, three post offices, and two primary schools have left or closed up (Davies 1994).

12. Our research was conducted before the present British government announced in 1994 its intention to apply Value Added Tax to domestic fuel. We can only speculate on the consequences of this decision for the new urban poor. We note that social agencies have started to refer to particular clients' situations as 'fuel poverty' – the inability to afford proper heat and fuel.

13. The new Metrolink urban transit system in Manchester was certainly deemed 'too expensive' (at £1 for an adult for a zone of four stations) by many of our poorer respondents in that city, who indicated that they would continue to have to rely almost entirely and very selectively on local buses to get around. Metrolink, indeed, has had a continuing problem with 'fare dodging', so that an intensive campaign against fare dodgers was launched in January 1995. Sheffields' Supertram – which, as we indicated in Chapter 4, opened after the completion of this research – was significantly cheaper that Metrolink when it first opened, at 50 pence per stage for an adult, 25 pence for a senior citizen and 15 pence for a child or a scholar. There are some echoes here of the subsidised bus fare policies of the late 1970s, but there is also a clear business interest: the Supertram's first route takes in some of the poorer outlying and inner estates to the north and east of the city, and, in many commentators' view, its further commercial development and, indeed, its public legitimacy in Sheffield will depend on its capacity to attract custom from those areas.

14. The data collected by the Department of Environment on homelessness are a count of the number of households that have been 'accepted' into permanent local authority accomodation under Part III of the 1985 Housing Act. Usually this refers to the offer of accommodation in a council house or in accommodation owned by a housing association. It is clear that such acceptance will depend on the recognition of a household as being eligible for such provision under the Act (a discretionary decision taken by local authority officials) and also on the availability of council housing or housing association alternatives in the local authority area. It is

widely thought that the homelessness statistics involve a very significant under-representation of the 'real rate' of homelessness in the country, and it is also accepted by the department itself that the measures are of house-holds and not people.

15. These data on homelessness in Manchester, and the size of the operation of the North-west *Big Issue*, arise out of a personal communication from Ruth Turner, editor, November 1994.

16. One such scheme by the local branch of Crisis, the charity for the homeless, in conjunction with the local Chamber of Commerce, involved the distri-bution of vouchers to beggars which could only be redeemed in centres run by the charity. Intriguingly for our purposes, the spokesperson for Man-chester Chamber of Commerce launching the scheme was quoted as saying that 'if Manchester gets a reputation for having a large number of beggars who pester shoppers, people are going to shove off to Meadowhall in Sheffield' (*Manchester Metropolitan News* 24 February 1995)

17. Pat Carlen's work on homelessness strongly suggests that the conscious and fearless interpretation of homelessness and its larger 'structural causes' is now confined to a few critically minded scholars and politicians, and also those who have become homeless themselves. Discussion of the homeless in the public media tends to focus on the individual characteristics and failings of those who find themselves without a home (Carlen 1994).

18. It is one of the many limitations of this study that we have not been able to ecplore, specifically, the home and neighbourhood life of the urban poor in our two cities: the struggle for economic survival and for some peace of mind in the inner city or the estates. We have concentrated instead – for example, in our analysis of subsistence shoppers – on some particular strategic uses of the wider city to which the poor are propelled. For an insightful set of interviews with poor residents of a London council estate in the early 1980s, see Parker (1983).

19. Claimant unemployment statistics, 13 October 1994, in *Employment Gazette* 102 (12) December 1994, Table 2.10.

20. The presence of beggars on the street in many cities of the world has been presented, usually by local 'growth coalitions', as a threat to the prospect of attracting incoming investment into those cities, especially when cities are involved in high-profile competitive bids – for example, to stage major international sporting events. The first campaign by a growth coalition in a major western city to clear beggars away from the urban centres was in Vancouver, Canada (evacuating the Gastown area of vagrants), in the lead-up to the Winter Games of 1982. This was then followed by the evacuation of downtown Barcelona prior to the 1982 World Cup finals and the Olympics of 1992. In May 1993, some five months before the decision over the staging of the Millennium Olympics, Manchester City Council and Greater Manchester Police released details of 'Operation Broom' to take poor and homeless people from the streets of the city centre, insisting that the motivation behind this initiative included the concern to help prevent young homeless people becoming launched on careers of shop-lifting and other crime (*Manchester Evening News* 24 May 1993).

21. 'Begging "Only Path" for the Young' *Guardian* 16 June 1993.

22. The idea of 'urban spectatorship' by suburban or middle-class visitors to the City is taken from Judith Walkowitz (1992).

23. There was, for example, some particular concern over the 'colonisation' during the early 1990s of the wall surrounding the Sir Stuart Goodwin fountain at the head of Fargate by small groups of lager drinkers and 'crusties', which was then linked, by some local councillors and correspon-dents to local papers, with the continuing presence of litter (lager tins and fast-food wrapping) around one of the city centre's few 'nice' architectural

landmarks. We have already mentioned the colonisation of Sheffield's Peace Gardens and Manchester's Piccadilly Gardens by 'winos' and the anxiety which this produces for many menbers of the larger public.

24. Less well-known nowadays are the earlier investigations associated, for example, with the Royal Commission into the Administration of the Poor Law in 1834. In this report, the problem of urban vagrancy was broken down by Harrison Gordon Codd, an expert witness, into a taxonomy consisting of (a) convicted vagrants on prison passes, (b) Scottish and Irish paupers and (c) 'trampers' or casual poor. A Mr Henderson from Lancashire was quoted as saying that the Manchester Vagrant Office in 1831–2 had 5942 vagrants claiming relief, a major increase on the previous year. About one-third of these claimants were 'Irish paupers' (Royal Commission for Inquiring into the Administration and Practical Operation of the Poor Laws, 1834, Appendix E: Vagrancy). There was no report to this national commission from any keeper of a pauper refuge in Sheffield or its wider region.

25. Lynch's idea of mental mapping has been applied, within the essentially positivistic framework of behavioural psychology, by Pocock with residents of two small British towns, Dundee (Pocock 1972) and Durham City (Pocock 1976).

26. In the first volume of his *Life and Labour of the People in London* (1889), Charles Booth described the whole of London in terms of a series of ecological maps, with what he called 'the areas of poverty' being presented in black and blue. In his discussion of these 'Maps of Poverty', he argued that 'local customs' and character, as well as specific features of the physical environment and factors like distance from the city centre, contributed to these areas, concentrated in the East End, having a 'peculiar' and distinctive quality (Walkowitz 1992: 32). The sheer diversity and idiosyncrasy of the accounts of urban poverty presented by Chadwick, Booth, Mayhew and other 'social missionaries' and 'urban explorers' in this period, according to Walkowitz, testifies to the insatiable popular demand 'for a comprehensive knowledge of the Other' (*ibid.*: 20).

27. One important criticism of Lynch's original work on mental maps, initially in Boston, and of many of the applications of it by human geographers elsewhere, is that it remains essentially descriptive in character and curiosity, unable to investigate the cultural and historical reasons for the idiosyncrasies of different maps and/or their relationshop to length and area of residence, the influences of social class and gender, or ethnic and subcultural difference in use of the city.

28. So, for example, we would not want to deny the influence in the construction of area difference and 'area reputation' of the policies of local housing departments in allocating so-called 'problem families' council houses only in particular areas. This is the primary focus of a widely quoted criminological study of Sheffield (Baldwin and Bottoms 1976), which has been the subject of some replication in the 1980s. The allocation of 'problem families' to individual estates or to individual areas within them in this way is seen to result in a self-fulfilling prophecy, as the reputation which these individual areas acquire renders then 'unlettable' to other council tenants. A process of amplification occurs *vis-à-vis* the area's reputation in the eyes of others, including Council workers, police and other visitors, and a spiral of despair sets in amongst the residents of these areas, which come to be seen as 'sink estates'. Baldwin and Bottoms are, in effect, describing a process which Michel Foucault would have recognised as the sequestration of each generation of 'problem families', not in total institutions so much as in pre-assigned public housing enclaves. The 'Sheffield study' has been very useful in describing these processes at work over some small areas of Sheffield's

stock of Council housing since 1979, but the authors would be the first to admit that they do not theorise the wider social processes which construct a household as 'a problem family' in the first instance (for example, in the North of England, the facts of ethnic difference, like Irishness), and they do not theorise the distribution of such problem families in relation to any larger explanation of the distribution of class, new imigrants, and other inequalities (for example, through some contemporary 'poverty map') across the city of Sheffield. In this sense, the Sheffield study attempts to discuss the epidemiology of crime in industrial Sheffield in the 1970s in isolation from any analysis of the nineteenth-century and twentieth-century economic geography of the City of Steel, as well as from what we would call its local 'cultural structure'. There is little sense, in the study, of the powerful local myths which assign particular 'moral qualities' – of friendliness (Hillsborough) or hardness (Firth Park, Pitsmoor) – to particular areas, and there is no sense in which the study (which is almost entirely focused on the allocation of the Council Housing Department in the 1970s and 1980s) could speak to a more broadly based account of changes and continuities in the epidemiology of crime of Sheffield over the whole period of industrial growth into the current period of crisis in the local labour market.

29. We should qualify this generalisation with the observation that many of these 'landscapes of fear' could provoke a level of anxiety as high when empty of people as when they were seen to be colonised by fearful Others. Frequently mentioned in this regard by our respondents were Manchester's rail and bus stations, whilst in Sheffield, almost inevitably, so were the 'Hole in the Road' and and the steps 'leading down to the Bus Station' from behind Josephine's night club on Arundel Gate. The fearfulness of empty spaces, or of spaces in which there is no obvious custodianship of safety, is by no means a simple issue in our two cities any more than it is elsewhere (cf. Stanko 1990). Women respondents in both our cities made particular frequent mention of their fear of the 'upper-deck' of double-decker buses, whether empty or occupied by only one Other, and also (especially in Greater Manchester) of empty, single-corridor, separate compartment carriages on local trains (cf. Taylor 1991a).

30. There is an attempt to outline a sociological explanation of this low level of expectation, as expressed in the toleration of litter, graffiti and other markers of urban dereliction, in North of England cities, in terms of a broader theory of the incomplete character of 'the bourgeois revolution' in England, in Taylor (1990).

31. In line with its origins, the word 'midden' is a commonly used Lancashire word for a rubbish tip or dump. In Yorkshire, the more common reference would be 'a tip' or 'a pit'.

32. In the late 1980s and early 1990s, residents of Greater Manchester would have had little option but to endure such levels of litter and dirt. The city of Manchester was identified by the *Daily Mail*, in the course of its own 'Tidy Up Britain' campaign, as one of 'the Dirty Dozen' most littered towns in Britain (*Daily Mail* 18 September 1989), and was accused of massive mismanagement of street-cleaning expenditure and practice. A similar set of criticisms emerged in a *Panorama* special, 'Sinking into Squalor', screened on BBC television early in 1990. The issue of letter – not as an expression of the level of (in)efficiency of local Councils but as a cultural index, a measure of the sense of shared collective and individual respon-sibility for public space, and therefore a measure of the 'stake' which citizens have in civil society as presently organised – was the topic of one of the present authors' Inaugural Lecture at the University of Salford in 1989 (cf. Taylor 1990).

33. It is quite clear that there was a very significant amount of 'avoidance' of the city centres in both our Northern cities, and that this avoidance had a highly patterned character. These strategies were the topic of particular 'focus groups'. In Chapter 8, for example, we will investigate how avoidance of city centres seems to be a particularly pronounced daily strategy of some black and Asian residents of Manchester and Sheffield alike, especially above adolescent age, as well as of women, Asian and otherwise.

34. This adaptation to places could take the form, as we indicated earlier in the chapter, of outright avoidance, but, as we are arguing here, this might not always be possible, given the unavoidability of using certain central urban thoroughfares. In this process of adaptation to these locales, quite subtle responses were evident. Doreen Dart and Pamela Reiss in Manchester both objected to the attempts being made by the local Council in 1993 to remove buskers and stalls from Market Street:

Doreen Dart: This thing about begging. You don't mind the buskers. That kind of people asking for money. They are doing it, but they are not actually confronting you – it's a voluntary situation. In fact, I quite like the idea of people doing whatever they want to do along Market Street. It gives it a bit of character.

Pamela Reiss: They had a petition going about the fact that there are people with stalls on Market Street. I don't think that's the kind of thing people are objecting to really. I don't mind if there's a chap selling pictures on a stall in Market Street. I think it adds to the atmosphere. The same with the buskers, with the music. So perhaps they are concentrating too much on what people don't object to – and not finding a way of cleaning up things that people do object to.

7 'OUT ON THE TOWN'

1. Claims have been made for Newcastle upon Tyne as a centre of gay life for the North-eastern region of England, but the 'scene' in this is mainly organised around a series of existing pubs. Cf. Lewis (1994).

2. As an aside, it should be added that the North American literature on gay urban enclaves (the new 'Gay Geography') is relatively inattentive to the situation of gay and lesbian peoples outside of these 'Meccas' – for example, in the 'Rust-Belt' old industrial cities like Detroit or Pittsburgh.

3. Hindle himself (1994) suggests one way of estimating the size of the gay population in an urban area, advancing the curious and unexplicated theorem that over 50,000 gay men over 20 years of age are required to support one male or mixed venue. Given that he identified 23 such venues in Manchester's Gay Village in 1993, this would have implied a gay population of over 1 million in the larger area in and around Greater Manchester.

4. James Anderton, a police officer of extremely fundamentalist views and notably homophobic sentiment, was appointed Chief Constable of Greater Manchester in 1976. Within two years, the Greater Manchester Police (GMP) were conducting regular raids on clubs in central Manchester thought to be used by homosexual people. One of these raids, on Napoleon's, and subsequent prosecutions (including one alleging 'licentious dancing') led to outcry, particularly amongst sections of the local student community. A period of very low-key policing followed, until 1984 when the newly elected left-wing Labour council in Manchester reinstated funding for the city's Gay Centre. The local press gave massive unfavourable coverage to this decision, proclaiming *inter alia* that the city was now the

'prisoner of gays'. A further raid on Napoleon's in November 1984 gave rise to further protest from 'the gay community'. Anderton resigned from office in June 1991, and the subsequent leadership of GMP was generally more conciliatory in its relationships with the organised gay community. In May 1993, GMP appointed its first police officer with responsibilities for gay and lesbian issues at the rank of Inspector, in part as a response to a few instances of 'queer-bashing' and robberies in the Village. The insistence of the newly appointed officer that his appointment was a matter of practical policing rather than 'a surrender to pink power' certainly did not help relationships, any more than did a raid on Rockies night club in the Gay Village in April 1994. One part of the police argument at this time, very similar to the arguments often marshalled by police spokespeople in respect of women's victimisation in public space (Stanko 1990), was that gay people should modify their behaviour in order to minimise risk – even in the restricted territory which gay people are wanting to claim is their own.

5. This process of 'liberalisation' was continuing in 1995. The Greater Manchester Police announced, in February 1995, that it was scrapping a computer database that could potentially have been used 'to monitor the gay and lesbian community' (*Guardian* 2 February 1995). This decision was taken in some quarters as further evidence of the improving links, developing over at least two years, between the police and the local 'gay community'.

6. It is interesting to see David subscribing here to the powerful local myth of the North of England mentioned earlier, namely, that everything of significance that happens in the city (like the emergence of clusters of ethnic restaurants) is *ipso facto* a result of City Council action, something decided by them, 'the Corporation'. There is actually every reason to think that the development of these areas, in their earliest form, occurred in many instances *against* the wishes of local councils.

8 WHITE CITY

1. For further discussion of the 'impossibilism' of local masculinism in Sheffield, and the translation of locally hegemonic forms of masculinity, in conditions of poverty, into what Connell (1995) has called 'protest masculinity', see Taylor and Jamieson (1996a)

2. The six sessions involved a group of six young black men, a group of retired West Indian people (in their own lunch club), and nine Asian women in Sheffield, and two groups of elderly Chinese people and seven Asian women in Manchester.

3. For detailed analysis of the experience of black women trying to find a place in the Sheffield labour market during the last decade, see Sheffield City Council, Department of Employment and Economic Development (1988), and for an account of the experience of Asian women in that city, see Sheffield City Council (1994). There is also a definitive account of black experience as a whole of the local Sheffield labour market in Fossu (1992), including some discussion of the various local training programmes (for example, S-PATC, the Sheffield Positive Action Training Consortium) and campaigns directed at local employers (for example, the local branches of major national banks) encouraging greater recruitment of staff from ethnic minority backgrounds. In Manchester, it may be one measure of the different local structure of opportunity that a significant amount of local authority effort has recently been put into the support of planning applications of people from ethnic minorities in the fast-moving local development process, through the ethnic monitoring of planning applications.

4. For a fascinating discussion of the angry refrains and commentaries which accompanied the transfer of Eric Cantona, the French international foot-

baller, from Leeds United to Manchester United in 1993, seen as an instance of the local feelings in Leeds about Manchester as the centre of excessive wealth, venality and sharp practice (by comparison with the less wealthy 'but honest' West Yorkshire centre of textiles and hard work), see King (1995).

5. For further discussion of the theme of guns and fashion style in Manchester and elsewhere in England in 1992–3, see Taylor (1993).

6. The most celebrated national example was Victor Headley's *Yardie* (Headley 1993): in 1995, a small Manchester publisher released a local version by one K. Smith, *Moss Side Massive* (Smith 1995).

7. *Criminal Statistics, England and Wales, 1993*: Tables 3.1, 3.4; US Department of Justice *Uniform Crime Reports 1993*.

8. The population of the Los Angeles and Long Beach conurbation was measured in 1992 at 9.2 million, with some 3.6 million in the city of Los Angeles itself.

9. Thomas de Quincey, who found notoriety for his *Confessions of an Opium Eater*, published in the *London Magazine* in 1821, was born at Greenheys, Moss Side, in 1785, and attended school in Salford and, briefly, in 1801, at Manchester Grammar. He left Manchester in 1802.

10. Kenyatta lived in Moss Side for some months during the last years of the Second World War, along with various African exiles. He returned to Kenya in 1944. Manchester itself hosted a meeting of the Pan-African Congress, attended by many locals but also by Clifford du Bois, Marcus Garvey, Kwame Nkrumah and many other famous names, in 1946 in Chorlton Town Hall.

11. Cheetham Hill is very much more heavily settled by an Asian population than Moss Side. In 1991, some 22.8 per cent of the local population of 14,100 was of Asian background, as against only 6.8 per cent 'black' and 6.1 per cent other non-whites. Greater Manchester Research *Census 1991: District and Ward Profile*.

12. James Kenney, reporter for *Chinese Times*, Manchester, personal communication 27 October 1994.

13. We were not able in this research to trace the development or impact of a powerful local myth about Chinatown in Manchester – the belief that it is home to a number of organised criminal gangs, or Triads. This theme has a continuing presence in local press reports in Manchester as well as being a preoccupation of the Greater Manchester Police, which has operated since 1993 a Dedicated Chinese Unit, liasing closely with Hong Kong police (*CJ Europe* 5(2) 1995: 2).

14. Politicians and 'concerned citizens' in the North of England have often been exercised by the absence of people from ethnic minorities from local countryside activity and related outdoor leisure pursuits. In 1992, for example, Sheffield City Council organised a conference in the Ponds Forge on 'Ethnic Minorities and the Environment', with a view to encouraging wider use of the city's 'Green Belt' and other opportunities, and *inter alia*, reported the results of a survey by the Countryside Commission in neighbouring Derbyshire, showing that the lowest frequency of visits to this country area was amongst residents of 'poor council estates' and 'multiracial areas'.

15. The wistful character of this activity, linking people of Asian backgrounds now 'in exile' to the international symbolic world beyond Britain through the exercise of imagination, is obvious. It is not an activity, however, that is so readily available to Asian peoples living at great distances from Manchester's international airport.

16. Research in London by Edwards and others on young Bengali men similarly showed that to be seen hanging around on the street 'could have serious consequences' if a young man's family was informed, perhaps even

affecting the level of standing of the family in the community or the young man's marriage possibilities (Edwards *et al.* 1987: 95).

17. In an article in the *Guardian* in August 1994 Sian Elisabeth Evans quoted a number of black disc-jockeys who claim they have been shown the door by Manchester's club owners (Evans 1994).

18. Similar problems clearly also exist for young black men in Manchester. The *Manchester Evening News* gave front-page coverage in 1994 to a survey released by Greater Manchester Police, in the interests of public account-ability, of their own policies with respect to 'stop and search'. The statistics released showed that in November–December 1993 black Mancunians were twice as likely to be stopped as whites (4,134 stops of blacks out of a total ethnic minority population of 152,500 as against 38,376 out of a white population of 2.4 million). Questioned about this survey, Ms Gabrielle Cox, secretary of the Moss Side and Hulme Community Forum, was quoted as saying that 'with the positive searches of young blacks being higher, then the police might say the search pattern is justified'. (*Manchester Evening News* 15 November 1994).

19. One of the different 'publics' we were not able to research to investigate directly was the adult Chinese population working in Chinatown or in Chinese restaurants across the Greater Manchester conurbation or in Sheffield. Anecdotal and other evidence confirms the importance in the daily round for Chinese men from Hong Kong, however, of gambling: Chinatown itself in Manchester is home to a small number of dedicated casinos.

20. This report also alleges that calls by Chinese take-away owners to local police for assistance were not taken very seriously, and that the response time to such calls was quite extended.

9 MEN'S TOWNS

1. For one detailed analysis of the circulation of rumour in a local neighbour-hood in south Manchester by one of the present authors, see Taylor (1995a).

2. We recognise that the distinction between the physical characteristics of an urban environment and its local cultural or symbolic definition should not be posed in too polarised or clear-cut a fashion: there is a close relationship between physical characteristics of places and their local cultural definition. In contrast to the architectural determinists who are so dominant, for example, in contemporary administrative criminology, we do want to insist that the relationship between physical and material reality and local cultural definitions is not straightforward. For example, one of the most troubled symbolic locations in Hale, south Manchester, is a quite well-maintained public park which, because unlit, in the winter evenings be-comes a dark space, evoking a variety of quite fascinating subliminal fears amongst the park's closest neighbours.

3. It is obviously not our position with respect to England that a male-dominated gender order is a feature only of the North. Many national institutions cited here, such as universities, seem to have a similar gender order across the country as a whole. There is a national political and sociological issue about the rigidity of the gender order in Britain. The question of regional difference is significant, however: it is only in the South of England, around London, that there is anything like an equivalent labour market for professional middle-class women (most noticeably in the media, advertising and related industries) to that which exists in many North American cities.

4. Male domination of the cotton trade in the North-west of England was a rather more contingent matter than male domination of the steel trades. Catherine Hall has traced the very active campaign waged by male cotton spinners to exclude women and children from the cotton factories, and, in particular, the attempt to define work on the mule in the cotton mill as male work, requiring the muscular power of 'experienced' men (Hall 1988). The struggle to maintain male hegemony in the cotton trade, however, was far less successful in the case of weaving, where the energy came to be provided by the power loom. The consequence was the development of a significant waged-labour market for women in the cotton districts, which over time became a matter of social convention, protected by local trade unionism (cf. Liddington 1979; Massey 1994).

5. The feminist geographer Doreen Massey recounts an early childhood memory of going to town from south Manchester on the top deck of a bus, and seeing the acres of football and rugby pitches (presumably, Hough End playing fields) stretching for miles 'like a vast animated Lowry painting'. 'I remember it striking me very clearly – even then, as a puzzled, slightly thoughtful little girl – that all this huge stretch of the Mersey flood plain had been entirely given over to men' (Massey 1994: 185).

6. We are aware of a host of methodological issues in this report of a gender difference in city use as measured by our street survey. For example, we are assuming that men and women are equally likely to stop in the street and answer a questionnaire. We should indicate that the majority of our interviewers were young women – a conscious decision on our part, intended to reduce the likelihood of women passers-by declining to stop and answer a questionnaire administered by a man. We also asked our interviewers to record all those who declined to answer in terms of their sex and any reason they gave for not wanting to stop. This strategy revealed that the numbers of men and women, of all ages, passing each spot roughly corresponded to the numbers and proportions responding to our survey. Thus, although our analysis of all those who declined to answer the questionnaire in the four city-centre sites in Sheffield shows that women were slightly more likely than men to do so, the fact remains that in three of these four city sites men nevertheless outnumbered women. In Manchester the findings were very similar, with women at five out of six sites declining to be interviewed more frequently than men. However, as with Sheffield, at five out of the six sites men still outnumbered women in total.

7. Women were twice as likely as men to mention fear or personal safety as the reason why they would avoid certain parts of the city; 28 per cent of all women respondents in Manchester gave this as the reason for avoidance, and 25 per cent in Sheffield.

8. The women invited to and attending these discussion groups, therefore, comprised mainly women 'of mature age', rather than adolescents or younger women, and they also tended to be women from middle-class or lower middle-class backgrounds, rather than from working-class or underclass backgrounds. This chapter should not be read, therefore, as an account of the practices of women in general in these two cities – although it could be argued that they may be representative of the practices that most women will feel they have to adopt when they attain adulthood or are defined as adult by others, in the absence of any change in the customary gender order or any major transformations in the policing, design, lighting or custodianship of public spaces 'in women's interest'.

9. Sharon Bedford, a Sheffield woman who confessed to going out only during the day, explained how she liked to walk some distance from her home to the city's Botanical Gardens, even on her own: 'It was always safe. There was always someone out tending the plants.'

10. We are aware, of course, that the definition of an activity as being for purposes of work or pleasure is a very crude instrument, which suppresses important gendered assumptions about the nature of 'real work'. For many of the women we interviewed, the routine practices of subsistence shopping were defined as a kind of leisure activity, in the sense that 'it gets you out of the house'.

11. It is difficult to avoid seeing some parallels between this statement and the comments made about Manchester by Engels, 150 years ago, on how the streets around the Cotton Exchange 'in all directions are lined . . . with an almost unbroken series of shops, and so are kept in the hands of the middle and lower bourgeoisie, which, out of self-interest, cares for a decent and cleanly external appearance . . . but [still] they suffice to conceal from the eyes of the wealthy men and women of strong stomachs and weak nerves the misery and grime which form the complement of their wealth' (Engels 1987: 86).

12. Fifteen thousand local Sheffield people applied for jobs in the Centre when the call for applications was announced in the run-up to Christmas in 1989: 2,000 were successful, but half of these lost their positions after the New Year. Meadowhall now employs fewer people from Sheffield than the various local Employment Services Outreach programmes of the Department of Employment. Most of the staff at the Meadowhall Centre are recruited and trained nationally by the chain stores that are tenants in the Centre (Rose Birks, personal communication 23 October 1992).

13. It is beyond the scope of this text to examine the prehistory of local community activism by women on 'sink estates', in the inner city or in other local urban neighbourhoods facing the consequences of de-industrialisation and the crisis of mass manufacturing. There are obvious parallels with the role played by women as 'Mothers of the Community' during the depression of the 1930s (cf. Davies 1992; Rice 1939; Roberts 1973) and also with the role played by women 'on the home front' during the Second World War. The recognition of this continuity does not specifically identify the kinds of aspiration that drive local women activists in defence of communities against market forces and the anger of uncontrolled 'protest masculinity' in the mid-1990s.

10 PENSIONED OFF

1. There is an important qualification to this generalisation. The population of the city area of Manchester (the City of Manchester) was reported in the 1991 Census to be slightly younger overall, with 17.2 per cent of its population defined as pensioners, compared to 18.5 per cent in 1981 (Manchester City Council, Planning Studies Group 1993: 2). We take it that this is a measure, in part, of the return of young professionals into city-centre apartments during the 1980s. All nine other boroughs of Greater Manchester, however, had a more elderly profile in 1991 than ten years before.

2. Current estimates, nationally, project that the number of people over 65 will rise from 9.1 million in 1989 (15.9 per cent of the total UK population) to 11.4 million (18.7 per cent) by 2025 (McHardy 1991).

3. For one account of the life of the elderly 'playing at youth' in retirement vacation homes and in other locales, especially in the United States, see Shurmer-Smith and Hannam (1994: Ch. 10).

4. Not the least of the important and sociologically interesting issues is the increasing recognition of elderly people in the North that the 'welfare net' they had assumed would be present, in the form of home helps, respite care and residential homes for the elderly, has been radically diminished in

scope, and that the provision of institutional care for the elderly has been one of the most rapidly growing private industries of the 1980s. The accelerating transfer of elderly care into the private sector (signalled further in the government's Community Care legislation of 1993) was a sub-theme in many of our discussions in Manchester and Sheffield, not least in terms of its impact on the network of local authority provision which had been widely assumed to be built into the infrastructure of the city.

5. This game was known in Salford, we were told, as 'putting on the knockers', since the string might on occasion be attached to door knockers, either causing passers-by to get entangled or, sometimes, causing several door knockers to knock simultaneously. In the Opies' famous study of children's games, this Salford devilment is known by another name of 'White Rabbit' (Opie and Opie 1969).

6. A similar reinvention of the past took place in England in the late 1970s, particularly around a notion of an Imperial England (cf. Hobsbawm and Ranger 1983) or the England of the Edwardian period. Granada Television screened Paul Scott's *The Jewel in the Crown*, an epic about the British empire in India, and also Evelyn Waugh's *Brideshead Revisited*, to mass audiences and mass acclaim; and the tradition was established of television dramas set firmly in the past, like the Conservative Government's recommended history curriculum for schools – before the 1960s.

7. What Lasch does not discuss is the changing role of nostalgic myths in the biography of individuals as they grew older, contemplating their past lives and perhaps the personal objectives or aspirations not achieved or the places not visited or seen. Graham Rowles's fascinating study of the 'geographical experience of older people' suggests that the 'construction of the realm of action' of older, infirm people is often accompanied by 'an expansion of the role of geographical fantasy', imagining what places that one would like to have visited but haven't are really like (Rowles 1978).

8. The nostalgic collective memory of the city's past is, however, not so marked amongst the elderly people we met from these Northern cities, black, Asian and Chinese populations (see Chapter 8).

9. For the same reason, we cannot claim that the material presented here, derived from 27 group discussions varying in size from some 5 to 10 people lasting an hour and a half each, are in any way equivalent to an exploration of individual biographies, which, like oral history, are enjoying new favour in sociological accounting for social behaviour (cf. Stanley 1992; special issue of *Sociology* 27(1) February 1993). Our discussion sessions can probably best be conceived as initial enquiries into certain sets of beliefs and memories that have some kind of public provenance in our two cities (and perhaps also, in some respects, like the recent demise of industrial work and its impact, across the North of England as a whole).

10. Historians of the collective memories of the organised working class have emphasised how these memories are usually organised in terms of heroic moments of struggle, particularly strikes (cf. Fentress and Wickham 1992 114–27; Portelli 1991). In industries whose recent history has not been punctuated by strikes, the memories and myths are far less distinct, and the importance of the time spent at work is perhaps less significant in local memories and/or nostalgia.

11. The exception to this generalisation might be the juxtaposition of certain key memories for some fans of particular football games, played out at certain grounds at particular stages of their architectural development or, for others, particularly memorable theatrical performances.

12. Portelli's concern is to try and make sense of the way that collective working-class memories in Terni, in the Lazio region of Italy, insist on locating the death of Luigi Trastulli, who died in a peace demonstration in

1949, at the centre of a series of violent struggles against loss of jobs in the local steelworks four years later, in 1953.

13. Sometimes, the groups are involved in collective discussion and in mutual assistance working out how to operate the ticketing machines. One of the areas of greatest problem for many elderly Northerners is dealing with the computerised technology, with no assistance from any public custodian.

14. The importance of such shopping routines to the elderly is well recognised by local social service departments in the North. Sheffield's Family and Community Service Department, for example, runs a Wheelchair Loan Service for the elderly from a location which is described in a locally distributed leaflet as being 'at the bottom of The Moor, opposite Thorntons'. Meadowhall has a similar provision, provided by the mall management itself.

15. In early 1994, there were some 330 such clubs in Sheffield, based in church and community rooms of various descriptions. Of these, 180 were described as 'lunch clubs' (charging a small fee for a midday meal), 107 as senior citizens' clubs, 22 as day centres and 21 in some other terms. Activities taking place at these centres included 'trips' (at 208 of the clubs), bingo (164), entertainment and speakers (95 mentions), as well as the provision of welfare and other advice. All but 16 of these centres were run by volunteers, but with continuing problems of attracting adequate numbers of such volunteer helpers (Sheffield City Council, Family and Community Services Department, 1994). There are currently some 40 such clubs for the elderly known to the Social Services Department of the City of Manchester. The departmental strategy in Manchester has been to concentrate provision for the elderly (home help, advice on pensions, mobility and medication, etc.) in a number of centrally located Resource Centres, with the primary objective of reducing numbers going into residential care (Roger Lightup, Public Relations Co-ordinator, Manchester Social Services Department, personal communication 24 February 1995).

16. This particular exchange very quickly took the form of a racialised description of place: so that, it was alleged, 'no white man [sic] can walk up there on his own'. (Cf. our discussion in Chapter 8.)

17. We have in mind here the host of studies of crime against the elderly that have taken as their starting point the famous essay on the 'invention' of a moral panic about crimes against the elderly by the press of New York City in 1976 (cf. Fishman 1978).

18. A senior social worker, in private communication, observed that the city of Manchester is 'long and thin', with very little information flowing from the north to south and south to north, and that the majority of the population spend most of their time in a number of 'little villages' (in the south, Chorlton and Stretford, and, to the north, in very deprived areas like Beswick and Bradford) (Roger Lightup, Public Relations Co-ordinator, City of Manchester Social Services Department, personal communication 24 February 1995). This containment of people within areas intensifies with the more elderly.

19. The process of social reproduction of the working-class neighbourhood and 'community' has also been the subject of an extensive, rather less critical literature by social scientific and other writers, most notably by Richard Hoggart (1957), Brian Jackson (1968) and, in a recent rewrite of the history of working-class fatherhood, Norman Dennis and George Erdos (1992).

11 THE URBAN OTHER

1. It is not surprising, perhaps, that this guarded sympathy with the young (largely white) men was not as widely expressed by adults from the different ethnic groups of Manchester. The Chinese elderly living in Chinatown in Manchester were particularly forthright in their dislike of the behaviours and demeanour of young men in groups.

2. In a recent analysis of nineteenth-century fears, Kumar also notes that the neat taxonomies of the poor developed by Mayhew and others broke down later, in periods of mass poverty, when the rhetorics attributing particular personal characteristics to the 'disorganised poor' came to be applied to working people in general (Kumar 1995). There is a sense in which any such formal taxonomies of poverty, differentiating between different categories of the poor, collapse when the precipitating circumstances take on a life of their own: the taxonomies are then replaced by a more generalised awareness in the minds of others of a 'dangerous class' – in this instance, of city-centre 'street people', both young and old.

3. On the idea of reading a city as a text, see Donald (1992).

4. We are aware that many recent forms of youth cultural behaviour ('raves', 'joy riding' and computer hacking) can be, and are, interpreted as forms of 'post-modern excess' and also of resistance, after Michel Foucault, to the Disciplinary Society (Stanley 1995). This approach carries insight but seems to us to over-emphasise, like many earlier forms of subcultural writing about young people, 'spectacular' aspects of youthful behaviour to the exclusion of more mundane continuities (for example, the routine reproduction of masculinist forms of identification amongst young English men), and also proceeds without regard to the social implications of any such show of resistance to legitimation (for example, in car theft and joy riding) or, for that matter, to the specifically local forms of neighbourhood reaction and response to youthful excess. The negative responses of local communities in Manchester and Sheffield, both on council estates and in the suburbs, to joy riding and similar forms of youthful excess by angry, undisciplined young men was unambiguous (Taylor 1995a, Taylor and Jamieson 1996b).

5. According to research at the Policy Studies Institute, four times as many children were driven to school in 1990 as in 1971, and only half of all 10- and 11-year-olds went to school alone in 1990, compared to 95 per cent in 1971 (Hillman et al. 1990).

6. In all this discussion of the culture of different cities as a source of fear for young children, we should not ignore the fact of children's actual experience of harassment and aggravation in cities, from older children and from adults, which may be more prevalent than conventional discussion wants to admit.

7. Chris Stanley actually argues that the attempted exercise of discipline over young people, in a post-modern age of computers and multimedia, has lost its specific relation to territoriality or place (Stanley 1995). This may be true for those, essentially, middle-class young adults who are equipped with the specific technology.

8. Dr Andrew Davies, personal communication 4 March 1995.

9. Given the frequency of such outbreaks of trouble in pubs in the long period of Fordism, it is surprising how infrequently they were subject to serious analysis. There are descriptions of incidents in the mid-sixties in Huddersfield in Jackson (1968) and in the 1920s in Manchester and Salford in Davies (1992). One of the most interesting analytical investigations of the relationship between public houses, young people, crime, local myths and fear, however, is a study of the down-town bars in St John's, Newfoundland

(Rapport 1987). There is nothing entirely new here: the Royal Commission on the Poor Laws of 1909 identified the most dangerous occupation in England and Wales as being that of publican (Ruth Jamieson, personal communication).

10. Manchester may have been at the forefront of youthful imaginations in the North of England, but there is evidence that other cities in Britain were more dynamic in their response to the changed circumstances of the 1980s. Lovatt quotes data from an unnamed Bristol consultancy which suggest that whilst Manchester's 'entertainment economy' grew by 3.7 per cent between 1979 and 1989, Glasgow's grew some 12 per cent in the five years to 1995. In the meantime, London's, 'entertainment economy', grew a full 20 per cent between 1979 and 1989 (Lovatt: 1995a 4). Given the absence of any definitions or sources in this paper, we have to treat the observations with some care. But there is no doubt that there has been great unevenness in the response of different cities across the North and South of England, and in Scotland, to the crisis of local manufacturing economies.

11. The bulk of this chapter will focus on the 'youth scene' and culture industry in Manchester, although our analysis of the recursive use of urban space by young people will draw on our discussions in both cities. Manchester is a particularly important focus for this chapter, because of the commercial and social significance of the recent transformations for the city itself (a central element in Manchester's bid to become a 'headquarter city'). They are also important for Manchester's standing *vis-à-vis* young people elsewhere within the North of England, as a mecca for music and youth cultural consumption generally. One other theme in our discussions in Sheffield, however, suggested that Manchester was now seen as the centre for distribution of hard drugs for large areas of the North of England, as well as for other activities involving organised, professional crime. The youth scene in Sheffield was seen by young people in that city as relatively restricted and very predictable. Students, teachers and social workers would be the patrons of The Leadmill, a large music and social club first opened in an old works building with the support of the City Council in the days of the 'Socialist Republic', and they would also be the main patrons of the adjoining 'Cultural Industries Quarter' (built around the Red Tape Studios, a subsidised recording studio). Young people from other backgrounds would gravitate to one of eight other clubs in the city centre, though there was very general agreement in our discussions that one of these clubs, Roxy's, was primarily the resort of 'the lads' and their girlfriends. According to Sean Temple, an engineer living in the south-west suburbs, Roxy's, was 'a cattle market ... for psychos [with] giros in their backpocket'. Isobelles and Josephines, by contrast, were seen by Jim Mellor, an ex-student from Stannington outside Sheffield, as a 'bit more upper class: you get Sheffield Wednesday footballers in there'. There was some recognition in our group discussions that this night-club scene was quite small, that the reputations attaching to particular clubs were very much a product of local experience and folklore, and that some of the distinctions made between clubs were based on local custom, developed over the years, rather than national or international music-cultural trends. This recognition of 'local difference' (Sheffield as a village within the larger youth cultural scene, 'keeping itself to itself') was deplored by some and celebrated by others, with only a few challenging voices, making reference to the city as the home of Joe Cocker or the Human League. We have not done the work that would sustain any such generalisation, but we suspect that Sheffield has more in common at this level as a youth cultural centre with cities like Bradford and Hull than it does with Leeds and Newcastle, where rather more elaborate night-time economies developed during the 1980s.

12. Champion's 'periodisation' of the Manchester scene locates it as arising from the Sex Pistols' concert in the Free Trade Hall in 1976, and identifies an interim climax as being the Festival of the Tenth Summer in 1986 (Champion 1990: 15). Talk of an end to the Manchester scene was hotly contested by young Mancunians in the early 1990s, in celebrations of a new fusion between the city's music scene and successful, European football, particularly at the time of Manchester United's victory in the European Cup Winners Cup in May 1991 (Redhead 1991) and, later, in the emergence of important new bands like Oasis.

13. In 1990, the number of licensed premises in central Manchester reached 220 – the highest since the 1960s. A further dozen purpose-built night-club venues have opened between 1990 and 1995, adding a capacity of 7,200 and bringing total night-club capacity in the city centre to 25,000. Over the same period, 28 new 'designer bars' have been opened by independent entrepreneurs (Lovatt 1995a).

14. In February 1995, for example, in one of several such stories run by the *Manchester Evening News*, the continuing growth of the local music industry was seen as creating 'a job bonanza' for young people. A consultant at the city-centre Manchester Business Consortium was quoted as saying that '87 per cent of new music-related businesses on his book were making a success of it' – a much higher success rate than for other new businesses (Taylor 1995). As in so many such reports, no figures are given for the numbers of 'new jobs' being created or, of course, their sustainability as full-time permanent positions.

15. The wine bars are the resort of the slightly older professional middle class, catering to a population aged 25 or 30 and above. With some exceptions, they are not patronised by adolescents.

16. 1991 Census: County Report: Greater Manchester, Table F.

17. 1991 Census: County Report, Greater Manchester, Table 8 Economic Position (p. 106).

18. Cf. the discussion in Brooks, Walklate and Taylor (1994).

19. The incidence of burglaries in South Yorkshire as a whole was 3,219 per 100,000.

20. We are also aware of the recent calls, originating in the United States but now finding favour in the United Kingdom, for 'legalisation' of drugs as the only conceivable next move. Our own work does not warrant entry into this debate, but we would commend our readers to the work, in this area, of the fine American criminologist Elliot Currie (1993).

21. For an ethnographic description of rave culture in the North-east of England and its association with Ecstasy, see Merchant and Macdonald (1994).

22. One of the most important aspects of the fears brought to the drugs/clubs connection in Manchester is the unfamiliarity of this kind of pleasure and its regulation, compared to the 'liminality' of pub life and drinking . As Bernice Martin (1981) demonstrated, many working-class wives in the North of England have been familiar, for years, with strategies for the regulation of 'drink' (and various other forbidden pleasures such as 'gambling', flirting, etc.). What would not be understood within these communities are the very different drugs circulating amongst young people in Manchester, and their function. In working-class areas, in particular, we suspect there would be a tendency for all drug use to be apprehended as being on a par with that of heroin or cocaine. The fact of Ecstasy and amphetamine use in clubs – and particularly its universal presence in house music clubs, as a support for long hours of dancing – would not be understood. Nor would the fact that this kind of drug use, whatever its dangers to personal health, is not (unlike alcohol) associated with trouble or violence.

23. The Lifeline agency in Manchester estimates that some 100,000 'E' tablets are consumed every week in the North-western region (at an average cost of £15 per tablet) (Lovatt 1995a).

24. For further discussion of this *Up Front* programme on 12 April 1991, see Taylor (1991c).

25. Two further heavily publicised shootings followed the Benji Stanley killing, one involving the use of a machine gun in the Sports pub in June 1993 in nearby Whalley Range, seriously wounding three people, and the other, in January 1994, resulting in the death of 20-year-old Julian Stewart. The Sports was described in the local press as the 'headquarters' of the 'Gooch Close gang' (*Manchester Evening News* 26 June 1993) whilst Julian Stewart was believed by police to be a member of the rival Doddington gang (*Guardian* 14 January 1994). These 'gangs' are discussed in the main body of our chapter.

26. 'Hell is a City: Behind the Drugs War in Moss Side' *Manchester Evening News* 29 April 1991.

27. These 'fashion accessories' were on sale at one particular shop in Afflecks Palace, patronised primarily by young poor white and Afro-Caribbean men.

28. The total number of homicides in Greater Manchester reported to the police in 1993 was 34, six down on 1992. Firearms were reported in 1049 case, a significant increase on 1992 (799), 1991 (619) and 1990 (502) (Greater Manchester Police: 1993: 12).

29. It is not our argument that heavy drinking is prevalent only in the North of England: the Home Counties have recently been the site of many expressions of concern in respect of 'lager louts' and also inebriated 'Hooray Henries'. But we do want to recognise the close historical connection between the industrial working-class life of men, especially in heavy manufacturing work, and consumption of beer (cf. also Taylor and Jamieson 1996a). The constant repositioning of beer and lager consumption in different regions of the country in the aftermath of de-industrialisation would be a separate area of study.

30. Andy Lovatt, currently actively engaged in researching Manchester's 'night-time economy' reports that every single night club in the centre is 'paying protection' (Lovatt 1995a).

31. Violence in pubs has become a topic of national concern in recent years, and the focus of several initiatives by the industry itself. Many of these new initiatives for the management of such violence are discussed in Marsh (1990). In Greater Manchester as a whole, in the early 1990s, many pubs, especially on the fringe of poor council estates, have taken an added reputation as centres for protection rackets, drugs and other illegal trades, and for the intimidation of any person wanting to speak to the police.

32. The move towards 'a 24-hour city' (at least conceptually) is, in part, the result of an article in *City Life* magazine in October 1992 by Steve Redhead and Andy Lovatt of Manchester Metropolitan University, where the authors argue that Manchester's 'reconstruction' as 'a European city' and also its bid to hold the Olympics required an expansion of night-time leisure provision in the city – including the introduction of sidewalk or pavement cafés on 'the continental model' and a challenge to existing licensing laws. In May 1993, Manchester City Council proposed revisions in local liquor licensing provisions, through the increased use of 'special exemptions' under the Licensing Act of 1964, allowing clubs to stay open until 4 a.m. These measures were put into effect in the summer months of August and September, during the recently established summer festival

sponsored by Boddington's brewery in part as an experimental measure with a view to the Olympics. The research and development branch of Greater Manchester Police later reported favourably on this experiment in an internal evaluation, concluding that the modification of licensing hours in the city centre had resulted in very few problems (Greater Manchester Police: Review of Licensing Hours, City Centre, September 1993).

33. In Salford, Greater Manchester, local crime-prevention workers have recognised the importance of this local industrial discourse as translated into local youth cultural argot: the campaign against bike theft, for example, goes under the name of 'Crucial Crew'. We ourselves noticed that 'the crews' operated after the fashion of work groups in the old steel works, with older and more experienced grafters inducting younger apprentices into 'the secrets of the trade'.

34. The use of Meadowhall in Sheffield (and of the Arndale Centre in Manchester) by disenfranchised, poor young people should be the subject of a separate and dedicated study. Meadowhall is 'policed' by a token two South Yorkshire Police constables, and some 75 security staff (50 on the ground), employed by the mall management with a particular view to excluding, we were told, any group of young people above four in number. We were given the impression that this policy is fairly gender-specific, and also that the wearing of football shirts was seen as an important signifier of suspicious intent. The shops and corridors of the mall and its outside car parks are constantly and very prominently under the surveillance of sophisticated, high-resolution CCTV and video cameras, and the management claims that this has all had a beneficial effect on levels of theft of cars and shoplifting at Meadowhall. Nonetheless, there were references in our interviews with Meadowhall security staff to 'problems with ethnic minority gangs', 'lads from the Manor' and also some 'locals from Attercliffe' (interview with John Weston, head of Security, Meadowhall, 15 July 1992). We were not able to follow up these last intriguing references, but there is no question that the mall, as what some commentators have called 'a temple of consumption', exercises an enormous fascination for the young men (and women) cut adrift from work and regular income. In the Arndale Centre, Manchester, there is a significant presence of uniformed police (10 in total in 1992, with a small police station underground in the main mall) as well as a significant security force (28 in 1992) and an older CCTV system. The reports we were given in 1992 by representatives of the Arndale insisted that problems with young people (for example, 'football gangs') were 'a thing of the past'. The main purpose of the Anti-Theft Group nowadays was to train new staff in the Arndale's shops in techniques of observation and awareness in respect of opportunistic shoplifters. About 75 arrests had been made in May 1992, compared to 123 in December 1991 (Bill Lowe, Arndale Anti-Theft Group, 2 June 1992). The research issue in the case of the Arndale was the sequestration of the Centre shops from the adjoining Market Street, in many ways the most problematic street in Manchester.

35. With all respect to the residents of Bents Green, we do need to point out that this is very much a mixed, predominantly lower middle-class, area, rather than a seriously rich Sheffield suburb. However, as criminological students of 'the journey to crime' would appreciate, it is easily accessible by bus from Sheffield city centre. It is also important to realise that from the perspectives of these young men, living in places like The Manor estate, *most other* areas of the city looked to be relatively affluent. Steff informed us that his latest offence, a particularly negativistic act of vandalism on a private house, had been on the Mosborough Estate, south-east of the city, which he thought to be 'a right posh area'. The bulk of the residents

of this modern estate are actually first-time buyers in the middle of the housing market.

36. This is the world which has been described most brilliantly of all, for the North of England, by the playwright Jim Cartwright in *Road* (Cartwright 1986).

37. This anguished disavowal of the presence of these 'Others' in their city, some of them '[calling] us white trash', invites further discussion, not least in terms of the pressing issue of gender and ethnic identity. We have argued throughout this book that both these Northern cities, but Sheffield in particular, have been dominated culturally for many years (ostensibly, for over 150 years) by a particular masculinist identity, valorising the particular kinds of skill (craft) and graft demanded by the developing local industries. In the aftermath of the demise of these industries, however, these masculinist class identities have to compete at least in the world of television and billboard advertising with a set of other images of masculinity – for example, of black English athletes and footballers (Nike running and football shoes) or of young men as sex objects (Calvin Klein jeans, 'Too Good to be True' ice cream, Chippendale male strippers on Heineken lager adverts – and also with other images of everyday consumption and everyday life, which further unsettle the idea of fixed, hegemonic, industrial, working-class masculinity in any old industrial locality.

38. The problem of recognition may be less of an issue for young shoplifters in Manchester, but the level of CCTV surveillance in Manchester city is quite well known throughout the city (with highly visible cameras on walls) and the Arndale Centre is very visibly policed by private security guards.

12 CONTESTED VISIONS OF THE CITY

1. We will pay particular attention here to the focus groups we held with 'professional workers' in Manchester and Sheffield.

2. Interviews were held in Manchester with representatives of the Central Manchester Development Corporation, P and O Shipping (the Arndale Centre), and various different department of the City Council; and in Sheffield with representatives of the Sheffield Development Corporation, the Chamber of Commerce, and the Director of Planning in the City Council.

3. To emphasise the continuing and widespread presence of residualised housing areas in Manchester is not to ignore the success of local partnerships in Manchester itself (or neighbouring boroughs) in 'rescuing' particular areas of the city, particularly Hulme in Manchester, via a substantial City Challenge award, from an apparently relentless process of 'sinking'. But it is to recognise the number and geographical spread of the housing areas occupied by a residualised, deindustrialised underclass in Greater Manchester.

4. There was a glimpse of the other side of this demonised Sheffield estate, as the site of a strong local popular community, in April and May 1995, when local residents and schoolteachers responded with speed and commitment to an arson attack on Waltheof School (one of the main, shared public facilities of the estate) that caused £3-million worth of damage (*Guardian* 1 April 1995). The 950-pupil school was fully operative in temporary accommodation within two weeks, as a result of local voluntary effort.

5. For the initial vision of a planned regeneration of bombed-out Sheffield, and the importance of new provision for housing, the zoning of the city centre, and the protection of the city's Green Belt – framed specifically in

the interest of 'children and future generations' – see Sheffield Town Planning Committee (1945).

6. There are currently very few initiatives being launched in cities like Manchester and Sheffield to rescue such areas. The few schemes which do exist are low on the national political agenda, and sometimes on local agendas as well (depending on the ebb and flow of local politics), and also that 'the rescue' of inner-city areas and outer estates must now be thought of by reference to 'multi-agency partnerships' between 'the state' (the local Council) and business with an actual or potential interest in a local area.

7. We are associating ourselves here with the kind of critique of 'cultural populism', the straightforwardly and appreciative approach to popular culture, advanced by Jim McGuigan (1992).

8. We frame the argument in this way to underline the fact that even the cultural professionals do not actually live (eat, sleep, and construct their daily lives) in the imaginary world of texts and images which is their cultural capital. Like all social groups at any point in history, they have a need for shelter and they also want to establish their home as a centre of some kind of life project. They are in that sense participants, like everyone else, in what Rex and Moore once insisted we should think of as 'the class struggle for housing' (Rex and Moore 1967).

9. Wynne and O'Connor's informed estimate was that there were some 10,000 people employed in the arts and cultural industries in Manchester in 1989 – by no means an insignificant local labour market, and, indeed, a significant proportion of the total number of people in employment in the city centre itself (O'Connor and Wynne 1993).

10. Wynne's and O'Connor's surveys of the 'cultural intermediary' exhibit residents of the gentrified apartments in city-centre Manchester actually identify significantly more diversity of life-strategy and cultural interest than popular stereotypes (of the 'yuppie' or the 'dink' – 'double-income no kids' – household) might suggest (Wynne and O'Connor 1995).

11. Fears about being victimised by burglary in Manchester city centre will almost certainly be influenced by the recognition that the city centre is surrounded on all sides by a ring of inner-city areas and council estates which are well established in the popular imagination as home to 'hundreds of young criminals'. The proximity of these areas also implies that the so-called 'journey to crime' will be quick and easy for many such marauding villains, especially since the arrival of the Metrolink. The evidence supporting these fears is thin: there is a great deal of evidence, as we suggest in Chapter 11, that young men engaged in crime on a regular and routine basis are rather reluctant to venture 'into town', preferring to work in areas where they can avoid police and private security.

12. Given the limited architectural merits and low level of physical amenities in these estates, the approval given them by some Mancunians and Shef-fielders would probably surprise technicians of 'residential or locational satisfaction' studied or those involved in the construction of 'quality of life' indices (see Chapter 1). But this is a comment on the inability of these students of 'well-being' to understand the *social dynamics* underlying the development of human community – especially the real compensations that can sometimes accompany the experience of contradictory subordi-nate cultures, even with their class and ethnic inequalities, in heavily divided societies.

13. The exception of Ollerenshaw's complaint was the non-commercial middle class, working in education and the local television and newspaper industry, whose preferred area of residence over the years was Didsbury, half-way between the centre of the city and the southern edge of the conurbation.

14. The Richmond area, in Sheffield's south-east, is an old village (actually

located in Derbyshire), around which was built, in the 1960s, a small overspill council estate. It is now located in Sheffield's postal district no. 13. We have not had the space in this volume to do an analysis of the local knowledge about postal district of phone numbers, but there is no question that this is a vital bit of local knowledge (especially in terms of area reputation) in larger North of England cities.

15. The separation of the English suburb from the troubled council estates and terraced houses of the old working class was not, however, as complete, we would argue, as the separation that has been effected in North America. In the crowded, condensed contribution of Greater Manchester, a defining feature of many suburbs is their proximity (within their particular zone of development) to areas known locally to suffer pronounced social problems connected with poverty, 'disorganisation' and crime (for example the proximity of suburban Prestwich to troubled Higher Broughton or the inner suburbs of Chorlton, Withington and Didsbury to Moss Side and Hulme). This spatial and geographical proximity of very differently advantaged areas, with a very different 'quality of life', situated cheek-by-jowl with each other, separated by a single thoroughfare, that suggests a parallel between the Los Angeles described by Mike Davis and the Greater Manchester conurbation as a whole, as first understood both by Engels and Leon Faucher (Taylor 1991b, 1991c).

16. It is impossible to escape the continuing nostalgia for the idea of 'the English village' as the very definition of 'community' and sociability.

17. These are precisely the issues which are built into the *Sim City 2000* CD-Rom computer game, released in 1994 by the Maxis Corporation, and no doubt played in many cultural intermediary and high-technology households in the North of England as well as in California.

18. One employment forecast by Sheffield City Council's Department of Employment and Economic Development in August 1994 extrapolated from data on change occurring in the local labour market between 1991 and 1994 to predict an increase, by the year 2002, of 29 per cent in the number of 'corporate administrators', 24.9 per cent in science and engineering professionals, 22.8 per cent in science-associated professionals, and 21.1 per cent in 'protective service professionals'. Some time before the creation of trusts in the Health Service, it predicted a 6.8 per cent growth in the number of health professionals and 35.9 per cent in health-related professions. This would be one of the projections being revised downwards in early 1995.

19. It does not always follow, of course, that the local 'rescue squads' are actually able to carry out the task conventionally given to the politicians by victory in local government elections, and devolved to these local partnerships by national government. A considerable amount of effort and energy is fed into struggles over jurisdiction ('turf wars') between national government and local partnerships over areas of cities or, indeed, whole cities for which neither wants full responsibility. In 1994, Manchester City Council tried unsuccessfully to encourage the Department of the Environment and the Home Office to assume new responsibilities for Moss Side, and in April 1995, the Sheffield City Council Chief Executive Pamela Gordon indicated to the local press that she would be writing to Environment Minister John Gummer to emphasise that the city would be in deep crisis if the government did not allow the Council to spend an extra £4.5 million above its capped limits (*Sheffield Telegraph* 28 April 1995). An interesting area of research for political science students is the role played in this turf warfare by the MPs who have been nominated by this government as 'ministers', outside the Cabinet, with responsibility for Manchester (Alistair Burt) and Sheffield (Ann Widdicombe).

20. We are not arguing here that a local growth coalition in a headquarter city

ever claims that such economic benefits will be equally spread or even universally accessible. At most, the rhetorics of the local growth coalition usually speak of such growth as creating a sense of economic opportunity in the locality – a kind of local version of the 'trickle-down theory' popularised at national level during the turn to the free market in the early 1980s. This may be a limited 'version', but it may still be a more optimistic scenario than those currently available in 'module production' cities.

21. For one attempt to examine this circulation of very local and fearful knowledge about crime in one south Manchester suburb, carried out by one of the authors of this study simultaneously with the large project, see Taylor (1995a).

22. For further elaboration of the connection between this 'fear of falling', the condition of the post-imperial, post-Thatcherite English middle class and crime fears in the late 1990s, see Taylor and Jamieson (1996b).

23. We do not enter here into the debate as to what percentage of this reduction in recorded crime might be a function of the widespread reported increases in the level of witness intimidation.

24. One of many leaflets released by Manchester Airport putting the case for this new runway claims that the existing level of increased use of the existing airport (13 million passengers a year compared to 4 million in 1983) is putting a strain on existing capacities. But the leaflet also specifically articulates the case for the new runway in terms of job creation, suggesting that some 50,000 new jobs could be created by this development. The argument is also, however, a specifically competitive one, directed against the claims of other cities, since local growth coalitions operate in a competitive market – in this instance, specifically, the claims being made for transfer of business to Liverpool Airport, less than 40 miles away. The leaflet therefore proclaims that 'Manchester is the only viable *international* airport in North West England.' (The concerns of local environmental groups over pollution, congestion and further demolition of local housing, as already scheduled for the village of Mobberley, are countered by the argument that a comprehensive Environmental Impact Assessment has accompanied the formal planning application, submitted to Manchester City Council, Macclesfield Borough Council and the Secretary of State.) The struggle for and against the second runway in Manchester in the mid-1990s is a fascinating case study in growth coalition politics, since the commercial arguments so directly conflict with the other interests of many of the suburban middle class who live in the vicinity of the airport, and whose 'quality of life' (not to say house values) would be directly affected by the opening of a second runway.

BIBLIOGRAPHY

Adburgham, Alison (1964) *Shops and Shopping 1800–1914: Where and in What Manner the Well-dressed Englishwoman Bought Her Clothes* London: George Allen and Unwin.

Adler, Sy and Brenner, Johanna (1992) 'Gender and Space: Lesbians and Gay Men in the City' *International Journal of Urban and Regional Research* 16 pp. 24–34.

Aitchison, Cathy (1994) 'Short-term Funds Go Down the Tube' *Independent on Sunday* 9 January.

Anderson, Simon, Kinsey, Richard, Loader, Ian and Smith, Connie (1994) *Cautionary Tales: Young People, Crime and Policing in Edinburgh* Aldershot: Avebury.

Atkins, Philip (1987) *Guide across Manchester* Swinton: North West Civic Trust (first published 1976; revised edition by Philip Atkins and Paul Daniels).

Bachelard, Gaston (1964) *Poetics of Space* New York and Boston: Beacon (reprinted 1969).

Bagguley, P., Mark-Lawson, J., Shapiro, D., Urry, J., Walby, S. and Warde, A. (1990) *Restructuring: Place, Class and Gender* London: Sage.

Baldwin, John and Bottoms, A.E. (1976) *The Urban Criminal* London: Tavistock.

Barker, Pat (1982) *Union Street* London: Virago.

Barth, G. (1980) *City People* Oxford: Oxford University Press.

Bartlett, J.E. and Preston, F.L. (1956) 'Pre-History: Iron Age and Roman Period' in David L. Linton (ed) *Sheffield and its Region: A Scientific and Historical Survey* Sheffield: Local Executive Committee of the British Association.

Bauman, Zygmunt (1992) *Intimations of Postmodernity* London: Routledge.

Bauman, Zygmunt (1993) *Post-modern Ethics* Oxford: Blackwell.

Baumgartner, M.P. (1988) *The Moral Order of a Suburb* New York: Oxford University Press.

Bean, J.P. (1981) *The Sheffield Gang Wars* Sheffield: D. and D. Publications.

Bean, J.P. (1987) *Crime in Sheffield* Sheffield: Sheffield City Libraries.

Beattie, Geoffrey (1986) *Survivors of Steel City: A Portrait of Sheffield* London: Chatto and Windus.

Beauregard, Robert A. (1993) *Voices of Decline: The Post-war Fate of US Cities* Oxford and Cambridge, MA: Blackwell.

Beck, Ulrich, Giddens, Anthony and Lash, Scott (1994) *Reflexive Modernization* Cambridge: Polity Press.

Bee, Malcolm (1984) *Industrial Revolution and Social Reform in the Manchester Region* Manchester: Neil Richardson.

Begg, I. and Moore, B. (1987) 'The Changing Economic Role of Britain's Cities' in Victor A. Hausner (ed) *Critical Issues in Urban Economic Development, Vol. II* Oxford: Clarendon Press.

Bell, David J. (1991) 'Insignificant Others: Lesbian and Gay Geographies' *Area* 23 pp. 332–9.

Bellos, Alex (1993) 'The Best Place to Live in Britain' *Sunday Telegraph* 15 August.

Benfield, Chris (1991) 'Moss Side: Living with a Reputation' *Yorkshire Post* 9 May.

Benhabib, Seyla (1992) *Situating the Self* Cambridge: Polity Press.

Bennett, Tony (1986) 'Hegemony, Ideology, Pleasure: Blackpool' in T. Bennett, C. Mercer and J. Woollacott (eds) *Popular Culture and Social Relations* Milton Keynes and Philadelphia: Open University Press.

Betjeman, John (1961) 'Men and Buildings: The Best and Worst of an Era' *Daily Telegraph and Morning Post*, 3 July (reprinted in Pybus, 1994)

Beynon, Huw, Hudson, Ray and Sadler, David (1994) *A Place called Teesside* Edinburgh: University of Edinburgh Press.

Bianchini, Franco, Fisher, Mark, Montgomery, John and Worpole, Ken (1988) *City Centres, City Cultures* Manchester: Centre for Local Economic Strategies.

Binfield, Clyde, Hey, David, Childs, Richard, Martin, David, Harper, Roger and Tweedale, Geoffrey (1993) *The History of the City of Sheffield 1843–1993* Sheffield: Sheffield Academic Press (three vols).

Blunkett, D. and Green G. (1983) *Building from the Bottom: The Sheffield Experience* Fabian Tract 481, London: Fabian Society.

Boddy, John (1993) *Improving the Quality of Service to Customers: Survey of Feelings, Views and Opinions of Personnel in a Bus Company* Report to the Greater Manchester Passenger Transport Executive.

Bourdieu, Pierre (1977) *Outline of a Theory of Practice* Cambridge: Cambridge University Press.

Bowlby, R. (1985) *Just Looking: Consumer Culture in Dreiser, Gissing and Zola* New York: Methuen.

Bowlby, S. (1984) Editorial *Built Environment* 10(1) pp. 5–7.

Bridges, M.J. and Lodwick, S.J. (1980) 'Changes in Shopping' in H.P. White (ed) *The Continuing Conurbation: Change and Development in Greater Manchester* Farnborough: Gower.

Briggs, Asa (1959) *The Age of Improvement 1783–1867* London: Longman (new revised edition 1979).

Briggs, Asa (1963) *Victorian Cities* London: Odhams (reprinted Penguin, 1968, 1990).

Brindle, David (1994) 'Ethnic Map Shows Racial Isolation' *Guardian* 14 December.

Bristow, Joseph (1989) 'Homophobia/Misogyny: Sexual Fears, Sexual Definitions' in Simon Shepherd and Mick Wallis (eds) *Coming on Strong: Gay Politics and Culture* London: Unwin Hyman.

Bronski, M. (1984) *Culture Clash: The Making of Gay Sensibility* Boston MA: South End Press.

Brooks, Kate, Walklate, Sandra and Taylor, Ian (1994) *Salford Wine Audit 1994*, obtainable on request from the City of Salford, Chief Executive's Department.

Brooks-Gardner, Carol (1989) 'Analysing Gender in Public Places: Rethinking Goffman's Vision of Everyday Life' *The American Sociologist* 20(1) pp. 42–56.

Brooks-Gardner, Carol (1990) 'Safe Conduct: Women, Crime and Self in Public Places' *Social Problems* 37(3) pp. 311–28.

Brown, Ivor (ed) (1955–6) *The Bedside Guardian 5: A Selection from the Manchester Guardian 1955–6* London: Collins.

Buck, Trevor W. (1979) 'Regional Class Differences: An International Study of Capitalism' *International Journal of Urban and Regional Research* 3 pp. 516–25.

Burgess, J. Limb, M. and Harrison C.M. (1988) 'Exploring Environmental Theory through the Medium of Small Groups' *Environment and Planning* 20 pp. 309–26, 457–76.

Burns, Richard (1991) 'The City as Not London' in M. Fisher and U. Owen (eds) *Whose Cities?* London: Penguin.

Burrell, Ian and Leppard, David (1994) 'Fall in Crime a Myth as Police Chiefs Massage the Figures' *Sunday Times*, 16 October.

Cahill, Michael (1994) *The New Social Policy* Oxford: Blackwell.

Campbell, Angus, Converse, Philip and Rodgers, Willard (1976) *The Quality of American Life* New York: Russell Sage.

Campbell, Beatrix (1993) *Goliath: Britain's Dangerous Places* London: Methuen.

Carlen, Pat (1994) 'The Governance of Homelessness: Legality and Lexicon in the Agency-maintenance of Homelessness' *Critical Social Policy* 41 (August) pp. 18–35.

Cartwright, Jim (1986) *Road* London: Methuen Original.

Castells, Manuel (1983) *The City and the Grassroots* Berkeley: University of California Press.

Castells, Manuel (1989) *The Informational City* Oxford: Blackwell.

Castells, M. and Murphy, K.A. (1982) 'Cultural Identity and Urban Structure: The Spatial Organisation of San Francisco's Gay Community' in N. Fainstain and S. Fainstain (eds) *Urban Policy under Capitalism* Beverly Hills: Sage.

Central Manchester Development Corporation (1994) 'Annual Report 1993–4'.

Champion, Sarah (1990) *And God Created Manchester* Manchester: Wordsmith.

Chaney, David (1990) 'Subtopia in Gateshead: The MetroCentre as a Cultural Form' *Theory, Culture and Society* 7(4) pp. 49–68.

Chaney, David (1994) *The Cultural Turn: Scene-Setting Essays on Contemporary Cultural Change* London: Routledge.

Chaney, David (1995) 'Authenticity and Suburbia' Paper presented to the Annual Conference of the British Sociological Association, University of Leicester.

Clarke, Alan (1987) *The Rise and Fall of the Socialist Republic* Sheffield: Sheaf Publishing.

Clarke, Alan H. and Lewis, Margaret J. (1982) 'Fear of Crime among the Elderly' *British Journal of Criminology* 33(1) pp. 109–25.

Coffield, Frank, Borrill, Carol and Marshall, Sarah (1986) *Growing Up at the Margins: Young People in the North East* Milton Keynes and Philadelphia: Open University Press.

Cohen, Phil (1979) 'Policing the Working-class City' in Bob Fine, Richard Kinsey, John Lea, Sol Picciotto and Jock Young (eds) *Capitalism and the Rule of Law* London: Hutchinson.

Cohen, Phil (n.d.) 'Credos and Credibilities: Introduction to a Theory of Proletarian Youth Formation' (Mimeo).

Cohen, Phil (1985) 'Towards Youthtopia' *Marxism Today* (October) pp. 33–7.

Collis, Robert and Lancaster, Bill (eds) (1992) *Geordies: Roots of Regionalism* Edinburgh: University of Edinburgh Press.

Collinson, Barbara (ed) (1986) *Kendals: One Hundred and Fifty Years 1836–1986* Manchester: Kendals.

Comedia, for the Greater Manchester Development Corporation (1991) *Manchester: Safe and Sound* (Final Report).

Common, Jack (1938) *The Freedom of the Streets* London: Secker and Warburg (reprinted People's Publications, Newcastle upon Tyne, 1988)

Connell, R.W. (1987) *Gender and Power: Society, the Person and Sexual Politics* Cambridge: Polity Press.

Connell, R.W. (1995) *Masculinities* Cambridge: Polity Press.

Cook, Dee and Hudson, Barbara (1993) *Racism and Criminology* London: Sage.

Cooke, Philip (ed) (1986) *Global Restructuring, Local Response* London: Economic and Social Research Council.

Cooke, Philip (1989a) 'Locality Theory and the Poverty of 'Spatial Variation'' *Antipode* 21(3) pp. 261–73.

Cooke, Philip (ed) (1989b) *Localities: The Changing Face of Urban Britain* London: Unwin Hyman.

Corrigan, Paul (1978) 'Doing Nothing' in S. Hall and T. Jefferson (eds) *Resistance through Rituals* London: Hutchinson.

Cox, K. and Mair, A. (1989) 'Levels of Abstraction in Locality Studies' *Antipode* 21(2) pp. 121–32.

Craine, Stephen F. (1994) 'Beggars Can't Be Choosers: An Ethnography of Post-school Transitions in a High Unemployment Area' Unpublished Ph.D., University of Salford, Department of Sociology.

Crampton, Robert (1992) 'From Steel City to Brass Farthing' *The Times* 23 June.

Cross, Malcolm and Keith, Michael (1993) *Racism, the City and the State* London: Routledge.

Currie, Elliott (1993) *Reckoning: Drugs, the Cities and the American Future* New York: Hill and Wang.

Cusick, James (1994) 'London Traffic Getting Worse as Car Use Rises' *Independent* 24 March.

Darke, Roy (1994) 'The 16th Universiade, Sheffield 1991' Paper presented to the World Congress of Sociology, Bielefeld, Germany (July).

Davies, Andrew (1987) 'Saturday Night Markets in Manchester and Salford 1840–1939' *Manchester Regional History Review* 1(2) pp. 3–12.

Davies, Andrew (1992) *Leisure, Gender and Poverty: Working-class Culture in Salford and Manchester 1900–1939* Buckingham: Open University Press.

Davies, Nick (1994) 'Nomad's Land' *Guardian* 1 September.

Davies, S.J. (1985) 'Classes and Police in Manchester' in Kidd A.J. and Roberts, K. (eds) *City, Class and Culture: Studies of Social Policy and Cultural Production in Victorian Manchester* Manchester: Manchester University Press.

Davis, Mike (1990) *City of Quartz: Excavating the Future of Los Angeles* London: Verso.

de Certeau, Michel (1984) *The Practice of Everyday Life* Berkeley: University of California Press.

Defoe, Daniel (1724–7) *Tour through the Whole Island of Great Britain* (three vols), Cornhill: G. Strahan (reprinted London: Cass, 1927).

Dennis, Norman and Erdos, George (1992) *Families without Fatherhood* London: Institute of Economic Affairs.

Department of the Environment (1994) 'Households Found Accomodation under the 'Homelessness Provisions of the 1985 Housing Act, England' Information Bulletin, 12 September.

Dickinson, Mark (1990) *Goodbye Piccadilly: The History of the Abolition of the Greater Manchester Council* Poynton, Cheshire: Intercommunication Publishing.

Donald, James (1992) 'Metropolis: The City as Text' in Robert Bocock and Kenneth Thompson (eds) *Social and Cultural Forms of Modernity* Oxford: Polity Press in association with the Open University.

Duncan, S.S. and Savage, M. (1989) 'Space, Scale and Locality' *Antipode* 21(3) pp. 179–206.

Dyos H.J. and Wolff, Michael (1973) *The Victorian City: Images and Realities* London: Routledge and Kegan Paul (two volumes).

East End Publishing (1990) *Who'd Have Thought It? The Changing Face of Sheffield's East End* Sheffield: East End Publishing.

Edwards, J., Oakley, R. and Carey, S. (eds) (1987) 'Street Life, Ethnicity and Social Policy' in G. Gaskell and R. Benewick (eds) *The Crowd in Contemporary Britain* London: Sage.

Ehrenreich, Barbara (1984) *Hearts of Men: American Dreams and the Flight from Commitment* Garden City, NY: Anchor Books.

Ehrenreich, Barbara (1989) *Fear of Falling: The Inner Life of the Middle Class* New York: Pantheon.

Engels, Friedrich (1987) ed. Victor Kiernan *The Condition of the Working Class in England* London: Penguin.

Evans, Karen (1987) *Ghetto-Building: Racism and Housing Policy since the Second World*

War University of Manchester, Faculty of Economic and Social Studies Working Papers No.11.

Evans, Karen and Fraser, Penny (1995) 'Difference in the City: Locating Marginal Use of Public Space' in C. Sampson and N. South (eds) *Conflict and Consensus in Social Policy* (Proceedings of the British Sociological Association 1993 Conference) Basingstoke: Macmillan.

Evans, Karen, Fraser, Penny and Taylor, Ian (1995) 'Going to Town: Routine Anxieties and Routine Accommodations in Respect of Public Space and Public Facilities in the North of England' in S. Edgell, S. Walklate and G. Williams (eds) *Debating the Future of the Public Sphere: Transforming the Public and Private Domains in Free Market Societies* Aldershot: Avebury.

Evans, Sian Elizabeth (1994) 'Blacklisted' *Guardian* 19 August.

Ewen, Stuart and Ewen, Elizabeth (1982) *Channels of Desire* New York: McGraw-Hill.

Farrow, Elaine (1990) *The Manchester Travel Survey (Summary Report)* Greater Manchester Passenger Transport Executive.

Farrow, Elaine (1993) *Trends and Statistics 1984–1993* Greater Manchester Passenger Transport Executive.

Faucher, M. Leon (1969) *Manchester in 1844* London: Frank Cass.

Felson, Marcus (1994) *Crime and Everyday Life: Insight and Implications for Society* Thousands Oaks and London: Pine Forge Press.

Fentress, James and Wickham, Chris (1992) *Social Memory: New Perspectives on the Past* Oxford: Blackwell.

Fielding, Neil (1993) 'Poverty Traps – A Damning Picture of Centenary Sheffield' *Star* 22 September.

Fielding, Nigel (1993) 'Interviews' in N. Gilbert (ed) *Researching Social Life* London: Sage.

Fine, David (1992) *Sheffield: History and Guide* (1992) Stroud: Alan Sutton.

Fisher, Kevin and Collins, John (eds) (1993) *Homelessness, Health Care and Welfare Provision* London: Routledge.

Fisher, Mark and Owen, Ursula (1991) *Whose Cities?* London: Penguin.

Fishman, Mark (1978) 'Crime Waves as Ideology' *Social Problems* 25(4) (June) (reprinted in S. Cohen and J. Young (eds) *The Manufacture of News* (second edition) London: Constable 1981).

Fitch, Robert (1994) 'New York's Road to Ruin: Explaining New York's Aberrant Economy' *New Left Review* 207 (Sept.–Oct.) pp. 17–48.

Foley, Paul and Lawless, Paul (1992) *The Sheffield Central Area Study: 2010 A Vision of Quality* Sheffield Chamber of Commerce, Sheffield City Council, Sheffield Development Corporation and University of Sheffield (September).

Forrest, Ray and Gordon, Dave (1993) *People and Places: A 1991 Census Atlas of England* University of Bristol: School for Advanced Urban Studies.

Fossu, Kingsley (1992) 'Race and the Labour Market' in M. Campbell and K. Duffy (eds) *Local Labour Markets* Basingstoke: Macmillan.

Foucault, Michel (1977) *Discipline and Punish: The Birth of the Prison* London: Penguin.

Frank, Bryn (1994) *Manchester: A Guidebook* London: André Deutsch.

Fried, Marc (1982) 'Residential Attachment: Sources of Residential and Community Attachment' *Journal of Social Issues* 38 pp. 107–19.

Gandy, Kenneth (1985) *Sheffield Corporation Tramways: An Illustrated History* Sheffield: Sheffield City Libraries.

Gardner, Carl and Sheppard, Julie (1989) *Consuming Passions: The Rise of Retail Culture* London: Unwin Hyman.

Garland, Steve (1984) *Climate of Sheffield* Sheffield City Museums Information Sheet No. 15.

Garreau, Joel (1991) *Edge City: Life on the New Frontier* New York: Doubleday.

Geertz, Clifford (1983) *Local Knowledge: Essays in Interpretative Anthropology* New York: Basic Books.

Giddens, Anthony (1984) *The Constitution of Society* Cambridge: Polity Press.

Giddens, Anthony (1991) *Modernity and Self-Identity: Self and Society in the Late Modern Age* Cambridge: Polity Press.

Gilliatt, Stephen (1992) 'Consumers at Work: The Private Life of Public Provision' *British Journal of Sociology* 32(2) (June) pp. 239–65.

Goffman, Erving (1963) *Behavior in Public Places* Glencoe: Free Press.

Goldberg, David Theo (1993) 'Polluting the Body Politic': Racist Discourse and Urban Location' in Malcolm Cross and Michael Keith (eds) *Racism, the City and the State* London: Routledge.

Greater Manchester Police (1993) 'Chief Constable's Report 1993'.

Greater Manchester Research and Information Planning Unit (1991) *Greater Manchester: Facts and Trends* Research and Information Paper 91/1.

Green, E., Hebron, S. and Woodward D. (1987) 'Women, Leisure and Social Control' in J. Hanmer and M. Maynard (eds) *Women, Violence and Social Control* London: Macmillan.

Green, L.P. (1959) *Provincial Metropolis: The Future of Local Government in South Lancashire. A Study in Metropolitan Analysis* London: Allen and Unwin.

Gregory, Derek and Urry, John (eds) (1985) *Social Relations and Spatial Structures* London: Macmillan.

Greig, Geordie (1994) 'From Motown to No Town: Detroit and the Decline of the Post-industrial City' *Sunday Times* (Supplement) 20 March.

Gunn, Simon (1988) 'The "Failure" of the Victorian Middle Class: A Critique' in Seed and Wolff, (1988)

Habermas, Jürgen (1989) *The New Conservatism* Cambridge: Polity Press.

Hägerstrand, T. (1970) 'What about People in Regional Science?' *Papers of the Regional Science Association* 24.

Hägerstrand, T. (1975) 'Survival and Arena: On the Life History of Individuals in Relation to their Geographical Environment' in T. Carlstein, D. Parker and N.Thrift (eds) *Human Activity and Time Geography* London: Edward Arnold.

Hall, Catherine (1988) 'The World Turned Upside Down: The Working-class Family in Cotton Textiles 1780–1850' in E.Whitelegg, M. Arnot, V. Beechey, L. Birke, S. Himmselweit, D. Leonard, S. Ruehl and M.-A. Speakman (eds) *The Changing Experience of Women* Oxford: Martin Robertson.

Hall, Stuart (1981) 'Cultural Studies: Two Paradigms' in Tony Bennett, Graham Martin, Colin Mercer and Janet Woollacott (eds) *Culture, Ideology and Social Process* London: Batsford, for the Open University Press.

Hall, Stuart and Jacques, Martin (1989) *New Times: The Changing Face of Politics in the 1990s* London: Lawrence and Wishart.

Hall, Stuart and Jefferson, Tony (eds) (1978) *Resistance through Rituals: Youth Subcultures in Post-War Britain* London: Hutchinson.

Halsall, Martin (1994) 'Sheffield Forges New Links to Help Pioneer Job Centres' *Guardian* 25 January.

Hambridge, John (1992) 'Leaner, Fitter City is Ready for the Upturn', *Business Review for 1992, Sheffield Telegraph* 16 October.

Hamilton, Kerry (1990) 'Driven to Distraction' *New Socialist* 67 (June–July) pp. 16–17.

Hampton, William (1993) 'Optimism and Growth 1951–1973' in Binfield *et al.* (1993) Vol. 1.

Hansen, Miriam (1993) 'Foreword' in Negt and Kluge (1993).

Harding, Mike (1994) 'This Park Belongs to the People' *Manchester Evening News* 19 September.

Hargreaves, W.D. (1956) 'Steelmaking and Engineering' in *Sheffield and its Region: A Scientific and Historical Survey* British Association for the Advancement of Science.

Harloe, Michael, Pickvance, Chris and Urry, John (eds) (1990) *Place, Policy and Politics: Do Localities Matter?* London: Unwin Hyman.

Harriss Research Centre (1991) *Sheffield Interchange Attitude Survey* Report prepared for the South Yorkshire Passenger Transport Executive, Manchester: Harriss Research Centre.

Harriss Research Centre (1994) *Sheffield Interchange Attitude Survey* Report prepared for the South Yorkshire Passenger Transport Executive, Manchester: Harriss Research Centre.

Hartnagel, T.F. (1979) 'The Perception and Fear of Crime: Implications for Neighbourhood, Social Activity and Community Affect' *Social Forces* 58(1) pp. 176–93.

Harvey, David (1985) *The Urban Experience* Oxford: Blackwell.

Harvey, David (1989) *The Condition of Postmodernity* Oxford: Blackwell.

Harvey, Sir Paul (ed) (1957) *The Oxford Companion to Classical Literature* Oxford: Oxford University Press.

Hattersley, Roy (1981) *A Yorkshire Boyhood* Oxford: Oxford University Press.

Headley, Victor (1993) *Yardie* London: Pan.

Health Education Authority (1990) *Measuring the Epidemic* London: Health Education Authority.

Henslin, James M. (1967) 'Craps and Magic' *American Journal of Sociology* 73(3) pp. 316–30.

Hillier, Bill and Hanson, Juliette (1984) *The Social Logic of Space* Cambridge: Cambridge University Press.

Hillman, M. Adams, J. and Whitelegg, J. (1990) *One False Move: A Study of Children's Independent Mobility* London: Policy Studies Institute.

Hindle, Paul (1994) 'Gay Communities and Gay Space in the City' in Stephen Whittle (ed) *The Margins of the City: Gay Men's Urban Lives* Newcastle upon Tyne: Athenaeum Press.

Hobbs, Dick (1989) *Doing the Business: Entrepreneurship, the Working Class and Detectives in the East End of London* Oxford: Oxford University Press.

Hobsbawm, E.J. (1994) *Age of Extremes: The Short Twentieth Century* London: Michael Joseph.

Hobsbawm, Eric and Ranger, Terence (eds) (1983) *The Invention of Tradition* Cambridge: Cambridge University Press.

Hofstader, Richard (1948) *The American Political Tradition and the Men Who Made It* New York: Random House.

Hoggart, Richard (1957) *The Uses of Literacy* London: Penguin.

Holcomb, B. (1984) 'Women in the Rebuilt Urban Environment: the United States experience' *Built Environment* 10(1) pp. 18–24.

Hollander, C.F. and Becker, H.A. (eds) (1987) *Growing Old in the Future: Scenarios on Health and Aging* Dordrecht: Martinus Nijhoff.

Holliday, Joyce (1987) *It's a Bit Lively Outside* Sheffield: Yorkshire Arts Circus in association with Crucible Theatre and Sheffield City Libraries.

Hudson, Ray (1993) 'A New Ball Game for the North-east' *Times Higher Education Supplement* 24 December.

Humphries, Stephen (1981) *Hooligans or Rebels: An Oral History of Working-class Childhood and Youth 1889–1939* Oxford: Blackwell.

Inglis, Simon (1987) *The Football Grounds of Great Britain* London: Willow Books.

Jackson, Brian (1968) *Working-class Community: Some Notions Raised by a Series of Studies in Northern England* London: Routledge.

Jackson, Peter (1989) *Maps of Meaning: An Introduction to Cultural Geography* London: Unwin Hyman.

Jackson, P.T. 'Supertram for South Yorkshire' *Modern Tramway* (April) pp. 115–23.

Jackson, P.T. (1992) 'South Yorkshire Supertram Update' (1992) *Modern Tramway* (November) pp. 231–8.

Jackson, P.T. (1994) 'South Yorkshire's Dream Becomes Reality' *Modern Tramway* (June) pp. 143–6.

Jewell, Helen M. (1994) *The North–South Divide: The Origins of Northern Consciousness in England* Manchester: Manchester University Press.

Jones, G.P. (1956) 'Industrial Evolution' in David L. Linton (ed) *Sheffield and its Region: A Scientific and Historical Survey* Sheffield: British Association (Local Executive Committee).

Jones, Stephen G. (1988) *Sport, Politics and the Working Class* Manchester: Manchester University Press.

Joyce, Patrick (1991) *Visions of the People: England and the Question of Class 1848–1914* Cambridge: Cambridge University Press.

Kahn, Peggy, Lewis, Norman, Livock, Rowland and Wiles, Paul (1983) *Picketing: Industrial Disputes, Tactics and the Law* London: Routledge and Kegan Paul.

Kay, Peter (1994a) 'After the Pain, the New Gain' *Sheffield Telegraph* 21 October.

Kay, Peter (1994b) 'City Aims for Top Ten Status' *Sheffield Telegraph* 21 October.

Keegan, Victor (1993) 'The City, Centre of Recovery' *Guardian* 6 September.

Keegan, Victor (1994) 'Girls on Top in Jobs Market' *Guardian* 9 April.

Kidd, Alan J. (1985) 'The Middle-class in Nineteenth-century Manchester' in A.J. Kidd, and K. Roberts (eds) *City, Class and Culture: Studies of Social Policy and Cultural Production in Victorian Manchester* Manchester: Manchester University Press.

Kidd, Alan J. (1993) *Manchester* Keele Ryburn Publishing (Keele University Press).

King, Anthony (1995) 'The Cult of Cantona' *Salford Working Papers in Sociology* No. 16.

Kinsey, A., Pomeroy, W.B. and Martin, C.E. (1949) *Sexual Behaviour in the Human Male* Chicago: Pocket Books.

Kirby, Terry (1993) 'Manchester Tops Car Crime Table' *Independent* 17 August.

Knopp, Lawrence (1990) 'Some Theoretical Implications of Gay Involvement in an Urban Landscape' *Political Geography Quarterly* 9(4) (October) pp. 337–52.

Knowles, Richard and Fairweather, Liz (1991) *The Impact of Rapid Transit* Metrolink Impact Study, Working Paper No. 2, University of Salford: Department of Geography.

Kozar, Christian (1992) 'Three Years Spent Reclaiming Lost Ground' in *Public Transport: Security and Environment* (Proceedings of International Conference, La Defence, Paris) Brussels: Union Internationale Des Transports Publiques.

Krieger, Eric (1984) *Bygone Manchester* Chichester Phillimore.

Kumar, Krishan (1995) 'Versions of the Pastoral: Poverty and the Poor in English Fiction from the 1840s to the 1950s' *Journal of Historical Sociology* 6(1) pp. 1–35.

Labour Party (1992) *Putting the Brakes on Car Crime* (December). London: Labour Party.

Laermans, Rudi (1993) 'Learning to Consume: Early Department Stores and the Shaping of the Modern Consumer Culture (1860–1914)' *Theory, Culture and Society* 10 pp. 79–102.

Laffin M. (1986) 'Professional Communities and Policy Communities in Central–Local Relations' in M. Goldsmith (ed) *New Research in Central–Local Relations* Aldershot: Gower.

Lane, Tony (1987) *Liverpool: Gateway of Empire* London: Lawrence and Wishart.

Langton, John (1984) 'The Industrial Revolution and the Regional Geography of England' *Transactions of the Institute of British Geographers* 9 pp. 145–67.

Lasch, Christopher (1991) *The True and Only Heaven: Progress and its Critics* New York: W.W. Norton.

Lasch, Christopher (1995) *The Revolt of the Elites and the Betrayal of Democracy* New York: W.W. Norton.

Lash, Scott and Urry, John (1994) *Economies of Signs and Space* London: Sage.

Lauria, Mickey and Knopp, Lawrence (1985) 'Towards an Analysis of the Role of Gay Communities in the Urban Renaissance' *Urban Geography* 6(2) pp. 152–69.

Law, Christopher (1986) 'The Uncertain Future of the City Centre: The case of Manchester' *Manchester Geographer* 6 pp. 26–43.

Law, Christopher (1988) 'From Manchester Docks to Salford Quays' *Manchester Geographer* 9 pp. 2–15.

Lawton, M.P. and Yaffee, Silvia (1980) 'Victimization and Fear of Crime in Elderly Public Housing Tenants' *Journal of Gerontology* 33(1) pp. 109–25.

Lederer, Laura (ed) (1980) *Take Back the Night: Women on Pornography* New York: William Morrow.

Lefebvre, Henri (1974) *La Production de l'Espace* Paris (English edition, Oxford: Blackwell, 1991).

Lewis, Marc (1994) 'A Sociological Pub-crawl around Gay Newcastle' in Stephen Whittle (ed) *The Margins of the City: Gay Men's Urban Lives* Newcastle upon Tyne: Athenaeum Press.

Lewis, N.B. (1956) 'History: The Middle Ages' in Linton (1956).

Liddington, Jill (1979) 'Women Cotton Workers and the Suffrage Campaign: The Radical Suffragettes in Lancashire 1893–1914' in S. Burman (ed) *Fit Work for Women* London: Croom Helm.

Linton, David L. (ed) (1956) *Sheffield and its Region: A Scientific and Historical Survey* Sheffield: British Association (Local Executive Committee).

Little, J., Peake, L. and Richardson, P. (1988) *Women in Cities: Gender and the Urban Environment* London: Macmillan Education.

Loader, Ian (1996) *Youth, Policing and Democracy* Basingstoke: Macmillan.

Logan, John R. and Molotch, Harvey L. (1987) *Urban Fortunes: The Political Economy of Place* Berkeley and Los Angeles: University of California Press.

Lovatt, Andy (1995a) 'After Dark: Investment in the Night-time Economy' Manchester Metropolitan University: Institute for Popular Culture (unpublished paper).

Lovatt, Andy (1995b) 'From Gun City to Fun City' Paper to the British Sociological Association Annual Conference, Contested Cities, University of Leicester (April).

Lowenthal, David (1961) 'Geography, Experience and Imagination: Towards a Geographical Epistemology' *Annals of the Association of American Geographers* 51(2) pp. 241–60.

Lowenthal, David (1975) 'Past Time, Present Place: Landscape and Memory' *Geographical Review* LXV(1) pp. 1–36.

Lowenthal, David and Bowden, Martyn J. (1976) *Geographies of the Mind: Essays in Historical Geography* New York: Oxford University Press

Lynch, Kevin (1960) *The Image of the City* Boston: Massachusetts Institute of Technology.

Lynch, Kevin (1972) *What Time is this Place?* Boston: Massachusetts Institute of Technology.

Lyotard, Jean-François (1984) *The Postmodern Condition* Manchester: Manchester University Press.

Manchester City Council (1994) *Community Care Plan, Update.*

Manchester City Council, Planning Studies Group (1993) *Manchester's Elderly Population (1991 Census Topics Paper).*

Manchester City Council, Economic Initiatives Group (1993) 'Manchester Economic Facts'.

Manchester, Salford and Trafford Councils (1994) 'City Pride: A Focus for the Future'.

Marans, Robert and Rodgers, William (1975) 'Towards an Understanding of Community Satisfaction' in A. Hawley and V. Rock (eds) *Metropolitan America in Contemporary Perspective* New York: John Wiley.

Marcus, Steven (1973) 'Reading the Illegible' in H.J. Dyos and Michael Wolff (eds) *The Victorian City: Images and Realities* London: Routledge and Kegan Paul.

Marsh, Peter (1990) *Conflict and Violence in Pubs* Oxford: MCM Research Ltd.

Marshall, Alfred (1919) *Industry and Trade* London: Macmillan.

Marshall, Alfred (1920) *Principles of Economics* London: Macmillan.

Martin, Bernice (1981) *A Sociology of Contemporary Cultural Change* Oxford: Blackwell.

Marwick, Arthur (1982) *British Society Since 1945* London: Penguin.

Marx, Karl and Engels, Friedrich (1986) *The Manifesto of the Communist Party* Moscow: Progress Publishers.

Massey, Doreen (1991) 'The Political Place of Locality Studies' *Environment and Planning A* (23) pp. 267–81 (reprinted in Massey, 1994).

Massey, Doreen (1992) 'A Place called Home?' *New Formations* 17 pp. 3–15 (reprinted in Massey, 1994).

Massey, Doreen (1994) *Space, Place and Gender* Cambridge: Polity Press.

Massey, Doreen and Meegan, Richard (1982) *The Anatomy of Job Loss: The How, Why and Where of Employment Decline* London: Methuen.

Mathews, Jessica (1994) 'Committed Citizens could Start to Reverse the Melting of America' *International Herald Tribune* 24 August.

Mathias, Peter (1969) *The First Industrial Nation* London: Methuen.

Maxwell, I.S. (1956) 'History: The Age of Settlement' in Linton (1956).

Mawby, Rob (1979) *Policing the City* Westmead: Saxon House.

McDowell, L. (1983) 'Towards an Understanding of the Gender Division of Urban Space' *Environment and Planning D: Society and Space* 1 pp. 59–72.

McGuigan, Jim (1992) *Cultural Populism* London: Routledge.

McHardy, Anne (1991) 'The Cost of Living' *Guardian* 8 May.

McKie, Linda and Edwards, Julia (1995) 'The Role of the Toilet in the Engendered City' Paper presented to the British Sociological Association Annual Conference, University of Leicester (April).

McRobbie, Angela (1978) 'Working-Class Girls and the Culture of Femininity' in Women's Studies Group (ed) *Women Take Issue* London: Hutchinson.

McRobbie, Angela (1980) 'Settling Accounts with Subcultures' *Screen Education* 34 pp. 37–49.

McRobbie, Angela (1989) 'The Role of the Ragmarket' in A. McRobbie *Zoot Suits and Second-Hand Dresses: An Anthology of Fashion and Music* London: Macmillan.

McRobbie, Angela (1994) *Postmodernism and Popular Culture* London: Routledge.

McRobbie, Angela and Garber, Jenny (1978) 'Girls and Subcultures' in Hall and Jefferson (1978).

McRobbie, Angela and Nava, Mica (eds) (1984) *Gender and Generation* London: Macmillan.

Measham, Fiona, Newcombe, Russell and Parker, Howard (1994) 'The Normalization of Recreational Drug Use among Young People in the North-west of England' *British Journal of Sociology* (Summer) pp. 287–312.

Melbin, Murray (1987) *Night as Frontier: Colonizing the World after Dark* New York: The Free Press.

Merchant, Jacqueline and Macdonald, Robert (1994) 'Youth, Rave Culture, Ecstasy and Health' *Youth and Policy* 45 (Summer) pp. 16–38.

Messinger, Gary S. (1985) *Manchester in the Victorian Age: The Half-known City* Manchester: Manchester University Press.

Meyrowitz, Joshua (1988) *No Sense of Place: The Impact of Electronic Media on Social Behaviour* New York: Oxford University Press.

Middleton, Michael (1991) *Cities in Transition: The Regeneration of Britain's Inner Cities* London: Michael Joseph.

Miliband, Ralph (1978) 'A State of De-subordination' *British Journal of Sociology* 29(4) (December) pp. 399–409.

Miller, Walter B. (1958) 'Lower Class Culture as a Generating Milieu of Gang Delinquency' *Journal of Social Issues* 15 pp. 5–19.

Mingione, Enzo (1994) 'Life Strategies and Social Economies in the Post-Fordist Age' *International Journal of Social and Economic Research* 18(1) pp. 24–45.

Mitchell, B. and Deane, P. (1962) *British Historical Statistics* Cambridge: Cambridge University Press.

Molotch, Harvey and Logan, John R. (1985) 'Urban Dependencies: New Forms of Use and Exchange in US Cities' *Urban Affairs Quarterly* 21(2) pp. 143–69.

Morgantau, Tom and McCormick, John (1991) 'Are Cities Obsolete?' *Newsweek* 9 September pp. 32–4.

Morris, Meaghan (1988) 'Things to do with Shopping Centres' in S. During (ed) *The Cultural Studies Reader* London: Routledge.

Mort, Frank (1987) *Dangerous Sexualities: Medico-moral Politics in England since 1930* London: Routledge and Kegan Paul.

Morton, James (1994) *Gangland 2* London: Little, Brown.

Murgatroyd, Linda, Savage, Mike, Shapiro, Dan, Urry, John, Walby, Sylvia, Warde, Alan and Mark-Lawson, Jane (1985) *Localities, Class and Gender* London: Pion.

Musgrove, Frank (1990) *The North of England: A History from Roman Times to the Present* Oxford: Blackwell.

Nava, Mica (1991) 'Consumerism Reconsidered: Buying Power' *Cultural Studies* 5 pp. 204–10.

Nava, Mica (1992) *Changing Cultures: Feminism, Youth and Consumerism* London: Sage.

Negt, Oskar and Kluge, Alexander (1993) *Public Sphere and Experience: Towards an Analysis of the Bourgeois and Proletarian Public Sphere* Minneapolis: University of Minnesota Press.

Newby, Howard, Bujra, Janet, Littlewood, Paul, Rees, Gareth and Rees, Teresa L. (1985) *Restructuring Capital: Recession and Reorganization in Industrial Society* London: Macmillan.

O'Connor, Justin and Wynne, Derek (1993) 'From the Margins to the Centre: Cultural Production and Consumption in the Post-industrial City' *Working Papers in Popular Cultural Studies* No.7 (Manchester Metropolitan University, Institute for Popular Culture).

Ogden, Eric and Senior, John (1991) *Metrolink Official Handbook* Glossop Transport Publishing.

Olive, Martin (ed) (1994) *Central Sheffield* Bath: Alan Sutton.

Ollerenshaw, Kathleen (1982) 'The Future of our City' *Manchester Literary and Philosophical Society Vol. 1 New Series* Manchester.

Opie, Iona and Opie Peter (1969) *Children's Games in Street and Playground* Oxford: Clarendon Press.

Orlowski, Andrew (1994) 'Metrolink Myths' *City Life* 267 16 Nov.–1 Dec.

Pahl, Ray (1984) *Divisions of Labour* Oxford: Blackwell.

Pain, R. (1991) 'Space, Sexual Violence and Social Control: Integrating Geographical and Feminist Analyses of Women's Fear of Crime' *Progress in Human Geography* 15 pp. 415–31.

Palmer, Bryan (1984) *Working Class Experience: The Rise and Reconstitution of Canadian Labour 1800–1980* Toronto: Butterworths.

Parker, Tony (1983) *The People of Providence* London: Hutchinson.

Pearson, Geoffrey (1983) *Hooligans: A History of Respectable Fears* London: Macmillan.

Pearson, Geoff, Ditton, Jason, Newcombe, Russell and Gilman, Mark (1991) 'Everything Starts with an E' *Druglink* (Nov.–Dec.) pp. 10–11.

Peck, J.A. and Emmerich, M. (1992a) *Recession, Restructuring and the Greater Manchester Labour Market: An Empirical Overview* University of Manchester, School of Geography Spatial Policy Analysis Working Paper No. 17 (July).

Peck, J.A. and Emmerich, M. (1992b) 'Recession, Restructuring . . . and Recession Again: The Transformation of the Greater Manchester Labour Market' *Manchester Geographer* 13 pp. 13–46.

Pepinsky, Hal (1987) 'Explaining Police-recorded Crime Trends in Sheffield' *Contemporary Crises* 11(1) pp. 55–73.

Pickup, L. (1988) 'Hard to Get Around: A Study of Women's Travel Mobility' in Little *et al.* (1988).

Pocock, D.C.D. (1972) 'City of the Mind: A Review of Mental Maps of Urban Areas' *Scottish Geographical Magazine* 88 pp. 115–24.

Pocock, D.C.D. (1976) 'A Comment on Images Derived from Invitation-to-map Exercises' *Professional Geographer* XXVIII(2) pp. 161–5.

Pollard, Sidney (1959) *A History of Labour in Sheffield* Liverpool: Liverpool University Press.

Pollard, Sidney (1993) 'Labour' in Binfield *et al.* (1993) Vol.2.

Pons, Valdo (1978) 'Contemporary Interpretations of Manchester in the 1830s and 1840s' in John D. Wirth and Robert L. Jones (eds) *Manchester and Sao Paulo: Problems of Rapid Urban Growth* Stanford, CA: Stanford University Press.

Pope, Nicki (1994) 'Over the Edge: Stressed Out Britain' *Today* 31 May.

Portelli, Alessandro (1991) *The Death of Luigi Trastulli and Other Stories* Albany: State University of New York.

Pratt, G. and Hanson, S. (1994) 'Geography and the Construction of Difference' *Gender, Place and Culture* 1(1) pp. 5–29.

Priestley, J.B. (1934) *English Journey* London: Heinemann.

Pybus, Sylvia (ed) (1994) *Damned Bad Place, Sheffield: An Anthology of Writing about Sheffield Through the ages* Sheffield: Sheffield Academic Press.

Rapport, Nigel (1987) *Talking Violence: An Anthropological Interpretation of Conversation in the City* St John's, Newfoundland: School of Social and Economic Studies No. 24, Institute for Social and Economic Research, Memorial University.

Read, Donald (1979) *England 1868–1914: The Age of Urban Democracy* London: Longman.

Redford, Arthur (1940) *The History of Local Government in Manchester* London: Longmans, Green.

Redhead, Brian (1993) *Manchester: A Celebration* London: André Deutsch.

Redhead, Steve (1990) *The End of the Century Party: Youth and Pop towards 2000* Manchester: Manchester University Press.

Redhead, Steve (1991) *Football with Attitude* Manchester: Wordsmith.

Redhead, Steve (1995) *Unpopular Cultures: The Birth of Law and Popular Culture* Manchester: Manchester University Press.

Reich, Robert (1991) *The Work of Nations: Preparing Ourselves for Twenty-first-century Capitalism* New York: Alfred A. Knopf.

Reisman, David (1957) 'The Suburban Dislocation' *Annals of the American Academy of Political and Social Science* 314 (November) reprinted in N.F. Cantor and M.S. Werthman (eds) *The History of Popular Culture* New York: Macmillan, London: Collier-Macmillan (1968).

Relph, E. (1976) *Place and Placelessness* London: Pion.

Renshaw, Patrick (1993) 'Aspects of Sports and Recreation' in Binfield *et al.* Vol. 2 (1993)

Rex, John (1973) *Race, Colonialism and the City* London: Routledge.

Rex, John (1988) *The Ghetto and the Underclass: Essays on Race and Social Policy* Aldershot: Avebury.

Rex, John and Moore, Robert (1967) *Race, Community and Conflict: A Study of Sparkbrook* Oxford: Oxford University Press.

Rice, Margery Spring (1939) *Working Class Wives: Their Health and Conditions* London: Penguin (reprinted Virago Press, 1981).

Richards, Jeffrey and Mackenzie, John M. (1986) *The Railway Station: A Social History* Oxford: Oxford University Press.

Richardson, Neil (1995) *Manchester's Pubs and Bars* Manchester: Campaign for Real Ale.

Robbins, Keith (1994) *The Eclipse of a Great Power: Modern Britain 1870–1992* London: Longman (second edition).

Roberts, Robert (1973) *The Classic Slum: Salford Life in the First Quarter of the Century* Harmondsworth: Penguin.

Robertson, George, Lash, Melinda, Truckner, Lisa, Bird, Jon and Curtis, Barry (1994) *Travellers' Tales: Narratives of Home and Displacement* London: Routledge.

Robins, David and Cohen, Phil (1978) *Knuckle Sandwich: Growing Up in the Working-Class City* Harmondsworth: Penguin.

Roche, Maurice (1991) *Mega-events and Urban Policy: A Study of Sheffield's World Student Games* University of Sheffield, Policy Studies Centre.

Roche, Maurice (1994) 'Mega-events, Popular Culture and Power' Paper presented to the World Congress of Sociology, University of Bielefeld, Germany.

Rock, Paul and Cohen, Stanley (eds) (1970) 'The Teddy Boy' in Vernon Bogdanor and Robert Skidelsky *The Age of Affluence 1951–1964* London: Penguin.

Rose, Michael E. (1985) 'Culture, Philanthropy and the Manchester Middle Class' in A.J. Kidd and K. Roberts (eds) *City, Class and Culture: Studies of Social Policy and Cultural Production in Victorian Manchester* Manchester: Manchester University Press.

Rowbotham, Sheila and Weeks, Jeffrey (1977) *Socialism and the New Life: The Personal and Sexual Politics of Edward Carpenter and Havelock Ellis* London: Pluto.

Rowles, Graham (1978) *Prisoners of Space? Exploring the Geographical Experience of Older People* Boulder, CO: Westview Press.

Sabel, C. and Zeitlin, J. (1985) 'Historical Alternatives to Mass Production: Politics, Markets and Technology in Nineteenth Century Industrialization' *Past and Present* 108 pp. 133–76.

Samuel, Raphael (1994) *Theatres of Memory. Vol. 1: Past and Present in Contemporary Culture* London: Verso.

Samuel, Raphael (1995) 'North and South' *London Review of Books* 3 (22 June) pp. 5–7.

Saunders, Peter (1981) *Social Theory and the Urban Question* London: Unwin and Hyman.

Savage, Jon (1992) 'Structures of Feeling' *New Statesman and Society* 18 September pp. 30–1.

Savage, Mike and Warde, Alan (1993) *Urban Sociology, Capitalism and Modernity* Basingstoke: Macmillan.

Saxenian, A. (1989) 'The Cheshire Cat's Grin: Innovation, Regional Development and the Cambridge Case' *Economy and Society* 18 pp. 448–77.

Sayer, Andrew (1989) 'Dualistic Thinking and Rhetoric in Geography' *Arena* 22 pp. 301–5.

Schivelbusch, Wolfgang (1986) *The Railway Journey: The Industrialisation of Time and Space in the Nineteenth Century* New York/Hamburg/Leamington Spa: Berg. First published as *Geschichte der Eisenbahnreise* Munich: Carl Hauser Verlag (1977).

Schwartz, John E. and Volgy, Thomas J. (1994) *The Forgotten Americans* New York: W.W. Norton.

Scola, Roger (1975) 'Food Markets and Shops in Manchester 1770–1870' *Journal of Historical Geography* 1(2) pp. 153–68.

Scola, Roger (1994) *Feeding the Victorian City: The Food Supply of Manchester 1770 to 1870* Manchester: Manchester University Press.

Seed, John and Wolff, Janet (eds) (1988) *The Culture of Capital: Art, Power and the Nineteenth century Middle Class* Manchester: Manchester University Press.

Sennett, Richard (1990) *The Conscience of the Eye: The Design and Social Life of Cities* New York: Alfred A. Knopf, London: Macmillan.

Sennett, Richard (1991) *The Conscience of the Eye: The Design and Social Life of Cities* London and Boston: Faber and Faber.

Sennett, Richard (1992) 'The Body and the City' (review essay) *Times Literary Supplement* 18 September pp. 3–4.

Seyd, Patrick (1993) 'The Political Management of Decline 1973–1993' in Binfield *et al.* (1993) Vol. 1.

Shaw, George (1993) *Sheffielder: A Life in the City* Stroud: Alan Sutton.

Sheffield City Council (1989) *Because the Skin is Black.*

Sheffield City Council (1991) *Sheffield: A City for People* (The Draft Unitary Development Plan).

Sheffield City Council (1993) *Sheffield: The Welcoming City* (City of Sheffield Centenary, Official Guide) Gloucester: British Publishing Company.

Sheffield City Council, Community Services Department (1994) *Sheffield's Community Care Plan 1994–5.*

Sheffield City Council, Department of Employment and Economic Development (1988) 'Black Women's Working Lives' Women in Sheffield No. 6.

Sheffield City Council, Department of Employment and Economic Development (1989) *Because they're Black.*

Sheffield City Council (1994) Department of Employment and Economic Development 'South Asian Women's Survey'.

Sheffield City Council, Department of Employment and Economic Development (1995) 'Sheffield Economic Plan, 1995–6, Part 2, Directory of Major Projects and Initiatives'.

Sheffield City Council, Department of Land and Planning (1988) *Black Sheffielders: An Information Pack.*

Sheffield City Council, Family and Community Services Department (1994) 'Review of Elderly Day Services'.

Sheffield, Director of Public Health (1993) *Sheffield's Health into 1993 . . . and a Century Ago* (Sixth Annual Report).

Sheffield, Town Planning Committee (1945) *Sheffield Replanned.*

Sheffield Trades Council (1982) *Sheffield: The Second Slump* Sheffield: Trades Council.

Sheffield, Tramway Department (1960) *The Tramway Era in Sheffield: Souvenir Brochure on the Closure of the Tramways* (8 October).

Shepherd, Simon and Wallis, Mick (1989) *Coming on Strong: Gay Politics and Culture* London: Unwin Hyman.

Shields, Rob (1989) 'Social Spatialization and the Built Environment: The West Edmonton Mall' *Environment and Planning D: Society and Space* 7 pp.147–64.

Shields, Rob (1991) *Places on the Margin: Alternative Geographies of Modernity* London: Routledge.

Shurmer-Smith, Pamela and Kevin Hannam (1994) *Worlds of Desire, Realms of Power: A Cultural Geography* London: Edward Arnold.

Sillitoe, Sir Percy (1953) *Cloak without Dagger* London: Quality Book Club (reprinted Penguin, 1955).

Simmel, George (1950) 'The Metropolis and Mental Life' in K. Wolff (ed) *The Sociology of George Simmel* New York: The Free Press, (reprinted in Sennett (1990).

Simmons, Michael (1993) 'Steel City on a Knife Edge' *Guardian* 15 December.

Simon, Alfred P. (1936) *Manchester Made Over* London: P.S. King and Son.

Simon, Shena D. (1938) *A Century of City Government: Manchester 1838–1938* London: George Allen and Unwin.

Sinfield, Adrian (1981) *What Unemployment Means* Oxford: Martin Robertson.

Skogan, Wesley (1990) *Disorder and Decline: Crime and the Spiral of Decay in American Neighbourhoods* New York: The Free Press.

Smith, Dennis (1982) *Conflict and Compromise: Class Formation in English Society 1830–1914: A Comparative Study in Birmingham and Sheffield* London: Routledge and Kegan Paul.

Smith, Gavin (1984) *Getting Around: Transport Today and Tomorrow* London: Pluto.

Smith, Gavin (1994) 'Towards an Ethnography of Idiosyncratic Forms of Livelihood' *International Journal of Urban and Regional Research* 18(1) pp. 71–87.

Smith, K. (1995) *Moss Side Massive* Manchester: X Press.

Smith, Susan J. (1989) *The Politics of Race and Residence* Cambridge: Polity Press.

South Yorkshire Transport (1994) 'Live Operators' Data Sheet' 31 October.

Stallybrass, Peter and White, Allon (1986) *The Politics and Poetics of Transgression* Ithaca NY: Cornell University Press.

Stanko, E. (1987) 'Typical Violence, Normal Precaution: Men, Women and Interpersonal Violence in England, Wales, Scotland and the USA' in J. Hanmer and M. Maynard (eds) *Women, Violence and Social Control* London: Macmillan.

Stanko, E. (1990) *Everyday Violence: How Men and Women Experience Sexual and Physical Danger* London: Pandora.

Stanley, Christopher (1993) 'Repression and Resistance: Problems of Regulation in Contemporary Urban Culture (Part 1: Towards Definition)' *International Journal of the Sociology of Law* 21 pp. 23–47.

Stanley, Christopher (1995) 'Urban Narratives of Dissent: Hacking-Wrecking-Raving' *Working Papers in Law and Popular Culture Series Two, No.1,* Manchester Metropolitan University.

Stanley, Liz (1992) *The Auto/Biographical I: Theory and Practice of Auto/Biography* Manchester: Manchester University Press.

Stedman-Jones, Gareth (1971) *Outcast London: A Study in the Relationships between Classes in Victorian Society* London: Peregrine.

Stevens, Rob (ed) (1993) *Health Inequalities in Manchester in the 1990s* Manchester City Council: Health for All Working Party.

Stokes, Gordon (1992) *Travel in South Yorkshire 1991: An Analysis of the South Yorkshire Household Travel Survey* Transport Studies Unit, University of Oxford.

Taylor, A.J.P. (1957) 'Manchester' *Encounter* 8 (March) pp. 3–13.

Taylor, Ian (1989) 'Hillsborough: 19 April 1989' *New Left Review* 177 (Oct.–Nov.) pp. 89–110.

Taylor, Ian (1990) 'Sociology and the Condition of the English City: Thoughts from a Returnee' (Inaugural Lecture) Salford Papers in Sociology 9.

Taylor, Ian (1991a) *Not Spaces in which You'd Linger: Public Transport and Public Well-being in Manchester* Report to the Greater Manchester Passenger Transport Executive (August).

Taylor, Ian (1991b) 'The Experience of Order and Disorder in Free Market Societies: New York versus Manchester' in Bryan S. Turner (ed) *Citizenship. Civil Society and Social Cohesion* Colchester: University of Essex for the ESRC (Mimeo) (November).

Taylor, Ian (1991c) 'Moral Panics, Crime and Urban Policy in Manchester' *Sociology Review* 1(1) pp. 28–30.

Taylor, Ian (1992) 'Public Sense of Well-being and Transport Provision in Older Industrial Cities in the North of England' in *Public Transport: Security and Environment* (Proceedings of International Conference, La Defence, Paris, May) Brussels: Union Internationale des Transports Publiques.

Taylor, Ian (1995a) 'Private Homes and Public Others: An analysis of talk about crime in suburban South Manchester in the mid-1990s' *British Journal of Criminology* 35(2) (Spring) pp. 263–85.

Taylor, Ian (1995b) 'Fear of Crime, Urban Fortunes and Suburban Social Movements' in Flemming Balvig (ed) *Arbog fur 1994* Kriminalistik Institut, Universitat Kopenhagn.

Taylor, Ian and Jamieson, Ruth (1996a) "Proper Little Mesters" – Nostalgia and Protest Masculinity in De-industrialised Sheffield', in S. Westwood and J. Williams (eds) *Imagining Cities*, London: Sage.

Taylor, Ian and Jamieson, Ruth (1996b) 'Fear of Crime and Fear of Falling' in Malin Akerstrom (ed) *Crime, Culture and Social Control* Stockholm: Carlssons Forlag.

Taylor, Ian, Walton, Paul and Young, Jock (1973) *The New Criminology: For a Social Theory of Deviance* London: Routledge and Kegan Paul.

Taylor, J.S. (1989–90) '"Set Down in a Large Manufacturing Town" – Sojourning Poor in Early Nineteenth Century Manchester' *Manchester Regional History Review* III(2) pp. 3–8.

Taylor, Paul (1995) '"Manchester" Magic Spells a Rich Spin-off' *Manchester Evening News* 23 February.

Taylor, Sally (1993) 'The Industrial Structure of the Sheffield Cutlery Trades 1870–1917' in Binfield *et al.* (1993) Vol. 2.

Tebbutt, Melanie (1992) 'You Can't Help but Know: Private and Public Space in the Life of Working-class Women' *Manchester Region History Review* V pp. 72–9.

Thame, David (1994) 'Down in the Dumplingtons' *Manchester Evening News Quota Magazine* 25 October pp. 22–3.

Thompson, E.P. (1963) *The Making of the English Working Class* London: Penguin.

Thompson, E.P. (1968) 'Time, Work-discipline and Industrial Capitalism' *Past and Present* 38 pp. 56–97.

Thorpe, Andrew (1993) 'The Consolidation of a Labour Stronghold 1926–1951' in Binfield *et al.* (1993) Vol. 1.

Thrift, Nigel (1987) 'The Geography of Nineteenth Century Class Formation' in N. Thrift and P. Williams (eds) *Class and Space: The Making of Urban Society* London: Routledge.

Townsend, Martin (1994) 'Return to Madchester' *Vox* (March) pp. 50–60.

Townsend, Peter, Phillimore, Peter and Beattie, Alistair (1988) *Health, Deprivation and Inequality in the North* London: Croom Helm.

Trafford Park Development Corporation (1994) 'Annual Report for the Year Ended 31st March 1994'.

Trafford Park Development Corporation (1995) 'Village Trafford Park' corporate brochure.

Tuan, Yi-Fu (1974) *Topophilia: A Study of Environmental Perception, Attitudes and Values* Englewood Cliffs, NJ: Prentice Hall.

Tuan, Yi-Fu (1975) 'Images and Mental Maps' *Annals of the Association of American Geographers* 65(2) pp. 205–13.

Tuan, Yi-Fu (1979) *Landscapes of Fear* Oxford: Blackwell.

Tupling, G.H. (1936) 'Greater Manchester: A Sketch of its Growth to the End of the Eighteenth Century' *Journal of the Manchester Geographical Society* (reprinted in *Manchester Geographer* 5 (1984) pp. 106–15).

Turner, Graham (1966) *The North Country* London: Eyre and Spottiswoode.

Turner, Ralph (1960) 'Sponsored and Contest Mobility in the School System' *American Sociological Review* XXV(5) (reprinted in A.H. Halsey, J. Floud and C.A. Anderson (eds) *Education, Economy and Society* New York: The Free Press 1961).

Tweedale, Geoffrey (1993) 'The Business and Technology of Sheffield Steelmaking' in Binfield *et al.* (1993) Vol. 2.

Tym and Partners (1986) *Greater Manchester Shopping Survey* London: Roger Tym and Partners.

Unger, Roberto M. (1987) *False Necessity: Anti-necessitarian Social Theory in the Service of Radical Social Democracy* Cambridge: Cambridge University Press.

University of Oxford Transport Studies Unit (1992) 'Travel in South Yorkshire 1991' Report prepared for the South Yorkshire Passenger Transport Executive.

Urry, John (1981) 'Localities, Regions and Social Class' *International Journal of Urban and Regional Research* 5 pp. 455–74.

Urry, John (1986) 'Locality Research: The Case of Lancaster' *Regional Studies* 20(3) pp. 233–42.

Urry, John (1990) 'Lancaster: Small Firms, Tourism and the "Locality" in Harloe, Pickvance and Urry.

Urry, John (1987) 'Society, Space and Locality' *Society and Space* 5(4) pp. 435–44.

Valentine, G. (1989) 'The Geography of Women's Fear' *Area* 21(4) pp. 385–90.

Valentine, G. (1992) 'Images of Danger: Women's Sources of Information about the Spatial Distribution of Male Violence' *Area* 24(1) pp. 22–9.

Vance, Carol S. (ed) (1984) *Pleasure and Danger: Exploring Female Sexuality* Boston: Routledge and Kegan Paul.

Vickers, J. Edward (1972) *Old Sheffield Town: An Historical Miscellany* Wakefield: E.P. Publishers (revised edition Applebaum Bookshop, Sheffield 1979)

Vickers, J. Edward (1992) *A Popular History of Sheffield* Sheffield: Applebaum Bookshop. First edition 1978.

Waddington, David, Jones, Karen and Crichter, Chas (1989) *Flashpoints: Studies in Public Disorder* London: Routledge and Kegan Paul.

Wainwright, Martin (1989) 'Sheffield Steels Itself' *Guardian* 12 July.

Wainwright, Martin (1993) 'Council Staff Ready to Go Short to Save Jobs' *Guardian*, 4 March.

Walker, Alan (1990) 'The Strategy of Inequality: Poverty and Income Distribution' in Ian Taylor (ed) *The Social Effects of Free Market Policies* Hemel Hempstead: Harvester Wheatsheaf.

Walker, Alan and Walker, Carol (eds) (1987) *The Growing Divide: A Social Audit 1979–1987* London: Child Poverty Action Group.

Walkowitz, Judith (1992) *City of Dreadful Night: Narratives of Sexual Danger in Late Victorian London* London: Virago.

Waller, P.J. (1987) 'Democracy and Dialect, Speech and Class' in P.J. Waller (ed) *Politics and Social Change in Modern Britain: Essays presented to A.F. Thompson* Brighton: Harvester.

Walsh, Peter (1994) 'Get Out of Town' *Manchester Evening News* 18 November.

Walter, E.V. (1988) *Placeways: A Theory of the Human Environment* Chapel Hill: University of North Carolina Press.

Walton, John (1992) 'Professor Musgrove's North of England: A Critique' *Journal of Regional and Local Studies* 12(2) pp. 25–31.

Walton, John (1995) 'Cooperation in Lancashire 1844–1914' *North West Labour History* 19 pp. 115–25.

Walton, Mary (1968) *Sheffield: Its Story and Achievements* (fourth edition) Sheffield: S.R. Publishers and the Corporation of Sheffield (first edition 1948).

Ward, Colin (1978) *The Child in the City* London: Architectural Press; New York: Pantheon.

Ward, Robin (1975) 'Residential Succession and Racism in Moss Side' Unpublished University of Manchester Ph.D. Thesis

Warde, Alan (1985) 'Comparable Localities: Some Problems of Method' in Murgatroyd *et al.* (1985).

Warde, Alan (1989) 'Recipe for a Pudding: A Comment on Locality' *Antipode* 21 (3) pp. 274–81.

Watney, Simon (1987) *Policing Desire: Pornography, AIDS and the Media* London: Methuen.

Watts, H.D., Smithson, P.A. and White P.E. (eds) (1989) *Sheffield Today* University of Sheffield, Department of Geography.

Weeks, Jeffrey (1991) *Against Nature: Essays on History, Sexuality and Identity* London: Rivers Oram Press.

Werlen, Bruno (1993) *Society, Action and Space: An Alternative Human Geography* London: Routledge.

Westergaard, John (1965) 'The Withering Away of Class: A Contemporary Myth' in Perry Anderson (ed) *Towards Socialism* London: Fontana.

Westergaard, John, Noble Iain and Walker, Alan (1989) *After Redundancy: The Experience of Economic Insecurity* Cambridge: Polity Press.

White, Alan (1988) 'Class, Culture and Control: The Sheffield Athenaeum Movement and the Middle Class' in Seed and Wolff (1988).

White, Alan (1993) "We Never Knew What Price We Were Going to Have Til We Got to the Warehouse". Nineteenth Century Sheffield and the Industrial District Debate' Unpublished paper, Department of Sociology, University of East London.

White, H.P. (ed) (1980a) *The Continuing Conurbation: Change and Development in Greater Manchester* London: Gower.

White, H.P. (1980b) 'Transport Change' in White (1980a).

Whitehead, A. (1992) 'Decisions in a Vacuum: Local Authorities and Out of Town Shopping 1980–1992' Unpublished paper for Centre for Local Economic Strategies (CLES) Summer School.

Whitehouse, Paul (1993) 'We're Bigger than Blackpool!' *Star* 18 September.

Whittle, Stephen and Jones, Angela (1993) 'Consuming Differences: The Collaboration of the Gay Body with the Cultural State – A Study in Manchester's Gay Village' Unpublished paper, Manchester Metropolitan University, Manchester Institute for Popular Culture.

Whyte, W.H. (1988) *City: Rediscovering the Center* New York: Doubleday.

Williams, Raymond (1965) *The Long Revolution* London: Penguin.

Williams, Raymond (1977) *Marxism and Literature* Oxford: Oxford University Press.

Willis, Paul (1977) *Profane Culture* London: Routledge.

Willis, Paul (1978) *Learning to Labour: How Working-class Kids get Working-class Jobs* Farnborough: Saxon House.

Wilson, Elisabeth (1991) *The Sphinx in the City: Urban Life, the Control of Disorder and Women* London: Virago.

Wilson, James Q. and Kelling, George (1982) 'Broken Windows' *Atlantic Monthly* (March) pp. 29–37.

Wilson, William Julius (1991) *The Truly Disadvantaged: The Inner City, Underclass and Public Policy* Chicago: University of Chicago Press.

Winyard, Steve (1987) 'Divided Britain' in Walker and Walker (1987)

Wirth, John D. and Jones, Robert L. (eds) (1978) *Manchester and Sao Paulo: Problems of Rapid Urban Growth* Stanford, CA: Stanford University Press.

Wirth, Louis (1938) *On Cities and Social Life* Selected papers, ed. and intro by Albert J. Reiss Jr, Chicago: University of Chicago Press.

Wolff Janet (1990) *Feminine Sentences*: Cambridge: Polity Press.

Worpole, Ken (1992) *Towns for People: Transforming Urban Life* Buckingham: Open University Press for Comedia and the Gulbenkian Foundation.

Wright, Patrick (1985) *On Living in an Old Country: The National Past in Contemporary Britain* London: Verso.

Wright Mills, C. (1959) 'The Big City: Private Troubles and Public Issues' in I.L. Horowitz (ed) *Power, Politics and People: The Collected Essays of C.Wright Mills* New York: Oxford University Press.

Wynne, Derek and O'Connor, Justin (1995) 'City Cultures and "New Cultural

Intermediaries" Paper presented to the British Sociological Association Annual Conference, University of Leicester (April)

Yin, Peter (1982) 'Fear of Crime as a Problem for the Elderly' *Social Problems* 30(2) pp. 240–5.

Zukin, Sharon (1988) *Loft Living: Cultural and Capital in Urban Change* London: Radius.

Zukin, Sharon (1991) *Landscapes of Power: From Detroit to Disneyworld* Los Angeles: University of California Press.

Zukin, Sharon (1995) *The Culture of Cities* Oxford: Blackwell.

NAME INDEX

PLACE INDEX

SUBJECT INDEX